The Stanley Fish Reader

The Stanley Fish Reader

Edited by
H. Aram Veeser

BLACKWELL
Publishers

Copyright © Blackwell Publishers Ltd 1999
Introduction, selection and arrangement copyright © H. Aram Veeser 1999

First published 1999

2 4 6 8 10 9 7 5 3 1

Blackwell Publishers Inc.
350 Main Street
Malden, Massachusetts 02148
USA

Blackwell Publishers Ltd
108 Cowley Road
Oxford OX4 1JF
UK

Library of Congress Cataloging-in-Publication Data
Fish, Stanley Eugene.
The Stanley Fish reader / edited by H. Aram Veeser.
p. cm
Includes bibliographical references and index.
ISBN 0–631–20438–5 (alk. paper)—ISBN 0–631–20439–3 (pbk. alk. paper)
1. English literature—Early modern, 1500–1700—History and criticism.   2. Literature—History and criticism—Theory, etc.   3. Aram), Civilization, Modern—20th century.
I. Veeser, H. Aram (Harold Aram), 1950– . II. Title
PE64.F57A5 1999   98–25152
809—dc21   CIP

British Library Cataloguing in Publication Data

A CIP catalogue record for this book is available from the British Library.

Typeset in 10½ on 12½ pt Bembo
by Pure Tech India Ltd, Pondicherry
Printed in Great Britain by
M. P. G. Books, Bodmin, Cornwall

This book is printed on acid-free paper

Contents

Notes on Contributors

Joan Bennett is the author of *Reviving Liberty: Radical Christian Humanism in Milton's Great Poems* (Cambridge, Mass., 1989) and additional articles about Milton. She works at the University of Delaware.

Judith Butler is Chancellor's Professor of Rhetoric and Comparative Literature at the University of California, Berkeley. She is the author of *Gender Trouble* (New York, 1990), *Bodies that Matter* (New York, 1993), *Excitable Speech* (New York and London, 1997), and *The Psychic Life of Power* (Stanford, 1997).

Jonathan Goldberg is Sir William Osler Professor of English Literature at the Johns Hopkins University and also has an appointment at Duke. His most recent book is *Desiring Women Writing: English Renaissance Examples* (Stanford, 1997).

Gerald Graff, who has played a lot of one-on-one basketball with Stanley Fish over the years, is the author most recently of *Beyond the Culture Wars* (New York and London, 1992) and of several textbooks designed to help students enter the kind of controversies stirred up by critics like Fish.

Geoffrey Galt Harpham is Professor and Chair in the English Department at Tulane University. He is the author of *One of Us: the Mastery of Joseph Conrad* (Chicago, 1996) and *In the Shadows of Ethics: Literature, Criticism, Culture* (Durham, NC, forthcoming).

Amitava Kumar teaches in the English Department at the University of Florida. He is the editor of *Class Issues: Cultural Studies, Pedagogy, and the Public*

Sphere (New York, 1997) and the author of *Passport Photos* (New York, forth-coming). He has recently completed a documentary (with Sanjeev Chatterjee) on Trinidadian Indians, *Pure Chutney*.

Steven Mailloux is Professor of English at the University of California, Irvine. He is editor of *Rhetoric, Sophistry, Pragmatism* (Cambridge and New York, 1995) and author of *Rhetorical Power* (Ithaca, 1989) and *Reception Histories: Rhetoric, Pragmatism, and American Cultural Politics* (forthcoming).

Stephen D. Moore is a Senior Lecturer in Biblical Studies at the University of Sheffield, England. His most recent book is *God's Gym: Divine Male Bodies in the Bible* (London, 1996).

Rick Perlstein is contributing editor at *Lingua Franca* and a contributor to *Slate* and *The Nation*.

Bruce Robbins is Professor in the English and Comparative Literature departments at Rutgers University. Most recently, he is co-editor of *Cosmopolitics: Thinking and Feeling beyond the Nation* (Minneapolis, 1998) and author of *Feeling Global: Internationalism in Distress* (New York, 1999).

Judith Roof is Professor of English at Indiana University. She is author of, most recently, *A Lure of Knowledge: Lesbian Sexuality and Theory* (New York, 1991), *Reproductions of Reproduction: Imaging Symbolic Change* (New York and London, 1996), and *Come as You Are: Sexuality and Narrative* (New York, 1996).

H. Aram Veeser is Associate Professor of English at the City University of New York-CUNY. He is editor of *The New Historicism* (New York and London, 1989), *The New Historicism Reader* (New York and London, 1994), and *Confessions of the Critics* (New York and London, 1996).

Acknowledgments

So invasive and sustained a career as Stanley Fish's touches many people, and some of them generously agreed to contribute headnotes. Other people have less directly shaped the *Stanley Fish Reader*. The School of Criticism and Theory class of 1985 included Ellen Messer-Davidow, Howard Horwitz, Melita Schaum, and Frank Lentricchia, all of whose encounters with Fish impressed me with the sheer range of reactions he could inspire, reactions that ranged from dislike to devotion. Ten years later, at Harvard's Center for Literary and Cultural Studies, the same rainbow of responses persisted. The Center's director, Marjorie Garber, and Dubois Center fellow Sabina Sielke altered my thinking about Fish. So did Laurie Stone. The lynx-eyed Juanita Bullough copyedited the manuscript. My editors at Blackwell, Louise Spencely and Alison Dunnett, expertly shaped the book as it now stands. Andrew McNeillie commissioned the book, agreed to its unconventional format, and encouraged me to take risks.

The introduction to this volume has benefited from the help and support of many able people. Gerald Graff, Steven Mailloux, Cyrus Veeser, Bruce Robbins, Stephen Moore, Amitava Kumar, and Mia Hindrell read my essay and improved it. My Kansas colleagues Roger Berger, Sarah Daugherty, Deborah Gordon, Peter Zoller, and, at the City Univeristy of New York, Carla Cappetti and Lawrence Hanley, gave of their time and insights. Their exceptional generosity can never be forgotten.

The editor and publisher gratefully acknowledge the following for permission to reproduce copyright material:

"Surprised by Sin,"reprinted by permission of the publisher, from Stanley Fish, *Surprised by Sin* (Cambridge, MA: Harvard Univerrsity Press), Copyright © 1967, 1997 by Stanley Fish and Macmillan Ltd; "Is There a Text in This Class?," reprinted by permission of the publisher, from Stanley Fish, *Is there a Text in This Class?* (Cambridge, MA: Harvard University Press), Copyright © 1980 by the President and Fellows of Harvard College; "With the Compliments of the Author: Reflections on Austin and Derrida," "No Bias, No Merit: The Case Against Blind Submission," "Anti-Professionalism," "Consequences", and "Rhetoric", from Stanley Fish, *Doing What Comes Naturally* (Durham, NC: Duke University Press, 1990 and permission of the author. All Rights Reserved); "There's no such thing as Free Speech," from *The Boston Review*, reprinted in Stanley Fish, *There's No Such Thing As Free Speech* (Oxford: Oxford University Press, 1994); "The Law Wishes to Have a Formal Existence," from Austin Sarat and Thomas Kearns, *The Fate of Law* (Ann Arbor, MI: University of Michigan Press, 1991); "The Young and the Restless," from H. Aram Veerser (ed.), *The New Historicism* (London and New York: Routledge, 1989); "Why Literary Criticism is Like Virtue," from *Professional Correctness* (Copyright © Stanley Fish 1995, reprinted from *Professional Correctness* by Stanley Fish, 1995, by permission of Oxford University Press).

The publishers apologize for any errors or omissions in the above list and would be grateful to be notified of any corrections that should be incorporated in the next edition or reprint of this book.

Introduction

It is high time a *Stanley Fish Reader* appeared.

By every measure Stanley Fish is a major figure. At present he is Professor of English and Professor of Law at Duke University, as well as Executive Director of Duke University Press. As a recent reviewer put it, Fish is "the most quoted, most controversial, most in demand and most feared English teacher in the world, and one of the very best essayists in any field."[1]

Fish confounds categories. He has been likened to everyone from the Greek malcontent Thersites to the Argentinean soccer star Diego Maradona. He is an "intellectual boot-boy,"[2] a "trafficker in scurrility, effrontery, misrepresentation of an opponent's views and every low rhetorical trick,"[3] a "happy gamesman" with a "disturbingly radical agenda,"[4] an Orwellian thought-control technician[5] and "a subtle but perverse intelligence determined to beat the critical theorists at their own demythologizing game."[6] Fish even knocks himself. How else to understand why he digs out and publishes for all to see an obscure Kenyon College student newspaper's report that Fish, during a campus visit, won his debate but lacked "the skill of a gentleman."[7]

The Stanley Fish Reader demonstrates why its subject has so persistently nettled his social betters. The *Reader* presents Fish's work in Milton, the English Renaissance, law and literature, linguistics, psychoanalysis, philosophy, professionalism, political correctness, affirmative action, free and regulated speech, and New Historicism. All of this work is introduced by well-known commentators who have written new headnotes expressly for this volume. And of course there are Fish's own essays, bounded, at first, by the university classroom and the scholar's study, then opening upon more expansive settings:

the convention hall ballroom, the federal courthouse, the baseball stadium, the op-ed page, the Oprah show.

Fish's biography is also a widening gyre. He grew up in a tenement block in a working-class neighborhood in Providence, Rhode Island and, as he rose to prominence, remained unembarrassed by his origins. He was the first member of his family to go to college.[8] In broadcasting his refusal to become a gentleman, Fish cut a path for later generations of brainy lower middle-class kids who wished to avoid the endemic weaknesses of social climbers – the pathetic traits that Groton headmaster Endicott Peabody identified as hesitancy, fear, self-loathing, and shame.[9] For better or worse, by boldly affirming his modest origins, Fish has done more than any Marxist to proletarianize the North Atlantic academy.

Fish measures his success in part by his notoriety. A reviewer of *Doing What Comes Naturally*, Fish's 1989 volume on rhetoric and the practice of theory in literary and legal studies, put it this way: "Fish has made his living from qualities more typically associated with careers in sports or venture capital: agility, pugnacity, tenacity, opportunism, inventiveness, risk, flair. His professional career would be considered exemplary if there were any who could follow his example."[10] But does Fish so offend as to make offense a skill? Yes, indeed. Fish's acknowledged talents – "agility, pugnacity, tenacity, opportunism, inventiveness, risk, flair" – are not the usual professorial profile. Only Fish would endow essays with titles such as "Why no One's Afraid of Wolfgang Iser," "Fish v. Fiss," and "Still Wrong After All These Years." Even Terry Eagleton, who sneezes at Fish's "sentimental populism," admits that Fish's offensiveness is a response commensurate with "the parlous situation of American intellectuals bleakly marooned in an extravagantly Philistine, money-obsessed society."[11]

The fact is that Fish embarrasses Marxists. While Eagleton trenches in at St Catherine's College, Oxford to await the long revolution, while Fredric Jameson digs deeper into the mysteries of Proust and Los Angeles's four star hotels, Fish is on the front lines, year in and year out, attending cramped special sessions of the MLA, watching graduate-student presenters at conferences, and writing op-ed pieces for *The New York Times*. Even his first major book was dedicated "to my students at the University of California, Berkeley, 1962–5." He was the first to advertise his proletarian interest in watching sports.

Fish offends the English especially. Valentine Cunningham fumed that Fish's 1993 Clarendon Lectures at Oxford were "intellectually sullying" and "morally disgusting." Fish's work was a "barbarous slight on every writer who has ever suffered at the hands of some inhuman regime."[12] Worst of all, Fish was "very crass." He had had the temerity to defend literary criticism as an end in itself. (For an example of the Clarendon Lectures, see Chapter 9 in this volume,

"Why Literary Criticism is Like Virtue.") In pieces such as "Profession Despise Thyself," Fish wages ruthless war on professors who, like Cunningham, "subscribe to a view of our enterprise in relation to which our activities can only be either superfluous or immoral."[13] Literary work can always surrender itself to a political agenda, but then, Fish believes, it will have lost the form that gave it distinctive life. Essays such as "Profession Despise Thyself: Fear and Self-Loathing in Literary Studies," "The Unbearable Ugliness of Volvos," and "Anti-Professionalism," are intended to muzzle those who would pretend to be more-political-than-thou while writing books, achieving tenure, and spending royalties, just like the rest of the profession.

Surrender holds no charm for Stanley Fish. Robert Scholes speaks from his own hard experience when he warns, "If you play cards with Stanley Fish, don't let him bring his own deck." Terry Eagleton also accuses Fish of cheating: "like any lawyer, he likes to win, and in a kind of intellectual equivalent to jury-stacking has so rigged his theories that he can never lose." Right-leaning playmates who claim to love the laissez-faire rough-and-tumble are in fact the worst sore-heads; one of them whines about Fish's "virtual enshrinement of cynicism as a principle."[14] The catalog of detraction leads one to ask: Is Fish a cynic and a sophist, a critic gone rogue, spurning principles and values? Or do bands of coherent theory hold together his diverse, controversial, and evidently offensive writings?

The answer is not simple. Fish's knowledge that people are basically greedy and selfish coexists with his urgings to community and solidarity. Much that same perplexing mixture can be found in Fish's primordial influence, John Milton, who was convinced that human beings had fallen into sin. He put *Paradise Lost* on hold for twenty years while he devoted himself to a political revolution that promised theocratic control of the sinful natures of English citizens. Milton's *Areopagitica* thus becomes, for Fish, not the anti-censorship polemic it is often mistaken for, but rather an early defense of speech codes and a precursor of rules to constrain hate-speech. Literary critics are like Adam and Eve: they, too, inhabit a rule-governed world where the penalty for transgression is expulsion, or at least under-employment. Fish reminds them they're in Paradise. Like our ruined parents in *Paradise Lost*, Fish's peers imagine themselves as free to obey or disobey constraints: in one case God's strictures, in the other, the profession's. *Surprised by Sin: The Reader in "Paradise Lost"* teaches that defiance breeds disaster.

Declaring that his mission was to save Milton from democracy, Fish attacked liberal idols such as free speech and the level playing field. The US media responded; they gave Fish a working-over the likes of which is "usually reserved for Afrocentrists and Satanists."[15] Whoever peruses the *Fish Reader* will perceive a through line connecting Fish's Milton work to his later inventions. Milton's attacks on papist idolatry echo in Fish's indictment of those who worship the US Constitution, the First Amendment, and academic freedom; the community of the saints resembles Fish's interpretive communities; the loss of Eden leads to Fish's love of rules and behavioral constraints and to his distrust of human reason and its principles. Fish's essays about Ben Jonson's "Community of the Same" and "The Common Touch" present society as a tense stand-off between redoubtable competitors, and his essays on law regard justice as the word for victory over weaker interests. Given Fish's adversarial approach to literary criticism and legal theory, his current joint appointment in the Duke Law School seems like destiny fulfilled.

The naturally greedy and selfish humanity envisaged by Fish sits ill with a liberal academy: unlike the authors of the Constitution, modern liberals subscribe to the doctrine of fundamental human generosity. Some liberals simply shut their ears to Fish's darkly Hobbesian view of human life. "The animating impulse of Fish's work," contends one legal scholar, "is democratic . . . anti-aristocratic. He wants to say that philosophers and theorists are nothing special."[16] Fish's politics are liberal and democratic, but he despises the shibboleths of liberal democratic culture. He has denounced, in *The New York Times* no less, fairness, merit, equal opportunity, color-blindness, race neutrality, individual rights, and academic freedom: terms he ridicules as "magic words."

In fact, Fish casts human society in his own combative image. His methods express his premise that, unless restrained, we would eat each other. Some critics admire Fish's ability to latch on to an opponent's text and cannibalize her arguments. Gerald Graff gives Fish credit: he "excels at . . . rewritings."[17] Steven Mailloux approves: Fish "resorts to the device of citing other readers' reactions" to literature and thereby succeeds in "making a usable past out of a text's interpretive history."[18] Fish performs a Rolfe massage, quips Harpham, rearranging the deep structure of his opponent's thought.[19]

These contradictory impulses allow critics to paint Fish in contrasting hues. To some, Fish is a master of the one-sided conversation. "Fish likes to tease his opponents, to refute their retaliations by getting them in first"; Fish cannot refute opponents because he "has no coherent account of disagreement" and sees it as "theological error."[20] Fish's "therapeutic rhetoric" is a ruse; he listens well and restates "the patient's delusions sympathetically ('Let's see if I understand you. You're saying that . . .')." But Fish is " 'unable' " – by his own admission – " 'even to hear an argument that constitutes a challenge.' " Fish embodies literary critics' "nightmare of not being able to talk to one another."[21] To one of the contributors of headnotes to this volume, however, Fish is no therapist; he is a patient, compulsively reeling off the endless imagined objections to his ideas.[22]

To other critics, Fish converses all too well. He is a typical liberal who ameliorates conflict and stifles change, reassures us with comments like "Not to worry!" and "this debate has no consequences." His "shadow-boxing techniques" are "diplomatic and not critical."[23] Fish's cream-puff polemics fit the "Rortian term 'conversation,'" the "nonconflictual, harmonious conception of interaction" (43). Christopher Norris also finds "Rorty...closest to Fish" because both "embrace a full-blown pragmatist doctrine of truth as what is (currently and contingently) 'good in the way of belief'" (155).

Fish, however, raises an objection: "Rorty wants to continue the conversation of humankind. I want to end it." Openness without penalties offends his Miltonic sensibility. "What 'independent value' could be invoked that would persuade [a militant believer] to relax the imperatives of faith when he or she enters the public square?" asks Fish. His answer is that liberty must be curtailed. "It is not," he knows, "an answer modern liberals find attractive."[24]

This answer instantly sets Fish at odds with Rorty. It's not because Rorty is a confessed Hubert Humphrey Democrat – Fish is, too – but because for Rorty, "no one can make sense of the notion of a last commentary, a last discussion note, a good piece of writing which is more than the occasion for a better piece."[25] Fish responds that if it is impossible to win in a final way, let me win now. Scholar and writer David Lodge has affectionately portrayed Fish as "Morris Zapp" in two campus novels, *Small World* and *Changing Places*; one burlesque episode involves Zapp's craving to give the last-ever paper on Jane Austen. The literary scholar whom Fish admires most is the one who imposed a fifteen-year moratorium on discussions of *Paradise Lost*.[26]

One can understand why Fish rarely wrote about drama.[27] In the drama, each character speaks in its own accents, whereas Fish's ventrilologues – his relentless rephrasings and summarizings – subordinate all opponents to a single authority: his own. Verbal modes that permit one voice decisively to check another prove more congenial. Fish was the first to hear Milton's narrator chastising the reader. Later, Fish wrote an entire book about the Anglican catechism – a most rigidly one-sided conversation.[28]

Fish admires the ability to silence others, and he objects to pluralism. Is Fish merely acting the *enfant terrible* or, if he is serious, who gets to silence whom?[29] Fish's debut as a public intellectual was his demonstration, in *The New York Times*, that (as his 1994 book title put it) *There's No Such Thing as Free Speech, and It's a Good Thing, Too*. "One cannot wake up in the morning and decide, 'today I am going to be more open,'" Fish writes, "that kind of openness is nothing more (or less) than a resolution to be differently closed" ("The Young and the Restless," 251). As opposed to Rorty's relaxed conversational world, Fish "invites you to join with your fellow men in a defensive compact based on mutual distrust." He sees "freedom as the danger and preaches the necessity of coercive constraint."[30] Constraint is the action in affirmative action, the might behind equal rights.

Fish can claim credit for intruding Miltonic censoriousness into *The New York Times*. His December 1996 op–ed piece entitled "When Principles Get In The Way" berates the idolatrous regard that liberals accord to certain catch-phrases, now that those phrases are demolishing liberal affirmative action: "Of course, you could also try to work within that vocabulary and fight over its terms, arguing that 'fairness,' 'equality' and 'color-blindness' really belong on your side. But even if you got good at the game, you would be playing on your opponent's field and thus buying into his position, and why would you want to do that?" "It would be far wiser," he concludes, "to refuse the lure of 'fairness,' 'merit,' and 'equality,' now code words for ignoring the effects of the long history of racial oppression."[31] "Far wiser" suggests a principled wisdom, which Fish ordinarily derides. A true rhetorician, he slides over this contradiction.

Self-destructive idol-worship receives a further drubbing in "How the Right Hijacked the Magic Words." As the title indicates, political reactionaries have co–opted "the vocabulary of America's civil religion – the vocabulary of equal opportunity, color-blindness, race neutrality, and, above all, individual rights."[32] Yet liberals remain awed by these words. With Miltonic exasperation, Fish denounces liberals who have made of that sacred vocabulary a brazen image even as affirmative action hiring, environmental protection, and Rodney King's civil rights disappear. The Miltonic theme of coercive community dominates "School for the Scandalous," where Fish makes clear that he hates academic freedom and deplores its invocation. The invoker was, in this case, Dr Bowen, a state university president who was attacked by the Governor of New York for sponsoring a controversial academic conference. "If Dr. Bowen thinks that the conference is defensible in academic terms, he should have said so and laid out the terms. Instead he went on about academic freedom. . . ."[33] Again, the college president must argue from a position *within* the community of the faithful.

In "Professor Sokal's Bad Joke," Fish delivers a Miltonic denunciation of a fellow professor who violated interpretive community rules. The Marxist Sokal had fooled the editors of a prominent leftist academic quarterly into publishing his nonsense article, which was billed as a postmodern physics. Sokal exposed the hoax on the day that the journal hit the newsstands. "Just as the criteria of an enterprise will be internal to its own history, so will the threat to its integrity be internal, posed not by presumptuous outsiders but by insiders who decide not to play by the rules or to put the rules in the service of a devious purpose . . . Remember, science is above all a communal effort."[34]

A career as substantial as Fish's defies summary. Yet even the partial collec-tion in this volume communicates his ability to change with the times, to reinvent himself as the occasion requires. Even Marxists have to admit that

Fish, who has always declared himself free of political commitments and devoid of radical political intentions, has yet had unparalleled clout when publicly defending leftist positions. Fish has sought the thickest parts of the fighting.

The essays in the *Reader* touch on many other debates and innovations: a high-profile battle (in *Critical Inquiry* and the *Times Literary Supplement*, among other places) to defend professionalism against anti-specialist detractors (Walter Jackson Bate, Edward Said, Walter Davis); the tendency, noted by Prasad, to make radical movements become, in Fish's work, "more like corporate undertakings than agencies of political struggle"; Fish's shattering impact on legal studies; his attacks on critics of the academy; and his unique style of writing literary history.

Fish has often been his own best explicator and historian. In the introduction and headnotes for *Is There a Text In This Class?*, Fish offers a replay of his sometimes-halting, sometimes-explosive changes of mind and position. The analyst will, however, always have certain advantages over the analysand. The headnote writers for this volume have seized the occasion to have the last word. One can sense the flavor of these contributions in Harpham's passing observation that Fish's compulsive repetitions of his opponents' views may well be beyond his conscious control.

What impresses me most? That Fish's literary studies have armed him to do battle in the public sphere. He has emerged as a public intellectual without following the deeply rutted, gentleman-and-scholar road. Like John Milton, Christian humanist and regicide, epic poet, flak-catcher, and political pamphleteer, Fish certainly frustrates easy classification.

Notes

1 Geoffrey Galt Harpham, "Constraints, not consequences," *Times Literary Supplement* 9–15 March 1990: 247.
2 Terry Eagleton, "The death of self-criticism," *Times Literary Supplement* 24 November 1995: 6.
3 Richard A. Posner, "The judging game," *Times Literary Supplement* 15 July 1994: 14.
4 Daniel J. Silver, "The Higher Gamesmanship," *Commentary* February 1994: 61.
5 Robert Scholes, "Tlön and Truth: Reflections on Literary Theory and philosophy," in *Realism and Representation: Essays on the Problem of Realism in Relation to Science, Literature and Culture* (Madison, WI: University of Wisconsin Press, 1993), 178.
6 Christopher Norris, "Right You Are (If You Think So): Stanley Fish and the Rhetoric of Assent," *Comparative Literature* 42 (Spring 1990): 144–82.
7 Stanley Fish, *Is There a Text in This Class?* (Cambridge, MA: Harvard University Press, 1980), 304.

8   Adam Begley, "Souped-Up Scholar," *New York Times Magazine* 3 May 1992: 52.

9   Peter W. Cookson, *Preparing for Power: America's Elite Boarding Schools* (New York: Basic Books, 1985), 128.

10 Harpham, "Constraints, not consequences," 247.

11 "The death of self-criticism," 6.

12 "Motormouth silliness" (review of *Professional Correctness: Literary Studies and Political Change*), *New Statesman & Society* 8 December 1995: 27–8.

13 "Profession Despise Thyself: Fear and Self-Loathing in Literary Studies," *Critical Inquiry*; reprinted in Stanley Fish, *Doing What Comes Naturally: Change, Rhetoric, and the Practice of Theory in Literary and Legal Studies* (Durham, NC: Duke University Press, 1989), 197–214.

14 Silver, "The Higher Gamesmanship," 60.

15 Michael Bérubé, *Public Access: Literary Theory and American Cultural Politics* (London and New York: Verso, 1994), 50.

16 Cass R. Sunstein, "The Professor's New Clothes," *The New Republic* 6 December 1993: 44.

17 Gerald Graff, "Interpretation on Tlön: A Response to Stanley Fish," *Critical Inquiry* 17.1 (Autumn 1985): 112.

18 Steven Mailloux, *Rhetorical Power* (Ithaca, NY: Cornell University Press, 1989), 43.

19 "Constraints, not consequences," 247.

20 Patrick C. Hogan, *On Interpretation* (Athens, GA: Georgia University Press, 1996), 106.

21 Ellen Rooney, "'Not To Worry': The Therapeutic Rhetoric of Stanley Fish," in Rooney, *Seductive Reasoning: Pluralism as the Problematic of Contemporary Literary Theory* (Ithaca, NY: Cornell University Press, 1989), 153.

22 See Geoffrey Galt Harpham's headnote to Ch. 4.

23 Madhava Prasad, "The New (International) Party of Order? Coalition Politics in the (Literary) Academy," *diacritics* 22.1 (Spring 1992): 35, 45.

24 Fish, "Mission Impossible: Settling the Just Bounds Between Church and State," unpublished typescript, 20.

25 Richard Rorty, "Philosophy as a Kind of Writing: An Essay on Derrida," *New Literary History* 10 (1978–79), 141–60; reprinted in *Pragmatism: A Reader*, ed. Louis Menand (New York: Vintage/Random House, 1997), 328.

26 The scholar is C. S. Lewis. Gary A. Olson, "Fish Tales: A Conversation with 'The Contemporary Sophist,'" *Journal of Advanced Composition* 12.2 (Fall 1992), reprinted in Stanley Fish, *There's No Such Thing as Free Speech, and It's a Good Thing, Too* (New York and Oxford: Oxford University Press, 1994), 283.

27 The exception is *Coriolanus*, in Fish's essay "How To Do Things with Austin and Searle: Speech-Act Theory and Literary Criticism," in *Is There a Text In This Class?* 197–245. He says there that he makes the exception for *Coriolanus* "because it is a speech-act play" (200).

28 *The Living Temple: George Herbert and Catechizing* (Berkeley, CA and London: University of California Press, 1978).

29 Gerald Graff has posed these questions.

30   "Mission Impossible," 23.
31   *New York Times* 26 December 1996.
32   "How the Right Hijacked the Magic Words," *New York Times* 13 August 1995.
33   *New York Times* 21 November 1997.
34   *New York Times* 21 May 1996.

H. Aram Veeser

1

Not so Much a Teaching as an Intangling

When Fish published *Surprised by Sin* in 1967, the "Milton Controversy" of the 1940s and 1950s still undergirded most criticism of *Paradise Lost* with its debates over the attractiveness of Satan, the unattractiveness of God, the judgments of the epic narrator and, in general, Milton's constant demand that we accept "his religious mood," making it hard for us to grant him a " 'willing suspension of disbelief' – the condition," according to academic commonplace, "on which alone most people today can enjoy religious poetry."[1]

Fish fundamentally changed the course of what was, by then, a tired discussion. Readers felt, in Samuel Johnson's word, "harassed" by contradictions, Fish announced, because they were, in fact, the locus of Milton's poetic performance. Indeed, as reporters of their own readerly reactions, they were providing valuable empirical evidence that could be accounted for by the new theory of reader response. And Milton's theology, instead of being a dispensable distraction, was central to his performative poetics. Fish's claim about Milton's readers quickly became critical orthodoxy, used as a base for other writers' own positions and as a teaching device for encouraging students to read a difficult poem very closely.

In the thirty years since *Surprised By Sin's* initial publication, critical discourse has shifted away from the issues that provoked Fish's deployment of reader-response theory. A younger generation has been educated under the dominance not only of Fish but of many theorists whose systems now threaten, some think, to bind the rich, contradictory particularities of Milton's text to rigid intellectual constructs while also occluding the poet's biography and political career, so that Western academics discuss "Milton" as a critical construct at a time when Milton and his poetry are sought as sources of real moral and political help by contemporary readers, from Eastern Europe to China and South Africa.[2] As the first (and for quite a while, the only) scholar to subject Milton's poetry to one of the European theoretical schools, Fish is now beginning to serve as a target for attacks on theory's perceived hegemony.[3]

In this process, a misreading of *Surprised by Sin* is under construction wherein the absolute truth, or being, of Milton's God is transmuted into an ideological absolut*ism* imposed on Milton's reader. Fish did not ascribe this kind of absolutism to Milton. In fact, Fish was drawing, in 1967, on a convergence of twentieth-century insights from physics, cognitive psychology, and moral and linguistic philosophy to study the implications of the old theological observation that the nature of divine Truth can always be known only in partial and mediated ways by a contingent creation. Fish saw Milton richly celebrating an understanding that this necessity for mediation exists by divine design. For although mediations do lead toward one eternally unified moral Truth, it makes all the difference that what that Truth absolutely requires is the exercise of human freedom-within-contingency.

Fish's own rhetorical style has made some readers feel that he is trying to coerce and contain them; for these readers Fish's critical writing has not affectively conveyed Milton's liberating vision. But the fact remains that Fish's theoretical perspective allowed him to see Milton's central paradox: that to be surprised by joy,[4] it is necessary to be surprised by sin, because the unavoidable condition of being always already forgiven is the Truth that in Milton's doctrine and poem "liberates," filling the plenitude of contingent experiences and powering the agents of reform.

Notes

1 L. A. Cormican, "Milton's Religious Verse," in *From Donne to Marvell*, vol. 3, *The New Pelican Guide to English Literature*, ed. Boris Ford (Harmondsworth; New York; Victoria, Australia; Markham, Ontario; Auckland, 1982; first published in *The Pelican Guide to English Literature*, 1956), p. 232.
2 On twentieth-century uses of Milton's religio-political inspiration and guidance, see Joan S. Bennett, "Asserting Eternal Providence: John

Milton Through the Window of Liberation Theology," in *Milton and Heresy*, ed. John P. Rumrich and Stephen Dobranski (Cambridge, forthcoming).
3 See John P. Rumrich, *Milton Unbound: Controversy and Reinterpretation* (Cambridge, 1996) and William Kolbrener, *Milton's Warring Angels: A Study of Critical Engagements* (Cambridge, 1997).
4 *Surprised by Joy* is the title of C. S. Lewis's spiritual autobiography.

Joan S. Bennett

> The right thing in speaking really is that we should be satisfied not to annoy our hearers, without trying to delight them: we ought in fairness to fight our case with no help beyond the bare facts: nothing, therefore, should matter except the proof of those facts. Still, as has been said, other things affect the result considerably, owing to the defects of our hearers.
>
> Aristotle, *Rhetoric*

1 The Defects of our Hearers

I would like to suggest something about *Paradise Lost* that is not new except for the literalness with which the point will be made: (1) the poem's center of reference is its reader who is also its subject; (2) Milton's purpose is to educate the reader to an awareness of his position and responsibilities as a fallen man, and to a sense of the distance which separates him from the innocence once his; (3) Milton's method is to re-create in the mind of the reader (which is, finally, the poem's scene) the drama of the Fall, to make him fall again exactly as Adam did and with Adam's troubled clarity, that is to say, "not deceived." In a limited sense few would deny the truth of my first two statements; Milton's concern with the ethical imperatives of political and social behavior would hardly allow him to write an epic which did not attempt to give his audience a basis for moral action; but I do not think the third has been accepted in the way that I intend it.

A. J. A. Waldock, one of many sensitive readers who have confronted the poem since 1940, writes: "*Paradise Lost* is an epic poem of singularly hard and definite outline, expressing itself (or so at least would be our first impressions) with unmistakable clarity and point."[1] In the course of his book Waldock expands the reservation indicated by his parenthesis into a reading which predicates a disparity between Milton's intention and his performance:

In a sense Milton's central theme denied him the full expression of his deepest interests. It was likely, then, that as his really deep interests could not find outlet in his poem in the right way they might find outlet in the wrong way. And to a certain extent they do;

they find vents and safety-valves often in inopportune places. Adam cannot give Milton much scope to express what he really feels about life; but Satan is there, Satan gives him scope. And the result is that the balance is somewhat disturbed; pressures are set up that are at times disquieting, that seem to threaten more than once, indeed, the equilibrium of the poem.[2]

The "unconscious meaning" portion of Waldock's thesis is, I think, as wrong as his description of the reading experience as "disquieting" is right. If we transfer the emphasis from Milton's interests and intentions which are available to us only from a distance, to our responses which are available directly, the disparity between intention and execution becomes a disparity between reader expectation and reading experience; and the resulting "pressures" can be seen as part of an intelligible pattern. In this way we are led to consider our own experience as a part of the poem's subject.

By "hard and definite outline" I take Waldock to mean the sense of continuity and direction evoked by the simultaneous introduction of the epic tradition and Christian myth. The "definiteness" of a genre classification leads the reader to expect a series of formal stimuli – martial encounters, complex similes, an epic voice – to which his response is more or less automatic; the hardness of the Christian myth predetermines his sympathies; the union of the two allows the assumption of a comfortable reading experience in which conveniently labeled protagonists act out rather simple roles in a succession of familiar situations. The reader is prepared to hiss the devil off the stage and applaud the pronouncements of a partisan and somewhat human deity who is not unlike Tasso's "il Padre eterno." But of course this is not the case; no sensitive reading of *Paradise Lost* tallies with these expectations, and it is my contention that Milton ostentatiously calls them up in order to provide his reader with the shock of their disappointment. This is not to say merely that Milton communicates a part of his meaning by a calculated departure from convention; every poet does that; but that Milton consciously wants to worry his reader, to force him to doubt the correctness of his responses, and to bring him to the realization that his inability to read the poem with any confidence in his own perception is its focus.

Milton's program of reader harassment begins in the opening lines; the reader, however, may not be aware of it until line 84 when Satan speaks for the first time. The speech is a powerful one, moving smoothly from the *exclamatio* of "But O how fall'n" (84) to the regret and apparent logic of "till then who knew / The force of those dire Arms" (93–4), the determination of "courage never to submit or yield" (108) and the grand defiance of "Irreconcilable to our grand Foe, / Who now triumphs, and in th' excess of joy / Sole reigning holds the Tyranny of Heav'n" (122–4). This is our first view of Satan and the impression given, reinforced by a succession of speeches in Book 1, is described by Waldock: "fortitude in adversity, enormous endurance, a certain splendid recklessness, remarkable powers of rising to an occasion, extraordinary qualities of leadership (shown not least in his salutary taunts)."[3] But in each case Milton follows the voice of Satan with a comment which complicates, and according to some, falsifies, our reaction to it:

> So spake th' Apostate Angel though in pain,
> Vaunting aloud, but rackt with deep despair. (125–6)

Waldock's indignation at this authorial intrusion is instructive:

If one observes what is happening one sees that there is hardly a great speech of Satan's that Milton is not at pains to correct, to damp down and neutralize. He will put some glorious thing in Satan's mouth, then, anxious about the effect of it, will pull us gently by the sleeve, saying (for this is what it amounts to): "Do not be carried away by this fellow: he *sounds* splendid, but take my word for it. . . ." Has there been much despair in what we have just been listening to? The speech would almost seem to be incompatible with that. To accept Milton's comment here . . . as if it had a validity equal to that of the speech itself is surely very naïve critical procedure . . . in any work of imaginative literature at all it is the demonstration, by the very nature of the case, that has the higher validity; an allegation can possess no comparable authority. Of course they should agree; but if they do not then the demonstration must carry the day. (pp. 77–8)

There are several assumptions here:

(1) There is a disparity between our response to the speech and the epic voice's evaluation of it.
(2) Ideally, there should be no disparity.
(3) Milton's intention is to correct *his* error.
(4) He wants us to discount the effect of the speech through a kind of mathematical cancellation.
(5) The question of relative authority is purely an aesthetic one. That is, the reader is obliged to hearken to the most dramatically persuasive of any conflicting voices.

Of these I can assent only to the first. The comment of the epic voice unsettles the reader, who sees in it at least a partial challenge to his own assessment of the speech. The implication is that there is more (or less) here than has met the ear; and since the only ear available is the reader's, the further implication is that he has failed in some way to evaluate properly what he has heard. One must begin by admitting with Waldock the impressiveness of the speech, if only as a *performance* that commands attention as would any forensic *tour de force*; and attention on that level involves a corresponding inattention on others. It is not enough to analyse, as Lewis and others have, the speciousness of Satan's rhetoric. It is the nature of sophistry to lull the reasoning process; logic is a safeguard against a rhetorical effect only after the effect has been noted. The deep distrust, even fear, of verbal manipulation in the seventeenth century is a recognition of the fact that there is no adequate defense against eloquence at the moment of impact. (The appeal of rhetoric was traditionally associated with the weakness of the fallen intellect – the defect of our hearers; its fine phrases flatter the desires of the cupidinous self and perpetuate the disorder which has reigned in the soul since the Fall.)[4] In other words one can analyze the process of deception only after it is successful. The reader who is stopped short by Milton's rebuke (for so it is) will, perhaps, retrace his steps and note more carefully the inconsistency of a Tyranny that involves an excess of joy, the perversity of "study of revenge, immortal hate" (a line that had slipped past him sandwiched respectably between will and courage), the sophistry of the transfer of power from the "Potent Victor" of 95 to the "Fate" of 116, and the irony, in the larger picture, of "that were *low* indeed" and "in *foresight* much advanc't." The fit reader Milton has in mind would go further and recognize in Satan's finest moment – "And courage never to submit or yield" – an almost literal translation of *Georgic* IV.84, "usque adeo obnixi non cedere." Virgil's "praise" is for his bees whose heroic posturing is presented in terms that are at least ambiguous:

> ipsi per medias acies insignibus alis
> ingentes animos angusto in pectore versant,
> usque adeo obnixi non cedere, dum gravis aut hos
> aut hos versa fuga victor dare terga subegit.
> hi motus animorum atque haec certamina tanta
> pulveris exigui iactu compressa quiescunt. (82–7)[5]

If we apply these verses to Satan, the line in question mocks him and in the unique time scheme of *Paradise Lost* looks both backward (the Victor has already driven the rebel host to flight) and forward (in terms of the reading experience, the event is yet to come). I believe that all this and more is there, but that the complexities of the passage will be apparent only when the reader has been led to them by the necessity of accounting for the distance between his initial response and the *obiter dictum* of the epic voice. When he is so led, the reader is made aware that Milton is correcting not a mistake of composition, but the weakness all men evince in the face of eloquence. The error is his, not Milton's; and when Waldock invokes some unidentified critical principle ("they should agree") he objects to an effect Milton anticipates and desires.

But this is more than a stylistic trick to ensure the perception of irony. For, as Waldock points out, this first epic interjection introduces a pattern that is operative throughout. In Books I and II these "correctives" are particularly numerous and, if the word can be used here, tactless. Waldock falsifies his experience of the poem, I think, when he characterizes Milton's countermands as gentle; we are not warned ("Do not be carried away by this fellow"), but accused, taunted by an imperious voice which says with no consideration of our feelings, "I know that you *have been* carried away by what you have just heard; you should not have been; you have made a mistake, just as I knew you would"; and we resent this rebuke, not, as Waldock suggests, because our aesthetic sense balks at a clumsy attempt to neutralize an unintentional effect, but because a failing has been exposed in a context that forces us to acknowledge it. We are angry at the epic voice, not for fudging, but for being right, for insisting that we become our own critics. There is little in the human situation more humiliating, in both senses of the word, than the public acceptance of a deserved rebuke.

Not that the reader falls and becomes one of Satan's party. His involvement in the speech does not *directly* compromise his position in a God-centered universe, since his response (somewhat unconscious) is to a performance rather than to a point of view that he might be led to adopt as his own. As Michael Krouse notes, "the readers for whom Milton wrote ... were prepared for a Devil equipped with what appear on the surface to be the best of arguments."[6] As a Christian who has been taught every day to steel himself against diabolical wiles, the reader is more than prepared to admit the justness of the epic voice's *judgment* on Satan. It is the phrase "vaunting aloud" that troubles, since it seems to deny even the academic admiration one might have for Satan's art as apart from his morality and to suggest that such admiration can never really be detached from the possibility of involvement (if only passive) in that morality. The sneer in "vaunting" is aimed equally at the performance and anyone who lingers to appreciate it. (Satan himself delivers the final judgment on this and on all his speeches at IV.83: "Whom I seduc'd / With other promises and other *vaunts*.") The danger is not so much that Satan's argument will persuade (one does not accord the father of lies an impartial hearing), but that its intricacy will engage the reader's attention and lead him into an error of omission. That is to say, in the attempt to follow and analyze Satan's soliloquy, the larger contexts in which it exists will be forgotten. The immediate experience of the poetry will not be qualified by the perspective of the poem's doctrinal assumptions. Arnold Stein writes, "the formal perspective does not force itself upon Satan's speech, does not label and editorialize the impressive wilfulness out of existence; but rather sets up a dramatic conflict between the local context of the immediate utterance and the larger context of which the formal perspective is expression.

This conflict marks . . . the tormented relationship between the external boast and the internal despair."[7] Stein's comment is valuable, but it ignores the way the reader is drawn into the poem, not as an observer who coolly notes the interaction of patterns (this is the mode of Jonsonian comedy and masque), but as a participant whose mind is the *locus* of that interaction. Milton insists on this since his concern with the reader is necessarily more direct than it might be in any other poem; and to grant the reader the status of the slightly arrogant perceiver-of-ironies Stein invents would be to deny him the full *benefit* (I use the word deliberately, confident that Milton would approve) of the reading experience. Stein's "dramatic conflict" is there, as are his various perspectives, but they are actualized, that is, translated into felt meaning, only through the more pervasive drama (between reader and poem) I hope to describe.

A Christian failure need not be dramatic; if the reader loses himself in the workings of the speech even for a moment, he places himself in a compromising position. He has taken his eye from its proper object – the glory of God, and the state of his own soul – and is at least in danger. Sin is a matter of degrees. To think "how fine this all sounds, even though it is Satan's," is to be but a few steps from thinking, "how fine this all sounds" – and no conscious qualification. One begins by simultaneously admitting the effectiveness of Satan's rhetoric and discounting it because it *is* Satan's, but at some point a reader trained to analyze as he reads will allow admiration for a technical skill to push aside the imperative of Christian watchfulness. To be sure, this is not sin. But from a disinterested appreciation of technique one moves easily to a grudging admiration for the technician and then to a guarded sympathy and finally, perhaps, to assent. In this case, the failure (if we can call it that) involves the momentary relaxation of a vigilance that must indeed be eternal. Richard Baxter warns: "Not only the open profane, the swearer, the drunkard, and the enemies of godliness, will prove hurtful companions to us, though these indeed are chiefly to be avoided: but too frequent society with persons merely civil and moral, whose conversation is empty and unedifying, may much divert our thoughts from heaven."[8] In Book IX, Eve is "yet sinless" when she talks with Satan and follows him to the forbidden tree; but Milton indicates the danger and its vehicle at line 550:

> Into the heart of Eve his words made way,
> Though at the voice much marvelling.

Eve (innocently) surrenders her mind to wonderment ("much marvelling") at the technical problem of the seeming-serpent's voice ("What may this mean? Language of Man pronounc't / By Tongue of Brute") and forgets Adam's injunction to "strictest watch" (363). There is at least one assertion of Satan's that Eve should challenge, since it contradicts something she herself has said earlier. The proper response to Satan's salutatory "Fairest resemblance of thy Maker fair" (538) has been given, in effect, by Eve when she recognizes Adam's superior "fairness" at iv.490 ("I . . . see / How beauty is excell'd by manly grace / And wisdom, which alone is truly fair"). Her failure to give that response again is hardly fatal, but it does involve a deviation (innocent but dangerous) from the strictness of her watch. Of course to rebuke the serpent for an excess in courtesy might seem rude; tact, however, is a social virtue and one which Milton's heroes are rarely guilty of. Eve is correct when she declares that the talking serpent's voice "claims attention due" (566), but attention *due* should not mean *complete* attention. Satan is the arch-conjurer here, calling his audience's attention to one hand (the mechanics of his articulation), doing his real work with the other ("Into the heart of Eve his words made way"). In Book 1, Milton is the conjurer: by naming Satan he disarms us, and allows us to feel secure in the identification of an enemy who traditionally succeeds through disguise (serpent, cherub). But as William Haller notes, in *The Rise of Puritanism*,[9] nothing is more indicative of a graceless state than a sense of security: "Thus we live in danger, our greatest danger being that we should feel no danger, and our safety lying in the very dread of feeling safe" (p. 156). Protected from one error (the possibility of listening sympathetically to a disguised enemy) we fall easily into another (spiritual inattentiveness) and fail to read Satan's speech with the critical acumen it demands. In the opening lines of Book x, Milton comments brusquely on Adam's and Eve's fall:

> For still they knew, and ought to have still remember'd, (12)

Paradise Lost is full of little moments of forgetfulness – for Satan, for Adam and Eve, and, most important, for the reader. At 1.125–6, the epic voice enters to point out to us the first of these moments and to say, in effect, " 'For still you knew and ought to have still remembered,' remembered who you are (Paradise has already been lost), where you are ('So spake th'Apostate Angel')," and what the issues are (salvation, justification). In this poem the isolation of an immediate poetic effect involves a surrender to that effect, and is a prelude to error, and possibly to sin. Milton challenges his reader in order to protect him from a mistake he must make before the challenge can be discerned. If this seems circular and even unfair, it is also, as I shall argue later, necessary and inevitable.

The result of such encounters is the adoption of a new way of reading. After 1.125–6 the reader proceeds determined not to be caught out again; but invariably he is. If Satanic pronouncements are now met with a certain caution, if there is a new willingness to search for complexities and ironies beneath simple surfaces, this mental armour is never quite strong enough to resist the insidious attack of verbal power; and always the irritatingly omniscient epic voice is there to point out a deception even as it succeeds. As the poem proceeds and this little drama is repeated, the reader's only gain is an awareness of what is happening to him; he understands that his responses are being controlled and mocked by the same authority, and realizes that while his efforts to extricate himself from this sequence are futile, that very futility becomes a way to self-knowledge. *Control* is the important concept here, for my claim is not merely that this pattern is in the poem (it would be difficult to find one that is not), but that Milton (a) consciously put it there and (b) expected his reader to notice it. Belial's speech in Book II is a case in point. It is the only speech that merits an introductory warning:

> On th'other side up rose
> *Belial*, in act more graceful and humane;
> A fairer person lost not Heav'n; he seem'd
> For dignity compos'd and high exploit:
> But all was false and hollow; though his Tongue
> Dropt Manna, and could make the worse appear
> The better reason to perplex and dash
> Maturest Counsels: for his thoughts were low;
> To vice industrious, but to Nobler deeds
> Timorous and slothful: yet he pleas'd the ear,
> And with persuasive accent thus began.
>
> (II. 108–18)

The intensity of the warning indicates the extent of the danger: Belial's apparent solidity, which is visible, must be contrasted to his hollowness, which is not, the manna of his tongue to the lowness of mind it obscures; and the "yet" in "yet he pleas'd the ear," more than a final admonition before the reader is to be left to his own resources, is an admission of wonder by the epic voice itself (*yet* he pleased...) and one of the early cracks in its façade of omniscience. Belial's appeal is a skilful union of logical machinery ("*First*, what Revenge?") and rhetorical insinuation. The easy roll of his periods literally cuts through the contortions of Moloch's bluster, and the series of *traductiones* around the word "worse" is an indirect comment on the "what can be worse" of the "Sceptr'd King's" desperation. The ploys are effective, and since in the attempt to measure the relative merits of the two devils we forget that their entire counsel is baseless, the return of the epic voice yields one more slight shock at this new evidence of our susceptibility. Again we are led to forget what we know; again we take our eye from the object (the centrality of God); again we are returned to it with an abruptness that is (designedly) disconcerting:

> Thus *Belial* with words cloth'd in reason's garb
> Counsell'd ignoble ease, and peaceful sloth,
> Not Peace: (226–8)

Waldock complains, "Belial's words are not only 'cloath'd in reason's garb': they *are* reasonable."[10] Belial's words are *not* reasonable, although a single uncritical reading will yield the appearance of reason rather than the reality of his ignoble ease. Again the flaw in the speech is to be located precisely at its strongest point. Belial cries at line 146: "for who would lose, / Though full of pain, this intellectual being, / Those thoughts that wander through Eternity, / To perish rather, swallow'd up and lost / In the wide womb of uncreated night." In other words, do we wish to give up our nature, our sense of identity? The rhetorical question evokes an emphatic "no" from the assembled devils and the reader. Yet at line 215 Belial offers his final argument, the possibility of adapting to their now noxious environment: "Our purer essence then will overcome / Thir noxious vapor, or enur'd not feel, / Or chang'd at length, and to the place conform'd / In temper and in nature, will receive / Familiar the fierce heat, and void of pain." If this is less spectacular than the question posed at 146, it is still a direct answer to that question. *Belial* is willing to lose "this intellectual being." The choice is not, as he suggests, between annihilation and continued existence, but between different kinds of annihilation – Moloch's suicidal thrust at the Almighty or his own gradual surrender of identity, no less suicidal, much less honest. This will be obvious on a second reading. My intention is not to refute Waldock, but to suggest that while his reaction to the epic voice ("they *are* reasonable") is the correct one, Milton expects his reader to go beyond it, to see in the explicitness of the before and after warnings a comment on his own evaluation of the speech.

Satan and his host need not speak in order to betray us to ourselves. When Satan and Beelzebub move from the lake of fire to dry land, "if it were Land that ever burn'd," their actions become their rhetoric. Milton's introductory stage direction (or is it a marginal note) "nor ever thence / Had ris'n or heav'd his head, but that the will / And high permission of all-ruling Heaven" (1.210–12) parallels the warning against Belial; and again the experience of the verse leads us (literally) to lose sight of the warning. If Belial's words seem reasonable, Satan's act certainly seems autonomous. He *rears* himself "from off the Pool," and the sense of directed force communicated by the verb is channelled into an image that suggests the rocket thrust of modern propellants: "on each hand the flames / Driv'n backward slope their pointing spires." Do the flames move upward ("pointing") or downward ("backward")? The answer is both; and the impression is one of great movement, Satan's movement. He steers "incumbent," and while his cumbrousness is introduced to impress us with the strain his unusual weight places on "the dusky air," we are finally impressed by his ability to manage that weight; Satan rather than the air is the hero of these lines. The "force" that "transports a Hill / Torn from *Pelorus*" is not identified, but since the "Archfiend" is the nearest available agent, it is attached to him, as is the entire image. Carried forward by the sequence that began at "Forthwith upright he rears" (a second reading will emphasize the irony in "upright"), the reader accepts "Both glorying to have scap't the *Stygian* flood" (239) as an accurate summary of the scene presented to him. Not that Satan and Beelzebub are consciously granted the status of self-sufficient agents; rather, the question of self-sufficiency does not seem at this point to be relevant to the reading experience. But of course it is the central question, or at least it was at 210 when the epic voice introduced the action; and is again as that same voice returns us to it – in stages: "Both glorying to have scap't the *Stygian* flood / As Gods, and by their own recover'd strength, / Not by the sufferance of Supernal Power" (239–41). First, the words "As Gods" recall "the high permission of all-ruling Heaven" and indicate the blasphemy of "glorying." To the reader, "As Gods" is less a continuation of line 239 than a qualification of the line's literal assertion that protects him (a half-second too late) against accepting it as true. "By thir own recover'd strength" changes as we read it, from an extension of the momentarily neutral "scap't the *Stygian* flood" to the ironic complement of "nor ever thence / Had ris'n...." "Not by the sufferance of Supernal Power" is a flat statement that disdains irony for the simple declarative of truth; the passage is suddenly and firmly placed in the larger perspective which the reader again enjoys after a defection to Satan's. Milton's point here is one he will make again and again; all acts are performed in God's service; what is left to any agent is a choice between service freely rendered and service exacted against his will. Satan continually deludes himself by supposing that he can act apart from God, and in this passage we come to understand that delusion by (momentarily) sharing it. The lesson will be repeated on a larger scale when the contrition Adam and Eve evidence at the close of the tenth book is attributed by the poet to "Prevenient Grace descending" (xi.3) and by God himself to the result of "My motions in him" (xi.91). Thomas Greene observes that "it is a little anti-climactic for the reader after following tremulously the fallen couple's gropings toward redemption...to hear from the Father's lips that he has decreed it – that all of this tenderly human scene, this triumph of conjugal affection and tentative moral searching, occurred only by divine fiat,"[11] while John Peter thinks God's claim "downright unfair."[12] By encouraging the reader to follow the "fallen couple's gropings" and by refraining all the while from direct references to grace or to heavenly powers, Milton allows the illusion of independent action on the human level; and when the reader has (predictably) acquiesced in the illusion, if only by failing to struggle against it, he then reminds him of the truth he ought to have remembered, but *somehow*, in the isolating persuasiveness of a seemingly self-contained experience, forgot.[13] (Life lived or viewed on the human level alone is itself a rhetorical deception.)

These are almost laboratory experiments, tests insulated by rigid controls, obviously didactic. The pattern that unites them is reminiscent of Spenser's technique in *The Faerie Queene*, I.ix. There the approach to Despair's cave is pointedly detailed and the detail is calculated to repel; the man himself is more terrible than the Blatant Beast or the dragon of I.xii, for his ugliness is something we recognize. Spenser's test of his reader is less stringent than Milton's; he makes his warning the experience of this description rather than an abstract statement of disapproval. It is, of course, not enough. Despair's adaptation of Christian rhetoric (guilt, grace) is masterful and the Redcross Knight (along with the reader) allows the impression of one set of appearances (the old man's ugliness) to be effaced by another (the Circean lure of his rhetoric): "Sleepe after toyle, port after stormie seas, / Ease after warre, death after life does greatly please" (40). Spenser eases us along by making it impossible to assign stanza 42 to either the knight or Despair. At that point the syntactical ambiguity is telling; the dialogue is over, and we have joined them both in a three-part unanimity that leads inexorably to the decision of 51:

> At last, resolv'd to worke his finall smart
> He lifted up his hand that backe again did start.

Una's exhortation and accusation — "Come, come away, fraile, feeble, fleshly wight" (53) — is for us as well as her St George, and we need the reminder that she brings to us from a context *outside* the experience of the poem: "In heavenly mercies has thou not a part?" Without this *deus ex machina* we could not escape; without Milton's "snubs" we could not be jolted out of a perspective that is after all *ours*. The lesson in both poems is that the only defense against verbal manipulation (or appearances) is a commitment that stands above the evidence of things that are seen, and the method of both poems is to lead us beyond our perspective by making us feel its inadequacies and the necessity of accepting something which baldly contradicts it. The result is instruction, and instruction is possible only because the reader is asked to observe, analyze, and *place* his experience, that is, to think about it.

In the divorce tracts Milton reveals the source of this poetic technique when he analyzes the teaching of Christ, "not so much a teaching, as an intangling."[14] Christ is found "not so much interpreting the Law with his words, as referring his owne words to be interpreted by the Law."[15] Those who would understand him must themselves decipher the obscurities of his sayings, "for

Christ gives no full comments or continu'd discourses...scattering the heavenly grain of his doctrin like pearle heer and there, which requires a skilfull
and laborious gatherer."[16] In order better to instruct his disciples, who "yet
retain'd the infection of loving old licentious customs," he does not scruple to
mislead them, temporarily: "But why did not Christ seeing their error informe
them? for good cause; it was his profest method not to teach them all things at
all times, but each thing in due place and season...the Disciples took it [one of
his gnomic utterances] in a manifest wrong sense, yet our Saviour did not there
informe them better.... Yet did he not omitt to sow within them the seeds of
sufficient determining, agen the time that his promis'd spirit should bring all
things to their memory."[17] "Due season" means when they are ready for it,
and they will be ready for it when the seeds he has sown obliquely have
brought them to the point where a more direct revelation of the truth will be
efficacious; until then they are allowed to linger in error or at least in partial
ignorance. Recently H. R. MacCallum has shown how Michael uses just this
strategy of indirection and misdirection to lead Adam from the sickness of
despair to faith and spiritual health.[18] Michael's strategy in Book XI is Milton's
strategy in the entire poem, whereby his reader becomes his pupil, taught
according to his present capacities in the hope that he can be educated, in tract
of time, to enlarge them. By first "intangling" us in the folds of Satan's rhetoric,
and then "informing us better" in "due season," Milton forces us to acknowledge the *personal* relevance of the Arch-fiend's existence; and, in the process, he
validates dramatically one of western man's most durable commonplaces, the
equation of the rhetorical appeal (representative of the world of appearances)
with the weakness of the "natural man," that is, with the "defects of our
hearers."

2   Yet Never Saw

The wariness these encounters with demonic attraction make us feel is part of a
larger pattern in which we are taught the hardest of all lessons, distrust of our
own abilities and perceptions. This distrust extends to all the conventional ways
of knowing that might enable a reader to locate himself in the world of any
poem. The questions we ask of our reading experience are in large part the
questions we ask of our day-to-day experience. Where are we, what are the
physical components of our surroundings, what time is it? And while the hard
and clear outline of *Paradise Lost* suggests that the answers to these questions are
readily available to us, immediate contexts repeatedly tell us that they are not.
Consider, for example, the case of Satan's spear. I have seen responsible critics
affirm, casually, that Satan's spear is as large as the mast of a ship; the poem of

course affirms nothing of the kind, but more important, it deliberately encourages such an affirmation, at least temporarily:

> His spear, to equal which the tallest Pine
> Hewn on *Norwegian* Hills to be the Mast
> Of some great Ammiral, were but a wand. (I.292–4)

Throughout *Paradise Lost*, Milton relies on the operation of three truths so obvious that many critics fail to take them into account: (1) the reading experience takes place in time, that is, we necessarily read one word after another; (2) the childish habit of moving the eyes along a page and back again is never really abandoned, although in maturity the movement is more mental than physical, and defies measurement; therefore the line as a unit is a resting place even when rhyme is absent; (3) a mind asked to order a succession of rapidly given bits of detail (mental or physical) seizes on the simplest scheme of organization which offers itself. In this simile, the first line supplies that scheme in the overt comparison between the spear and the tallest pine, and the impression given is one of equality. This is not necessarily so, since logically the following lines could assert any number of things about the relationship between the two objects; but because they are objects, offering the mind the convenience of focal points that are concrete, and because they are linked in the reading sequence by an abstract term of relationship (equal), the reader is encouraged to take from the line an image, however faint and wavering, of the two side by side. As he proceeds that image will be reinforced, since Milton demands that he attach to it the information given in 293 and the first half of 294; that is, in order to maintain the control over the text that a long syntactical unit tends to diminish, the reader will accept "hewn on *Norwegian* hills" as an adjunct of the tallest pine in a very real way. By providing a scene or background (*memoria*) the phrase allows him to strengthen his hold on what now promises to be an increasingly complex statement of relationships. And in the construction of that background the pine frees itself from the hypothetical blur of the first line; it is now real, and through an unavoidable process of association the spear which stood in an undefined relationship to an undefined pine is seen (and I mean the word literally) in a kind of apposition to a conveniently visual pine. (This all happens very quickly in the mind of the reader, who does not have time to analyze the cerebral adjustments forced upon him by the simile.) In short, the equation (in size) of the two objects, in 292 only a possibility, is posited by the reader in 292–4 because it simplifies his task; and this movement towards simplification will be encouraged, for Milton's fit reader, by the obvious reference in "to be the Mast / Of some great Ammiral" to the staff of the Cyclops Polyphemus, identified in the *Aeneid* as a lopped pine[19] and likened in the *Odyssey* to "the mast of some black ship of twenty oars."[20]

The construction of the image and the formulation of the relationship between its components are blocked by the second half of line 294, "were but a wand." This does several things, and I must resort to the mechanical aid of enumeration:

(1) In the confusion that follows this rupture of the reading sequence, the reader loses his hold on the visual focal points, and is unable to associate firmly the wand with either of them. The result is the momentary diminution of Satan's spear as well as the pine, although a second, and more wary reading, will correct this; but corrected, the impression remains (in line 295 a miniature Satan supports himself on a wand-like spear) and in the larger perspective, this aspect of the simile is one of many instances in the poem where Milton's praise of Satan is qualified even as it is bestowed.

(2) The simile illustrates Milton's solution of an apparently insoluble problem. How does a poet provide for his audience a perspective that is beyond the field of its perception? To put the case in terms of *Paradise Lost*, the simile as it functions in other poems will not do here. A simile, especially an epic simile, is an attempt to place persons and/or things, perceived in *a* time and *a* space, in the larger perspective from which their significance must finally be determined. This is possible because the components of the simile have a point of contact – their existence in the larger perspective – which allows the poem to yoke them together without identifying them. Often, part of the statement a simile makes concerns the relationship between the components and the larger perspective in addition to the more obvious relationship between the components themselves; poets suggest this perspective with words like "smaller" and "greater." Thus a trapped hero is at once like and unlike a trapped wolf, and the difference involves their respective positions in a hierarchy that includes more than the physical comparison. A complex and "tight" simile, then, can be an almost scientific description of a bit of the world in which for "the immediate relations of the crude data of experience" are substituted "more refined logical entities, such as relations between relations, or classes of relations, or classes of classes of relations."[21] In Milton's poem, however, the components of a simile often do not have a point of contact that makes their comparison possible in a meaningful (relatable or comprehensible) way. A man exists and a wolf exists, and if categories are enlarged sufficiently it can be said without distortion that they exist on a comparable level; a man exists and Satan (or God) exists, but any statement that considers their respective existences from a human perspective, however inclusive, is necessarily reductive, and is liable to falsify rather than clarify; and of course the human perspective is the only one available. To return to Book I, had Milton asserted the identity of

Satan's spear and the tallest pine, he would not only have sacrificed the awe that attends incomprehensibility; he would also have lied, since clearly the *personae* of his extraterrestrial drama are not confined within the limitations of our time and space. On the other hand, had he said that the spear is larger than one can imagine, he would have sacrificed the concreteness so necessary to the for-mulation of an effective image. What he does instead is grant the reader the convenience of concreteness (indeed fill his mind with it) and then tell him that what he sees is not what is there ("there" is never located). The result is almost a feat of prestidigitation: for the rhetorical negation of the scene so painstak-ingly constructed does not erase it; we are relieved of the necessity of believing the image true, but permitted to retain the solidity it offers our straining imaginations. Paradoxically, our awareness of the inadequacy of what is described and what we can apprehend provides, if only negatively, a sense of what cannot be described and what we cannot apprehend. Thus Milton is able to suggest a reality beyond this one by forcing us to feel, dramatically, its unavailability.

(3) Finally, the experience of reading the simile tells us a great deal about ourselves. How large is Satan's spear? The answer is, we don't know, although it is important that for a moment we think we do. Of course, one can construct, as James Whaler does, a statement of relative magnitudes (spear is to pine as pine is to wand)[22] but while this may be logical, it is not encouraged by the logic of the reading experience which says to us: If one were to compare Satan's spear with the tallest pine the comparison would be inadequate. I submit that any attempt either to search out masts of Norwegian ships or to determine the mean length of wands is irrelevant.

Another instance may make the case clearer. In Book III, Satan lands on the Sun:

> There lands the Fiend, a spot like which perhaps
> Astronomer in the Sun's lucent Orb
> Through his glaz'd optic Tube yet never saw. (588–90)

Again in the first line two focal points (spot and fiend) are offered the reader who sets them side by side in his mind; again the detail of the next one and one half lines is attached to the image, and a scene is formed, strengthening the implied equality of spot and fiend; indeed the physicality of the impression is so persuasive that the reader is led to join the astronomer and looks with him through a reassuringly specific telescope ("glaz'd optic Tube") to see – nothing at all ("yet never saw"). In both similes the reader is encouraged to assume that his perceptions extend to the object the poet would present, only to be informed that he is in error; and both similes are constructed in such a way that the error must be made before it can be acknowledged by a surprised reader. (The parallel to the rhetorical drama between demonic attraction and authorial rebuke should be obvious.) For, however many times the simile is reread, the "yet never saw" is unexpected. The mind cannot perform two operations at the same time, and one can either cling to the imminence of the disclaimer and repeat, silently, " 'yet never saw' is coming, 'yet never saw' is coming," or yield to the demands of the image and attend to its construction; and since the choice is really no choice at all – after each reading the negative is only a memory and cannot compete with the immediacy of the sensory evocation – the taillike half line always surprises.

Of course Milton wants the reader to pull himself up and reread, for this provides a controlled framework within which he is able to realize the extent and implication of his difficulty, much like the framework provided by the before and after warnings surrounding Belial's speech. The implication is personal; the similes and many other effects say to the reader: "I know that you rely upon your senses for your apprehension of reality, but they are unreliable and hopelessly limited." Significantly, Galileo is introduced in both similes; the Tuscan artist's glass represents the furthest extension of human perception, and that is not enough. The entire pattern, of which the instances I analyze here are the smallest part, is, among other things, a preparation for the moment in Book VIII when Adam responds to Raphael's astronomical dissertation: "To whom thus Adam clear'd of doubt." Reader reaction is involuntary: cleared of doubt? by that impossibly tortuous and equivocal description of two all too probable universes?[23] By this point, however, we are able to place our reaction, since Adam's experience here parallels ours in so many places (and a large part of the poem's meaning is communicated by our awareness of the relationship between Adam and ourselves). He *is* cleared of doubt, not because he now knows how the universe is constructed, but because he knows that he cannot know; what clears him of doubt is the certainty of self-doubt, and as with us this certainty is the result of a superior's willingness to grant him, momentarily, the security of his perspective. Milton's lesson is one that twentieth-century science is just now beginning to learn:

Finally, I come to what it seems to me may well be from the long-range point of view the most revolutionary of the insights to be derived from our recent experiences in physics, more revolutionary than the insights afforded by the discoveries of Galileo and Newton, or of Darwin. This is the insight that it is impossible to transcend the human reference point. . . . The new insight comes from a realization that the structure of nature may eventually be such that our processes of thought do not correspond to it sufficiently to permit us to think about it at all.[24]

In *Paradise Lost*, our sense of time proves as illusory as our sense of space and physicality. Jackson Cope quotes with approval Sigfried Giedion and Joseph Frank, who find in modern literature a new way of thinking about time:

The flow of time which has its literary reflection in the Aristotelian development of an action having beginning, middle and end is . . . frozen into the labyrinthine planes of a spatial block which . . . can only be perceived by travelling both temporally and physically from point to point, but whose form has neither beginning, middle, end nor center, and must be effectively conceived as a simultaneity of multiple views.[25]

And Mrs Isabel MacCaffrey identifies the "simultaneity of multiple views" with the eternal moment of God, a moment, she argues, that Milton makes ours:

The long view of time as illusory, telescoped into a single vision, had been often adopted in fancy by Christian writers. . . . Writing of Heaven and the little heaven of Paradise, Milton by a powerful releasing act of the imagination transposed the intuitive single glance of God into the poem's mythical structure. Our vision of history becomes for the time being that of the Creator "whose eye Views all things at one view" (ii. 189–90); like him, we are stationed on a "prospect high Wherin past, present, future he beholds." (iii. 77–8)[26]

The experience of every reader, I think, affirms the truth of these statements; Milton does convince us that the world of his poem is a static one which "slights chronology in favor of a folded structure which continually returns upon itself, or a spiral that circles about a single center."[27] The question I would ask is how does he so convince us? His insistence on simultaneity is easily documented. How many times do we see Christ ascend, after the war in Heaven, after the passion, after Harrowing Hell, after giving Satan his death wound, after the creation, after the final conflagration, at the day of final judgment? How many times do our first parents fall, and how many times are they accorded grace? The answer to all these questions is, "many times" or is it all the time (at each point of time) or perhaps at one, and the same, time. My difficulty with the preceding sentence is a part of my point: I cannot let go of the word "time" and the idea of sequence; timelessness (I am forced to resort to a question-begging negative) is an interesting concept, but we are all of us trapped in the necessity of experiencing in time, and the attempt even to conceive of a state where words like day and evening measure space rather than duration is a difficult one; Chaucer's Troilus, among others, is defeated by it. Mrs MacCaffrey asserts that "spatial imagining" is part of Milton's "mental climate" and the researches of Walter Ong, among others, support her; but if Milton has implanted the eternal moment "into the poem's mythical structure," how does the reader, who, in Cope's words, must travel temporally and physically from point to point,' root it out? Obviously many readers do not; witness the critics who are troubled by contradictory or "impossible" sequences and inartistic repetitions. Again the reactions of these anti-Miltonists are the surest guide to the poet's method; for it is only by encouraging and then "breaking" conventional responses and expectations that Milton can point his reader beyond them. To return to Waldock, part of the poem's apparently "hard and definite" outline is the easy chronology it seems to offer; but the pressures of innumerable local contexts demand adjustments that give the lie to the illusion of sequence and reveal in still another way the inability of the reader to consider this poem as he would any other.

In the opening lines of Book I, chronology and sequence are suggested at once in what is almost a plot line: man disobeys, eats fruit, suffers woe, and awaits rescue. It is a very old and simple story, one that promises a comfortable correlation of plot station and emotional response: horror and fear at the act, sorrow at the result, joy at the happy ending, the whole bound up in the certain knowledge of cause and effect. As Milton crowds more history into his invocation the reader, who likes to know what time it is, will attempt to locate each detail on the continuum of his story line. The inspiration of the shepherd, Moses, is easily placed between the Fall and the restoration; at this point many readers will feel the first twinge of complication, for Moses is a type of Christ who, as the second Adam, restores the first by persevering when he could not; as one begins to construct statements of relationship between the three, the clarity of lines 1–3 fades. Of course there is nothing to force the construction of such statements, and Milton thoughtfully provides in the very next line the sequence-establishing phrase, "In the Beginning." Reassured both by the ordering power of "beginning" and by the allusion to Genesis (which is, after all, the original of all once-upon-a-times), the reader proceeds with the invocation, noting, no doubt, all the riches unearthed by generations of critical exegesis, but still firmly in control of chronology; and that sense of control is reinforced by the two-word introduction to the story proper: "Say first," for with the first we automatically posit a second and then a third, and in sum, a neat row of causal statements leading all the way to an end already known.

The security of sequence, however, is soon taken away. I have for some time conducted a private poll with a single question: "What is your reaction when the second half of line 54 – 'for *now* the thought' – tells you that you are *now* with Satan, in Hell?" The unanimous reply is, "surprise," and an involuntary question: how did I come to be here? Upon rereading, the descent to Hell is again easy and again unchartable. At line 26 the time scheme is still manageable: there is (a) poem time, the *now* in which the reader sits in his chair and listens, with Milton, to the muse, and (b) the named point in the past when the

story ("our Grand Parents . . . so highly to fall off") and our understanding of it
("say first what cause") is assumed to begin. At 33, the "first" is set back to the
act of Satan, now suggested but not firmly identified as the "cause" of 27, and a
third time (c) is introduced, further from (a) than (b), yet still manageable; but
Satan's act also has its antecedent: "what time his Pride / Had cast him out from
Heav'n" (36–7); by this point, "what time" is both an assertion and a question
as the reader struggles to maintain an awkward, backward-moving perspective.
There is now a time (d) and after (that is, before) that an (e) "aspiring . . . He
trusted to have equall'd the most High" (38, 40). Time (f) breaks the pattern,
returning to (d) and providing, in the extended description of 44–53, a respite
from sudden shifts. To summarize: the reader has been asked repeatedly to
readjust his idea of "in the beginning" while holding in suspension two plot
lines (Adam's and Eve's and Satan's) that are eventually, he knows, to be
connected. The effort strains the mind to its capacity, and the relief offered
by the vivid and easy picture of Satan falling is more than welcome.[28] It is at
this time, when the reader's attention has relaxed, that Milton slips by him the
"now" of 54 and the present tense of "torments," the first present in the
passage. The effect is to alert the reader both to his location (Hell) and to his
inability to retrace the journey that brought him there. Rereading leads him
only to repeat the mental occupations the passage demands, and while the
arrival in Hell is anticipated, it is always a surprise. The technique is of course
the technique of the spot and spear similes, and of the clash between involuntary response and authorial rebuke, and again, Milton's intention is to strip
from us another of the natural aids we bring to the task of reading. The passage
itself tells us this in lines 50–1, although the message may pass unnoted at first:
"Nine times the Space that measures Day and Night." Does space measure day
and night? Are day and night space? The line raises these questions, and the
half-line that follows answers them, not "to mortal men" who think in terms of
duration and sequence, not to us. In this poem we must, we will, learn a new
time.

The learning process is slow at first; the reader does not necessarily draw the
inferences I do from this early passage; but again it is the frequency of such
instances that makes my case. In Book II, when the fallen Angels disperse,
some of them explore "on bold adventure" their new home. One of the
landmarks they pass is "Lethe the River of Oblivion," and Milton pauses to
describe its part in God's future plans: "At certain revolutions all the damn'd/
. . . They ferry over this *Lethean* Sound / Both to and fro, thir sorrow to
augment, / And wish and struggle, as they pass to reach / The tempting
stream, with one small drop to lose / In sweet forgetfulness all pain and woe,
/ All in one moment and so near the brink; / But Fate withstands" (597–8,
604–10). At 614 the poet continues with "Thus roving on / In confus'd march

forlorn," and only the phrase "advent'rous bands" in 615 tells the reader that the poet has returned to the fallen angels. The mistake is a natural one: "forlorn" describes perfectly the state of the damned, as does "Confus'd march" their movements "to and fro": indeed a second reflection suggests no mistake at all; the fallen angels *are* the damned, and one drop of Lethe *would* allow them to lose their woe in the oblivion Moloch would welcome. Fate *does* withstand. What Milton has done by allowing this momentary confusion is to point to the identity of these damned and all damned. As they fly past Lethe the fallen angels are all those who will become them; they do not stand for their successors (the word defeats me), they *state* them. In *Paradise Lost*, history and the historical sense are denied and the reader is forced to see events he necessarily perceives in sequence as time-identities. Milton cannot re-create the eternal moment, but by encouraging and then blocking the construction of sequential relationships he can lead the reader to accept the necessity of, and perhaps even apprehend, negatively, a time that is ultimately unavailable to him because of his limitations.

This translation of felt ambiguities, confusions, and tautologies into a conviction of timelessness in the narrative is assured partially by the uniqueness of Milton's "fable." "For the Renaissance", notes Mrs MacCaffrey, "all myths are reflections, distorted or mutilated though they may be, of the one true myth."[29] For Milton all history is a replay of the history he is telling, all rebellions one rebellion, all falls one fall, all heroism the heroism of Christ. And his readers who share this Christian view of history will be prepared to make the connection that exists potentially in the detail of the narrative. The similes are particularly relevant here. The first of these compares Satan to Leviathan, but the comparison, to the informed reader, is a tautology; Satan *is* Leviathan and the simile presents two aspects of one, rather than the juxtaposition of two, components. This implies that Satan is, at the moment of the simile, already deceiving "The Pilot of some small night- founder'd Skiff'; and if the reader has attended to the lesson of his recent encounter with the epic voice he recognizes himself as that pilot, moored during the speech of 1.84–126 by the side of Leviathan. The contests between Satan and Adam, Leviathan and the pilot, rhetoric and the reader – the simile compresses them, and all deceptions, into a single instant, forever recurring. The celebrated falling-leaves simile moves from angel-form to leaves to sedge to Busiris and his Memphian Chivalry, or in typological terms (Pharaoh and Herod are the most common types of Satan), from fallen angels to fallen angels. The compression here is so complex that it defies analysis: the fallen angels as they *lie* on the burning lake (the Red Sea) are already *pursuing* the Sojourners of Goshen (Adam and Eve, the Israelites, the reader) who are for the moment *standing* on the safe shore (Paradise, the reader's chair). In XII.191, Pharoah becomes the River-Dragon or Leviathan (Isaiah 27: I), pointing to the ultimate unity of the Leviathan and falling leaves similes themselves. As similes they are uninformative; how numberless are the falling angels? They are as numberless as Pharaoh's host, that is, as fallen angels, and Pharaoh's host encompasses all the damned who have been, are, and will be, all the damned who will fly longingly above Lethe. As vehicles of perception, however, they tell us a great deal, about the cosmos as it is in a reality we necessarily distort, about the ultimate subjectivity of sequential time, about ourselves.

There are many such instances in the early books, and together they create a sensitivity to the difficulties of writing and reading this particular poem. When Milton's epic voice remarks that pagan fablers err relating the story of Mulciber's ejection from Heaven (I.747), he does not mean to say that the story is not true, but that it is a distorted version of the story he is telling, and that any attempt to apprehend the nature of the angels' fall by comparing it to the fall of Mulciber or of Hesiod's giants involves another distortion that cannot be allowed if *Paradise Lost* is to be read correctly. On the other hand the attempt is hazarded (the reader cannot help it), the distortion is acknowledged along with the unavailability of the correct reading, and Milton's point is made despite, or rather because of, the intractability of his material. When Satan's flight from the judgment of God's scales (IV. 1015) is presented in a line that paraphrases the last line of the *Aeneid*, the first impulse is to translate the allusion into a comparison that might begin, "Satan is like Turnus in that...". but of course, the relationship as it exists in a reality beyond that formed by our sense of literary history, is quite the opposite. Turnus's defiance of the fates and his inevitable defeat are significant and comprehensible only in the light of what Satan did in a past that our time signatures cannot name and is about to do in a present (poem time) that is increasingly difficult to identify. Whatever the allusion adds to the richness of the poem's texture or to Milton's case for superiority in the epic genre, it is also one more assault on the confidence of a reader who is met at every turn with demands his intellect cannot even consider.

Notes

This chapter incorporates, with some additions, two articles published in the Summer and Autumn issues of *The Critical Quarterly* (1965).
1   *Paradise Lost and its Critics* (Cambridge, 1947), p. 15. I consider Waldock's book to be the most forthright statement of an anti-Miltonism that can be found in the criticism of Leavis and Eliot, and, more recently, of Empson, R. J. Zwi Werblowsky, H. R. Swardson, and John Peter. Bernard Bergonzi concludes his analysis

of Waldock by saying, "no attempt has been made to defend the poem in the same detailed and specific manner in which it has been attacked" (*The Living Milton*, ed. Frank Kermode, London, 1960, p. 171). This essay is such an attempt. Bergonzi goes on to assert that "a successful answer to Waldock would have to show that narrative structure of *Paradise Lost does* possess the kind of coherence and psychological plausibility that we have come to expect from the novel. Again there can be no doubt that it does not" (p. 174). I shall argue that the coherence and psychological plausibility of the poem are to be found in the relationship between its effects and the mind of its reader. To some extent my reading has been anticipated by Joseph Summers in his brilliant study, *The Muse's Method* (Harvard, 1962). See especially pp. 30–1: "Milton anticipated . . . the technique of the 'guilty reader' . . . The readers as well as the characters have been involved in the evil and have been forced to recognize and to judge their involvement." See also Anne Ferry's *Milton's Epic Voice: The Narrator in Paradise Lost* (Harvard, 1963), pp. 44–66: "We are meant to remember that the events of the poem have already occurred . . . and that it is because of what happens in the poem, because we and all men were corrupted by the Fall, that we stand in need of a guide to correct our reading of it. The narrative voice is our guide" (p. 47). Finally I refer the reader to Douglas Knight's excellent article, "The Dramatic Center of *Paradise Lost*," *South Atlantic Quarterly* (1964), pp. 44–59, which reached me only after this manuscript was substantially completed. Mr Knight argues, as I do, for the analytic nature of the reading experience. Our emphases are different (he focuses mainly on the similes) but our general conclusions accord perfectly: "The poem's material and structure fuse as they put pressure on the reader to assess and estimate the place where he is to stand; Adam and Eve can almost be said to dramatize for him a mode of action which is his own if he reads the poem properly. For *Paradise Lost* is a work of art whose full achievement is one of mediation and interactivity among three things: a way of reading the poem, an estimate of it as a whole work, and a reader's proper conduct of his life" (pp. 56–7).

2   *Paradise Lost and its Critics*, p. 24.

3   Ibid., p. 77.

4   The tradition begins with Plato's opposition of rhetoric to dialectic. Socrates' interlocutors *discover* the truth for themselves, when, in response to his searching questions, they are led to examine their opinions and, perhaps, to refute them. The rhetorician, on the other hand, creates a situation in which his auditors have no choice but to accept the beliefs he urges on them. In *The Testimony of the President, Professors, Tutors, and Hebrew Instructor of Harvard College in Cambridge, Against the Reverend Mr. George Whitefield, And his Conduct* (Boston, 1744), Whitefield is censured because of "his power to raise the People to any Degree of Warmth he pleases, whereby they stand ready to receive almost any Doctrine he is pleased to broach . . ." (p. 13). The danger lies in the weakness of the fallen intellect which is more likely to be swayed by appearances than by the naked presentation of the truth. In recognition of this danger, the Puritan preacher first sets out the points of doctrine in the form of a Ramist "proof" before turning in the "uses" to the figures

of exhortation. "For a minister to lure men to an emotional reception of the creed before their imaginations had conceived it, before their intellects were convinced of it and their wills had deliberately chosen to live by it, was fully as immoral as openly to persuade them to wrong doing" (Perry Miller, *The New England Mind: The Seventeenth Century*, Beacon Press Edition, Boston, 1961, p. 308). A similar distrust of rhetoric manifests itself in the writings of the Baconian empiricists. Figurative language is said to be useless for the description of experiments or the formulation of conclusions, and rhetorical appeals are disdained because they dull intellects which should be alertly analytic. Bacon protests against the delivery (presentation) of knowledge "in such form as may be best believed, and not as may be best examined" and advises instead "the method of the mathematiques" (*Selected Writings*, ed. H. G. Dick, New York, 1955, p. 304). To Hobbes geometry is "the only science that it has pleased God hitherto to bestow on mankind," a science which, as Aristotle said, no one uses fine language in teaching (*Leviathan*, ed. H. W. Schneider, New York, 1958, p. 41). Sprat believes that eloquence, "this vicious volubility of *Tongue*," should be "banish'd out of all *civil Societies*" because the ornaments of speaking "are in open defiance against *Reason*" and hold too much correspondence with the passions, giving the mind "a motion too changeable, and bewitching, to consist with *right practice*" (*The History of the Royal Society of London*, 1667, p. 111). [Fish examines the philosophical-linguistic objections to rhetoric at greater length in chapter 3 of *Surprised by Sin*.] Complementing the fear of rhetoric is a faith in the safeguards provided by the use of analytical method. Where one short-circuits the rational and panders to the emotions, the other speaks directly to the reason. Where one compels assent without allowing due deliberation, the other encourages the auditor or reader to examine the progress of a composition at every point, whether it be a poem, a sermon, or the report of an experiment. "Now my plan," announces Bacon, "is to proceed regularly and gradually from one axiom to another." However complex the experiment, he proposes to "subjoin a clear account of the manner in which I made it; that men knowing exactly how each point was made out, may see whether there be any error connected with it" (*Preface to the Great Instauration*, in *The English Philosophers From Bacon to Mill*, ed. E. A. Burtt, New York, 1939, p. 21). Puritan preachers dispose their texts with the same care so that their auditors can receive the discourse according to the manner of its composition. The focus is always on the mind, which must be led, step by step, and with a consciousness of an answering obligation, to a clear understanding of conceptual content. (Again we see the similarity to Platonic dialectic.) In writing *Paradise Lost*, then, Milton is able to draw upon a tradition of didacticism which finds its expression in a distrust of the affective and an insistence on the intellectual involvement of the listener-pupil; in addition he could rely on his readers to associate logic and the capacity for logical reasoning with the godly instinct in man, and the passions, to which rhetoric appeals, with his carnal instincts.

5   As Davis Harding points out (*The Club of Hercules*, Urbana, Ill., 1962, pp. 103–8), this passage is also the basis of the bee simile at line 768. The reader who catches the allusion here at line 108 will carry it with him to the end of the book and to the

simile. One should also note the parallel between the epic voice's comment at 126 and Virgil's comment on Aeneas' first speech (as Milton's early editors noted it): "Talia voce refert, curisque ingentibus aeger/spem voltu simulat, premit altum corde dolorem." But as is always the case in such comparisons, Satan suffers by it, since his deception is self-deception and involves an attempt to deny (to himself) the reality of an authority greater than his, while Aeneas' deception is, in context, an evidence of his faith in the promise of a higher authority. The hope he feigns is only partially a pretense; if it were all pretense, he would not bother.

6 Michael Krouse, *Milton's Samson and the Christian Tradition* (Princeton, 1949), p. 102.

7 *Answerable Style: Essays on Paradise Lost* (Minneapolis, 1953), p. 124. Frank Kermode's analysis in *The Living Milton* (p. 106) supports my position: "He uses the epic poet's privilege of intervening in his own voice, and he does this to regulate the reader's reaction; but some of the effects he gets from this device are far more complicated than is sometimes supposed. The corrective comments inserted after Satan has been making out a good case for himself are not to be lightly attributed to a crude didacticism; naturally they are meant to keep the reader on the right track, but they also allow Milton to preserve the energy of the myth. While we are hearing Satan we are not hearing the comment; for the benefit of a fallen audience the moral correction is then applied, but its force is calculatedly lower; and the long-established custom of claiming that one understands Satan better than Milton did is strong testimony to the tact with which it is done." Anne Ferry (*Milton's Epic Voice*) is closer to Stein: "The speech is meant to belie the inner experience and the comment to point out the power of the contradiction. Satan's words do not sound despairing precisely because the division within him is so serious. Only the inspired narrator can penetrate the appearance to discover the reality" (p. 120). Mrs Ferry's discussion of this pattern focuses on her conception of the narrator as a divided being: "These didactic comments remind us of the narrator's presence and his special vision in order that we may accept his moral interpretation of the story. . . . They are not *opposed* to the action of the poem, but are part of the total pattern of that action, not checks upon our immediate responses to drama, but a means of expressing the speaker's double point of view, his fallen knowledge and his inspired vision" (p. 56). It seems to me that the didactic comments *are* checks upon our immediate responses; nor do I believe it an oversimplification "to make the speaker" a judge "who lectures us like a prig just when we are most involved in the story." I agree wholeheartedly, however, with Mrs Ferry's arranging of interpretative hierarchies: "So that when we find complexity in our response to the behavior or speech of a character and to the statement of the narrator which interprets it, we must judge the character by the interpretation, not the interpretation by the character's words or acts" (p. 16). I would add (and this is the heart of my thesis) that we must judge ourselves in the same way.

8 Richard Baxter, *The Saints Everlasting Rest* (London, 1658).

9 New York/London, 1957.

10 *Paradise Lost and its Critics*, p. 79. Cf. John Peter, *A Critique of Paradise Lost* (London, 1960), p. 44: "the comments [of the epic voice] seem simply biased. . . . His premises are correct and he deduces from them a perfectly feasible plan."

11 *The Descent from Heaven: A Study in Epic Continuity* (New Haven, 1963), p. 407.

12 *A Critique of Paradise Lost*, p. 145.

13 Cf. *The Pilgrim's Progress*, ed. J. B. Wharey, rev. R. Sharrock (Oxford, 1960), p. 134. "He asked them then, If they had not of them Shepherds *a note of direction for the way?* They answered; Yes. But did you, said he, when you was at a stand, pluck out and read your note? They answered, No. He asked him why? They said they forgot. He asked moreover, If the Shepherds did not bid them beware of the *Flatterer?* They answered, Yes: But we did not imagine, said they, that this fine-speaking man had been he . . . So they . . . went softly along in the right way, Singing. *Come hither, you that walk along the way; / See how the Pilgrims fare, that go a stray! / They catched are in an intangling Net, / 'Cause they good Counsel lightly did forget:/ . . . Let this your caution be.*"

14 *Complete Prose Works of John Milton*, vol. ii, ed. Ernest Sirluck (New Haven, 1959), p. 642.

15 Ibid., p. 301.

16 Ibid., p. 338.

17 Ibid., pp. 678–9.

18 "Milton and Sacred History: Books XI and XII of *Paradise Lost*", in *Essays in English Literature from the Renaissance to the Victorian Age, Presented to A. S. P. Woodhouse*, ed. Millar MacLure and F. W. Watt (Toronto, 1964), pp. 149–68.

19 iii. 659. Harding insists that "if this passage does not conjure up a mental picture of Polyphemus on the mountaintop, steadying his footsteps with a lopped pine . . . it has not communicated its full meaning to us" (*The Club of Hercules*, p. 63). In my reading a "full reading" of the passage involves the recognition of the inadequacy of the mental picture so conjured up.

20 The translation is E. V. Rieu's in the Penguin Classic Edition (Baltimore, 1946), p. 148.

21 A. N. Whitehead in *The Limits of Language*, ed. Walker Gibson (New York, 1962), pp. 13–14. In classical theory, metaphor is the figure of speech whose operation bears the closest resemblance to the operations of dialectic and logic. Aristotle defines it in the *Poetics* as "a transference either from genus to species or from species to genus, or from species to species."

22 "The Miltonic Simile," *PMLA* xlvi (1931), 1064.

23 Milton clearly anticipates this reaction when he describes the dialogue in the "argument"; "Adam inquires concerning celestial Motions, is *doubtfully* answer'd" (emphasis mine). See also v. 261–6: "As when by night the Glass/of *Galileo*, less assur'd, observes/Imagin'd Lands and Regions in the Moon: / Or Pilot from amidst the *Cyclades/Delos* or *Samos* first appearing kens/A cloudy spot." It should be noted that in all these passages certain details form a consistent pattern: Galileo, the moon, spots (representing an unclear vision), etc. The pattern is fulfilled in Raphael's disquisition on the possible arrangement of the heavens. See Greene's

excellent reading of Raphael's descent (*The Descent from Heaven*, p. 387): "The fallen reader's imperfect reason must strain to make out relations as the pilot strains with his physical eyes, as Galileo strains with his telescope, as the fowls gaze with mistaken recognition on the angel, as Adam and Eve will fail to strain and so blur our vision." See also Northrop Frye, *The Return of Eden* (Toronto, 1965), p. 58: "Galileo thus appears to symbolize, for Milton, the gaze outward on physical nature, as opposed to the concentration inward on human nature, the speculative reason that searches for new places, rather than the moral reason that tries to create a new state of mind."

24 P.W. Bridgman, quoted in *The Limits of Language*, p. 21.

25 *The Metaphoric Structure of Paradise Lost* (Baltimore, 1962), pp. 14–15.

26 *Paradise Lost as "Myth"* (Cambridge, Mass., 1959), p. 53.

27 Ibid., p. 45.

28 The technique is reminiscent of Virgil's "historical present," which is used to bring the action of the epic before the reader's eyes. Recently Helen Gardner has reached conclusions similar to those offered here concerning the operation of time and space in the poem. See her *A Reading of Paradise Lost* (Oxford, 1965), pp. 39–51: "Milton's poem must move in time, yet he continually suggests that the time of the poem is an illusion" (39); "Milton, as he plays us into his poem, is using our human measurement to convey vastness sensuously" (40); "He continually satisfies and then defeats our powers of visualization" (41). See also Roy Daniells, *Milton, Mannerism and Baroque* (Toronto, 1963), p. 98; W. B. C. Watkins, *An Anatomy of Milton's Verse* (Baton Rouge, 1955), p. 44; Anne Ferry, *Milton's Epic Voice*, pp. 46–7.

29 *Paradise Lost as "Myth,"* p. 14.

2
Is There a Text in This Class?

Stanley Fish's contribution to our intellectual life has been enormous. Literary criticism will never be the same after his demonstration that interpreters run in packs, and that how we read texts has as much to do with the interests of these "interpretive communities" as with the texts themselves. This deeply enabling insight makes it possible to talk about interpretation as a collective and institutional phenomenon, not just a random set of individual responses.

Fish has never denied that there is such a thing as getting texts right, as vulgar Fish-bashers have taken him to be saying. His point, rather, is that getting texts right is a matter of negotiation within a community, not arriving at the Holy Grail of the text itself or at fixed rules of interpretation. According to Fish, however, we have been falsely trained to believe that, without stable rules, interpretation degenerates into a relativism in which anything goes and whatever is is right. Fish argues that though such relativism may be a problem in theory, it cannot be in practice, since we always have recourse to some "system of intelligibility" that guides us.

But these challenging arguments are better taken as provocations to further thought than as final truths. Can Fish be right, for example, in arguing that interpreters "create" meanings without prompting from any preexistent text? Can it be true, as Fish argues in "How to Recognize a Poem When You See One," that the "act of recognition" is not "triggered" by the features of texts or other objects, but itself "produces" or "creates" those features that we then imagine to exist independent of us?

(325–7). And can the fact that interpreters come in subcommunities sufficiently explain how they change their minds? Don't we necessarily assume
that our readings are answerable to something outside our orbit of
expectations?

These problems arise in the essay, "Is There a Text in This Class?" On the
first day of the semester, a professor misconstrues a student's question, "Is
there a text in this class?" as a question about the assigned reading. On
being corrected – "No, no. I mean in this class do we believe in poems
and things, or is it just us?" – the professor recognizes that the
question is really about the theory of interpretation that will guide the
course.

The example is hard to square with the theoretical conclusions Fish
draws from it. How, after at first misconstruing the student's question, is
the professor able to revise his interpretation? After considerable wrest-
ling with the question, Fish concludes that the professor adjusts his understanding of the student's words "not because she has reformulated or
refined them," but because her words can "now be read or heard within
the same system of intelligibility from which they issue" (315–16).

But this description patently misrepresents what happens in the
exchange. For it is only after the student "has reformulated or refined"
her words that the professor is able to perceive them "within the same
system of intelligibility from which they issue." If mere membership in the
same "system of intelligiblllty" were sufficient to produce understanding,
then how could the professor have ever got the student's question wrong
in the first place?

It seems impossible to avoid the commonsense, if banal, assumption
that an external stimulus "triggered" the revised reading. To support his
theory, however, Fish has to deny the possibility of such an external
stimulus. He argues that we never have access to anything "outside" the
"situation" or interpretive community that we're in at any given moment.
For him the incident illustrates that understanding is always "specific" to
particular "systems of intelligibility" and never "operates above or across
situations."

So Fish's argument ultimately hinges on our ability to know where one
"system of intelligibility," "situation," or "interpretive community" ends
and another begins, without messy overlap. But no such distinctions are
possible. Indeed, the ability to operate across (if not above) "situations" is
intrinsic to any coherent notion of understanding or belief. For example,
contrary to Fish, the idea on which the student–professor exchange turns,
that the objects we encounter may be projections of our minds or languages, is not "specific" to any particular discourse-community, such as
those au courant with recent literary theory. The idea is a familiar one

across many different communities, thereby accounting for how this essay can be explained to students who at first may not understand it.

At least three critics – Scholes, Dasenbrock, and me – have argued that Fish too readily treats beliefs as if they comprise consistent, monolithic, and discrete "systems" with a clear inside and outside.[1] Dasenbrock, following Donald Davidson, argues that our beliefs are not structured in this systematic, consistent way, a fact that explains how we can inhabit the beliefs of others and even differ from our own beliefs. Fish assumes that we always believe our own beliefs, but arguably we never quite do, and this explains how it is possible to communicate across interpretive communities and why, contrary to Fish, it is legitimate to "worry" about conflicts of belief.

Note

1 See Reed Way Dasenbrock, "Do We Write the Text We Read?," *College English* 53: 1 (January, 1991), 7–17; Robert Scholes, *Textual Power* (New Haven: Yale University Press, 1985), 149–65; Gerald Graff, "Interpretation in Tlön: A Response to Stanley Fish," *New Literary History* XVII: 1 (Autumn, 1985), 109–17. See also Fish's response to my essay in the same volume, "Resistance and Independence: A Reply to Gerald Graff" (119–27), in which Fish concedes that interpretive communities overlap but fails to acknowledge the problems such a concession poses for his argument.

Gerald Graff

[The essays in my 1980 volume, *Is There a Text in This Class?*, have a double origin, in the incident that gave them their title, and in Meyer Abrams's recently published paper "How To Do Things with Texts," a forthright attack on the work of Jacques Derrida, Harold Bloom, and me. I was present when Abrams delivered the paper at the Lionel Trilling Seminar of 1978, and I remember laughing very hard when he took on Bloom and Derrida and trying very hard to laugh when he turned his attention to me. Abrams's arguments are familiar; they are essentially the same he deployed against J. Hillis Miller in the "pluralism" debate. Specifically, he accuses each "Newreader" of playing a double game, of "introducing his own interpretive strategy when reading someone else's text, but tacitly relying on communal norms when undertaking to communicate the methods and results of his interpretations to his own readers" (*Partisan Review*, no. 4 (1979) 587). Miller, Derrida, and the others write books and essays, and engage in symposia and debates, and in so doing use the standard language in order to deconstruct the standard language. The very presumption that they are understood is an argument against the position they urge.

As a counterargument this has a certain prima facie plausibility, if only because it imagines as its object a theory that renders understanding impossible. But in the theory of this Newreader, understanding is always possible, but not from the outside. That is, the reason that I can speak and presume to be understood by someone like Abrams is that I speak to him *from within* a set of interests and concerns, and it is in relation to those interests and concerns that I assume he will hear my words. If what follows is communication or understanding, it will not be because he and I share a language, in the sense of knowing the meanings of individual words and the rules for combining them, but because a way of thinking, a form of life, shares us, and implicates us in a world of already-in-place objects, purposes, goals, procedures, values, and so on; and it is to the features of that world that any words we utter will be heard as necessarily referring. Thus Abrams and I could talk about whether or not a poem was a pastoral, advance and counter arguments, dispute evidence, concede points, and so forth, but we could do these things only because "poem" and "pastoral" are possible labels of identification within a universe of discourse that also includes stipulations as to what would count as an identifying mark, and ways of arguing that such a mark is or is not there. It would be within the assumption of such ways, stipulations, and classifications that Abrams and I would proceed, and we could not proceed at all if either of us were someone for whom they were not already assumed. Nor would it be enough to give someone "on the outside" a set of definitions (of the order "a poem is...," "a genre is...") because in order to grasp the meaning of an individual term, you must already have grasped the general activity (in this case academic literary criticism) in relation to which it could be thought to be meaningful; a system of intelligibility cannot be reduced to a list of the things it renders intelligible. What Abrams and those who agree with him do not realize is that communication occurs only *within* such a system (or context, or situation, or interpretive community) and that the understanding achieved by two or more persons is specific to that system and determinate only within its confines. Nor do they realize that such an understanding is enough and that the more perfect understanding they desire – an understanding that operates above or across situations – would have no place in the world even if it were available, because it is only in situations – with their interested specifications as to what counts as a fact, what it is possible to say, what will be heard as an argument – that one is called on to understand.

These essays were originally delivered as the John Crowe Ransom Memorial Lectures, and were given at Kenyon College from April 8 through 13, 1979. In effect, I was engaged in a week-long seminar consisting of some three hundred members, and I found the experience both exhilarating and exhausting. Apparently, some of the same feelings were shared by the audience, for in an editorial written for the college newspaper (entitled "Fish Baits Audience") generous praise of my "intellectual skill" was immediately qualified by the observation that, needless to say, "it was not always the skill of a gentleman."]

On the first day of the new semester a colleague at Johns Hopkins University was approached by a student who, as it turned out, had just taken a course from me. She put to him what I think you would agree is a perfectly straightforward question: "Is there a text in this class?" Responding with a confidence so perfect that he was unaware of it (although in telling the story, he refers to this moment as "walking into the trap"), my colleague said, "Yes; it's the *Norton Anthology of Literature*," whereupon the trap (set not by the student but by the infinite capacity of language for being appropriated) was sprung: "No, no," she said, "I mean in this class do we believe in poems and things, or is it just us?" Now it is possible (and for many tempting) to read this anecdote as an illustration of the dangers that follow upon listening to people like me who preach the instability of the text and the unavailability of determinate meanings; but in what follows I will try to read it as an illustration of how baseless the fear of these dangers finally is.

Of the charges levied against what Meyer Abrams has recently called the New Readers (Derrida, Bloom, Fish) the most persistent is that these apostles of indeterminacy and undecidability ignore, even as they rely upon, the "norms and possibilities" embedded in language, the "linguistic meanings" words undeniably have, and thereby invite us to abandon "our ordinary realm of experience in speaking, hearing, reading and understanding" for a world in which "no text can mean anything in particular" and where "we can never say just what anyone means by anything he writes."[1] The charge is that literal or normative meanings are overriden by the actions of willful interpreters. Suppose we examine this indictment in the context of the present example. What, exactly, is the normative or literal or linguistic meaning of "Is there a text in this class?"

Within the framework of contemporary critical debate (as it is reflected in the pages, say, of *Critical Inquiry*) there would seem to be only two ways of answering this question: either there *is* a literal meaning of the utterance and we should be able to say what it is, or there are as many meanings as there are readers and no one of them is literal. But the answer suggested by my little story is that the utterance has *two* literal meanings: within the circumstances assumed by my colleague (I don't mean that he took the step of assuming them, but that he was already stepping within them) the utterance is obviously a question about whether or not there is a required textbook in this particular course; but within the circumstances to which he was alerted by his student's corrective response, the utterance is just as obviously a question about the instructor's position (within the range of positions available in contemporary literary theory) on the status of the text. Notice that we do not have here a case of indeterminacy or undecidability but of a determinacy and decidability that do not always have the same shape and that can, and in this instance do, change. My colleague was not hesitating between two (or more) possible meanings of the utterance; rather, he immediately apprehended what seemed to be an inescapable meaning, given his prestructured understanding of the situation, and then he immediately apprehended another inescapable meaning when that understanding was altered. Neither meaning was imposed (a favorite word in the anti-newreader polemics) on a more normal one by a private, idiosyncratic interpretive act; both interpretations were a function of precisely the public and constituting norms (of language and understanding) invoked by Abrams. It is just that these norms are not embedded in the language (where they may be read out by anyone with sufficiently clear, that is, unbiased, eyes) but in here in an institutional structure within which one hears utterances as already organized with reference to certain assumed purposes and goals. Because both my colleague and his student are situated in that institution, their interpretive activities are not free, but what constrains them are the understood practices and assumptions of the institution and not the rules and fixed meanings of a language system.

Another way to put this would be to say that neither reading of the question – which we might for convenience's sake label as "Is there a text in this class?"$_1$ and "Is there a text in this class?"$_2$ – would be immediately available to any native speaker of the language. "Is there a text in this class?"$_1$ is interpretable or readable only by someone who already knows what is included under the general rubric "first day of class" (what concerns animate students, what bureaucratic matters must be attended to before instruction begins) and who therefore hears the utterance under the aegis of that knowledge, which is not applied after the fact but is responsible for the shape the fact immediately has. To someone whose consciousness is not already informed by that knowledge, "Is there a text in this class?"$_1$ would be just as unavailable as "Is there a text in this class?"$_2$ would be to someone who was not already aware of the disputed issues in contemporary literary theory. I am not saying that for some readers or hearers the question would be wholly unintelligible (indeed, in the course of this essay I will be arguing that unintelligibility, in the strict or pure sense, is an impossibility), but that there are readers and hearers for whom the intelligibility of the question would have neither of the shapes it had, in a temporal succession, for my colleague. It is possible, for example, to imagine someone who would hear or intend the question as an inquiry about the location of an object, that is, "I think I left my text in this class; have you seen it?" We would then have an "Is there a text in this class?"$_3$ and the possibility, feared by the defenders of the normative and determinate, of an endless succession of numbers, that is, of a world in which every utterance has an infinite plurality of meanings. But that is not what the example, however it might be extended, suggests at all. In any of the situations I have imagined (and in any that I might be able to imagine) the meaning of the utterance would be severely constrained, not after it was heard but in the ways in which it *could*, in the first place, be heard. An infinite plurality of meanings would be a fear only if sentences existed in a state in which they were not already embedded in, and had come into view as a function of, some situation or other. That state, if it could be located, would be the normative one, and it would be disturbing indeed if the norm were free-floating and indeterminate. But there is no such state; sentences emerge only in situations, and within those situations, the normative meaning of an utterance will always be obvious or at least accessible, although within another situation that same utterance, no longer the same, will have another normative meaning that will be no less obvious and accessible. (My colleague's experience is precisely an illustration.) This does not mean that there is no way to discriminate between the meanings an utterance will have in different situations, but that the discrimination will already have been made by virtue of our being in a situation (we are never not in one) and that in another situation the discrimination will also have already been made, but differently. In other words, while at any one point it is always possible to order and rank "Is there a text in this class?"$_1$ and "Is there a text in this class?"$_2$ (because they will always have already been ranked), it will never be possible to give them an immutable once-and-for-all ranking, a ranking that is independent of their appearance or nonappearance in situations (because it is only in situations that they do or do not appear).

Nevertheless, there is a distinction to be made between the two that allows us to say that, in a limited sense, one is more normal than the other: for while each is perfectly normal in the context in which their literalness is immediately obvious (the successive contexts occupied by my colleague), as things stand now, one of those contexts is surely more available, and therefore more likely to be the perspective within which the utterance is heard, than the other. Indeed, we seem to have here an instance of what I would call "institutional nesting": if "Is there a text in this class?"$_1$ is hearable only by those who know what is included under the rubric "first day of class," and if "Is there a text in this class?"$_2$ is hearable only by those whose categories of understanding include the concerns of contemporary literary theory, then it is obvious that in a random population presented with the utterance, more people would "hear" "Is there a text in this class?"$_1$ than "Is there a text in this class?"$_2$ and, moreover, that while "Is there a text in this class?"$_1$ could be immediately hearable by someone for whom "Is there a text in this class?"$_2$ would have to be laboriously explained, it is difficult to imagine someone capable of hearing "Is there a text in this class?"₂ who was not already capable of hearing "Is there a text in this class."₁ (One is hearable by anyone in the profession and by most students and by many workers in the book trade, and the other only by those in the profession who would not think it peculiar to find, as I did recently, a critic referring to a phrase "made popular by Lacan.") To admit as much is not to weaken my argument by reinstating the category of the normal, because the category as it appears in that argument is not transcendental but institutional; and while no institution is so universally in force and so perdurable that the meanings it enables will be normal for ever, some institutions or forms of life are so widely lived in that for a great many people the meanings they enable seem "naturally" available and it takes a special effort to see that they are the products of circumstances.

The point is an important one, because it accounts for the success with which an Abrams or an E. D. Hirsch can appeal to a shared understanding of ordinary language and argue from that understanding to the availability of a core of determinate meanings. When Hirsch offers "The air is crisp" as an example of a "verbal meaning" that is accessible to all speakers of the language, and distinguishes what is sharable and determinate about it from the associations that may, in certain circumstances, accompany it (for example, "I should have eaten less at supper," "Crisp air reminds me of my childhood in Vermont"),[2] he is counting on his readers to agree so completely with his sense of what that shared and normative verbal meaning is that he does not bother even to specify it; and although I have not taken a survey, I would venture to guess that his optimism, with respect to this particular example, is well founded. That is, most, if not all, of his readers immediately understand the utterance as a rough meteorological description predicting a certain quality of the local atmosphere. But the "happiness" of the example, far from making Hirsch's point (which is always, as he has recently reaffirmed, to maintain "the stable determinacy of meaning")[3] makes mine. The obviousness of the utterance's meaning is not a function of the values its words have in a linguistic system that is independent of context; rather, it is because the words are heard as already embedded in a context that they have a meaning that Hirsch can then cite as obvious. One can see this by embedding the words in another context and observing how quickly another "obvious" meaning emerges. Suppose, for example, we came upon "The air is crisp" (which you are even now hearing as Hirsch assumes you hear it) in the middle of a discussion of music ("When the piece is played correctly the air is crisp"); it would immediately be heard as a comment on the performance by an instrument or instruments of a musical air. Moreover, it would *only* be heard that way, and to hear it in Hirsch's way would require an effort on the order of a strain. It could be objected that in

Hirsch's text "The air is crisp"₁ has no contextual setting at all; it is merely presented, and therefore any agreement as to its meaning must be because of the utterance's acontextual properties. But there *is* a contextual setting and the sign of its presence is precisely the absence of any reference to it. That is, it is impossible even to think of a sentence independently of a context, and when we are asked to consider a sentence for which no context has been specified, we will automatically hear it in the context in which it has been most often encountered. Thus Hirsch invokes a context by not invoking it; by not surrounding the utterance with circumstances, he directs us to imagine it in the circumstances in which it is most likely to have been produced; and to so imagine it is already to have given it a shape that seems at the moment to be the only one possible.

What conclusions can be drawn from these two examples? First of all, neither my colleague nor the reader of Hirsch's sentence is constrained by the meanings words have in a normative linguistic system; and yet neither is free to confer on an utterance any meaning he likes. Indeed, "confer" is exactly the wrong word because it implies a two-stage procedure in which a reader or hearer first scrutinizes an utterance and *then* gives it a meaning. The argument of the preceding pages can be reduced to the assertion that there is no such first stage, that one hears an utterance within, and not as preliminary to determin- ing, a knowledge of its purposes and concerns, and that to so hear it is already to have assigned it a shape and given it a meaning. In other words, the problem of how meaning is determined is only a problem if there is a point at which its determination has not yet been made, and I am saying that there is no such point.

I am *not* saying that one is never in the position of having to self-consciously figure out what an utterance means. Indeed, my colleague is in just such a position when he is informed by his student that he has not heard her question as she intended it ("No, No, I mean in this class do we believe in poems and things, or is it just us?") and therefore must now figure it out. But the "it" in this (or any other) case is not a collection of words waiting to be assigned a meaning but an utterance whose already assigned meaning has been found to be inappropriate. While my colleague has to begin all over again, he does not have to begin from square one; and indeed he never was at square one, since from the very first his hearing of the student's question was informed by his assumption of what its concerns could possibly be. (That is why he is not "free" even if he is unconstrained by determinate meanings.) It is that assumption rather than his performance within it that is challenged by the student's correction. She tells him that he has mistaken her meaning, but this is not to say that he has made a mistake in combining her words and syntax into a meaningful unit; it is rather that the meaningful unit he immediately discerns is a function of a mistaken identification (made before she speaks) of her intention. He was prepared as she stood before him to hear the kind of thing students ordinarily say on the first day of class, and therefore that is precisely what he heard. He has not misread the text (his is not an error in calculation) but mis*pre*read the text, and if he is to correct himself he must make another (pre)determination of the structure of interests from which her question issues. This, of course, is exactly what he does and the question of how he does it is a crucial one, which can best be answered by first considering the ways in which he *didn't* do it.

He didn't do it by attending to the literal meaning of her response. That is, this is not a case in which someone who has been misunderstood clarifies her meaning by making more explicit, by varying or adding to her words in such a way as to render their sense inescapable. Within the circumstances of utterance as he has assumed them her words are perfectly clear, and what she is doing is asking him to imagine other circumstances in which the same words will be equally, but differently, clear. Nor is it that the words she does add ("No, No, I mean...") direct him to those other circumstances by picking them out from an inventory of all possible ones. For this to be the case there would have to be an inherent relationship between the words she speaks and a particular set of circumstances (this would be a higher-level literalism) such that any competent speaker of the language hearing those words would immediately be referred to that set. But I have told the story to several competent speakers of the language who simply didn't get it, and one friend – a professor of philosophy – reported to me that in the interval between his hearing the story and my explaining it to him (and just how I was able to do that is another crucial question) he found himself asking "What kind of joke is this and have I missed it?" For a time at least he remained able only to hear "Is there a text in this class" as my colleague first heard it; the student's additional words, far from leading him to another hearing, only made him aware of his distance from it. In contrast, there are those who not only get the story but get it before I tell it; that is, they know in advance what is coming as soon as I say that a colleague of mine was recently asked, "Is there a text in this class?" Who are these people and what is it that makes their comprehension of the story so immediate and easy? Well, one could say, without being the least bit facetious, that they are the people who come to hear me speak because they are the people who already know my position on certain matters (or know that I will *have* a position). That is, they hear "Is there a text in this class?", even as it appears at the beginning of the anecdote (or for that matter as a title of an essay), in the light of their knowledge of what I am likely to do with it. They hear it coming from *me*, in circumstances which have committed me to declaring myself on a range of issues that are sharply delimited.

My colleague was finally able to hear it in just that way, as coming from me, not because I was there in his classroom, nor because the words of the student's question pointed to me in a way that would have been obvious to any hearer, but because he was able to think of me in an office three doors down from his, telling students that there are no determinate meanings and that the stability of the text is an illusion. Indeed, as he reports it, the moment of recognition and comprehension consisted of his saying to himself, "Ah, there's one of Fish's victims!" He did not say this because her words identified her as such but because his ability to see her as such informed his perception of her words. The answer to the question "How did he get from her words to the circumstances within which she intended him to hear them?" is that he must already be thinking within those circumstances in order to be able to hear her words as referring to them. The question, then, must be rejected, because it assumes that the construing of sense leads to the identification of the context of utterance rather than the other way around. This does not mean that the context comes first and that once it has been identified the construing of sense can begin. This would be only to reverse the order of precedence, whereas precedence is beside the point because the two actions it would order (the identification of context and the making of sense) occur simultaneously. One does not say "Here I am in a situation; now I can begin to determine what these words mean." To be in a situation is to see the words, these or any other, as already meaningful. For my colleague to realize that he may be confronting one of my victims is *at the same time* to hear what she says as a question about his theoretical beliefs.

But to dispose of one "how" question is only to raise another: if her words do not lead him to the context of her utterance, how does he get there? Why did he think of me telling students that there were no determinate meanings and not think of someone or something else? First of all, he might well have. That is, he might well have guessed that she was coming from another direction (inquiring, let us say, as to whether the focus of this class was to be the poems and essays or our responses to them, a question in the same line of country as hers but quite distinct from it) or he might have simply been stymied, like my philosopher friend, confined, in the absence of an explanation, to his first determination of her concerns and unable to make any sense of her words other than the sense he originally made. How, then, did he do it? In part, he did it because he *could* do it; he was able to get to this context because it was already part of his repertoire for organizing the world and its events. The category "one of Fish's victims" was one he already had and didn't have to work for. Of course, *it* did not always have *him*, in that his world was not always being organized by it, and it certainly did not have him at the beginning of the conversation; but it was available to him, and he to it, and all he had to do was to recall it or be recalled to it for the meanings it subtended to emerge. (Had it not been available to him, the career of his comprehension would have been different, and we will come to a consideration of that difference shortly.)

This, however, only pushes our inquiry back further. How or why was he recalled to it? The answer to this question must be probabilistic and it begins with the recognition that when something changes, not everything changes. Although my colleague's understanding of his circumstances is transformed in the course of this conversation, the circumstances are still understood to be academic ones, and within that continuing (if modified) understanding, the directions his thought might take are already severely limited. He still presumes, as he did at first, that the student's question has something to do with university business in general, and with English literature in particular, and it is the organizing rubrics associated with these areas of experience that are likely to occur to him. One of those rubrics is "what-goes-on-in-other-classes" and one of those other classes is mine. And so, by a route that is neither entirely unmarked nor wholly determined, he comes to me and to the notion "one of Fish's victims" and to a new construing of what his student has been saying.

Of course that route would have been much more circuitous if the category "one of Fish's victims" was not already available to him as a device for producing intelligibility. Had that device not been part of his repertoire, had he been incapable of being recalled to it because he never knew it in the first place, how would he have proceeded? The answer is that he could not have proceeded at all, which does not mean that one is trapped for ever in the categories of understanding at one's disposal (or the categories at whose disposal one is), but that the introduction of new categories or the expansion of old ones to include new (and therefore newly seen) data must always come from the outside or from what is perceived, for a time, to be the outside. In the event that he was unable to identify the structure of her concerns because it had never been his (or he its), it would have been her obligation to explain it to him. And here we run up against another instance of the problem we have been considering all along. She could not explain it to him by varying or adding to her words, by being more explicit, because her words will only be intelligible if he already has the knowledge they are supposed to convey, the knowledge of the assumptions and interests from which they issue. It is clear, then, that she would have to make a new start, although she would not have to start from scratch (indeed, starting from scratch is never a possibility); but she would have to back up to some point at which there was a shared agreement as to what was reasonable to say so that a new and wider basis for agreement could be fashioned. In this particular case, for example, she might begin with the fact that her interlocutor already knows what a text is; that is, he has a way of thinking about it that is responsible for his hearing of her first question as one about bureaucratic classroom procedures. (You will remember that "he" in these sentences is no longer my colleague but someone who does not have his special knowledge.) It is that way of thinking that she must labor to extend or challenge, first, perhaps, by pointing out that there are those who think about the text in other ways, and then by trying to find a category of his own understanding which might serve as an analogue to the understanding he does not yet share. He might, for example, be familiar with those psychologists who argue for the constitutive power of perception, or with Gombrich's theory of the beholder's share, or with that philosophical tradition in which the stability of objects has always been a matter of dispute. The example must remain hypothetical and skeletal, because it can only be fleshed out after a determination of the particular beliefs and assumptions that would make the explanation necessary in the first place; for whatever they were, they would dictate the strategy by which she would work to supplant or change them. It is when such a strategy has been successful that the import of her words will become clear, not because she has reformulated or refined them but because they will now be read or heard within the same system of intelligibility from which they issue.

In short, this hypothetical interlocutor will in time be brought to the same point of comprehension my colleague enjoys when he is able to say to himself, "Ah, there's one of Fish's victims," although presumably he will say something very different to himself if he says anything at all. The difference, however, should not obscure the basic similarities between the two experiences, one reported, the other imagined. In both cases the words that are uttered are immediately heard within a set of assumptions about the direction from which they could possibly be coming, and in both cases what is required is that the hearing occur within another set of assumptions in relation to which the same words ("Is there a text in this class?") will no longer be the same. It is just that while my colleague is able to meet that requirement by calling to mind a context of utterance that is already a part of his repertoire, the repertoire of his hypothetical stand-in must be expanded to include that context so that should he some day be in an analogous situation, he would be able to call it to mind.

The distinction, then, is between already having an ability and having to acquire it, but it is not finally an essential distinction, because the routes by which that ability could be exercised on the one hand, and learned on the other, are so similar. They are similar first of all because they are similarly *not* determined by words. Just as the student's words will not direct my colleague to a context he already has, so will they fail to direct someone not furnished with that context to its discovery. And yet in neither case does the absence of such a mechanical determination mean that the route one travels is randomly found. The change from one structure of understanding to another is not a rupture but a modification of the interests and concerns that are already in place; and because they are already in place, they constrain the direction of their own modification. That is, in both cases the hearer is already in a situation informed by tacitly known purposes and goals, and in both cases he ends up in another situation whose purposes and goals stand in some elaborated relation (of contrast, opposition, expansion, extension) to those they supplant. (The one relation in which they could not stand is no relation at all.) It is just that in one case the network of elaboration (from the text as an obviously physical object to the question of whether or not the text is a physical object) has already been articulated (although not all of its articulations are in focus at one time; selection is always occurring), while in the other the articulation of the network is the business of the teacher (here the student) who begins, necessarily, with what is already given.

The final similarity between the two cases is that in neither is success assured. It was no more inevitable that my colleague tumble to the context of his student's utterance than it would be inevitable that she could introduce that context to someone previously unaware of it; and, indeed, had my colleague remained puzzled (had he simply not thought of me), it would have been necessary for the student to bring him along in a way that was finally indistinguishable from the way she would bring someone to a new knowledge, that is, by beginning with the shape of his present understanding.

I have lingered so long over the unpacking of this anecdote that its relationship to the problem of authority in the classroom and in literary criticism may seem obscure. Let me recall you to it by recalling the contention of Abrams and others that authority depends upon the existence of a determinate core of meanings because in the absence of such a core there is no normative or public way of construing what anyone says or writes, with the result that interpretation becomes a matter of individual and private construings, none of which is subject to challenge or correction. In literary criticism this means that no interpretation can be said to be better or worse than any other, and in the classroom this means that we have no answer to the student who says my interpretation is as valid as yours. It is only if there is a shared basis of agreement at once guiding interpretation and providing a mechanism for deciding between interpretations that a total and debilitating relativism can be avoided.

But the point of my analysis has been to show that while "Is there a text in this class?" does not have a determinate meaning, a meaning that survives the sea change of situations, in any situation we might imagine the meaning of the utterance is either perfectly clear or capable, in the course of time, of being clarified. What is it that makes this possible, if it is not the 'possibilities and norms' already encoded in language? How does communication ever occur if not by reference to a public and stable norm? The answer, implicit in everything I have already said, is that communication occurs within situations and that to be in a situation is already to be in possession of (or to be possessed by) a structure of assumptions, of practices understood to be relevant in relation to purposes and goals that are already in place; and it is within the assumption of these purposes and goals that any utterance is *immediately* heard. I stress immediately because it seems to me that the problem of communication, as someone like Abrams poses it, is a problem only because he assumes a distance between one's receiving of an utterance and the determination of its meaning – a kind of dead space when one has only the words and then faces the task of construing them. If there were such a space, a moment before interpretation began, then it would be necessary to have recourse to some mechanical and algorithmic procedure by means of which meanings could be calculated and in relation to which one could recognize mistakes. What I have been arguing is that meanings come already calculated, not because of norms embedded in the language but because language is always perceived, from the very first, within a structure of norms. That structure, however, is not abstract and independent but social; and therefore it is not a single structure with a privileged relationship to the process of communication as it occurs in any situation but a structure that changes when one situation, with its assumed background of practices, purposes, and goals, has given way to another. In other words, the shared basis of agreement sought by Abrams and others is never not already found, although it is not always the same one.

Many will find in this last sentence, and in the argument to which it is a conclusion, nothing more than a sophisticated version of the relativism they fear. It will do no good, they say, to speak of norms and standards that are context-specific, because this is merely to authorize an infinite plurality of norms and standards, and we are still left without any way of adjudicating between them and between the competing systems of value of which they are functions. In short, to have many standards is to have no standards at all.

On one level this counterargument is unassailable, but on another level it is finally beside the point. It is unassailable as a general and theoretical conclusion: the positing of context- or institution-specific norms surely rules out the possibility of a norm whose validity would be recognized by everyone, no matter what his situation. But it is beside the point for any particular individual, for since everyone is situated somewhere, there is no one for whom the absence of an asituational norm would be of any practical consequence, in the sense that his performance or his confidence in his ability to perform would be impaired. So that while it is generally true that to have many standards is to have none at all, it is not true for anyone in particular (for there is no one in a position to speak "generally"), and therefore it is a truth of which one can say "it doesn't matter."

In other words, while relativism is a position one can entertain, it is not a position one can occupy. No one can *be* a relativist, because no one can achieve the distance from his own beliefs and assumptions which would result in their being no more authoritative *for him* than the beliefs and assumptions held by others, or, for that matter, the beliefs and assumptions he himself used to hold. The fear that in a world of indifferently authorized norms and values the individual is without a basis for action is groundless because no one is indifferent to the norms and values that enable his consciousness. It is in the name of personally held (in fact they are doing the holding) norms and values that the individual acts and argues, and he does so with the full confidence that attends belief. When his beliefs change, the norms and values to which he once gave unthinking assent will have been demoted to the status of opinions and become the objects of an analytical and critical attention; but that attention will itself be enabled by a new set of norms and values that are, for the time being, as unexamined and undoubted as those they displace. The point is that there is never a moment when one believes nothing, when consciousness is innocent of any and all categories of thought, and whatever categories of thought are operative at a given moment will serve as an undoubted ground.

Here, I suspect, a defender of determinate meaning would cry "solipsist" and argue that a confidence that had its source in the individual's categories of thought would have no public value. That is, unconnected to any shared and stable system of meanings, it would not enable one to transact the verbal business of everyday life; a shared intelligibility would be impossible in a world where everyone was trapped in the circle of his own assumptions and opinions. The reply to this is that an individual's assumptions and opinions are not "his own" in any sense that would give body to the fear of solipsism. That is, *he* is not their origin (in fact it might be more accurate to say that they are his); rather, it is their prior availability which delimits in advance the paths that his consciousness can possibly take. When my colleague is in the act of construing his student's question ("Is there a text in this class?"), none of the interpretive strategies at his disposal are uniquely his, in the sense that he thought them up; they follow from his preunderstanding of the interests and goals that could possibly animate the speech of someone functioning within the institution of academic America, interests and goals that are the particular property of no one in particular but which link everyone for whom their assumption is so habitual as to be unthinking. They certainly link my colleague and his student, who are able to communicate and even to reason about one another's intentions, not, however, because their interpretive efforts are constrained by the shape of an independent language but because their shared understanding of what could possibly be at stake in a classroom situation results in language appearing to them in the same shape (or successions of shapes).

That shared understanding is the basis of the confidence with which they speak and reason, but its categories are their own only in the sense that as actors within an institution they automatically fall heir to the institution's way of making sense, its systems of intelligibility. That is why it is so hard for someone whose very being is defined by his position within an institution (and if not this one, then some other) to explain to someone outside it a practice or a meaning that seems to him to require no explanation, because he regards it as natural. Such a person, when pressed, is likely to say, "but that's just the way it's done" or "but isn't it obvious" and so testify that the practice or meaning in question is community property, as, in a sense, he is too.

We see then that (1) communication does occur, despite the absence of an independent and context-free system of meanings, that (2) those who participate in this communication do so confidently rather than provisionally (they are not relativists), and that (3) while their confidence has its source in a set of beliefs, those beliefs are not individual-specific or idiosyncratic but communal and conventional (they are not solipsists).

Of course, solipsism and relativism are what Abrams and Hirsch fear and what lead them to argue for the necessity of determinate meaning. But if, rather than acting on their own, interpreters act as extensions of an institutional community, solipsism and relativism are removed as fears because they are not possible modes of being. That is to say, the condition required for someone to be a solipsist or relativist, the condition of being independent of institutional assumptions and free to originate one's own purposes and goals, could never be realized, and therefore there is no point in trying to guard against it. Abrams, Hirsch, and company spend a great deal of time in a search for the ways to limit and constrain interpretation, but if the example of my colleague and his student can be generalized (and obviously I think it can be), what they are searching for is never not already found. In short, my message to them is finally not challenging, but consoling – not to worry.

Notes

1   M. H. Abrams, "The Deconstructive Angel," *Critical Inquiry* vol. 3, no. 3 (Spring 1977), 431, 434.
2   *Validity in Interpretation* (New Haven: Yale University Press, 1967), pp. 218–19.
3   *The Aims of Interpretation* (Chicago: University of Chicago Press, 1976), p. 1.

3

With the Compliments of the Author: Reflections on Austin and Derrida

Readers who turn to this essay in eager anticipation of a heavyweight slugfest – Fish vs Derrida, neopragmatism vs deconstruction, the Vanishing Text vs the Infinite Text – are in for a bitter disappointment. No ears are bitten off in this essay. The essay is itself an intervention in an earlier confrontation, that between deconstruction, in the person of Derrida, and speech-act theory, in the person of J. L. Austin. But what Fish has to say of this "confrontation" – that it "never quite takes place because there finally is not enough space between [Austin and Derrida] for there to be a confrontation" (p. 74) – is even more true of the "confrontation" between Fish and Derrida.

In this essay, Fish *translates* Derrida (just as Derrida had earlier translated Austin). The dense, lyrical discourse of Derridean deconstruction is transformed into the crisp, commonsensical idiolect of Fishian neopragmatism ("Derrida's argument is that..."; "By this Derrida means..."; "That is why Derrida..."). Such translation is an uncharacteristic undertaking for Fish; small wonder if he appears somewhat insecure at fleeting moments (the extreme unlikelihood of this spectacle is not the least interesting feature of the essay). Fish conjures up an imaginary utterance, for example, delivered to him in person by Derrida, adding: "the way would be open to hearing his utterance as an assertion both of precedence and superiority" (p. 61). One is reminded of Lacan's arch remark to Derrida, "You can't bear my having already said what you want to say."

So how does Fish's translation proceed? The opening of a Derridean essay is often its most tortuous stretch. Singularly un-Derridean is the inaugural anecdote with which Fish's essay begins – a *personal* anecdote, what is more (although not *too* personal; that would be singularly un-Fishian). In general, Fish appears to have dressed down for his day in court with Derrida. Derrida likes to focus on the marginal, the lateral, and the eccentric rather than on what *seems* to be of central importance. In light of this proclivity, it is interesting to note the marginality of Fish's textual witnesses in this essay. No *Paradise Lost* this time, no *Coriolanus*, no legal or constitutional examples. His chief witness is an enigmatic publisher's card that rudely accosted him when he opened his copy of Derrida's *Of Grammatology*, secondary testimony being supplied by a cartoon from *The New Yorker*.

So what is the challenge that Fish sets himself in this essay? Five pages into the essay, Fish sets the bar at an improbable height and steps back to surmise it: "Presumably, if in 1977 I had been in possession of more precise information and had been able to meet my benefactor face-to-face [the individual who had sent him the copy of *Of Grammatology*], the uncertainty and indeterminacy that characterized my efforts to construe WITH THE COMPLIMENTS OF THE AUTHOR [the legend on the publisher's card] would have been lessened and perhaps eliminated entirely" (p. 60). Admittedly, the suspense is hardly killing. We have no doubt but that Fish will clear the bar; the interest will be in seeing how the maneuver will be executed, how the commonsensical will (once again) be surmounted, how that which appears to ground interpretation will be shown (once again) to be generated by it. And the interest will be in hearing Stanley Fish pronounce on "the metaphysics of presence," his voice echoing eerily across the great divide that supposedly separates "Anglo-American" philosophy from its "continental" cousin.

Stephen D. Moore

> The most important thing in acting is honesty; once you learn to fake that, you're in. – Sam Goldwyn

I

In the summer of 1977, as I was preparing to teach Jacques Derrida's *Of Grammatology* to a class at the School of Criticism and Theory in Irvine, a card floated out of the text and presented itself for interpretation. It read:

WITH THE COMPLIMENTS OF THE AUTHOR

Immediately I was faced with an interpretive problem, not only in the ordinary and everyday sense of having to determine the meaning and the intention (they are the same thing) of the utterance, but in the special sense (or so it might seem) occasioned by the fact that I didn't know who the author named or, rather, not named by the card was. It might have been Derrida himself, whom I had met, but only in passing. Or it might have been Derrida's translator, Gayatri Spivak, whom I had known for some time and who might well have put me on the publisher's list. Or it might have been the publisher, in this case the Johns Hopkins University Press, of whose editorial board I was then a member. In the absence (a key word) of any explicit identification, I found myself a very emblem of the difficulties or infelicities that attend distanced or etiolated communication: unable to proceed because the words were cut off from their anchoring source in a unique and clearly present intention. That is to say, I seemed, in the very moment of my perplexity, to be proving on my pulse the superiority of face-to-face communication, where one can know intentions directly, to communication mediated by the marks of writing and in this case by a writing that materialized without any clues as to its context of origin. It may not have been a message found in a bottle, but it certainly was a message found in a book.

Philosophers and literary critics have long had a way of talking about such situations by contrasting them with others in which questions of meaning and intention are less indeterminate. The principle underlying this exercise has often been formulated, but nowhere more succinctly than in this pronouncement by Jonathan Culler: "Some texts are more orphaned than others."[1] Given such a principle, it might seem reasonable to construct a taxonomy of contexts of communication, arranged in a hierarchy from the least to the most orphaned. The elaboration of such a taxonomy is not my purpose here, but a sketch might afford us a perspective on some crucial issues in philosophy and literary theory.

One would begin, of course, with the optimal context, a face-to-face exchange of utterances between two people who know each other and who are able, in the event of confusion or discontinuity or obscurity, to put questions to one another. A less certain but still relatively risk-free form of communication would occur between persons who know each other but who are separated either by time or by space and are therefore reduced to the medium of letter or telegram or telephone; such persons would be hearing or reading one another against the background of a history of shared experiences and common concerns, and that background would operate in the absence of physical proximity as a constraint on interpretation. Constraints of another kind are operative when communication is between persons who don't know each other but who speak from within a context that stabilizes the direction and shape of their understandings: clerks and customers in a department store, teachers and students on the first day of class, waiters and patrons in a restaurant, and so on. Serious difficulties begin to set in when that kind of stabilizing context is absent. A coincidence of concerns is serendipitous rather than probable because one party is speaking or writing to a heterogenous audience and hoping that the right-minded listener or reader is tuning in; television commentators, direct-mail advertisers, and newspaper columnists are in this situation and are always in danger of being misunderstood because of miscalculation, special vocabularies, and unanticipated responses. As we continue down the scale, things go from bad to worse as the incommensurabilities of other times and other cultures are added to the difficulties occasioned by physical distance. Finally, at the outermost reaches of this declination from sure and transparent verbal encounters we arrive at literature, and especially at fiction; here interpretive hazards seem to be everywhere and without a check as we attempt to fix the meanings and intentions of long-dead authors whose words have reference not to a world that has passed from the earth but to a world that never was except in the interior reaches of their imaginations. In other cases the interpretive efforts of readers and listeners are tied, even if in some attenuated way, to specifiable empirical conditions, but in the case of fiction and drama those conditions are a construct of the author and in turn must be reconstructed, without the aid of extramental entities, by readers and listeners.

The picture I have just drawn is commonsensical and powerful, and something like it underlies the pronouncements of many of our most influential theorists. Culler assumes it when he says that words in a poem "do not refer us to an external context but force us to construct a fictional situation of utterance" because poems are by definition removed "from an ordinary circuit of communication" (p. 166); the same reasoning leads John Ellis to declare that once something is identified as literature "we do not generally concern ourselves with whether what it says is true or false, or regard it as relevant to any specific practical purpose," because it is not perceived "as part of the immediate context we live in."[2] Indeed, Barbara Herrnstein Smith concludes in the same vein: "A poem does not reflect but *creates* the context in which its meanings are located"; like a letter a poem "will be read in a context both temporally and spatially remote from that in which it was composed," but the limitations under which poets and their readers must operate are even more severe because a poet "must convey to his readers not only a context remote from space and time, but one that may have never existed in history or nature."[3] Wolfgang Iser is even more explicit and categorical: "Fictional texts constitute their own objects and do not copy something already in existence"; "everyday pragmatic language ... presupposes reference to a given object," and therefore the "multiplicity of possible meanings [is] narrowed down"; fictional language on the other hand "opens up an increasing number of possibilities," which entail decisions and acts of construction on the part of the reader.[4] For Iser, this increased reader activity is characteristic of literary experience as opposed, for example, to the experience of a scientific text where acts of construction are not required because the object – that is, the world – is already given. The same point is made somewhat more elegantly by Richard Ohmann: in ordinary discourse, Ohmann asserts, "we assume the real world and judge the felicity of the speech acts"; but in fictional discourse "we assume the felicity of the speech acts and infer a world."[5] The mechanics of how we do this are explained by John Searle. Fictional discourse is made possible, according to Searle, by "a set of conventions which suspend the normal operation of the rules relating illocutionary acts to the world."[6] In place of this normal operation, in which language is tied to an already existing referent, a writer of fiction, Searle explains, *pretends* to refer to real characters and events and by so pretending creates fictional characters and events (pp. 71–2); as readers we fall in with this pretense, we share in it, and thus share in the construction of the fictional world and its meanings (p. 73).

It may seem that in the course of this brief survey the focus has shifted from the question of distanced or orphaned speech to the question of fictional language; but the survey shows that the two questions are one. Both orphaned speech and fictional speech are regarded by these and other theorists as deviations from the full presence and normative contextuality of face-to-face communication; and in both cases the consequences are the same, an increase in the interpretive work required of readers and listeners (here there is an implicit formula: the more distance, the more work) which means, in turn, an increase in the risks and hazards attendant on any effort to fix and determine meanings. Indeed, it is remarkable how many issues in philosophy and critical theory finally resolve to the basic issue raised by the privileging of proximate or anchored speech. There are any number of paired terms that line up with orphaned versus full speech and ordinary versus fictional language to form a related and interdependent set of oppositions. The few theorists I have already cited yield the following list of examples, which is by no means exhaustive:

literal language	vs	metaphorical language
determinate	vs	indeterminate
brute facts	vs	institutional facts
objective discourse	vs	subjective discourse
real people	vs	fictional characters

direct speech acts	vs	indirect speech acts
real objects	vs	fictional objects
scientific language	vs	expressive language
explicit performative	vs	implicit performative
locutionary	vs	illocutionary
meaning	vs	significance
perception	vs	interpretation
real experience	vs	aesthetic experience
constative	vs	performative

What makes these oppositions transformations of one another is the epistemological premise underlying each of them: that the first or left-hand term
stands for a mode of knowing that is, at least relatively if not purely, direct,
transparent, without difficulties, unmediated, independently verifiable, unproblematic, preinterpretive, and sure; and, conversely, that the mode of knowing
named by the right-hand term is indirect, opaque, context-dependent, unconstrained, derivative, and full of risk. One reason for the extraordinary appeal of
this distinction in its many forms is the support it seems to derive from the
evidence of common sense. Here, we can say (imitating Dr Johnson), is a
stone; it is more available for inspection and description than a rock in France
or a rock in a novel by Dickens. Or, alternatively, here am I, standing before
you; you know me and you know what I mean by what I say, and if you don't,
you can just ask me, something you couldn't do if I were in China or dead or
alive only in the pages of an epic poem. The appeal, in short, is to the
experience of *immediacy* in contrast to the experience of objects and persons
that can only be apprehended at a remove, and it is a contrast that seems
confirmed by the anecdote with which I began. Presumably, if in 1977 I had
been in possession of more precise information and had been able to meet my
benefactor face-to-face, the uncertainty and indeterminacy that characterized
my efforts to construe WITH THE COMPLIMENTS OF THE AUTHOR would
have been lessened and perhaps eliminated entirely.[7]

Let us, for the sake of argument, test this presumption by imagining the
happy or felicitous circumstances in which this particular speech act would
have been more certain of success. First of all, let us assume that I had been able
to determine that the gift and therefore the card announcing it were sent to me
by Derrida. Would my position with respect to interpretive certainty be
improved? Well, in some sense, the answer is, "Of course"; I would no longer
be attempting to interpret a message from Spivak or the Johns Hopkins
University Press; but I would still be left with the problem of interpreting a
message from Derrida, and the fact that I now knew his name would not in and
of itself be decisive, for what I would *want* to know are his intentions, his

purposes, his reasons. That is, I would want to know in what *spirit* Derrida had sent me his book. It could be that mine is only one name on a very long list submitted by an editor or a publicist and that in response to its suggestion Derrida replied, "Stanley Who?" Nor would my perplexity necessarily be removed if the message were to be delivered in person, if Derrida were to walk into my office and say, "Aha, here is Stanley Fish, let me present this to you, with the compliments of the author." I might still suspect that he was being ironic rather than complimentary and that he was really saying, "With the compliments of *the* author," in which case the way would be open to hearing his utterance as an assertion both of precedence and superiority.

Of course, in the event of such a suspicion, I could simply ask. That is, I could put to Derrida any number of direct and piercing questions, like "What did you mean by that?" or "How am I to take it?" or "Do you expect something in return?" It is entirely possible that the answer to one or more of these questions would satisfy me, perhaps because it invoked a formula that was for me a particularly powerful marker of sincerity, or perhaps because it was accompanied by information about some past action of Derrida's that appeared to me to be strong evidence of his goodwill. However, it is also possible that my suspicions would not be allayed at all because they were deeply rooted in some professional insecurity – an insecurity which, rather than being removed by verbal (or other) assurances, simply made them into its renewed occasion. The point is not that I could never be certain about the meaning of WITH THE COMPLIMENTS OF THE AUTHOR but that neither the achievement of certainty nor the failure to achieve it will have a necessary relationship to the fact of physical proximity. The evidence that might convince me of Derrida's goodwill could have its effect on me even if it were relayed to me in a letter or by some third person; for its status as evidence does not depend only or even chiefly on my ability to eyeball it but on my holding a belief about the relationship of certain acts and formulas to the presence of goodwill. And, conversely, the physical proximity of such evidence, in the form of Derrida's words or gestures, might still fail to be convincing if my professional anxiety (which is also a belief that can also function at long distance as well as "close up") were strong enough to override it.

The fact of a face-to-face exchange, then, is no assurance that communication will be certain or even relatively trouble- free. The point is illustrated nicely by a cartoon that appeared some years ago in the *New Yorker*. It shows a man sitting in front of a television set, his eyes locked on the picture; standing above him is a woman, presumably his wife, who is obviously angry. The caption reads, "You look sorry, you act sorry, you say you're sorry, but you're not sorry." The supposed advantage of face-to-face communication is that it allows us to deduce the meaning of an utterance from the direct inspection of the speaker's words and actions; but the cartoon seems to be reminding us that the direction of inference is often the other way around: the woman knows in advance what will be meant by what her husband says because she knows, and knows with the passion of belief, what kind of person he is; and therefore she is able to hear whatever words issue from him as confirmation of what she already knows. He could present witnessed affidavits; he could secure testimonials from his minister, his doctor, or her mother, and she might still continue to interpret his words and all supporting documents as evidence of his insincerity.[8]

The juxtaposition of the cartoon with my anecdote is illuminating in part because at first they seem to be illustrative of quite different situations — of a particularly attenuated speech act, on the one hand, and a speech act tied firmly to its context, on the other. But in fact the two situations are finally very much alike because in both of them the crucial role in the attempt to fix meaning is played by assumptions and beliefs. In one case, a wife's tenaciously held assumption about the kind of man her husband is generates a single and unswerving interpretation of his words; in the other, my inability to believe wholeheartedly in Derrida's sincerity leaves me in doubt as to the right interpretation of his message. In both cases the shape of belief (either about another or about oneself) is responsible for the shape of interpretation, irre- spective of whether those beliefs operate at a remove or in a proximate encounter. My "reading" of Derrida's intention would not necessarily be stabilized by his presence; and if the husband were to leave his wife a note saying he was sorry, her reception of it would be as sure as her reception of his spoken words. What this means is that the difference between the two cases (and differences remain) cannot be explained as the difference between direct and mediated communication; and, indeed, if we are to generalize from these examples, there is no epistemological difference between direct and mediated communications because, in a fundamental sense, all communications are mediated. That is, communications of every kind are characterized by exactly the same conditions — the necessity of interpretive work, the unavoidability of perspective, and the construction by acts of interpretation of that which supposedly grounds interpretation, intentions, characters, and pieces of the world.

It would seem that rather than confirming "Culler's law," our analysis has led us to its reversal, to the conclusion that all texts are equally and radically orphaned in the sense that no one of them is securely fastened to an independ- ently specifiable state of affairs. With this assertion I at last approach Derrida's critique of J. L. Austin, for the issue between them (or so it would seem) is the possibility of identifying a kind of speech act that is not orphaned, that is "tethered to [its] origin" (HT, p. 61). In "Signature Event Context," Derrida questions that possibility when he reaches "a paradoxical but unavoidable conclusion – a successful performative is necessarily an 'impure' performative" ("SEC," p. 191). A pure performative would be one that was *assured* of success because a combination of verbal explicitness, a clear-cut context, and a transparency of intention so constrained its reception that there was no room for doubt and therefore no need for interpretation. Derrida's argument is that the optimal conditions that would be required for such a success do not exist because the risk attending the so-called impure cases – cases in which illocutionary force must be inferred through a screen of assumptions rather than read out directly – is constitutive of *all* cases. Derrida is struck by the fact that while Austin spends more than a little time on the "doctrine of the infelicities," or "the doctrine of the things that can be and go wrong," he remains committed to the ideal of a speech situation in which everything goes right (*HT*, p. 14). That is, Austin acknowledges the pervasiveness of infelicity but continues to think of infelicity as "accidental," as an unfortunate deviation from the norm "of an exhaustively definable context, of a free consciousness present to the totality of the operation, and of absolutely meaningful speech" ("SEC," p. 188). Derrida, on the other hand, regards infelicity not as accidental but as structural and founding, and he makes his case in part by posing a series of questions:

Is this general possibility necessarily one of a failure or trap into which language may *fall* or lose itself as in an abyss situated outside of or in front of itself? . . . In other words, does the quality of risk admitted by Austin *surround* language like a kind of *ditch* or external place of perdition which speech could never hope to leave, but which it can escape by remaining "at home?" . . . Or, on the contrary, is this risk rather its internal and positive condition of possibility? Is that outside its inside, the very force and law of its emergence? ("SEC," p. 190)

By "general possibility" Derrida means the possibility that language may fall prey to interpretation rather than being anchored to an originating and constraining center; interpretation, with all its hazards and uncertainties, is the source of infelicity; it *is* the "risk." In the traditional or classical view the risk of interpretation is only incurred when the conditions of communication are characterized by distance and etiolation; ordinary or basic communication takes place in a space of grounded or tethered security where meanings cannot go astray. Given such a view, it makes sense to proceed as Austin does in the early chapters of his book – by first isolating normative and clear-cut cases and then building up to difficult and derivative cases. But as Derrida observes, such a procedure, however methodologically innocent it may seem, conceals behind its reasonableness an entire metaphysics, the metaphysics of presence, of objects and/or intentions that possess a purity which can either be preserved or compromised in the act of communication.

In the first part of "Signature Event Context," Derrida offers as an example of that metaphysics Condillac's account of the origin of writing: "'Men in a state of communicating their thoughts by means of sounds, felt the necessity of imagining new signs capable of perpetuating those thoughts and of making them *known* to persons who are *absent*'" ("SEC," p. 176). This account is exemplary in the tradition because it assumes and, by assuming, fixes the secondary status of writing, which is here a means of conveying something prior to it, something that was in its moment of occurrence immediate and transparent, something once *present*. As a conveyer, the responsibility of writing is to transmit that presence with as little alteration as possible: "The same content, formerly communicated by gestures and sounds, will henceforth be transmitted by writing" ("SEC," p. 176). Writing so conceived is thus not a break in presence but a modification of presence, a modification made necessary by the unhappy fact of distance (absence), and yet a modification that is always connected to its originating source and is therefore always "at home." The situation becomes dangerous only when writing loses contact with this origin and is therefore no longer subordinated, as it should be, to a more substantial reality, to the reality of independent objects and intentions.

Derrida's challenge to this comfortable picture begins with an apparently trivial observation: "To be what it is, all writing . . . must be capable of functioning in the radical absence of every empirically determined receiver" ("SEC," p. 180). That is to say, writing is such that even someone who has no relationship whatsoever to the original receiver or sender will be able to construe it, to make something of it. If this were not so, if a piece of writing or speech could only function in the context of its original production, it would not be a representation of that context but a part of it; it would be a piece of presence. "A writing that is not structurally readable – iterable – beyond the death of the addressee would not be writing" ("SEC," p. 180). In this characterization, writing and language in general become too powerful for assimilation by the classical view in which writing "stands in" for an absent presence of which it is a mere representation; for if writing is readable even by those who know nothing of its original source or of its intended recipient, then it is doing its "standing in" without the anchoring presence, even at a remove, of anything to stand in for. As Derrida puts it, "The mark can do without the referent" ("SEC," p. 183); that is, the mark can be construed as referring to persons or objects or intentions to which readers have no independent or extralinguistic access either in person or in memory.

To put the matter this way, however, is to invite misunderstanding by suggesting that such construings are necessary only in the case of an empirical absence, that is, when the intended receiver or the object referred to are "actually" not there. It is a misunderstanding that is also courted when Derrida observes of the marks that he produces that their functioning will not be hindered by "my future disappearance." As it stands, this allows a reading in which at one time, in the original context of its production, the mark was stabilized by his "appearance"; but this reading, which has been deliberately encouraged, is immediately blocked by a qualifying statement:

When I say "my future disappearance," it is in order to render this proposition more immediately acceptable. I ought to be able to say my disappearance, pure and simple, my non-presence in general, for instance the non-presence of my intention of saying something meaningful. ("SEC," pp. 180–1)

By this Derrida means that, even in the original moment of production, his is an interpreted presence, a presence that comes into view in the act of construing performed *necessarily* by those who hear him even in a face-to-face situation. Moreover, this is as true for him as it is for others, since in order to "know" his own intention he must consult himself and interrogate his motives with categories of interrogation that limit in advance the image he can have of himself.[9] Even when he is physically present, he will not be an unmediated entity either in his own eyes (or ears) or in the eyes of his interlocutors. (The same can be said of the nonpresent presence, the disappearance in general, of the husband in the *New Yorker* cartoon or of Derrida in my anecdote.) So that when Derrida declares that "the sign possesses the characteristic of being readable even if the moment of its production is irrevocably lost" ("SEC," p. 182), we must understand that the moment of production is *itself* a moment of loss, in that its components – including sender, receiver, referents, and message – are never transparently present but must be interpreted or "read" into being. Thus, Derrida's argument in this section moves from the assertion that utterances are readable even in the special conditions of empirical absence to the assertion that utterances are *only* readable (as opposed to being deciphered or seen through) even in the supposedly optimal condition of physical proximity.

It is this insight that informs Derrida's vexing use of the term "iterability." To say that something is iterable is usually understood to mean that after an original use it can be used *again* (iter); but for Derrida, iterability is a *general* condition that applies to the original use, which is therefore not original in the sense of being known or experienced without reference to anything but itself. This becomes clear when we consider what would have to be the case for there to be something like what Derrida says there could not be, the "non-iteration of an event" ("SEC," p. 192). The noniteration of an event would be an event that was apprehended not by a relationship of sameness or difference to something else (something prior) but directly, simply as itself; but if the components of an event – however simple or complex, near or far – come into view only in the act of reading, then there can be no such instance of a noniteration, and every event is always and already a representation or a repetition. To this someone like Searle would reply, not unreasonably, "Repetition or representation of what?" The answer is repetition or representation of itself, which seems a contradiction until we understand that the assertion is precisely that "itself" (the event, its agents, its objects, its meanings) is never apprehended except in an interpreted – hence repeated or represented – form. That is what Derrida means when he speaks of "the logic that ties repetition to alterity" ("SEC," p. 180). The repetition or representation of something is different from that something, which becomes its other; but since the repetition or representation is all one can have, it will always be "other" than itself. In Samuel Weber's words, "If something must be iterable in order to become an object of consciousness, then it can never be entirely grasped, having already been split in and by its being-repeated (or more precisely: by its *repeated being*)."[10] Iterability, then, stands for the general condition of having-to-be-read, and noninterability stands for the condition of availability-independent-of-reading, a condition which in Derrida's argument we can never enjoy. Noniterability, in short, is another word for full and unmediated presence, and iterability is another word for readability, not as a possibility but as a necessity. It is a necessity that has already been demonstrated by the example of the *New Yorker* cartoon: even in the most favorable of circumstances, when the woman is within earshot of her husband, his appearance (a word nicely hesitating between substance and surface), his intentions, and his meaning only emerge in the act of construing for which they are supposedly the ground; they are all iterated, repeated, represented, or, in a word, "read," entities. The moment of face- to-face exchange that founds Condillac's account of communication is the moment of the production within reading of that which is thought anterior to reading. In Derridean terms, the interpretive gesture which threatens to infect the center (that is, presence) is responsible for the very form of the center and of everything it contains, including persons, their messages, and their very worlds. That outside is its inside, the very force and law of its emergence.

II

One effect of this account of everyday or face-to-face communication is to raise in an immediate and urgent form the question of fictional language: for it is fictional language, in the traditional characterization, that brings worlds, complete with objects, persons, events, and intentions, into being, while ordinary or serious language is said to be responsible to the world of empirical fact. It is this distinction that underlies Austin's decision to exclude from his account of speech acts fictional and dramatic utterances, and it is that decision which is more or less the occasion of Derrida's critique. This key passage occurs in Austin's second chapter:

A performative utterance will, for example, be *in a peculiar way* hollow or void if said by an actor on the stage, or if introduced in a poem, or spoken in soliloquy. This applies in a similar manner to any and every utterance – a sea-change in special circumstances. Language in such circumstances is in special ways . . . used not seriously, but in ways *parasitic* upon its normal uses – ways which fall under the doctrine of the *etiolations* of language. (*HT*, p. 22)

The reasoning behind this declaration is clear enough: a speaker in a poem or an actor on a stage does not produce his utterance with a full and present intention but with the intention of someone behind him, a poet or a play-wright; his is a *stage utterance*, and in order to get at its true meaning we have to go behind the stage to its originating source in the consciousness of an author. In construing the illocutionary force of stage utterances, we are, in short, at a remove.

Derrida's reply is that we are always and already at such a remove, and it is a reply that is implicit in the examples with which this essay began. If Derrida were to stand before me with his book and his message and his "presence," I would still be in the position of a playgoer, inferring his intention and his meaning not directly from his words but through the screen, already in place, of what I assumed to be his purposes, goals, concerns, and so on. I would be proceeding, that is, on the basis of the role I conceived him to be playing in relation to his "real" or interior or "offstage" intention; and the wife in the *New Yorker* cartoon proceeds in the same way when she hears her husband say that he is sorry, but she decides, because she knows what kind of person he "really" is, that he isn't sorry at all, that he is only acting. And even if I immediately accepted Derrida's words at face value, or if the wife never for a moment doubted her husband's sincerity, she and I would still be operating from within a prior construction of the character of our interlocutors. If by "stage utterances" one understands utterances whose illocutionary force must be inferred or constructed, then all utterances are stage utterances, and one cannot mark them off from utterances that are "serious."[11]

There is, however, another way to maintain the position that stage or literary utterances are not "used seriously"; one can point to their perlocu-tionary effects or, rather, as Austin does, to the absence of those effects: "There are parasitic uses of language, which are 'not serious,' not the 'full normal use.' The normal conditions of reference may be suspended, or no attempt made at a standard perlocutionary act, no attempt to make you do anything, as Walt Whitman does not seriously incite the eagle of liberty to soar" (*HT*, p. 104). Here the argument turns on the word "seriously," which seems to mean straightforwardly or nonmetaphorically and *therefore* productive of action in the world. The claim, in short, is that only when the words of an utterance refer to empirically specifiable conditions can it be called serious. But such a rigorous definition of serious would exclude many of the perlocutionary acts we perform daily. Surely, for example, the politician who incites the eagle of liberty to soar would be doing so seriously, in part because he would be attempting to make his hearers *do* something by making them think of themselves as extensions of the eagle of liberty. Someone intent on saving the difference between the serious and the literary might argue from "use" and point out that the politician would simply be saying one (metaphorical) thing while meaning another (real-world) thing; but the same observation could be made of a poet or a dramatist who uses an allegorical fable to urge a political action. However the relationship between perlocutionary effect and metaphor is characterized, that characterization cannot be turned into a distinction between serious and literary utterances, since perlocutions and metaphors will be found indifferently in both. The point would not even have to be made in relation to pre-Romantic aesthetics which were frankly didactic and hortatory (one cannot imagine telling Milton or Herbert or Jonson that they of course did not expect their readers to do anything in response to their works); and while some modernist aesthetics tell us that literature must be rigorously divorced from action of any kind, the reading or hearing of any play or poem involves the making of judgments, the reaching of decisions, the forming of attitudes, the registering of approval and disapproval, the feeling of empathy or distaste, and a hundred other things that are as much perlocutionary effects as the most overt of physical movements. The most one can say finally is that the kinds of perlocutionary effects produced by literary and nonliterary discourse are sometimes, but not always or necessarily, different, and this is not enough to warrant the distinctions Austin wants to make between ordinary and special circumstances, between normal and parasitic usage, between real-world utterances and stage or fictional utterances; at every point the conditions that supposedly mark off the lesser or derivative case can be shown to be defining of the normative case as well. In Derrida's words, "What Austin excludes as anomaly, exception, 'non-serious,' *citation* (on stage, in a poem, or a soliloquy) is the determined modification of a general citationality," that is, a highlighted instance of a general condition ("SEC," p. 191).

There are two obvious objections to this line of reasoning. The first one is posed by Derrida himself: If all utterances, serious as well as fictional, are detached from a centering origin and abandoned to an "essential drift"

("SEC," p. 182), then how is it that any of the world's verbal business gets satisfactorily done? One cannot deny, acknowledges Derrida, "that there are also performatives that succeed, and one has to account for them: meetings are called to order, . . . people say: 'I pose a question'; they bet, challenge, christen ships, and sometimes even marry. It would seem that such events have occurred. And even if only one had taken place only once, we would still be obliged to account for it" ("SEC," p. 191).

Derrida responds to his own objection first by saying "perhaps," and then by proceeding to inquire more closely into the notion of "occurrence." If by occurrence is meant an event whose certainty can be verified by independent evidence from the *outside*, then such events do not occur, because there is no "totally saturated context," no context so perspicuous that its interpretive cues can be read off by anyone no matter what his position; no context that precludes interpretation because it wears its meaning on its face. But if by occurrence is meant the conviction on the part of two or more contextually linked speakers that a particular speech act has taken place, then such events occur all the time, although independently of that conviction no external evidence could verify the communication. (Of course, speakers often subsequently *act* on the conviction that communication has occurred, and that continuing action is a kind of verification; but it *springs* from the conviction and does not stand outside it.)

Derrida offers as an example the context in which he originally delivered – orally, of course – the text of "Signature Event Context," a colloquium on philosophy in the French language whose theme was communication. Derrida calls this colloquium a "conventional context – produced by a kind of consensus that is implicit but structurally vague" ("SEC," p. 174). That is, while it is certainly in force, the consensus cannot be identified with an explicit statement of it because that statement itself would be "consensually" readable only by those whose consciousnesses were already informed by the goals and assumptions that give the colloquium its identity. The point is made by one of Derrida's typical jokes when he offers his own account – formal and written – of that consensus. It is understood, he explains, that at this colloquium one is to "propose 'communications' concerning communication, communications in a discursive form, colloquial communications, oral communications destined to be listened to, and to engage or to pursue dialogues within the horizon of an intelligibility and truth that is meaningful" ("SEC," p. 174). But all of this, he says, is "evident; and those who doubt it need only consult our program to be convinced" ("SEC," p. 174). The joke is that it will be evident only to those who are *able* to consult the program or who know what it is to consult the program of a philosophical colloquium, and they will *already* be convinced since their ability to consult is coextensive with the knowledge of why they are there. Someone who was without that ability – a passerby who happened to wander into the meeting room – might be convinced only that he didn't belong.

This, then, is how successful performatives occur, by means of the shared assumptions which enable speakers and hearers to make the same kind of sense of the words they exchange. And this also explains why the occurrence of successful performatives is not assured, because those who hear within different assumptions will be making a different kind of sense. One way to resist this argument, while appearing to assent to it, is to make the body of assumptions into an object by making a project of its description. Derrida believes that this is the project Austin pursues in the name of "context" when he declares in a famous passage that "what we have to study is *not* the sentence but the issuing of an utterance in a speech situation" (*HT*, p. 138). This dislodgment of the freestanding sentence from its traditional position of privilege is usually regarded as Austin's most powerful move; but Derrida sees that the move will have made very little difference if speech situations or contexts are conceived of as self-identifying; for then all that will have happened is that one self-interpreting entity will have been replaced by another; rather than sentences that declare their own meaning, we will now have contexts that declare their own meaning.

The issue here is between two notions of context: traditionally a context has been defined as a collection of features and therefore as something that can be identified by any clear-eyed observer; but Derrida thinks of a context as a structure of assumptions, and it is only by those who hold those assumptions or are held by them that the features in question can first be picked out and then identified as belonging to a context. It is the difference between thinking of a context as something *in* the world and thinking of a context as a construction *of* the world, a construction that is itself performed under contextualized conditions. Under the latter understanding one can no longer have any simple (that is, noninterpretive) recourse to context in order to settle disputes or resolve doubts about meaning, because contexts, while they are productive of interpretation, are also the products of interpretation. It would be useless, for example, to adjudicate the quarrel between the husband and wife in the *New Yorker* cartoon by appealing to the context, since it is precisely because they conceive the contextual conditions of their conversation differently that there is a quarrel at all. Of course, it is still the case, as Derrida acknowledges, that apologies are successfully offered and accepted ("there are also performatives that succeed"), but when that happens it is because the parties share or are shared by the same contextual assumptions and not because each can check what the other says against the independently available features of an empirical context. The contextual features of a simple exchange are no less "read" and therefore no more "absolutely" constraining than the contextual features of a stage performance or of a conversation reported in a poem.

This brings me directly to the second of the objections to this line of argument, that it denies the obvious differences between fiction and real life. But in fact it denies nothing. It simply asserts that the differences, whatever they are (and they are not always the same), do not arrange themselves around a basic or underlying difference between unmediated experience and experience that is the product of interpretive activity. If it is true, as Searle, Ohmann, and others contend, that we build up the world of a novel by reading it within a set of shaping conventions or interpretive strategies, it is no less true of the emergence into palpable form of the equally conventional worlds within which we experience real life. The "facts" of a baseball game, of a classroom situation, of a family reunion, of a trip to the grocery store, of a philosophical colloquium on the French language are only facts for those who are proceeding within a prior knowledge of the purposes, goals, and practices that underlie those activities. Again, this does not mean that there is no difference between them, only that they are all conventional as are the facts they entail.

The result is not to deny distinctions but to recharacterize them as distinctions between different kinds of interpretive practice. Thus, one might contrast the law, where interpretive practice is such that it demands a single reading (verdict), with the practice of literary criticism, where the pressure is for multiple readings (so much so that a text for which only one reading seemed available would be in danger of losing the designation "literary"). And if the contrast were extended to "ordinary conversation," that interpretive practice would be found to be more like the law than literary criticism in that a single reading is the understood norm; but, unlike the law, it is a reading for which one is not supposed to work, since it is a tacit rule of ordinary conversation that you accept things at their (contextually determined) face value and don't try to penetrate below the surface (again contextually determined) of an utterance. (Austin makes this into an ethical principle on pages 10 and 11 of *How to Do Things with Words*.) The violation of this rule is what makes the *New Yorker* cartoon funny; you're not supposed to question the surface currency of sincerity in everyday exchanges, and when you do, the resulting dislocation is at once irritating (as it is to the husband in the cartoon) and humorous (as it is to the readers of the *New Yorker*). One might say, then, that ordinary or everyday discourse is characterized by interpretive confidence and consequently by a minimum of self-conscious interpretive work; but this should not be understood to mean that the empirical conditions of ordinary discourse *compel* interpretive confidence: rather, interpretive confidence, as an assumption that produces behavior, also produces the empirical conditions it assumes.

Of course, this could be said of all conventional activities, each of which is carried on in a setting that it also elaborates and each of which is constitutive of the facts in its field of reference. This suggests the possibility of a new project or a new metaphysics, a taxonomic account of conventional activities and of the different kinds of fact they make available. Such an account, however, would itself be a conventional activity and thus could not escape the "interestedness" it claimed to describe. Moreover, such an account would never be able to catch up with the ability of conventional practices to modify themselves, to shrink or expand so that the boundaries between them, along with the facts marked off by those boundaries, are continually changing. In short, conventional differences are themselves a matter of convention and are no more available for direct inspection than the facts they entail. That is why the determination both of whether or not something is a fact and of what kind of fact it is can be a matter of dispute, as different criteria of difference are put into operation; and that is also why such disputes can only be adjudicated by invoking evidentiary procedures that will be no less conventional than the facts they are called on to establish. My morning newspaper reports that a plaque has been set up in Annapolis to commemorate the landing in America of Kunta Kinte, a displaced African. At the same time the Dublin city fathers are resisting efforts by a committee of Joyceans to have a plaque placed on the door of the house where Leopold Bloom was born on the grounds that he was only a fictional character. The two cases seem clear-cut until one begins to examine them. The primary documentary evidence of Kunta Kinte's independent existence is Alex Haley's *Roots*, a work whose integrity as a piece of research is very much in question; while, as Hugh Kenner has recently commented, Bloom is a personage more fully documented than the Irish national hero Cuchulain, whose statue stands in a Dublin post office. Nor can a fact/fiction boundary be definitively drawn by saying that, however imperfectly documented, there really was once a Kunta Kinte or a slave by a similar name of whom Haley's character is a representation; for the same thing can be said of Bloom who is a representation, many scholars believe, of a man named Hunter, a Dubliner who had himself changed his name (perhaps from Bloom) because it marked him as Jewish. It is not that these boundaries can't be settled but that when they are settled it will be by interpretive or institutional acts and not by evidence that is available independently of such acts. If Kunta Kinte has a plaque commemorating him in Annapolis, it is not because he has been objectively certified as a real person; rather his certification as a real person, when and if it is complete, will be the cumulative product of acts like the setting-up of a plaque to commemorate him, and the force of *that* act depends upon a convention linking the setting up of plaques and the validation of historical persons.

The point again is not that there are no such things as historical persons but that the category is no less a conventional one (with a membership conventionally established) than the category of fictional persons. The fact that it is a conventional category doesn't mean that the distinction is itself conventional; either Kunta Kinte was real or he was not. But the procedures for establishing the *fact* of his reality will always be conventional; that is, the fact will always have the status of something determined within a system of intelligibility and will never have the status of something determined outside of any system whatsoever. Nevertheless, since there always is a system, complete with evidentiary procedures and rules for applying them, the determination can always be made (although, given the claims of other systems, it can always be challenged).

That is why Derrida ostentatiously *refuses* to conclude that there "is no performative effect, no effect of ordinary language, no effect of presence or of discursive event (speech act). It is simply," he says, "that those effects do not exclude what is generally opposed to them, term by term; on the contrary, they presuppose it . . . as the general space of their possibility" ("SEC," p. 193). That is to say, there *are* differences in the experienced world of discourse that correspond to the differences traditionally posited between face-to-face and etiolated communication, between historical and fictional persons. It is just that those differences, rather than deriving from a *basic* difference between unmediated and mediated experience, mark off varieties of meditation. It is true that those varieties can be ordered with respect to their distance from an ideal or normative case, the case of ordinary circumstances, but that case, as we have seen, is nothing more than a set of interpretive practices (such as the practice of assuming sincerity) that produces what supposedly underlies the practices. Distance is not a special condition in relation to which interpretation becomes necessary; it is a general condition ("the general space of . . . possibility") that is productive of everything, including the circumstances – ordinary or presencefull circumstances – from which it is supposedly a falling away. Whatever hierarchy of communication situations may be in force, it is not a natural hierarchy, although within the space made available by the institutional and the conventional – finally the only available space – it will be received as natural, at least until it is challenged and reconstituted in another, equally institutional, form.[12] While there is no pure performative in the sense that authorizes Austin's exclusion of stage utterances, there is, as Derrida explains, a "relative purity" of performatives; but, he continues, "this relative purity does not emerge *in opposition* to citationality or iterability [Derrida's words in "Signature Event Context" for the institutional], but in opposition to other kinds of iteration within a general iterability" ("SEC," p. 192). That iterability – the condition of having-to-be-read – covers the field and can never be opposed to the "singular and original event-utterance," the transparent and simple speech act for which *How to Do Things with Words* is an extended but unsuccessful search.

III

The Derrida who emerges in the preceding pages may strike some readers as not at all like the apostle of "free play" they have learned either to fear or admire. While he is certainly not a believer in determinate meaning in a way that would give comfort to, say, M. H. Abrams or Frederick Crews, he does believe that communications between two or more persons regularly occur and occur with a "relative" certainty that ensures the continuity of everyday life. Rather than a subverter of common sense, this Derrida is very much a philosopher of common sense, that is, of the underlying assumptions and conventions within which the shape of common sense is specified and acquires its powerful force. One might even say, with the proper qualifications, that he is a philosopher of ordinary language. In so saying I am suggesting that Derrida and Austin may not be so far apart as some have thought. Searle begins his reply to Derrida by asserting that the confrontation between the two philosophers "never quite takes place" because the gulf that separates them is so wide and is made even wider by Derrida's "mistakes."[13] I want to argue, on the contrary, that the confrontation never quite takes place because there finally is not enough space between them for there to be a confrontation; and in the remainder of this essay I want to make that argument from the opposite direction by focusing on the process by which, at the conclusion of *How to Do Things with Words*, the supposedly normative class of constatives is shown to be a member of the supposedly exceptional class of performatives. Once that reversal has been effected, everything that Derrida says follows, including his challenge to the exclusion of stage or fictional utterances.

As it is first offered, the original distinction contrasts utterances that are responsible to the facts of an independent world with utterances that bring facts, of a certain kind, into being. Utterances of the first type are constatives, and the business of a constative is to " 'describe' some state of affairs, or to 'state some fact', which it must do either truly or falsely" (*HT*, p. I). Performatives, on the other hand, are actions in the sense that, rather than reporting on a state of affairs, they produce and create states of affairs. If I say, "I promise (to do X)," the effect of that "speech action" is to establish a future obligation (that is what a promise, by definition, is); that obligation was not a prior fact on whose existence I was reporting by saying "I promise" but a fact that came into the world by virtue of my saying "I promise." Of course, the creation of an obligation depends not simply on the words but on the uttering of the words within appropriate circumstances; if I promise to do something that I have already done or something that would not be of benefit to the promisee or something that I was obviously about to do anyway, the promise will be hollow or void or infelicitous for a variety of reasons analyzed by Searle in *Speech Acts*. Appropriateness, then, stands to performatives as truth and falsehood stand to constatives. The difference is that appropriateness as a standard varies with circumstances – it is a social or institutional judgment – while truth and falsehood as a standard refer to a relationship (between word and world) that *always* obtains.

Although Austin makes this distinction very firmly in the opening pages, much of the book is devoted to blurring it. The blurring begins with the last sentence of the first chapter: " 'False' is not necessarily used of statements only" (*HT*, p. II). By the end of chapter 4, we are being told that "in order to explain what can go wrong with statements we cannot just concentrate on the proposition involved (whatever that is) as has been done traditionally" (*HT*, p. 52). The parenthesis tells its own story: if you can't isolate a proposition, it is going to be hard to isolate the properties of statements. At the beginning of chapter 5 Austin admits that "there is danger of our initial... distinction between constative and performative breaking down," and chapter 6 opens by suggesting that "the performative is not altogether so obviously distinct from the constative" (*HT*, pp. 54, 67). In chapter 7 Austin pauses to "consider where we stand" and reports that we have now "found sufficient indications that unhappiness nevertheless seems to characterize both kinds of utterance... and that the requirement of conforming or bearing some relation to the facts... seems to characterize performatives... similarly to the way which is characterized of supposed constatives" (*HT*, p. 91).

The fact that constatives are now being referred to as "supposed" alerts us to the significance of what has been happening; terms are not merely blurring but a hierarchy is becoming undone. That is, the drawing together of performative and constative is finally to the benefit of performatives which under the traditional model were a subsidiary and inferior class because they were dependent on circumstances and not on judgments of truth and falsehood; but now judgments on truth and falsehood have been shown to be just as circumstantial as judgments of felicity (which themselves have been shown to be inseparable from questions of "fact"), with the result that constatives can no longer be defined as having a transparent relationship to the facts. Indeed, the notion of "fact" has been destabilized by the very same process; for since facts are established by means of true–false judgments (is it the case or is it not?) the circumstantialization of those judgments is also the circumstantialization of fact; that is, the question of whether something is or is not a fact will receive a different answer in different circumstances.

Austin makes this explicit in his last chapter when he declares that "truth and falsity are . . . not names for relations, qualities, or what not but for a dimension of assessment" (*HT*, p. 148). By "dimension of assessment," he means "a general dimension of being a right or proper thing to say as opposed to a wrong thing, in these circumstances, to this audience, for these purposes and with these intentions" (*HT*, p. 144). His example, "France is hexagonal," is surely a constative if anything is (*HT*, p. 142). Is it true or false? he asks. Well, perhaps, for certain intents and purposes, it might be true, if uttered in a military dimension of assessment by a general; but it might well be thought false if uttered in another dimension of assessment at a convention of geographers. It is not only that the terms within which the judgment is made change; the object of fact in relation to which one judges changes too. In one dimension France is conceived of as a military objective, in the other as a shape that must be reduced to a mapmaker's scale. One is tempted to say that underlying these different perspectives is a single factual entity, the "real" France, but that phrase can only stand for a France conceived within no dimension of assessment whatsoever, and that is precisely what it is impossible to do. France can only be thought of or even *thought* within some dimension of assessment, and so it will always be thought of as having or not having the kind of shape that is appropriate to that dimension. The France you are talking about will always be the product of the kind of talk (military, geographical, culinary, economic, literary) you are engaging in and will never be available *outside* any kind of talk whatsoever where it could function as an objective point of verification.

The point is made even clearer by Austin's next example. "Lord Raglan won the battle of Alma." True or false? Well, it depends on, among other things, whether it appears in a schoolbook or in a work of historical research. In a schoolbook it might be accepted as true because of the in-force assumptions as to what a battle is, what constitutes winning, the relationship of a general to success or failure, and so on; in a work of historical research all of these assumptions may have been replaced by others with the result that the very notions "battle" and "won" have a different shape. The mistake would be to think that "battle of Alma" was or ever could be an interpretation-free fact. Like France it is the product of the interpretive context – dimension of assessment – within which it has been conceived.

These accounts of France and the battle of Alma retroactively complicate the examples Austin had earlier offered to illustrate his original distinction. In chapter 4 he had cited the utterance "He is running" as a model constative because its truth can be determined simply by checking it against "the fact that he is running" (*HT*, p. 47). But once we realize that facts are only facts within a dimension of assessment, the relationship of transparency between the constative and the state of affairs on which it "reports" is immediately compromised. One need only imagine someone saying to the speaker. "You call that running, it's barely jogging," to see that the fit between the description and the "fact" will only be obvious to those for whom the articulations of the language of description correspond to their beliefs about the articulations in nature. If two speakers conceive of the distinction between running and jogging differently (or if one doesn't hold to any distinction at all), then they will disagree about the accuracy of "He is running" because each will be checking the utterance against a different set of "dimension-of-assessment" specific facts. Of course, it is always possible that a third party will enter the dispute and say, somewhat smugly, "You two are arguing about semantics; what you want is a vocabulary uninvolved in any particular perspective. If you were to describe the activity in terms of force, ratio of distance to speed, resistance, angles, velocity, and so on, you would have a neutral account of it, and *then* you could argue about whether to call it running or jogging." There is no reason to doubt that this could succeed as a strategy, since one can always have recourse to a vocabulary at a higher level of generality (a higher level of shared assumptions) than the level at which there is a dispute. But while the vocabulary may rise above and include the differing perspectives of the disputants, it will itself proceed from, and refer to the facts of, some or other perspective, and therefore the account it produces, while persuasive and convincing to all parties, will have no epistemological priority over the accounts it transcends. Talk of angles and ratios and velocities may have more cachet in the game of "accurate" description than talk of running and jogging, but it is still talk made possible in its intelligibility by a dimension of assessment; and therefore the accuracy such talk achieves will be relative to the facts as they are within that dimension.

On this analysis there is still a line of business for constatives to be in: but that business can no longer be thought of as involving a privileged relationship to reality. Whereas in the opening chapters of *How to Do Things with Words*, constatives are responsible to the world "as it is," by chapter II a constative is responsible to the world *as it is given within a dimension of assessment*. Rather than occupying a position of centrality in relation to which other uses of language are derivative and parasitic, constative speech acts are like all others in that the condition of their possibility (the condition of always operating within a dimension of assessment or interpretive community) forever removes them from any contact with an unmediated presence. By Austin's own argument, then, the exclusion of stage and other etiolated utterances as deviations from ordinary circumstances loses its warrant; for ordinary circumstances, circumstances in which objects, events, and intentions are transparently accessible, are shown to be an impossible ideal the moment the absolute (as opposed to conventional) distinction between constatives and performatives can no longer be made.

It would seem, then, that Derrida is right when he finds a contradiction at the heart of Austin's enterprise between his acknowledgement of the risk or infelicity inherent in all speech acts and his attempt to regulate that risk by excluding from consideration one class of speech acts because they are infected by risk. Derrida finds this strategy "curious," but he himself has directed us to a more generous reading of Austin's text when he characterizes it as "patient, open, aporetical, in constant transformation, often more fruitful in the acknowledgment of its impasses than in its positions" ("SEC," p. 187). That seems to me to be exactly right; the one thing that remains constant in *How to Do Things with Words* is that nothing remains constant: no term, no definition, no distinction survives the length of the argument, and many do not survive the paragraph or sentence in which they are first presented. The overturning of the distinction with which the book begins is of course the most dramatic instance of the pattern, but smaller and related instances abound, and they are all alike in that they simultaneously advance and retard the argument. Quite early on, Austin provides us with an account of his "method" when he remarks on the tendency of philosophy to begin by getting things wrong and says, cheerfully, "We must learn to run before we can walk" (*HT*, p. 12). By inverting the traditional proverb, Austin lets us know in advance that progress in this book will be a matter of declaring definitions that one must then take back, and moving forward will mean moving less quickly and perhaps, if we think of our goal as the achieving of undoubted rigor and clarity, not moving at all. Something of the feel of this experience is communicated in a remarkable series of sentences at the opening of the second chapter: "So far then we have merely felt the firm ground of prejudice slide away beneath our feet. But now how, as philosophers, are we to proceed? One thing we might go on to do, of course, is to take it all back: another would be to bog, by logical stages, down. But all this must take time" (*HT*, p. 13). The first sentence leaves us uncomfortable with either the past on which it reports or the future it promises. No one wants to feel that he is grounded in prejudice; but still less do we like to think that we may not be grounded at all. This Hobson's choice is immediately reproduced in the two alternative courses of action, taking everything back or bogging, by logical stages, down. When Austin then says, "But all this must take time," it is not at all clear what "all this" is or whether, at the end of it, we will once again have something under our feet.

Once Austin gets started (if that is the word), he regularly imitates God by first giving and then taking away. Later in chapter 3 he makes a distinction between those failures in communication that result from "botched procedures" and those failures that result when the procedures have been correctly executed but improperly invoked. He calls the first "misfires" and the second "abuses" and then admonishes the reader, one-half second too late, "Do not stress the normal connotations of these names" (*HT*, p. 16). The effect of this is complex: the names are on record and the distinction is in force, but at the same time the names are under a cloud, and the distinctions, as Austin almost immediately says, are "not hard and fast." Of course, hard and fast distinctions are not to be expected from an author who warns you that any new keys he puts in your hand will also be two skids under your feet (*HT*, p. 25). If one were to label this kind of writing, one might very well term it writing "under erasure," that is, writing which simultaneously uses and calls into question a vocabulary and a set of concepts. Of course, writing "under erasure" is a phrase that is associated with Derrida (who borrows it from Heidegger), and by invoking it I am easing into a claim that might at first seem counterintuitive: when all is said and done Derrida and Austin are very much alike. They are alike in writing a prose that complicates its initial assertions and obfuscates the oppositions on which it supposedly turns; and they are alike in the use to which that prose is put, a simultaneous proffering and withdrawing of procedural tests for determining the force and significance of utterances.

This has always been recognized in the case of Derrida, in part because the notorious difficulty of his prose, even at the surface level, flags the degree to which this discourse is concerned, not to say obsessed, with its own status. In Austin's case, however, it has been possible to overlook the fact of his style, either because it was thought irrelevant to the content of his philosophy or because it was regarded as a mannerism appropriate to a professor at Oxford. But in fact it is not a mannerism at all but a self-consciously employed strategy that is intended to produce, among other things, impatience and irritation. At one point Austin says as much. "Many of you will be getting impatient at this approach – and to some extent quite justifiably. You will say, 'Why not cut the cackle? . . . Why not get down to discussing the thing bang off in terms of linguistics and psychology in a straightforward fashion? Why be so devious?' " (*HT*, p. 122). To discuss the thing in terms of linguistics would be to produce criteria by which performatives could be marked off from constatives, and illocutionary acts distinguished from perlocutionary; and to discuss the thing in terms of psychology would be to correlate internal states with a list of verbs. In the course of his book Austin attempts more than once to do exactly that, but in each instance the formulas he considers turn out to be unworkable. Here on page 122 the address to the reader follows a chapter-long discussion of the prepositions "in" and "by" as possible ways of identifying different kinds of speech acts. He now asks, "Will these . . . formulas provide us with a test for distinguishing illocutionary from perlocutionary acts?" That is, will they do what we have been assuming all along that they could do? The answer is brief and crushing: "They will not." At times it seems that the only point of the book is to devise tests that will *not* work. In chapter 5 a succession of "absolute" criteria for picking out performatives is offered and rejected: the first person singular, the present indicative, tense, and mood – each of them is passed in review and of each of them Austin finally says, this "will not do." We are, he admits, at an "impasse over any *single simple* criterion of grammar or vocabulary" (*HT*, p. 59); but perhaps, he speculates, it may not be impossible to "produce a complex criterion" or "at least a set of criteria"; perhaps, for example, "one of the criteria might be that everything with the verb in the imperative mood is performative." But this proposal is no sooner made than it is threatened by an infinite regress: "This leads, however, to many troubles over . . . when a verb is in the imperative mood and when it is not, into which I do not propose to go" (*HT*, pp. 59–60). Presumably, if he did go into it, he would encounter the same difficulty he encounters here: the test for whether or not a verb was in the imperative mood would turn out to be no less vulnerable to exceptions and counterexamples than the tests that have already failed.

As his argument unfolds (exactly the wrong word), Austin continues to pursue this double strategy: he searches for a criterion of which it can be said, "it is only to be used in circumstances which make it unambiguously clear that it is being used," but the search yields only the repeated demonstration that such a criterion is unavailable because, as he immediately declares, it rests on "a counsel of perfection" (*HT*, p. 34). That counsel impels his enterprise forward and draws us on with its promise – the promise of a pure performative, of a mechanical procedure for distinguishing one kind of speech act from another, of a point of transparency – but the promise is never redeemed, as Austin teases out his examples until the distinctions they supposedly illustrate are blurred and even reversed. The pattern is particularly clear in the extended discussion through several chapters of the so-called explicit performative. An explicit performative is a verb that serves "the special purpose of *making explicit* . . . what precise action it is that is being performed by the issuing of the utterance" (*HT*, p. 61). In other words, the illocutionary force is named in the utterance itself by a performative verb, as in "I *promise* to pay you five dollars," or "I *order* you to leave the room." The position occupied by the explicit performative in the theory is thus a familiar one in philosophy: it stands for a core or paradigm case in relation to which other more doubtful cases are to be evaluated and understood. The explicit performative, in short, centers or anchors a system that at its outermost edges is characterized by uncertainty. The presence of an explicit performative affords a clear indication of the intention with which an utterance is issued; whereas in its absence the way in which an utterance can be taken is "open" (*HT*, p. 33).

Almost immediately, however, Austin complicates this picture by presenting an example in which the presence of an explicit performative does not in and of itself determine the force of an utterance. "Suppose I say 'I promise to send you to a nunnery' – when I think, but you do not, that this will be for your good, or again when you think it will but I do not, or even when we both think it will, but in fact, as may transpire, it will not?" (*HT*, pp. 37–8). Have I promised? Or "have I invoked a non-existent convention in inappropriate circumstances?" Austin does not answer his own questions but merely points out that "there can be no satisfactory choice between these alternatives, which are too unsubtle to fit subtle cases" (*HT*, p. 38). There is no "short-cut": no mechanical procedure for making these decisions; instead, one must expound "the full complexity of the situation which does not exactly fit any common classification" (*HT*, p. 38). But what this and other examples suggest is that *all* cases may be similarly subtle and that the situation which would fit the common classification – the situation in which illocutionary force is perfectly explicit – will never be encountered.

Whenever the explicit performative reappears, it is in contexts like this one, contexts that take away the interpretive comfort it promises to provide. In chapter 6 Austin offers a speculative genealogy in which the explicit performative and the "pure" statement emerge not before but *after* "certain more primary utterances, many of which are already implicit performatives" (*HT*, p. 71). In this account vagueness and indeterminacy, rather than being a departure from a more basic condition of precision, are in fact primitive, and we are very close to Derrida's assertion that "the quality of risk" is internal to the very structure of language and not something that infects only peripheral and nonnormative cases. In the same chapter the strong claim for the explicit performative is made once again when Austin says "the explicit performative rules out equivocation and keeps the performance fixed," but he then softens the claim almost to nothing by adding to his sentence a single word, "relatively" (*HT*, p. 76). On the very next page he declares explicitly what his examples have been all the while implying: "The existence and even the use of explicit performative does not remove all our troubles" (*HT*, p. 77). By troubles Austin means the "uncertainty of sure reception," and the reason that the explicit performative does not remove that uncertainty is because it is uncertain – that is, a matter of interpretation – as to whether or not a particular locution is in fact explicit in the way required. Rather than resolving an interpretive dispute, the citing of an explicit performative merely adds another component to the dispute. The final judgment on the explicit performative is delivered in chapter 9, and it is a judgment that renders the term incapable of performing the function it was introduced to serve: "We have found . . . that it is often not easy to be sure that, even when it is apparently in explicit form, an utterance is performative or that it is not" (*HT*, p. 91). "Apparently" is a master word here; it carries with it all the force of the critique Derrida will later make of this same book. "It is time," Austin declares in the very next sentence, "to make a fresh start on the problem." Of course by now making a fresh start means that the problem has itself been reconceived in a way so radical that even its outlines are no longer what they were when it was initially posed.

"It is difficult," Austin says at the end of chapter 9, "to say where conventions begin and end" (*HT*, p. 118). At times in the book this seems to be a difficulty that, once acknowledged, can be overcome, but in fact that difficulty, with all its implications for the possibility of certain formal projects, is finally triumphant in *How to Do Things with Words*. The rhetoric of the book's opening pages suggests a modest proposal: a type of utterance that had not been sufficiently attended to, and was in danger of escaping serious attention altogether, was to be brought into the circle that had been drawn around language by traditional philosophy; but, once in, the attempt to provide an account of that type begins to undermine the assumptions that allow the circle to be drawn in the first place, and in the end we have the revolution so elegantly reported by Searle: the special cases swallow the general case.[14] It is important to see that this is not a mere reversal in which two terms change places within a system whose structural shape remains the same. The revisionary effect of this discourse is much more wholesale; it challenges and dislodges the picture of things that at once gave the terms their shape and made conceivable the project of formally relating them. That project (of getting things straight "bang off") is what gives the book its apparent structure, but the true structure is its gradual dissolution as the distinctions with which it begins are blurred and finally collapsed. It is this double structure that is responsible for the fact that the book has given rise to two versions of speech-act theory, one committed to reabsorbing illocutionary force into a formal theory of the Chomsky type (here representative figures are John Ross, Jerrold Katz, and Jerrold Saddock)[15] and the other committed to making illocutionary force a function of pragmatic – that is, unformalizable – circumstances (here one might cite the work of H. P. Grice and Mary Pratt).[16] In a third version, represented at times by Searle and more recently by Kent Bach and Robert Harnisch, there is an attempt to reconcile the formal and the pragmatic, but this usually involves granting them an independence that the pragmatic view, if taken seriously, inherently destabilizes.[17] For Austin, the formal and the pragmatic are neither alternatives to be chosen nor simple opposites to be reconciled but the components of a dialectic that works itself out in his argument, a tacking back and forth between the commitment to intelligibility and the realization that intelligibility, although always possible, can never be reduced to the operation of a formal mechanism. That is why Derrida's reading of Austin is finally not a critique but a tribute to the radical provisionality of a text that has too often been domesticated, and it is a reading that is more faithful than many that have been offered by the master's disciples. Indeed, had he thought of it, Derrida might well have dedicated "Signature Event Context" to Austin; and it is pleasant to think that in some philosopher's heaven he will be able to present it to him, WITH THE COMPLIMENTS OF THE AUTHOR.

Notes

What follows is a carefully circumscribed and limited attempt to explicate for an Anglo-American audience the arguments of Derrida's "Signature Event Context" (*Glyph* I [1977]: 172–97) as they relate the project begun by J. L. Austin in *How to Do Things with Words* (Oxford, 1962); all further references to these works, abbreviated "SEC" and *HT*, respectively, will be included in the text. It is also an attempt, as some of my readers will recognize, to assimilate the Derrida of this and related essays to the theory of "interpretive communities" as it is elaborated in my *Is There a Text in This Class? The Authority of Interpretive Communities* (Cambridge, Mass., 1980). Such an effort may appear to be simply one more American domestication of Derridean thought, but it is intended as a counterweight to the more familiar domestication associated with words like "undecidability" and the "abyss." The narrowness of my focus precludes any consideration of Derrida's "Limited Inc." or of the essay by John Searle to which "Limited Inc." is a response. It also precludes a consideration of the other perspectives – psychoanalysis, feminism, sociolinguistics – that have been brought to bear on the issues raised by the Searle–Derrida debate. I refer the reader to the helpful and illuminating analyses of Gayatri Spivak ("Revolutions That as Yet Have No Model," *Diacritics* 8 [Winter 1980]: 29–49); Mary Pratt ("The Ideology of Speech-Act Theory," *Centrum*, n. s. I, no. I [Spring 1981]: 5–18); Samuel Weber ("It," *Glyph* 4 [1978]: 1–31); and Barbara Johnson ("Mallarmé and Austin," *The Critical Difference* [Baltimore, 1980], pp. 52–66). I am indebted to Kenneth Abraham, Michael Fried, and Walter Benn Michaels who worked through these texts with me in a succession of team-taught courses and who have contributed to the result in ways they will immediately recognize. I am grateful for the criticisms and suggestions of Steven Knapp, W. J. T. Mitchell, and Robert Viscusi.

1 Jonathan Culler, *Structuralist Poetics* (Ithaca, NY, 1975), p. 133; all further references to this work will be included in the text.

2 John M. Ellis, *The Theory of Literary Criticism: A Logical Analysis* (Berkeley and Los Angeles, 1974), p. 43.

3 Barbara Herrnstein Smith, *On the Margins of Discourse: The Relation of Literature to Language* (Chicago, 1978), pp. 35, 36.

4 Wolfgang Iser, *The Act of Reading* (Baltimore, 1978), pp. 24, 184.

5 Richard Ohmann, "Speech Acts and the Response to Literature" (paper delivered at the December 1976 meeting of the Modern Language Association).

6 John Searle, "The Logical Status of Fictional Discourse," *Expression and Meaning* (Cambridge, Eng., 1979), p. 67; all further references to this work will be included in the text.

7   The argument that the more information one has about a context the more sure will be the interpretation of utterances produced in that context is parallel to the argument that the more words in an utterance (the more explicit it is), the less likely it is to be misinterpreted or interpreted in a plurality of ways. They are both arguments for a state of saturation (either of words or things) so total that interpretation can find no entering wedge. For a counterargument, see my *Is There a Text in This Class?* pp. 282–3, 311.

8   Of course, it is possible that she could change her mind, but only if he succeeded in changing the belief she now holds about his character. This might happen, for example, if he were to do something he had often promised but failed to do or said something ("I love you") he had been unwilling to say before. The fact that she might be convinced by this or some other piece of behavior does not mean that her belief would have been altered by a direct encounter with unmediated evidence; for that behavior will have the status of evidence only in the context of the particular form her belief takes (it will be belief-specific evidence). If, for example, her belief about his character takes the form of her thinking "he will never do this or say that," then certain pieces of behavior (his doing this or saying that) will count as possible reasons for altering her belief, although those reasons will themselves have their source in belief. Moreover, the force of the behavior as evidence might be felt even if it were only reported to her or conveyed in a letter. Again, the fact of physical proximity is not as decisive or even necessarily relevant.

9   See Derrida, *Of Grammatology*. trans. Gayatri Spivak (Baltimore, 1976), pp. 107–40, for a powerful analysis of the appearance–disappearance of persons within a system.

10   Weber, "It," p. 7.

11   See Johnson, "Mallarmé and Austin," p. 60:

> The performative utterance . . . automatically fictionalizes its utterer when it makes him the mouthpiece of a conventionalized authority. Where else, for example, but at a party *convention* could a presidential candidate be nominated? Behind the fiction of the subject stands the fiction of society. . . . It is, of course, not our intention to nullify all the differences between a poem and, say, a verdict, but only to problematize the assumptions on which such distinctions are based. If people are put to death by a verdict and not by a poem, it is not because the law is not a fiction.

See also Pratt, "Ideology," p. 10:

> "Authorship" is a certain, socially constituted position occupied by a speaking subject and endowed with certain characteristics and certain relationships to other dimensions of that subject. Alternatively, we could say that an implied author exists in all speech acts – an author is implied in a text only in the same way subjects are implied in any speech act they perform.

There is an extended discussion of these matters in my "How to Do Things with Austin and Searle" in *Is There a Text in This Class?*, pp. 197–245; see esp. pp. 231–44.

12 See Derrida, *Of Grammatology*, p. 44: "If 'writing' signifies inscription and especially the durable institution of a sign . . . writing in general covers the entire field of linguistic signs. In that field a certain sort of instituted signifiers may then appear, 'graphic' in the narrow and derivative sense of the word, ordered by a certain relationship with other instituted – hence 'written,' even if they are 'phonic' – signifiers." That is to say, within the field of instituted signifiers, some one sort will occupy the position – within the institution – of 'natural.' See also p. 46: "The rupture of that 'natural attachment' puts in question the idea of naturalness rather than that of attachment. That is why the word 'institution' should not be too quickly interpreted within the classical system of oppositions." That is, the fact that everything is institutional does not mean that there are no distinctions or norms or standards – no "attachments" – only that those attachments, because they are institutional or socially constituted, are not eternal and can therefore change.

13 John Searle, "Reiterating the Differences: A Reply to Derrida," *Glyph* I (1977): 198.

14 See John Searle, *The Philosophy of Language* (Oxford, 1971), p. 7.

15 See John Ross, "On Declarative Sentences," in *Readings in English Transformational Grammar*, ed. Roderick Jacobs and Peter Rosenbaum (Lexington, Mass., 1970); Jerrold Katz, *Propositional Structure and Illocutionary Force* (Cambridge, Mass., 1980); and Jerrold Saddock, *Toward a Linguistic Theory of Speech Acts* (New York, 1974).

16 See H. P. Grice, "Logic and Conversation" (delivered as part of the William James Lectures, Harvard University, 1967), and Mary Pratt, *Toward a Speech Act Theory of Literary Discourse* (Bloomington, Ind., 1977).

17 See Kent Bach and Robert M. Harnisch, *Linguistic Communication and Speech Acts* (Cambridge, Mass., 1979).

4

Consequences

When I think of Stanley Fish in the 1980s, this essay is one of the two or three that come to mind. What bravura spirit, what dazzling intelligence, what boldness, what eagerness for argumentation! Reading "Consequences," any reader must be impressed with the energy and inventiveness with which Fish prosecutes his case.

And what a brilliantly heedless case it is. Always ahead of the curve, Fish had been arguing for several years that "theory," the new plaything – and a word with which he himself had been prominently associated – was not just old but dead, and not just dead but impossible on the face of it, sustained in a semblance of vitality only by a massive group hallucination. What people, especially literary academics and law professors, believed was that theory, a set of principles that held true all the time, both existed and made a difference in the world of practice. Writing on "Consequences" in a book called *Doing What Comes Naturally*, Fish argued, as he has always done, for "precisely the opposite" position. In the world, one generally suffers for doing what comes naturally, but in the academy, he said, theory *was* natural – just more practice, misnamed – and therefore had no consequences.

To prove this point, which he well knew would be both counterintuitive and unwelcome to people who had grown accustomed to "theory hope" and "theory fear," Fish constructs numerous little scenarios in which hopeful gestures come to grief and fears go unrealized. He considers the problem from every possible angle, entertaining objections to his case that his opponents probably hadn't even considered. So persistent and resourceful is he in discovering counter-examples that one suspects that these engage his imagination to a curious degree, given the absolute commitment to his position he professes. Indeed, Fish seems almost law-yerly in his willingness to argue a case he may not personally believe.

He is wise to withhold his full credence from this argument, for it takes so many twists and turns, undergoing more than one "dramatic reversal," as he points out, that it is very difficult to attach conviction to the entirety. If, for example, we believe Fish's first claim that theory is a "special pro-ject," then how can we go along with the later claim that it is just more practice with no specialness whatsoever? And how are we to reconcile the argument that real theory does not and cannot exist with the fact that, as Fish demonstrates, the sense, at least, of theory is everywhere? In full view of a world he knows to be incredulous, Fish actually makes a show, which is not without a certain Houdini-esque quality of escaping from his own confinements, of believing it all; and much of the charm of the essay results from the ingenuity and relentlessness of his argumentation.

Perhaps the most daring escape comes at the moment when Fish acknowledges, in the course of his compulsive elaboration of objections, that theory actually has lots of consequences – but that they are "polit-ical" and not theoretical. This move has always mystified me. What sort of consequences, a pragmatist might ask, could theory ever have or hope for? How would these consequences, occurring as they would in the world of practice, ever be anything but "political"? So full of words, Fish seems here to have one too many, for he has first identified theory and politics and then declared theory nonexistent.

In fact, however, one finishes "Consequences" with an augmented rather than a diminished view of the possibilities of theory as a powerfully peculiar but startlingly effective all-and-nothing, everywhere-and-nowhere enterprise. This may not be Fish's intention, but who can say what he really intends? In fact, the subject of theory takes us where Fish does not, or does not seem to, want to go. A theory is a belief in advance of the evidence. If there were full and sufficient evidence for a theory, it wouldn't be a theory, but a determined fact. To hold a theory, one needs a certain well-camouflaged disposition to believe something. Theory may, in short, be an ambassador of the unconscious in the court of thought; what Fish calls "belief" may be the unconscious roots of theory.

This may, in fact, be why arguments about theory suffer dramatic reversals: their kernels are deeply unconscious but their expression is highly conscious; reversal is their destiny. It may also be why Fish, whose entire mental outlook is hostile to the idea of the unconscious, is so committed to trashing theory. Clearly, the subject has not yet had a final analysis.

Geoffrey Galt Harpham

Nothing I wrote in *Is There a Text in This Class?* has provoked more opposition or consternation than my (negative) claim that the argument of the book has no consequences for the practice of literary criticism.[1] To many it seemed counterintuitive to maintain (as I did) that an argument in theory could leave untouched the practice it considers: After all, isn't the very point of theory to throw light on or reform or guide practice? In answer to this question I want to say, first, that this is certainly theory's claim – so much so that independently of the claim there is no reason to think of it as a separate activity – and, second, that the claim is unsupportable. Here, I am in agreement with Steven Knapp and Walter Benn Michaels, who are almost alone in agreeing with me and who fault me not for making the "no consequences" argument but for occasionally falling away from it. Those who dislike *Is There a Text in This Class?* tend to dislike "Against Theory" even more, and it is part of my purpose here to account for the hostility to both pieces. But since the issues at stake are fundamental, it is incumbent to begin at the beginning with a discussion of what theory is and is not.

"Against Theory" opens with a straightforward (if compressed) definition: "By 'theory' we mean a special project in literary criticism: the attempt to govern interpretations of particular texts by appealing to an account of inter- pretation in general" (p. 723). In the second sentence the authors declare that this definition of theory excludes much that has been thought to fall under its rubric and especially excludes projects of a general nature "such as narratology, stylistics, and prosody" (p. 723). On first blush this exclusion seems arbitrary and appears to be vulnerable to the charge (made by several respondents) that by defining theory so narrowly Knapp and Michaels at once assure the impregnability of their thesis and render it trivial. I believe, on the contrary, that the definition is correct and that, moreover, it is a reformulation of a familiar and even uncontroversial distinction. In E. D. Hirsch's work, for example, we meet it as a distinction between general and local hermeneutics. "Local hermeneutics," Hirsch explains,

consists of rules of thumb rather than rules. . . . Local hermeneutics can . . . provide models and methods that are reliable most of the time. General hermeneutics lays claim to principles that hold true all of the time. . . . That is why general hermeneutics is, so far, the only aspect of interpretation that has earned the right to be named a "theory."[2]

By "general hermeneutics," Hirsch means a procedure whose steps, if they are faithfully and strictly followed, will "always yield correct results";[3] "local hermeneutics," on the other hand, are calculations of probability based on an insider's knowledge of what is likely to be successful in a particular field of practice. When Cicero advises that in cases where a client's character is an issue a lawyer should attribute a bad reputation to "the envy of a few people, or back biting, or false opinion" or, failing that, argue that "the defendant's life and character are not under investigation, but only the crime of which he is accused," he is presenting and urging a local hermeneutics. But when Raoul Berger insists that the meaning of the Constitution can be determined only by determining the intentions of the framers, he is presenting and urging a general hermeneutics.[4] In one case the practitioner is being told "[i]n a situation like this, here are some of the things you can do," where it is left to the agent to determine whether or not he has encountered a situation "like this" and which of the possible courses of action is relevant. In the other case the practitioner is being told "[w]hen you want to know the truth or discover the meaning, do this," where "this" is a set of wholly explicit instructions that leaves no room for interpretive decisions by the agent. In one case the practitioner is being given a "rule of thumb," something that would in certain circumstances be a good thing to try if you want to succeed in the game; in the other he is being given a rule, something that is necessary to do if you want to be right, where "being right" is not a matter of being in tune with the temporary and shifting norms of a context but of having adhered to the dictates of an abiding and general rationality. A rule is formalizable: it can be programmed on a computer and, therefore, can be followed by anyone who has been equipped with explicit (noncircular) definitions and equally explicit directions for carrying out a procedure. A rule of thumb, on the other hand, cannot be formalized, because the conditions of its application vary with the contextual circumstances of an ongoing practice; as those circumstances change, the very meaning of the rule (the instructions it is understood to give) changes too, at least for someone sufficiently inside the practice to be sensitive to its shifting demands. To put it another way, the rule-of-thumb reader begins with a knowledge of the outcome he desires, and it is within such knowledge that the rule assumes a shape, becomes readable; the rule follower, in contrast, defers to the self-declaring shape of the rule, which then generates the correct outcome independently of his judgment. The model for the "true" rule and, therefore, for theory is mathematics, for as John Lyons points out, if two people apply the rules of mathematics and come up with different results, we can be sure that one of them is mistaken, that is, has misapplied the rules.[5]

Lyons turns to the analogy from mathematics in the course of an explication of Chomskian linguistics, and the Chomsky project provides an excellent example of what a model of the formal, or rule-governed, type would be like. The Chomskian revolution, as Jerrold Katz and Thomas Bever have written, involved "the shift from a conception of grammar as cataloging the data of a corpus to a conception of grammar as explicating the internalized rules

underlying the speaker's ability to produce and understand sentences."[6] Basically this is a turn from an empirical activity – the deriving of grammatical rules
from a finite body of observed sentences – to a rational activity – the discovery
of a set of constraints which, rather than being generalizations from observed
behavior, are explanatory of that behavior in the sense that they are what make
it possible. These constraints are not acquired through experience (education,
historical conditioning, local habits) but are innate; experience serves only to
actualize or "trigger" them. They have their source not in culture but in
nature, and therefore they are *abstract* (without empirical content), *general*
(not to be identified with any particular race, location, or historical period
but with the species), and *invariant* (do not differ from language to language).
As a system of rules, they are "independent of the features of the actual world
and thus hold in any possible one" ("FRE," p. 40).

It follows that any attempt to model these constraints – to construct a device
that will replicate their operations – must be equally independent in all these
ways, that is, it must be formal, abstract, general, and invariant. It is Chomsky's
project to construct such a device, a model of an innate human ability, a
"competence model" which reflects the timeless and contextless workings of
an abiding formalism, as opposed to a "performance model" which would
reflect the empirical and contingent regularities of the behavior of some
particular linguistic community. Once constructed, a competence model
would function in the manner of a "mechanical computation" ("FRE," p.
38); that is, to "apply" it would be to set in motion a self-executing machine or
calculus that would assign, without any interpretive activity on the part of the
applier, the same description to a sentence that would be assigned by "an ideal
speaker-listener, in a completely homogeneous speech-community, who
knows its language perfectly."[7] If such a speaker were presented with the
sentence "He danced his did," he would reject it as ungrammatical or irregular
or deviant. Accordingly, a grammar modeled on his ability (or intuition) would
refuse to assign the sentence a description – the generative device would find
itself blocked by an item that violated its rules. If such a speaker were presented
with the sentence "Flying planes can be dangerous," he would recognize it as
ambiguous; accordingly, a generative grammar would assign the sentence not
one but two structural (or "deep") descriptions. And if such a speaker were
presented with the pair of sentences "John hit the ball" and "The ball was hit
by John," he would recognize them as being synonymous, and, accordingly,
the generative grammar would assign them a single structural description.

It is important to realize that this ideal speaker and the grammar modeled on
his competence would perform their tasks without taking into account the
circumstances of a sentence's production, or the beliefs of the speaker and
hearer, or the idiomatic patterns of a particular community.[8] The speaker who

knows the language of his community "perfectly" in Chomsky's idealization knows that system independently of its actualization in real-life situations: that knowledge is his competence, and the grammar that captures it divides strings in a language "into the well-formed and the ill-formed just on the basis of their syntactic structure, without reference to the way things are in the world, what speakers, hearers, or anyone else believe, etc." ("FRE," p. 31). That is why, as Judith Greene puts it, "the only real test... of a grammar is to devise a set of formal rules which, if fed to a computer operating with no prior knowledge of the language, would still be capable of generating only correct grammatical sentences."[9]

This is precisely the goal of Chomskian theory – the construction of "a system of rules that in some explicit and well-defined way assigns structural descriptions to sentences," where "explicit" means mechanical or algorithmic and the assigning is done not by the agent but by the system (*ATS*, p. 8). Needless to say, there has been much dispute concerning the possibility (and even desirability) of achieving that goal, and there have been many challenges to the basic distinctions (between competence and performance, between grammaticality and acceptability, between syntax and semantics, between grammatical knowledge and the knowledge of the world) that permit the goal, first, to be formulated and, then, to guide a program of research. But putting aside the merits of the Chomsky program and the question of whether it could ever succeed, the point I want to make here is that as a program it is theoretical and can stand as a fully developed example of what Knapp and Michaels mean when they say that theory is a *special* project and what Hirsch means when he insists that only such a project – a general hermeneutics – "has earned the right to be named a 'theory.'" The Chomsky project is theoretical because what it seeks is a method, a recipe with premeasured ingredients which when ordered and combined according to absolutely explicit instructions – instructions that "[do] not rely on the intelligence of the understanding reader" (*ATS*, p. 4) – will produce the desired result. In linguistics that result would be the assigning of correct descriptions to sentences; in literary studies the result would be the assigning of valid interpretations to works of literature. In both cases (and in any other that could be imagined) the practitioner gives himself over to the theoretical machine, surrenders his judgment to it, in order to reach conclusions that in no way depend on his education, or point of view, or cultural situation, conclusions that can then be checked by anyone who similarly binds himself to those rules and carries out their instructions.

Thus understood, theory can be seen as an effort to govern practice in two senses: (1) it is an attempt to *guide* practice from a position above or outside it (see pp. 723 and 742), and (2) it is an attempt to *reform* practice by neutralizing interest, by substituting for the parochial perspective of some local or partisan

point of view the perspective of a general rationality to which the individual
subordinates his contextually conditioned opinions and beliefs. (Not incidentally, this is the claim and the dream of Baconian method, of which so many
modern theoretical projects are heirs.) Only if this substitution is accomplished
will interpretation be principled, that is, impelled by formal and universal rules
that apply always and everywhere rather than by rules of thumb that reflect the
contingent practices of particular communities.

The argument *against* theory is simply that this substitution of the general for
the local has never been and will never be achieved. Theory is an impossible
project which will never succeed. It will never succeed simply because the
primary data and formal laws necessary to its success will always be spied or
picked out from within the contextual circumstances of which they are
supposedly independent. The objective facts and rules of calculation that are
to ground interpretation and render it principled are themselves interpretive
products: they are, therefore, always and already contaminated by the interested judgments they claim to transcend. The contingencies that are to be
excluded in favor of the invariant constitute the field within which what will
(for a time) be termed the invariant emerges.

Once again, a ready example offers itself in the history of Chomskian
linguistics. In order to get started, Chomsky must exclude from his "absolute
formulations . . . any factor that should be considered as a matter of performance rather than competence." He does this, as Katz and Bever observe, "by
simply considering the former [performance] as something to be abstracted
away from, the way the physicist excludes friction, air resistance, and so on
from the formulation of mechanical laws" ("FRE," p. 21). This act of abstract-
ing-away-from must of course begin with data, and in this case the data are (or
are supposed to be) sentences that depend for their interpretation not on
performance factors – on the knowledge of a speaker's beliefs or of particular
customs or conventions – but on the rules of grammar.[10] The trick then is to
think of sentences that would be heard in the same way by all competent
speakers no matter what their educational experience, or class membership, or
partisan affiliation, or special knowledge, sentences which, invariant across
contexts, could form the basis of an acontextual and formal description of the
language and its rules.

The trouble is that there are no such sentences. As I have argued elsewhere,
even to think of a sentence is to have already assumed the conditions both of its
production and its intelligibility – conditions that include a speaker, with an
intention and a purpose, in a situation.[11] To be sure, there are sentences which,
when presented, seem to be intelligible in isolation, independently of any
contextual setting. This simply means, however, that the context is so established, so deeply assumed, that it is invisible to the observer – he does not

realize that what appears to him to be immediately obvious and readable is a function of its being in place. It follows, then, that any rules arrived at by abstracting away from such sentences will be rules only within the silent or deep context that allowed them to emerge and become describable. Rather than being distinct from circumstantial (and therefore variable) conditions, linguistic knowledge is unthinkable apart from these circumstances. Linguistic knowledge is contextual rather than abstract, local rather than general, dynamic rather than invariant; every rule is a rule of thumb; every competence grammar is a performance grammar in disguise.[12]

This, then, is why theory will never succeed: it cannot help but borrow its terms and its contents from that which it claims to transcend, the mutable world of practice, belief, assumptions, point of view, and so forth. And, by definition, something that cannot succeed cannot have consequences, cannot achieve the goals it has set for itself by being or claiming to be theory, the goals of guiding and/or reforming practice. Theory cannot guide practice because its rules and procedures are no more than generalizations from practice's history (and from only a small piece of that history), and theory cannot reform practice because, rather than neutralizing interest, it begins and ends in interest and raises the imperatives of interest – of some local, particular, partisan project – to the status of universals.

Thus far I have been talking about "foundationalist" theory (what Knapp and Michaels call "positive theory"), theory that promises to put our calculations and determinations on a firmer footing than can be provided by mere belief or unjustified practice. In recent years, however, the focus of attention has been more on "anti-foundationalist" theory (what Knapp and Michaels call "negative theory"), on arguments whose force it is precisely to deny the possibility (and even the intelligibility) of what foundationalist theory promises. Anti-foundationalist theory is sometimes Kuhnian, sometimes Derridean, sometimes pragmatist, sometimes Marxist, sometimes anarchist, but it is always historicist; that is, its strategy is always the one I have pursued in the previous paragraphs, namely, to demonstrate that the norms and standards and rules that foundationalist theory would oppose to history, convention, and local practice are in every instance a function or extension of history, convention, and local practice. As Richard Rorty puts it: "There are no essences anywhere in the area. There is no wholesale, epistemological way to direct, or criticize or underwrite the course of inquiry.... It is the vocabulary of practice rather than of theory...in which one can say something useful about truth."[13] (Notice that this does not mean that a notion like "truth" ceases to be operative, only that it will always have reference to a moment in the history of inquiry rather than to some God or material objectivity or invariant calculus that underwrites all our inquiries.)

The fact that there are two kinds of theory (or, rather, theoretical discourse – anti-foundationalism really isn't a theory at all; it is an argument against the possibility of theory) complicates the question of consequences, although in the end the relationship of both kinds of theory to the question turns out to be the same. As we have seen, those who believe in the consequences of foundationalist theory are possessed by a hope – let us call it "theory hope" – the hope that our claims to knowledge can be "justified on the basis of some objective method of assessing such claims" rather than on the basis of the individual beliefs that have been derived from the accidents of education and experience.[14] Anti-foundationalist theory tells us that no such justification will ever be available and that therefore there is no way of testing our beliefs against something whose source is not also a belief. As we shall see, anti-foundationalism comes with its own version of "theory hope," but the emotion its arguments more often provoke is "theory fear," the fear that those who have been persuaded by such arguments will abandon principled inquiry and go their unconstrained way in response to the dictates of fashion, opinion, or whim. Expressions of theory fear abound (one can find them now even in daily newspapers and popular magazines), and in their more dramatic forms they approach the status of prophecies of doom. Here, for example, is Israel Scheffler's view of what will happen if we are persuaded by the writings of Thomas Kuhn:

Independent and public controls are no more, communication has failed, the common universe of things is a delusion, reality itself is made ... rather than discovered. ... In place of a community of rational men following objective procedures in the pursuit of truth, we have a set of isolated monads, within each of which belief forms without systematic constraints.[15]

For Scheffler (and many others) the consequences of anti-foundationalist theory are disastrous and amount to the loss of everything we associate with rational inquiry: public and shared standards, criteria for preferring one reading of a text or of the world to another, checks against irresponsibility, etc. But this follows only if anti-foundationalism is an argument for unbridled subjectivity, for the absence of constraints on the individual; whereas, in fact, it is an argument for the situated subject, for the individual who is always constrained by the local or community standards and criteria of which his judgment is an extension. Thus the lesson of anti-foundationalism is not only that external and independent guides will never be found but that it is unnecessary to seek them, because you will always be guided by the rules or rules of thumb that are the content of any settled practice, by the assumed definitions, distinctions, criteria of evidence, measures of adequacy, and such, which not only define the practice but structure the understanding of the agent who thinks of himself as a "competent member." That agent cannot distance himself from these rules, because it is only within them that he can think about alternative courses of action or, indeed, think at all. Thus anti-foundationalism cannot possibly have the consequences Scheffler fears; for, rather than unmooring the subject, it reveals the subject to be always and already tethered to the contextual setting that constitutes him and enables his "rational" acts.

Neither can anti-foundationalism have the consequences for which some of its proponents *hope*, the consequences of freeing us from the hold of unwarranted absolutes so that we may more flexibly pursue the goals of human flourishing or liberal conversation. The reasoning behind this hope is that since we now know that our convictions about truth and factuality have not been imposed on us by the world, or imprinted in our brains, but are derived from the practices of ideologically motivated communities, we can set them aside in favor of convictions that we choose freely. But this is simply to imagine the moment of unconstrained choice from the other direction, as a goal rather than as an abyss. Anti-foundationalist fear and anti- foundationalist hope turn out to differ only in emphasis. Those who express the one are concerned lest we kick ourselves loose from constraints; those who profess the other look forward to finally being able to do so. Both make the mistake of thinking than anti-foundationalism, by demonstrating the contextual source of conviction, cuts the ground out from under conviction – it is just that, for one party, this is the good news and, for the other, it is the news that chaos has come again. But, in fact, anti-foundationalism says nothing about what we can now do or not do; it is an account of what we have always been doing and cannot help but do (no matter what our views on epistemology) – act in accordance with the standards and norms that are the content of our beliefs and, therefore, the very structure of our consciousnesses. The fact that we now have a new explanation of how we got our beliefs – the fact, in short, that we now have a new belief – does not free us from our other beliefs or cause us to doubt them. I may now be convinced that what I think about *Paradise Lost* is a function of my education, professional training, the history of Milton studies, and so on, but that conviction does not lead me to think something else about *Paradise Lost* or to lose confidence in what I think. These consequences would follow only if I also believed in the possibility of a method independent of belief by which the truth about *Paradise Lost* could be determined; but if I believed that, I wouldn't be an anti-foundationalist at all. In short, the theory hope expressed by some anti-foundationalists is incoherent within the anti-foundationalist perspective, since it assumes, in its dream of beginning anew, everything that anti-foundationalism rejects.

Of course, it could be the case that if I were shown that some of my convictions (about Milton or anything else) could be traced to sources in sets of assumptions or points of view I found distressing, I might be moved either to alter those convictions or reexamine my sense of what is and is not distressing. This, however, would be a quite specific reconsideration provoked by a perceived inconsistency in my beliefs (and it would have to be an inconsistency that struck me as intolerable), not a general reconsideration of my beliefs in the face of a belief about their source. To be sure, such a general reconsideration would be possible if the source to which I had come to attribute them was deemed by me to be discreditable (hallucinatory drugs, political indoctrination) – although even then I could still decide that I was sticking with what I now knew no matter where it came from – but human history could not be that kind of discreditable source for me as an anti-foundationalist, since anti-foundationalism teaches (and teaches without regret or nostalgia) that human history is the context within which we know. To put it another way, an anti-foundationalist (like anyone else) can always reject something because its source has been shown to be some piece of human history he finds reprehensible, but an anti-foundationalist cannot (without at that moment becoming a foundationalist) reject something simply because its source has been shown to be human history as opposed to something independent of it.

All of which is to say again what I have been saying all along: theory has no consequences. Foundationalist theory has no consequences because its project cannot succeed, and anti- foundationalist theory has no consequences because, as a belief about how we got our beliefs, it leaves untouched (at least in principle) the beliefs of whose history it is an explanation. The case seems open-and-shut, but I am aware that many will maintain that theory *must* have consequences. It is to their objections and arguments that I now turn.

The first objection has already been disposed of, at least implicitly. It is Adena Rosmarin's objection and amounts to asking, Why restrict theory either to foundationalist attempts to ground practice by some Archimedean principle or to anti-foundationalist demonstrations that all such attempts will necessarily fail? Why exclude from the category "theory" much that has always been regarded as theory – works like W. J. Harvey's *Character in the Novel*, or Barbara Herrnstein Smith's *Poetic Closure*, or William Empson's *Seven Types of Ambiguity* – works whose claims are general and extend beyond the interpretation of specific texts to the uncovering of regularities that are common to a great many texts? The answer is that the regularities thus uncovered, rather than standing apart from practice and constituting an abstract picture of its possibilities, would be derived from practice and constitute a report on its current shape or on the shape it once had in an earlier period. It is possible to think of these regularities as rules, but they would be neither invariant nor predictive since they would be drawn from a finite corpus of data and would hold (if they did hold) only for that corpus; each time history brought forward new instances, it would be necessary to rewrite the "rules," that is, recharacterize the regularities. In Chomsky's terms, the result would be a succession of performance grammars, grammars that reflect the shifting and contingent conditions of a community's practice rather than capture the laws that constrain what the members of a community can possibly do. The result, in short, would be *empirical generalizations* rather than a general hermeneutics.

Still, one might ask, Why not call such generalizations "theory"? Of course, there is nothing to prevent us from doing so, but the effect of such a liberal definition would be to blur the distinction between theory and everything that is not theory, so that, for example, essays on the functions of prefaces in Renaissance drama would be theory, and books on the pastoral would be theory, and studies of Renaissance self-fashioning or self-consuming artifacts would be theory. One is tempted to call such efforts theory in part because they often serve as models for subsequent work: one could study self-fashioning in the eighteenth century or self-consuming artifacts as a feature of modernism. Such activities, though, would be instances not of following a theory but of extending a practice, of employing a set of heuristic questions, or a thematics, or a trenchant distinction in such a way as to produce a new or at least novel description of familiar material. Much of what is done in literary studies and elsewhere conforms to this pattern. If we like, we can always call such imitations of a powerful practice "theory," but nothing whatsoever will have been gained, and we will have lost any sense that theory is special. After all, it is only if theory is special that the question of its consequences is in any way urgent. In other words, the consequentiality of theory goes without saying and is, therefore, totally uninteresting if *everything* is theory.

And yet the argument that everything is theory is sometimes put forward in *support* of theory's special status. Those who make this argument think it follows from the chief lesson of anti-foundationalism, the lesson that there are no unmediated facts nor any neutral perception and that everything we know and see is known and seen under a description or as a function of some paradigm. The conclusion drawn from this lesson is that every practice presupposes a structure of assumptions within which it is intelligible – there is no such thing as *simply* acting – and the conclusion drawn from that conclusion is that every practice is underwritten by a theory. The first conclusion seems to me to be correct – any practice one engages in is conceivable only in relation to some belief or set of beliefs – but the second conclusion is, I think, false, because beliefs are not theories. A theory is a special achievement of consciousness; a belief is a prerequisite for being conscious at all. Beliefs are not what you think *about* but what you think *with*, and it is within the space provided by their articulations that mental activity – including the activity of theorizing – goes on. Theories are something you can have – you can wield them and hold them at a distance; beliefs have *you*, in the sense that there can be no distance between them and the acts they enable. In order to make even the simplest of assertions or perform the most elementary action, I must already be proceeding in the context of innumerable beliefs which cannot be the object of my attention because they are the content of my attention: beliefs on the order of the identity of persons, the existence of animate and inanimate entities, the stability of objects, in addition to the countless beliefs that underwrite the possibility and intelligibility of events in my local culture – beliefs that give me, without reflection, a world populated by streets, sidewalks, telephone poles, restaurants, figures of authority and figures of fun, worthy and unworthy tasks, achievable and unachievable goals, and so on. The description of what assumptions must already be in place for me to enter an elevator, or stand in line in a supermarket, or ask for the check in a restaurant would fill volumes, volumes that would themselves be intelligible only within a set of assumptions they in turn did not contain. Do these volumes – and the volumes that would be necessary to *their* description – constitute a theory? Am I following or enacting a theory when I stop for a red light, or use my American Express card, or rise to speak at a conference? Are you now furiously theorizing as you sit reading what I have to say? And if you are persuaded by me to alter your understanding of what is and is not a theory, is your new definition of theory a new theory of theory? Clearly it is possible to answer yes to all these questions, but just as clearly that answer will render the notion "theory" *and* the issue of its consequences trivial by making "theory" the name for ordinary, contingent, unpredictable, everyday behavior.

Now it may be easy enough to see the absurdity of giving the label "theoretical" to everyday actions that follow from the first or ground-level beliefs that give us our world. The difficulty arises with actions that seem more momentous and are attached to large questions of policy and morality; such actions, we tend to feel, must follow from something more "considered" than a mere belief, must follow, rather, from a theory. Thus, for example, consider the case of two legislators who must vote on a fair housing bill: one is committed to the protection of individual freedom and insists that it trump all competing considerations; the other is some kind of utilitarian and is committed to the greatest good for the greatest number. Isn't it accurate to say that these two hold different theories and that their respective theories will lead them to cast different votes – the first, against, and the second, in favor of, fair housing? Well, first, it is not at all certain that the actions of the two are predictable on the basis of what we are for now calling their "theories." A utilitarian may well think that, in the long run, the greatest number will reap the greatest good if property rights are given more weight than access rights; a libertarian could well decide that access rights are more crucial to the promotion of individual freedom and choice than property rights. In short, nothing particular follows from the fact that the two agents in my example would, if asked, declare themselves adherents of different theories. But would they even be theories? I would say not. Someone who declares himself committed to the promotion of individual freedom does not have a theory; he has a belief. He believes that something is more important than something else – and if you were to inquire into the grounds of his belief, you would discover not a theory but other beliefs that at once support and are supported by the belief to which he is currently testifying. Now, to be sure, these clustered beliefs affect behavior – not because they are consulted when a problem presents itself, however, but because it is within the world they deliver that the problem and its possible solutions take shape. To put it another way, when one acts on the basis of a belief, one is just engaged in reasoning, not in theoretical reasoning, and it makes no difference whether the belief is so deep as to be invisible or is invoked within a highly dramatic, even spectacular, situation. The sequence "I believe in the promotion of individual freedom, and therefore I will vote in this rather than in that way" is not different in kind from the sequence "I believe in the solidity of matter and therefore I will open the door rather than attempt to walk through the walls." It seems curious to call the reasoning (if that is the word) in the second sequence "theoretical," and I am saying that it would be no less curious to give that name to the reasoning in the first. The fact that someone has a very general, even philosophical, belief – a belief concerning recognizably "big" issues – does not mean that he has a theory; it just means that he has a very general belief. If someone wants to say that his very general belief has a consequential (although not predictable) relationship to his action, I am certainly not going to argue, since to say that is to say what I said at the beginning of this essay: it is belief and not theory that underwrites action.

It is simply a mistake, then, to think that someone who identifies himself as a believer in individual freedom or in the greatest good for the greatest number has declared his allegiance to a theory. But there are instances in which it is indeed proper to say that someone who takes this rather than that position is opting for this rather than that theory, and in those instances the question of the consequences of theory is once again alive. Here, a recent essay by Thomas Grey of the Stanford Law School provides a useful example. Grey is concerned with the consequences for the judicial process of two theories of constitutional interpretation. Those who hold the first theory he calls "textualists," and in their view "judges should get operative norms only from the text," that is, from the Constitution. Those who hold the other theory he calls "supplementers," and in their view "judges may find supplemental norms through [the] interpretation of text analogs" such as previous judicial decisions or background social phenomena.[16] I regard these two positions as theoretical because they

amount to alternative sets of instructions for reaching correct or valid interpretive conclusions. Someone who says "I am committed to promoting individual freedom" still has the task, in every situation, of deciding which among
the alternative courses of action will further his ends. But a judge who says "I
get my operative norms only from the text" knows exactly what to do in every
situation: he looks to the text and restricts himself to the norms he finds there.
On the other side, his "supplementalist" opponent also knows what to do: he
looks for norms not only in the text but in a number of other, authorized,
places. Grey forthrightly identifies himself as a supplementer, arguing that if
lawyers and judges come to think of themselves as supplementers rather than
textualists, as one kind of theorist rather than as another, they "will thereby be
marginally more free than they otherwise would be to infuse into constitutional law their current interpretations of our society's values."

For Grey, then, the consequences of theory are real and important. It seems
obvious to him that (1) if two judges, one a textualist and the other a
supplementer, were presented with the same case they would decide it differently, and (2) the differences in their decisions would be a function of the
differences in their theories. This assumes, however, that the two theories give
instructions that it is possible to follow and that someone *could* first identify the
norms encoded in the text and then choose either to abide by them or to
supplement them. But as Grey himself acknowledges, interpretation is not a
two-stage process in which the interpreter first picks out a "context-independent semantic meaning" and then, if he chooses, consults this or that context;
rather, it is within some or other context – of assumptions, concerns, priorities,
expectations – that what an interpreter sees as the "semantic meaning"
emerges, and therefore he is never in the position of being able to focus on
that meaning independently of background or "supplemental" considerations.
The semantic meaning of the text does not announce itself; it must be decided
upon, that is, interpreted. Since this is also true of contexts – they too must be
construed – the distinction between text and context is impossible to maintain
and cannot be the basis of demarcating alternative theories with their attendant
consequences. In short, no text reads itself, and anything you decide to take
into account – any supplement – is a text; therefore interpreters of the Constitution are always and *necessarily* both textualists and supplementers, and the
only argument between them is an argument over which text it is that is going
to be read or, if you prefer, which set of background conditions will be
specified as the text. Those arguments have substance, and on many occasions
their outcomes will have consequences, but they will not be the consequences
of having followed one or the other of these two theories because, while they
truly are theories, they cannot be followed. If the two judges in our example
did in fact happen to reach different decisions about the same case, it would not

be because they have different theories of interpretation but because they interpret from within different sets of priorities or concerns, that is, from within different sets of beliefs. It is entirely possible, moreover, that despite the declared differences in theoretical allegiance, the two could reach exactly the same decision whenever the text to which the one has confined himself is perspicuous against the same set of supplemental concerns or perspectives that forms the other's text.

And yet it would be too much to say that declarations of theoretical allegiances – even allegiances to theories that cannot be made operative – are inconsequential. As Grey notes, such declarations have a political force. "Most lawyers," he points out, "share with the public a 'pre-realist' consensus that in doing judicial review, judges should generate their decisive norms by constitutional interpretation only." In short, there is a consensus that they should be textualists; therefore, Grey contends, "For me to call my views 'noninterpretive' [supplementalist] will obviously not improve my chances of winning the argument." Now one could dismiss this as a piece of cynical advice ("Call yourself a textualist no matter how you proceed"), but it seems to me to point to a significant truth: rather than dictating or generating arguments, theoretical positions are parts of arguments and are often invoked because of a perceived connection between them and certain political and ideological stands. That is, given a certain set of political circumstances, one or another theory will be a component in this or that agenda or program. So, for example, in a struggle for power between the judiciary and the legislature, one party may gravitate "naturally" – that is, in terms of its current goals – toward one theory while the other party – just as naturally and just as politically – identifies itself with the opposite theory. Moreover, in the course of a generation or two, the identifications may be reversed, as new circumstances find the onetime textualists now calling themselves supplementers (or legal realists, or "noninterpretivists") and vice versa. In short, declaring a theoretical allegiance will often be consequential – not, however, because the declaration dictates a course of action but because a course of action already in full flower appropriates it and gives it significance.

Thus we see that even when something is a theory and is consequential – in the sense that espousing it counts for something – it is not consequential in the way theorists claim. Indeed, on the evidence of the examples we have so far considered, the possible relationships between theories and consequences reduce to three: either (1) it *is* a theory but has no consequences because, as a set of directions purged of interest and independent of presuppositions, it cannot be implemented, or (2) it has consequences but is not a theory – rather, it is a belief or a conviction, as in the case of the promotion of individual freedom, or (3) it is a theory and does have consequences, but they are political rather than theoretical, as when, for very good practical reasons, somebody calls himself a textualist or a supplementer.

Nevertheless there still is a position to which a "consequentialist" might retreat: perhaps theory, strictly speaking, is an impossible project that could never succeed, and perhaps beliefs and assumptions, while consequential, are not theories – but, Isn't the foregrounding of beliefs and assumptions "theory"? – and, Doesn't the foregrounding of beliefs and assumptions make us more aware of them? – and, Isn't that a consequence, and one which will itself have consequences? In short, theory may be just an activity within practice, but – as this position would have it – Isn't it a special *kind* of activity? This claim has two versions, one weak and one strong. The strong version is untenable because it reinvents foundationalism, and the weak version is so weak that to grant it is to have granted nothing at all. The strong claim reinvents foundationalism because it imagines a position from which our beliefs can be scrutinized; that is, it imagines a position outside belief, the transcendental position assumed and sought by theorists of the Chomsky type. The argument against the strong claim is the anti-foundationalist argument: we can never get to the side of our beliefs and, therefore, any perspective we have on one or more of them will be grounded in others of them in relation to which we can have no perspective because we have no distance. The weak claim begins by accepting this argument but still manages to find a space in which theory does its special work: although we can never get an absolute perspective on our beliefs, we can still get a perspective on *some* of our beliefs in relation to some others; and if this happens, it may be that from within the enclosure of our beliefs we will spy contradictions of which we had been unaware and, thereby, be provoked to ask and answer some fundamental questions. In short, and in familiar language, theory – or the foregrounding of assumptions – promotes critical self-consciousness.

Now it is certainly the case that people are on occasion moved to reconsider their assumptions and beliefs and then to change them, and it is also the case that – as a consequence – there may be a corresponding change in practice. The trouble is, such reconsiderations can be brought about by almost anything and have no unique relationship to something called "theory." Some years ago Lawrance Thompson published a biography of Robert Frost in which the poet was revealed to have been a most unpleasant, not to say evil, person. The book produced much consternation, especially among those who had assumed that there was (or should be) a correlation between the quality of a man's art and his character. Underlying this assumption was a traditional and powerful view of the nature and function of literature. In that view (still held by many today), literature is ennobling: it enlarges and refines the sensibility and operates to make its readers better persons. It follows, then, that those who are able to produce nobility in others should themselves be noble – but here was an undeniably great artist who was, by all the evidence Thompson had marshaled, perfectly vile. Presumably, Thompson's book induced some who held this view to reconsider it; that is, they had been made aware of their assumptions. What moved them, however, was not theory but a work of traditional scholarship that did not even pretend to be criticism.

The impulse to reexamine the principles underlying one's practice can be provoked, moreover, by something that is not even within the field of practice: by turning forty, or by a dramatic alteration in one's economic situation, by a marriage, or by a divorce. Of course, it can also be provoked by theory – but not necessarily. That is, you could engage in the exercise of foregrounding your assumptions and even come to see that some of them were incompatible with some piece of your practice and, nevertheless, respond with a shrug, and decide to let things be. The man who declares himself committed to the redistribution of authority and the diffusion of power may be an absolute autocrat in the classroom, and when this is pointed out to him or when he points it out to himself, he may mutter something about the limited attention span of today's youth and go on as before. Even when theory (so called) produces self-consciousness, it need not be "critical"; it need not be the prelude to change. Once again, we reach the conclusion that there is no sense in which theory is special: it cannot provide us with a perspective independent of our beliefs, and the perspective it can occasionally (but not necessarily) provide on some of our beliefs relative to others can be provided by much that is not theory.

If one has followed the argument thus far, it begins to be difficult to understand why anyone has ever thought that theory should have consequences. Yet, since many have thought so and will continue to think so even after I have done, it is time to inquire into the reasons for their conviction. One reason, and a very powerful one, is the institutional success of philosophy in persuading us that the answers to its questions are directly relevant to everything we do when we are not doing philosophy. As Richard Rorty has put it:

Philosophers usually think of their discipline as one which discusses perennial, eternal problems – problems which arise as soon as one reflects. . . . Philosophy can be foundational in respect to the rest of culture because culture is the assemblage of claims to knowledge, and philosophy adjudicates such claims.[17]

The idea, then, is that whatever the surface configurations of our actions, *at bottom* we are being guided by principles of the kind that philosophy takes as its special province. Thus it is to philosophy that we should look to get a perspective on those principles and on the actions we perform in everyday life.

The relevance of philosophy to every aspect of human culture has been assumed for so long that it now seems less an assertion or an argument than a piece of plain common sense. But it is, in fact, an argument, and one whose content is the debatable proposition that almost everything we do is a disguised and probably confused version of philosophy. That proposition will begin to seem less plausible if we remember that philosophy is not the name of a natural kind but of an academic discipline and, moreover, of a discipline whose traditions are so special as to constitute a prima facie denial of its territorial ambitions. Philosophy is that area of inquiry in which one asks questions about the nature of knowledge, truth, fact, meaning, mind, action, and so forth, and gives answers that fall within a predictable range of positions called realism, idealism, relativism, pragmatism, materialism, mentalism, Platonism, Aristotelianism, Kantianism, etc. Of course, other areas of inquiry are similarly well developed and articulated and come complete with their own array of positions, problems, solutions, and decorums. One of these is literary criticism, where the task is the description and evaluation of verbal artifacts and the categories of interrogation are historical (is it Romantic or neoclassic?), generic (is it masque or drama?), formal (is it episodic or organic?), stylistic (is it Senecan or Ciceronian?).

Now, although the traditions of philosophy and literary criticism display certain points of intersection and occasionally refer to each other, they are for all intents and purposes distinct, so much so that it is perfectly possible for someone wholly ignorant of one to operate quite successfully in the other. It makes no sense, then, to think that one is radically dependent on the other, to think, for example, that since there is something called "the philosophy of action" and since literary criticism is an action, anyone who wants to know how to do literary criticism should consult the philosophy of action. A literary critic already knows what to do simply by virtue of his being embedded in a field of practice; it is hard to see why his performance would be improved or altered by bringing to bear the categories and urgencies of another field of practice. Of course, it is always possible to step back from a field and put to it the kinds of questions that belong properly (that is, by history and convention) to philosophy, to ask, for example, what literary critics must believe about the world, truth, meaning, fact, evidence, etc., in order to go about their work in a way that seems to them at once routine and natural. But the lessons learned from such an interrogation would be philosophical, not literary, and the fact that it was possible to learn them would not prove that those who do criticism are really doing philosophy any more than the fact that every activity is potentially the object of philosophical analysis means that every activity is at base philosophical and should be ruled by philosophy's norms.

The point is obvious and, one would have thought, inescapable: philosophy is one thing, and literary criticism is another. But the point has been obscured by the fact that in the past twenty-five years philosophy has become something that literary critics also do or attempt to do. That is, they attempt to do theory, which is another name for philosophy; and if the argument for the consequences of theory seems strong when theory is a separate discipline, it seems even stronger when theory is a component of the field it purports to govern. But if theory (or philosophy) is now a practice in literary studies, it differs more from its fellow practices than they do from each other. A formalist and a critic of myth may be at odds, but they are in the same line of work and contesting for the same privilege, the privilege of saying what this poem or novel or play means. Theory, on the other hand disdains particular acts of interpretation and aspires to provide an account of interpretation in general – and just as a philosophical analysis of an activity is not an instance of that activity but of philosophy, so an account of interpretation is not an interpretation but an account. They are different games, and they remain different even when they are played by the same person.

That is to say, as things stand now, a worker in the field may hold this or that theoretical position – think of himself as a foundationalist or an anti-foundationalist – and *also* be a practicing critic – think of himself as a Wordsworthian or a Miltonist. But, when he is performing as a Wordsworthian or a Miltonist, he will be asking the questions and giving the answers that belong to that tradition of inquiry, and his theoretical position will quite literally be beside the point. I may be convinced, as in fact I am, that my sense of what is going on in a literary work is a function of my history, education, professional training, ideological affiliation, and so on, but that conviction will be of no effect when I set out to determine who is the hero of *Paradise Lost*; for at that moment all of the categories, distinctions, imperatives, and urgencies that might at some other time become the object of a metacritical investigation will be firmly in place and form the enabling conditions of my actions. In short, theory is not consequential even when the practitioner is himself a theorist. Indeed, the practitioner may cease to be a theorist or may awake one morning (as I predict we all will) to find that theory has passed from the scene and still continue in his life's work without ever missing a beat.

This conclusion may seem to fly in the face of the evidence provided by those critics who, apparently, changed their practice when they changed their theory, who now discover aporias and radical de-centerings where they used to discover irony and unity. Doesn't this evidence itself constitute a strong empirical case for the consequences of theory?[18] Not at all – what it indicates is that thematizing remains the primary mode of literary criticism and that, as an action, thematizing can find its materials in theory as well as in anything else. In thematic criticism a work is discovered to be the literary expression or consideration of such and such concerns, be they economic or psychological, political or military, sexual, culinary, or whatever. What the thematic critic then produces are economic or psychological or sociological or political or philosophical readings. He does *not* produce – that is, he does not do – economics, psychology, sociology, political science, or philosophy. He may *quarry* these and other disciplines for vocabulary, distinctions, concerns, etc. – indeed, it is hard to see what else he could do – but to quarry from a discipline is not to become a practitioner of it. If I propose a religious reading of George Herbert's lyrics, am I practicing religion? If I read Gustave Flaubert in the light of medical knowledge in the nineteenth century, am I practicing medicine? Obviously not – and neither, when I find that a work is "about" the limits of language, or the conditions of assertion, or the relativity of truth, am I doing theory. If I were practicing religion, I would be urging, chastising, and preaching; if I were practicing medicine, I would be setting bones and handing out prescriptions; and if I were practicing theory, I would either be arguing for a set of formal and explicit rules or arguing that rules of that kind are never available. I would not be analyzing the way in which such arguments are distributed over a range of characters in a novel or underlie the dramatic structure of the Romantic lyric. It is only because theory as a form of practice now shares an institutional or disciplinary home with literary criticism that its thematization is taken as evidence of its power to alter literary criticism. In fact, the power flows in the other direction: like any other discipline or body of materials that is made into thematic hay, theory is not so much the consequential agent of a change as it is the passive object of an appropriation.

We have now achieved what appears to be a dramatic reversal. At the outset, the strong thesis in the field was that theory has consequences and that they are far-reaching and fundamental, but now theory has been deprived of any consequentiality whatsoever and stands revealed as the helpless plaything of the practice it claimed to inform. But certainly we have gone too far, and it is time to admit what everyone knows: theory has consequences; not, however, because it stands apart from and can guide practice but because it is itself a form of practice and therefore is consequential for practice as a matter of definition.[19] That is, any account of what now makes up the practice of literary criticism must include theory, which means that there was a time when theory was not a part of criticism's practice, and the fact that it now is has made a difference, has been consequential.

Of course, as consequences go, this is pretty low-level, but there is more. As a practice, theory has all the political and institutional consequences of other practices. Those who do it can be published, promoted, fired, feted, celebrated, reviled; there can be symposia devoted to it, journals committed to it; there can be departments of theory, schools of theory; it can be a rallying cry ("Give me theory or give me death!"), a banner, a target, a program, an agenda. All of these (and more) are consequences, and they would not be possible if there were no theory. But although these are certainly the consequences of theory, they are not theoretical consequences; that is, they are not the consequences of a practice that stands in a relationship of precedence and mastery to other practices. There is a world of difference between saying that theory is a form of practice and saying that theory informs practice: to say the one is to claim for theory no more than can be claimed for anything else; to say the other is to claim everything. So, even though the thesis that theory has no consequences holds only when the consequences are of a certain kind, they are the only consequences that matter, since they are the consequences that would mark theory off as special.

We can test this by thinking about the consequences that would satisfy a theorist. Surely Chomsky's theory has had consequences: it has revolutionized a discipline and extended its sway; its terms and goals structure everything that happens in the field; but it has not had (and, by my argument, could not have) the consequences of its claims – it has not provided the formal and algorithmic model of language acquisition and use whose promise generated all the activity in the first place. The theory's success, in short, has been largely political; as such, it is a success that can hardly be comforting to Chomsky since the political is what he, like every other theorist, desires to rise above. Paradoxically, the triumph of Chomskian theory from an institutional point of view is an illustration of its failure from the point of view of its fondest hope, the hope to transcend point of view by producing a picture of the language that holds for any or all institutions and is beholden to none Chomsky is in the position of every other theorist: the consequences he seeks are impossible, and the consequences to which he has clear right and title make him indistinguishable from any other political agent and render theory a category about which there is nothing particular – because there is nothing general – to say.

There is nothing either particular or general to say about theory's political consequences because, while they are palpable, they are not predictable; they do not follow *from* theory but are something that *befalls* theory – although, again, not necessarily and not always in the same way. As a practice, theory will cut a different figure in different disciplines; only in philosophy will changes in theory receive immediate and consequential attention. But that is because philosophy (at least in the analytic tradition) *is* theory, is the foundational project Rorty describes. Thus to say that in philosophy a change in theory will change practice is only to say that when practice changes, it changes. In literary criticism, on the other hand, theory is only one practice among many, and its impact has varied with different locations and universities. In some places in the United States the appearance of a theoretical manifesto in *New Literary History, Diacritics*, or *Critical Inquiry* will be Monday-morning news to which one must respond; in other places it will be heard, if it is heard at all, as the report of a minor skirmish on a foreign field of battle. In a discipline of such diversity with respect to theory, the question of its consequences cannot even be meaningfully put.

In the world of legal studies the case is different again. There theory has recently become the center of debate, in large part because of a single issue, the legitimacy of judicial review, or, as it is sometimes called, the "countermajoritarian difficulty."[20] The difficulty takes the form of a question: How, in a democratic system, can one justify the fact that a group of men and women, who are appointed for life, pass judgment on the validity of legislation enacted by the elected representatives of the people? This question is quite literally a demand for theory, for a justifying argument that does not presuppose the interests of any party or the supremacy of any political goal or borrow its terms from the practice it would regulate. For the foundationalists, only such an argument will guarantee the coherence of the legal process – it simply *must* be found; the failure so far of the efforts to find it leads the anti-foundationalists, on the other hand, to conclude that the legal process is political through and through and is therefore a sham. Both parties agree that the issue of judicial review is "the most fundamental in the extensive domain of constitutional law" and that the stakes are very high.[21] As long as that agreement continues, theory is likely to flourish as a consequential form of legal practice.

Here, then, are three disciplines, in each of which theory is differently consequential, and those differences themselves are not stable but contingent and changeable. Philosophy and theory have not always been one, and still are not in some parts of the world – and may not even be so in our part of the world if Rorty and some others have anything to say about it. Theory has not always been a glamour stock in literary studies and has already ceased to be a growth industry; if the urgency attached in the legal world to the issue of judicial review should ever fade, theory could fade with it (although if it has become well enough established, it might migrate to another issue). Will it fade? Will it rise in other disciplines hitherto innocent of it? Will the consequences of its appearance or demise be large or small? These and other questions could be answered only if there were a general account of theory's career, but since the determining factors will always be local and contingent – who could have predicted that the emigration of European scholars in the late 1930s would bring literary theory to the United States or that marketplace conditions in the humanities would bring it (by way of disgruntled Ph.D.'s) to the law – no such account is available and we must wait upon the event. If the question of theory's consequences is itself not theoretical but empirical, it can only receive an empirical answer in the form of specific and historical investigations into the consequences that this or that theory did or did not have. The result of such investigations will vary – in some cases, there will be virtually nothing to report and, in others, the report will fill volumes – but in no case will the chronicling of theory's consequences demonstrate that theory has – by right, as an inherent property – consequences.

Will there be consequences to an argument against theory's consequences? Since that too is an empirical question, the answer is "time will tell," but there are some consequences that would seem to be either likely or unlikely. A likely consequence attaches to the issue of justification. Should it happen that everyone were persuaded by the "no consequences" argument (an outcome that is itself extremely unlikely), the search for certain kinds of justification might very well cease or, at least, be carried on with altered hopes, and that would be a consequence. To return for a moment to the context of legal studies and the "countermajoritarian difficulty," the issue would lose its urgency and the debate would continue, if it continued, on different terms, if all parties were brought to see (1) that the demand for a justification of judicial review which did not presuppose but bracketed the interests, goals, agendas, lines of authority, and so on, already in place was a demand for something at once unobtainable and empty, and (2) that the unavailability of such a justification proved not that everything was a sham but that justifications are always interested and acquire their intelligibility and force from the very practices of which they are a public defense. That is, if both parties could be brought to see that political justifications are the only kind there are and that this fact does not render argument nugatory but necessary, they might fall to recommending their contrasting agendas for the frankly political consequences they would be likely to have and not for a theoretical purity they could never achieve. Such a turn of events would not change very much, since, if I am right, every argument is already interested and political no matter what its theoretical trappings – but at least certain kinds of objections would no longer have very much force and certain kinds of appeals would no longer seem tainted.

On the other side, there is at least one consequence of the success of the "no consequences" argument that is not only unlikely, but impossible, and can be ruled out in advance. The case for theory's inconsequentiality, even if it is persuasive, will not return us to some precritical state, whether it be thought of as a state of innocence or of know nothing ignorance. The consequences of theory as a form of practice are real even if the consequences of theory as a foundational or antifoundational project could not possibly exist – indeed, theory's "practical" consequences are real *because* its "theoretical" consequences could not exist. The discrediting of theory could have the consequence of returning us to some uncontaminated or unredeemed practice only if theory were the independent and abstract calculus of its strongest claims. The fact that theory is not and could not be that calculus and therefore could not have the

consequences of its claims assures that it will always have the political consequences I have been describing. Although theory cannot be a lever for
change from the outside, its existence on the inside – within the field of
practice – is evidence that a change has already occurred, a change in which
its mode of interrogation has now joined or displaced others. That change
cannot be reversed, and its effects will continue long after the formal program
of theory has been abandoned.

Will it be abandoned? Will theory stop? Certainly not as a result of arguments against it, mine, or anyone else's. Arguments against theory only keep it
alive, by marking it as a site of general concern. Theory will stop only when
it has played out its string, run its course, when the urgencies and fears of which
it is the expression either fade or come to be expressed by something else. This
is already happening in literary studies, and there could be no surer sign of it
than the appearance in recent years of several major anthologies – by Josué
Harari, Jane Tompkins, Robert Young – and of series that bear titles like New
Accents but report only on what is old and well digested. The fading away of
theory is signaled not by silence but by more and more talk, more journals,
more symposia, and more entries in the contest for the right to sum up theory's
story. There will come a time when it is a contest no one will want to win,
when the announcement of still another survey of critical method is received
not as a promise but as a threat, and when the calling of still another conference
on the function of theory in our time will elicit only a groan. That time may
have come: theory's day is dying; the hour is late; and the only thing left for a
theorist to do is to say so, which is what I have been saying here, and, I think,
not a moment too soon.

Notes

1 See my *Is There a Text in This Class?: The Authority of Interpretive Communities*
(Cambridge, Mass., 1980), p. 370. For a response to the "no consequences" claim,
see Mary Louise Pratt, "Interpretive Strategies/Strategic Interpretations: On
Anglo-American Reader Response Criticism," *Boundary 2* 11 (Fall–Winter
1982–3): 222.

2 E. D. Hirsch, Jr, *The Aims of Interpretation* (Chicago, 1976), p. 18. I should note here
that while I agree in general with Steven Knapp and Walter Benn Michaels on what
is and is not a theoretical enterprise, I think them mistaken in their choice of
particular examples. Stylistics, narratology, and prosody are, it seems to me, paradigm instances of theory in the strong sense. As I have argued elsewhere (see *Is
There a Text in This Class?* chapters 2 and 10), the entire project of stylistics is an
effort to produce a taxonomy of observable formal features which can then be
correlated in some mechanical or rule-governed way with a set of corresponding

significances and/or effects. In short, if stylistics were ever to succeed (and I am certain that it will not), it would be an engine of interpretation, a method, a theory. One sure sign of a theoretical enterprise is the lengths its proponents will go in order to pursue it. It seems to me extremely unlikely that stylisticians would have built their formidable apparatuses and worked out their complex formulations only so as to be able to produce a new reading of James Joyce's "Eveline." The same goes for narratology and for prosody, at least in its transformational or Halle-Keyser version.

3   Hirsch, *The Aims of Interpretation*, p. 18.

4   Cicero, *De inventione* 2. 11. 37; and see Raoul Berger, *Government by Judiciary: The Transformation of the Fourteenth Amendment* (Cambridge, Mass., 1977).

5   See John Lyons, *Noam Chomsky*, rev. ed. (New York, 1978), p. 37.

6   Jerrold J. Katz and Thomas G. Bever, "The Fall and Rise of Empiricism," in Bever, Katz, and D. Terrence Langendoen, *An Integrated Theory of Linguistic Ability* (New York, 1976), p. 12; all further references to this work, abbreviated "FRE," will be included in the text.

7   Noam Chomsky, *Aspects of the Theory of Syntax* (Cambridge, Mass., 1965), p. 3; all further references to this work, abbreviated *ATS*, will be included in the text.

8   In the jargon of the trade these are called "performance factors" and belong to the study of utterances as opposed to sentences: "Sentences are abstract objects which are not tied to a particular context, speaker, or time of utterance. Utterances, on the other hand, are datable events, tied to a particular speaker, occasion and context" (Neil Smith and Deirdre Wilson, *Modern Linguistics: The Results of Chomsky's Revolution* [Bloomington, Ind., 1979], p. 45). Utterances are ranked on a scale of "acceptability" according to the conditions – cultural and, therefore, variable – of their production; sentences, on the other hand, are ranked on a scale of grammaticality or well-formedness according to the invariant rules of a formal system. On this point, see F. R. Palmer, *Semantics: A New Outline* (Cambridge, 1976), p. 8.

9   Judith Greene, *Psycholinguistics: Chomsky and Psychology* (Baltimore, 1972), p. 28.

10 That is, one must begin, as Smith and Wilson observe, by "separating linguistic from non-linguistic knowledge" (*Modern Linguistics*, p. 32), but it is precisely the possibility of that separation that is denied by the argument I am mounting here.

11 See my *Is There a Text in This Class?* pp. 281–92.

12 That is why the history of Chomskian linguistics is a history of counter-examples to what are offered as *the* rules: since rules have been extrapolated from an assumed (if unacknowledged) context, the descriptions they assign will not seem perspicuous to someone who is operating from within *another* assumed (if unacknowledged) context. Of course, any proposed alternative system of rules will be vulnerable to exactly the same challenge.

In a searching and rigorous critique of a draft of this paper, Joseph Graham objects that I misrepresent the Chomsky project in several respects. Echoing some of the arguments in Chomsky's *Rules and Representations* (Woodbridge Lectures, nos. 3, 11, 78 [New York, 1980]), Graham contends, among other things, that the notion of "theory" as it appears in my discussion of Chomsky is far too strong and does not correspond to any claims Chomsky actually makes; that I fail to distinguish between "universal grammar" as an innate biological constraint on the set of possible "core" grammars and one or more of those possible grammars; that I blur the crucial distinction, on which so much depends, between grammatical and pragmatic competence and, thereby, ask more of the grammar than it could ever deliver; and that no theoretical enterprise is "demonstrative" in the sense that I use the word, for all scientific inquiry proceeds on the basis of "abduction or inference to the best explanation." To this I would reply, first, that my account of the Chomsky project and its claims is derived from statements made by Chomsky and some of his more faithful followers and that even if, as Graham says, that theory has been modified and clarified in recent years, the euphoria with which it was received and promoted in its early stages shows that it was for many the basis of what I call foundationalist "theory hope." Moreover, some of the differences between Graham and me stem from the different and opposing traditions in which we stand – he in the tradition of cognitive psychology with its interest in innate properties and inaccessible mental operations, and I in the practice and convention-centered tradition that includes Ludwig Wittgenstein, W. V. Quine, Hilary Putnam, Richard Rorty, and Donald Davidson, in addition to Jacques Derrida, Michel Foucault, and other continental thinkers. Presumably, for example, Graham would hear with equanimity and even with approval Chomsky's suggestion that knowledge and certainty may have little or nothing to do with grounding, justification, reasons, habits, skill, induction, and learning, and everything to do with genetic mechanisms that have yet to be specified, while to my ears the same suggestion sounds counterintuitive and even uninteresting (see Chomsky, *Rules and Representations*, pp. 92–109, 134–6, and 234). To be sure, there is more to be said about these matters, and Graham promises to say them in a series of forthcoming essays, but for the time being I will stick with my present formulations.

13   Rorty, *Consequences of Pragmatism (Essays 1972–1980)* (Minneapolis, 1982), p. 162.

14   Keith Lehrer, *Knowledge* (Oxford, 1974), p. 17.

15   Israel Scheffler, *Science and Subjectivity* (Indianapolis, 1967), p. 19. For similar statements, see Hirsch, *The Aims of Interpretation*, pp. 152–5, and Owen M. Fiss, "Objectivity and Interpretation," *Stanford Law Review* 34 (April 1982): 763.

16   Thomas Grey, "Supplementing the Constitution"; unpublished paper, quoted with permission of the author.

17   Rorty, *Philosophy and the Mirror of Nature* (Princeton, NJ, 1979), p. 3.

18   This is the argument made by Steven Mailloux in "Truth or Consequences: On Being Against Theory," *Critical Inquiry* 9: 4 (June 1983).

19   See ibid., pp. 765–6. Mailloux also asserts that theory is a form of practice, but we differ in our conclusions. He concludes that "theory does change practice" and cites as two examples the "theoretical assumptions" that "guide" Edward Said's "practical analyses of Orientalism" and the "New Critical proscriptions against the intentional and affective fallacies" which led critics to avoid "extrinsic approaches"

and focus instead on "intrinsic elements in the literary text itself" (ibid., pp. 765, 764, 765). To take the second example first, the Wimsatt-Beardsley injunction against taking into account the intentions of the author or the responses of the reader is exactly parallel to the injunction in the legal institution against looking beyond the Constitution itself to supplemental contexts: both make the same impossible recommendations and give the same unfollowable advice. That is, one may *say* "Consider only the text and not its extrinsic circumstances or the accident of its variable effects," but in fact any text one considers will will have come into view only against the contextual – including intentional and affective – circumstances that are supposedly being excluded or bracketed. In short, someone may well think that he is adhering to Wimsatt and Beardsley's theoretical strictures, but the truth is that he could not possibly do so. What he can do is present his argument in terms that make no mention of intention or affect; although that will certainly be a consequence of the pressure exerted by Wimsatt and Beardsley's pronouncements, it will not be a consequence of their theory in the sense of being answerable to its claims and hopes. One cannot, as I have said above, attribute consequences of a theoretical kind to a program that cannot be executed.

The example of Said and *Orientalism* can be assimilated to the discussion of the two legislators who are committed respectively to libertarian and utilitarian principles. It is certainly the case, as Mailloux asserts, that Said's assumptions guide his practice, but assumptions aren't theories, that is, they are not systematic procedures for generating valid conclusions – they are the *assertion* of conclusions which, when put to work as an interpretive "window," will generate or validate themselves. Said's assumption – or conviction, or belief – is that Western discourse, including diplomatic and academic as well as fictional texts, has projected an image of the Orient that has, for all intents and purposes, become its reality. Armed with this assumption, indeed operating as an extension of it, Said proceeds to redescribe texts as instances of a colonialism that does not know itself and is therefore even more powerful and insidious in its effects. But in producing these redescriptions, Said is not consulting a theory but extending a belief: when he urges his redescriptions on others, he is saying "Try on this belief; make it, rather than some other assumption, the content of your perception, and see what you see." It is a recommendation no more theoretical than a recommendation to think of the prefaces to Renaissance plays as part of the texts they introduce; either recommendation, if it is persuasive, will certainly alter practice but only because it will be a *practical* (not theoretical) recommendation, a recommendation to look at it this way rather than that way. To return to a formula used above, the Said example is an instance of something that has consequences but isn't a theory, and the Wimsatt-Beardsley example is an instance of something that is a theory and has consequences but not theoretical ones.

20   For a review and a discussion, see James A. Thomson, "An Endless but Productive Dialogue: Some Reflections on Efforts to Legitimize Judicial Review," *Texas Law Review* 61 (December 1982): 743–64.

21   Ibid., p. 745.

5

Rhetoric

Rhetoric, as strategy and topic, has played a prominent role at every stage in the critical career of Stanley Fish. In his early "Affective Stylistics," Fish established his name outside Renaissance studies by promoting a reader-response criticism that focused precisely on how the language of literary texts manipulated and transformed their intended readers. In *Surprised by Sin* he argued that Milton orchestrated the effects of *Paradise Lost* in ways that encouraged readers to re-enact the original sin of Adam, to commit mistakes that the text then corrected in order to teach anew. In *Self-Consuming Artifacts* Fish conjured up a brand-new genre based on the Platonic distinction between rhetoric and dialectic: while comforting rhetorical texts flattered readers and told them what they wanted to hear, self-consuming dialectical texts humiliated readers, leading them to discover for themselves the inadequacies of their own beliefs. Later, when Fish was asked whether there *really* were such things as self-consuming artifacts, he replied in symptomatic fashion, "There are now." He meant, of course, that his argument had been successful; he had persuaded his readers to begin identifying a new genre called self-consuming artifacts. This acknowledgment of his own rhetorical power was theorized explicitly at the end of his book on Herbert's *The Temple*, an epilogue he entitled "A Conclusion In Which It May Appear That Everything Is Taken Back." Here he makes clear that he now sees his critical interpretations to be acts of persuasion rather than demonstration. "If anyone is persuaded by my reading," Fish writes, "it will not be because he has assented to a disinterested marshaling of facts, but because he has been initiated into a way of seeing as a consequence of which the facts could not be otherwise than I report them." In the concluding chapter of *Is There a Text in This Class?*, Fish again contrasts the demonstration model of critical activity to his own persuasion model. But it might have been better if he had argued instead that the former is subsumed by the latter; that is, "demonstration" is the name we give to an act of persuasion that works and continues to work.

To characterize Fish's theoretical transformation differently, we might say he has moved from a Platonic view of rhetoric in his early Affective Stylistics to a Sophistic notion in his neopragmatist theory of interpretive communities. In *Surprised by Sin* he described the Christianized Platonic attitude toward the "speciousness of Satan's rhetoric," the critical view that "It is the nature of sophistry to lull the reasoning process." Fish summarized this tradition of anti-sophistic philosophy, which "begins with Plato's opposition of rhetoric to dialectic": "Socrates' interlocutors *discover* the truth for themselves, when, In response to his searching questions, they are led to examine their opinions and, perhaps, to refute them. The rhetorician, on the other hand, creates a situation in which his auditors have no choice but to accept the beliefs he urges on them." In this footnote, we see in embryo the Platonic distinction Fish later developed into a whole book. *Self-Consuming Artifacts* begins on its very first page with Fish citing Plato's invidious definition in the *Gorgias* – rhetoric as deceptive flattery – and he goes on to read out of the *Phaedrus* a point-by-point opposition between the "Bad Lover-Rhetorician" and the "Good Lover-Dialectician."

It is this opposition that Fish completely reverses in his later work, as he champions Sophistic Rhetoric over Platonic foundationalist philosophy. In the following essay, Fish provides his most detailed account of this opposition, its historical pedigree and its contemporary versions, and he makes quite clear on which side of the contest his own sympathies now lie. Fish sees his anti-foundationalist conventionalism, what I would call his rhetorical pragmatism, as squarely within the Sophistic Rhetorical tradition. Yet he also suggests that this tradition will never win out completely. To make such a prediction might be justified based on the history Fish tells. On the other hand, if in fact Plato "merely" invented the distinction between rhetoric (language use) and philosophy (truth seeking), if he strategically coined and defined the term *rhetorike* in the *Gorgias* to serve his own historical purposes against the Sophists, it might also happen that this contingent opposition upon which Fish has based so much of his provocative work might one day wither away, that the term "rhetoric" might cover the field, losing its polemical force, and be retired as a useless piece of vocabulary. In that case, the latest rebirth of rhetoric, its much-vaunted return to the humanities, might result in its eventual demise, a victim not of anxious censure or scornful neglect but of its own rhetorical success. This would be an irony that the Sophistic Rhetorician Stanley Fish would undoubtedly appreciate.

Steven Mailloux

> . . . up rose
> *Belial*, in act more graceful and humane;
> A fairer person lost not Heav'n; he seem'd
> For dignity compos'd and high exploit:
> But all was false and hollow; though his Tongue
> Dropt Manna, and could make the worse appear
> The better reason, to perplex and dash
> Maturest counsels: for his thoughts were low; . . .
> . . . yet he pleas'd the ear,
> And with persuasive accent thus began.
> *Paradise Lost*, II, 108–15, 117–18

I

For Milton's seventeenth-century readers this passage, introducing one of the more prominent of the fallen angels, would have been immediately recognizable as a brief but trenchant essay on the art and character of the rhetorician. Indeed, in these few lines Milton has managed to gather and restate with great rhetorical force (a paradox of which more later) all of the traditional arguments against rhetoric. Even Belial's gesture of rising is to the (negative) point: he catches the eye even before he begins to speak, just as Satan will in book IX when he too raises himself and moves so that "each part, / Motion, each act won audience ere the tongue" (673–4). That is, he draws attention to his appearance, to his surface, and the suggestion of superficiality (a word to be understood in its literal meaning) extends to the word "act"; that is, that which can be seen. That act is said to be "graceful," the first in a succession of double meanings (one of the stigmatized attributes of rhetorical speech) we find in the passage. Belial is precisely *not* full of grace; that is simply his outward aspect, and the same is true for "humane" and "fairer." The verse's judgment on all of his apparent virtues is delivered in the last two words of line 110 – "he seem'd" – and the shadow of "seeming" falls across the next line which in isolation might "seem" to be high praise. But under the pressure of what precedes it, the assertion of praise undoes itself with every Janus-faced word (the verse now begins to imitate the object of its criticism by displaying a pervasive disjunction between its outer and inner meanings; indicting seeming, it itself repeatedly seems): "compos'd" now carries its pejorative meaning of affected or made-up;

"high" at once refers to the favored style of bombastic orators and awaits its ironic and demeaning contrast with the lowness of his thoughts; "dignity" is an etymological joke, for Belial is anything but worthy; in fact, he is just what the next line says he is, "false and hollow," an accusation that repeats one of the perennial antirhetorical topoi, that rhetoric, the art of fine speaking, is all show, grounded in nothing but its own empty pretensions, unsupported by any relation to truth. "There is no need," declares Socrates in Plato's *Gorgias*, "for rhetoric to know the facts at all, for it has hit upon a means of persuasion that enables it to appear in the eyes of the ignorant to know more than those who really know" (459),[1] and in the *Phaedrus* the title figure admits that the "man who plans to be an orator" need not "learn what is really just and true, but only what seems so to the crowd" (260).[2]

This reference to the vulgar popular ear indicates that rhetoric's deficiencies are not only epistemological (sundered from truth and fact) and moral (sundered from true knowledge and sincerity) but social: it panders to the worst in people and moves them to base actions, exactly as Belial is said to do in the next famous run-on statement, "and could make the worse appear / The better reason." This is an explicit reference to a nest of classical sources: the most familiar is Aristotle, *Rhetoric*, II, 1402, 23, condemning the skill of being able to make arguments on either side of a question: "This . . . illustrates what is meant by making the worse argument appear the better. Hence people were right in objecting to the training Protagoras undertook to give them."[3] Socrates makes the same point in the *Phaedrus:* "an orator who knows nothing about good or evil undertakes to persuade a city in the same state of ignorance . . . by recommending evil as though it were good" (260). Behind Belial (or descending from him; the direction of genealogy in *Paradise Lost* is always problematic) is the line of sophists – Protagoras, Hippias, Gorgias, shadowy figures known to us mostly through the writings of Plato where they appear always as relativist foils for the idealistic Socrates. The judgment made on them by a philosophic tradition dominated by Plato is the judgment here made on Belial; their thoughts were low, centered on the suspect skills they taught for hire; the danger they represented is the danger Belial represents: despite the lowness of their thoughts, perhaps *because* of the lowness of their thoughts, they pleased the ear, at least the ear of the promiscuous crowd (there is always just beneath the surface of the antirhetorical stance a powerful and corrosive elitism), and the explanation of their unfortunate success is the power Belial now begins to exercise, the power of "persuasive accent." Encoded in this phrase is a continuing debate about the essence of rhetoric, a debate whose two poles are represented by Gorgias's praise in the *Encomium of Helen* of rhetoric as an irresistible force and the stoic Cato's characterization of the rhetorician as a good man skilled at speaking (*"vir bonus, dicendi peritus"*). The difference is that for Gorgias the skill is detached from any necessary moral center and represents a self-sustaining power ("persuasion allied to words can mold men's minds"), while for Cato the skill is a by-product of a focus on goodness and truth (thus the other of his famous aphorisms, "seize the thing, the words will follow" – "*rem tene, verba sequentur*" – which later flowers in the Renaissance distinction between *res et verba*.[4] In one position eloquence is the hard-won creation of a special and technical facility, a facility one acquires by mastering a set of complicated – and morally neutral – rules; in the other eloquence is what naturally issues when a man is in close touch with the Truth and allows it to inspire him. Born, it would seem, in a posture of defensiveness, rhetoric has often gravitated toward this latter view in an effort to defuse the charge that it is amoral. Quintilian's formulation (itself gathered from the writings of Cicero) is one that will later be echoed in countless treatises: "no man can speak well who is not good himself" ("*bene dicere non possit nisi bonus,*" *Institutes*, II, xv, 34). As a defense, however, this declaration has the disadvantage of implying the super-fluousness of rhetoric, an implication fully realized in Augustine's *On Christian Doctrine*, where eloquence is so much subordinated to wisdom that it disappears as a distinct and separable property. Belial, in contrast, is wholly defined by that property, by his ability to produce "persuasive accents." "Accent" here is a powerfully resonant word, one of whose relevant meanings is "mode of utterance peculiar to an individual, locality or nation" (*OED*). He who speaks "in accent" speaks from a particular *angled* perspective into which he tries to draw his auditors; he also speaks in the rhythms of song (etymologically, accent means "song added to speech") which, as Milton will soon observe, "*charms* the sense" (II, 556). "Persuasive accent," then, is almost a redundancy: the two words mean the same thing and what they tell the reader is that he is about to be exposed to a force whose exercise is unconstrained by any sense of respons-ibility either to the Truth or to the Good. Indeed, so dangerous does Milton consider this force that he feels it necessary to provide a corrective gloss as soon as Belial stops speaking: "Thus *Belial* with words cloth'd in reason's garb / Counsell'd ignoble ease and peaceful sloth" (II, 226–7). Just in case you hadn't noticed.

I have lingered so long over this passage because we can extrapolate from it almost all of the binary oppositions in relation to which rhetoric has received its (largely negative) definition: inner/outer, deep/surface, essential/peripheral, unmediated/mediated, clear/colored, necessary/contingent, straightforward/angled, abiding/fleeting, reason/passion, things/words, realities/illusions, fact/opinion, neutral/partisan. Underlying this list, which is by no means exhaust-ive, are three basic oppositions: first, between a truth that exists independently of all perspectives and points of view and the many truths that emerge and seem perspicuous when a particular perspective or point of view has been established and is in force; second, an opposition between true knowledge, which is knowledge as it exists apart from any and all systems of belief, and the knowledge, which because it flows from some or other system of belief, is incomplete and partial (in the sense of biased); and third, an opposition between a self or consciousness that is turned outward in an effort to apprehend and attach itself to truth and true knowledge and a self or consciousness that is turned inward in the direction of its own prejudices, which, far from being transcended, continue to inform its every word and action. Each of these oppositions is attached in turn to an opposition between two kinds of language: on the one hand, language that faithfully reflects or reports on matters of fact uncolored by any personal or partisan agenda or desire; and on the other hand, language that is infected by partisan agendas and desires, and therefore colors and distorts the facts which it purports to reflect. It is use of the second kind of language that makes one a rhetorician, while adherence to the first kind makes one a seeker after truth and an objective observer of the way things are. It is this distinction that, as Thomas Kuhn notes, underwrites the claims of science to be a privileged form of discourse because it has recourse to a "neutral observation language,"[5] a language uninflected by any mediating presuppositions or preconceptions; and it is the same distinction that informs Aristotle's observation (*Rhetoric*, III, 1404, 13) that "Nobody uses fine language when teaching geometry." The language of geometry – of formal rules with no substantive content – is contrasted by Aristotle to all those languages that are intended only to "charm the hearer," the languages of manipulation, deception, and self-consciously deployed strategy.

It is this understanding of linguistic possibilities and dangers that generates a succession of efforts to construct a language from which all perspectival bias (a redundant phrase) has been eliminated, efforts that have sometimes taken as a model the notations of mathematics, at other times the operations of logic, and more recently the purely formal calculations of a digital computer. Whether it issues in the elaborate linguistic machines of seventeenth-century "projectors" like Bishop Wilkins (*An Essay Towards a Real Character and a Philosophical Language*, 1668), or in the building (à la Chomsky) of a "competence" model of language abstracted from any particular performance, or in the project of Esperanto or some other artificial language claiming universality,[6] or in the fashioning of a Habermasian "ideal speech situation" in which all assertions express "a 'rational will' in relation to a common interest ascertained without deception,"[7] the impulse behind the effort is always the same: to establish a form of communication that escapes partiality and aids us in first determining and then affirming what is absolutely and objectively true, a form of communication that in its structure and operations is the very antithesis of rhetoric, of passionate partisan discourse.

That desideratum and the fears behind it have received countless articulations, but never have they been articulated with more precision than in these sentences from Bishop Sprat's *History of the Royal Society of London*, 1667:

When I consider the means of *happy living*, and the causes of their *corruption*, I can hardly forbear... concluding that *eloquence* ought to be banish'd out of all *civil societies*, as a thing fatal to Peace and good Manners.... They [the ornaments of speaking] are in open defiance against *Reason*; professing not to hold much correspondence with that; but with its slaves, the *Passions*: they give the mind a motion too changeable, and bewitching, to consist with *right practice*. Who can behold, without indignation, how many mists and uncertainties, these specious *Tropes* and *Figures* have brought on our Knowledge? How many rewards, which are due to more profitable, and difficult arts, have been snatch'd away by the easie vanity of *fine speaking?* (pp. 111–13)

The terms of banishment are exactly those invoked by Plato against the poets in book X of his *Republic*: Homer, Socrates says, may be "the most poetic of poets and the first of tragedians, but we must know the truth [and] we can admit no poetry into our city save only hymns to the gods and the praises of good men; for if you grant admission to the honeyed Muse...pleasure and pain will be lords of your city instead of law and that which shall...have approved itself to the general reason as the best" (607a). The "honeyed muse" is precisely what Belial becomes when his tongue drops Manna (113), a quintessentially idolatrous act in which he substitutes his own word for the word sent down to us by God and therefore deprives us of the direction that God's word might have given us. Although the transition from classical to Christian thought is marked by many changes, one thing that does not change is the status of rhetoric in relation to a foundational vision of truth and meaning. Whether the center of that vision is a personalized deity or an abstract geometric reason, rhetoric is the force that pulls us away from that center and into its own world of ever-shifting shapes and shimmering surfaces.

Of course, the allure of surfaces and shapes, of "specious *Tropes* and *Figures*," would not be felt if there were not something already in us that inclined to it. Rhetoric may be a danger that assaults us from without, but its possible success is a function of an *inner* weakness. The entire art, as Aristotle explains regretfully, is predicated on "the defects of our hearers" (*Rhetoric*, III, 1404, 8), on the assumption that members of the audience will be naturally susceptible to the rhetorician's appeal. The anti-rhetorical stance can only be coherent if it posits an *in*coherence at the heart (literally) of the self that is both rhetoric's victim and its source. That self is always presented as divided, as the site of contesting forces; in Christian terms the forces are named the carnal and the spiritual; in secular psychologies the names are passion and reason or the willful and the rational; but whatever the names, the result is a relationship of homology between the inner and outer landscapes, both of which contain a core element of truth and knowledge that is continually threatened by a penumbra of irrationality.[8] If tropes and figures "give the mind a motion too changeable," it is because the principle of change, in the form of the passions, already lives in the mind, and it follows then that banishing eloquence and the poets from your republic will only do half the job. As Milton puts it in the *Areopagitica*, "they are not skillful considerers of human things who imagine to remove sin by removing the matter of sin";[9] policing the outer landscape will be of little effect if the inner landscape remains host to the enemy, to sin, to error, to show.

It is the view of the anti-rhetoricians that this double task of inner and outer regulation can be accomplished by linguistic reform, by the institution of conditions of communication that at once protect discourse from the irrelevancies and contingencies that would compromise its universality and insulate the discoursing mind from those contingencies and irrelevancies it itself harbors. Wilkins proposes to fashion a language that will admit neither *Superfluities* – plural signifiers of a single signified, more than one word for a particular thing – nor *Equivocals* – signifiers doing multiple duty, single words that refer to several things – nor *Metaphor* – a form of speech that interposes itself between the observer and the referent and therefore contributes "to the disguising of it with false appearances" (pp. 17–18). The idea is that such a language, purged of ambiguity, redundancy, and indirection, will be an appropriate instrument for the registering of an independent reality, and that if men will only submit themselves to that language and remain within the structure of its stipulated definitions and exclusions, they will be incapable of formulating and expressing wayward, subjective thoughts and will cease to be a danger either to themselves or to those who hearken to them. In this way, says Wilkins, they will be returned to that original state in which the language spoken was the language God gave Adam, a language in which every word perfectly expressed its referent (on the model of Adam's simultaneously understanding the nature of the animals and conferring upon them their names), a language that in the course of time and "emergencies" has unfortunately "admitted various and *casual alterations*" (p. 19).

In the twentieth century Wilkins's program is echoed point for point (absent the theological scaffolding) by Rudolf Carnap: Carnap would admit into the lexicon only words that can be tied firmly to "protocol" or "observation" sentences, sentences that satisfy certain truth conditions and are therefore verifiable by reference to the facts of the world. The stipulation of this criterion, Carnap asserts, "takes away one's freedom to decide what one wishes to 'mean' by [a] word."[10] The freedom of individual speakers and hearers would be further taken away if the words of a verifiable lexicon were embedded in a grammar that "corresponded exactly to logical syntax," for if that were the case "pseudo-statements could not arise" (p. 68). That is, no one could be misled either by the words of another or by that part of his consciousness inclined to wander from the path of truth; the tendency of language to perform in excess of its proper duty – to report or reflect matters of fact – would be curbed in advance, and the mind's susceptibility to the power of a language unconstrained by its empirical moorings would be neutralized. In short, the danger posed by rhetoric, both to the field of discourse and the discoursing consciousness, would have been eliminated. Of course, there are important differences to be noted between the idealism of Plato, the anti-enthusiasm of a Restoration bishop, and the logical positivism of a member of the Vienna Circle, but together (and in the company of countless others) they stand on the same side of a quarrel that Plato was already calling "old" in the fifth century before Christ. That quarrel, the quarrel between philosophy and rhetoric, survives every sea change in the history of Western thought, continually presenting us with the (skewed) choice between the plain unvarnished truth straightforwardly presented and the powerful but insidious appeal of "fine language," language that has transgressed the limits of representation and substituted its own forms for the forms of reality.[11]

II

To this point my presentation has been as skewed as this choice, because it has suggested that rhetoric has received only negative characterizations. In fact, there have always been friends of rhetoric, from the sophists to the anti-foundationalists of the present day, and in response to the realist critique they have devised (and repeated) a number of standard defenses. Two of these defenses are offered by Aristotle in the *Rhetoric*. First, he defines rhetoric as a faculty or art whose practice will help us to observe "in any given case the available means of persuasion" (I, 1355, 27) and points out that as a faculty it is not in and of itself inclined away from truth. Of course, bad men may abuse it, but that after all "is a charge which may be made in common against all good things." "What makes a man a 'sophist,'" he declares, "is not his faculty, but his moral purpose" (I, 1355, 17). To the anticipated objection that rhetoric's potential for misuse is a reason for eschewing it, Aristotle replies that it is sometimes a necessary adjunct to the cause of truth, first, because if we leave the art to be cultivated by deceivers, they will lead truth-seekers astray, and, second, because, regrettable though it may be, "before some audiences not even the possession of the exactest knowledge will make it easy for what we say to produce conviction" and on those occasions "we must use, as our modes of persuasion and argument, notions possessed by everybody" (I, 1355, 27). That is, because of the defects of our hearers the truth itself must often be rhetorically dressed so that it will gain acceptance.[12]

Aristotle's second defense is more aggressively positive and responds directly to one of the most damaging characterizations of rhetoric: "We must be able to employ persuasion, just as strict reasoning can be employed, on opposite sides of a question, not in order that we may in practice employ it in both ways (for we must not make people believe what is wrong), but in order that we may see clearly what the facts are" (I, 1355, 28–33). In short, properly used, rhetoric is a heuristic, helping us not to distort the facts, but to discover them; moreover, adds Aristotle, the setting forth of contrary views of a matter will have the beneficial effect of showing us which of those views most accords with the truth because "the underlying facts do not lend themselves equally well to the contrary views." By this argument, as Peter Dixon has pointed out, Aristotle "removes rhetoric from the realm of the haphazard and the fanciful"[13] and rejoins it to that very realm of which it was said to be the great subverter.

But if this is the strength of Aristotle's defense, it is also its weakness, for in making it he reinforces the very assumptions in relation to which rhetoric will always be suspect, assumptions of an independent reality whose outlines can be perceived by a sufficiently clear-eyed observer who can then represent them in a transparent verbal medium. The stronger defense, because it hits at the heart of the opposing tradition, is one that embraces the accusations of that tradition and makes of them a claim. The chief accusation, as we have seen, is that rhetoricians hold "the probable (or likely-seeming, plausible) in more honour than the true" (*Phaedrus*, 267a). The sophist response is to assert that the realm of the probable – of what is likely to be so given particular conditions within some local perspective – is the only relevant realm of consideration for human beings. The argument is contained in two statements attributed famously to Protagoras. The first declares the unavailability (not the unreality) of the gods: "About gods I cannot say either that they are or that they are not."[14] And the second follows necessarily from the absence of godly guidance: "Man is the measure of all things, of the things that are that they are, and of the things that are not that they are not" (quoted in Plato, *Theaetetus*, 152a). What this means, as W. K. C. Guthrie has pointed out, is "that the Sophists recognized only accidental as opposed to essential being, . . . the conditional and relative as opposed to the self-existent."[15] This is not to say that the categories of the true and good are abandoned, but that in different contexts they will be filled differently and that there exists no master context (for that could only be occupied by the unavailable gods) from the vantage point of which the differences could be assessed and judged.

The result is to move rhetoric from the disreputable periphery to the necessary center: for if the highest truth for any man is what he believes it to be (*Theaetetus*, 152a), the skill which produces belief and therefore establishes what, in a particular time and particular place, is true, is the skill essential to the building and maintaining of a civilized society. In the absence of a revealed truth, rhetoric is that skill, and in teaching it the sophists were teaching "the one thing that mattered, how to take care of one's own affairs and the business of the state."[16] The rhetorician is like a physician; it is his job "to diagnose the particular institution and prescribe the best course of action for a man or a state under given conditions"[17] (see Plato, *Theaetetus*, 167b–d, *Protagoras*, 318e–19a); and when Socrates asks Protagoras if he is "promising to make men good citizens," the reply is firm: "That . . . is exactly what I profess to do" (*Protagoras*, 319a). Of course, in this context words like "good" and "best" do not have the meanings a Plato or Socrates would want them to have – good and best in any and all circumstances; rather, they refer to what would appear to be the better of the courses that seem available in what are generally understood to be the circumstantial constraints of a particular situation; but since, according to the sophist view, particular situations are the only kind there are, circumstantial determinations of what is good are as good as you're going to get.

That is, as I have already said, the strongest of the defenses rhetoric has received because it challenges the basic premise of the antirhetorical stance, the premise that any discourse must be measured against a stable and independent reality. To the accusation that rhetoric deals only with the realms of the probable and contingent and forsakes truth, the sophists and their successors respond that truth itself is a contingent affair and assumes a different shape in the light of differing local urgencies and the convictions associated with them. "Truth was individual and temporary, not universal and lasting, for the truth for any man was . . . what he could be persuaded of."[18] Not only does this make rhetoric – the art of analyzing and presenting local exigencies – a form of discourse no one can afford to ignore, it renders the opposing discourse – formal philosophy – beside the point. This is precisely Isocrates' thesis in his *Antidosis*. Abstract studies like geometry and astronomy, he says, do not have any "useful application either to private or public affairs; . . . after they are learned . . . they do not attend us through life nor do they lend aid in what we do, but are wholly divorced from our necessities."[19] Indeed, he goes so far as to deny to such disciplines the label "philosophy," for "I hold that man to be wise who is able by his powers of conjecture to arrive generally at the best course, and I hold that man to be a philosopher who occupies himself with the studies from which he will most quickly gain that kind of insight" (p. 271). Men who want to do some good in the world, he concludes, "must banish utterly from their interests all vain speculations and all activities which have no bearing on our lives."

What Isocrates does (at least rhetorically) is shift the balance of power between philosophy and rhetoric by putting philosophy on the defensive. This same strategy is pursued after him by Cicero and Quintilian, the most influential of the Roman rhetoricians. In the opening pages of his *De Inventione* Cicero elaborates the myth that will subsequently be invoked in every defense of humanism and belles lettres. There was a time, he says, when "men wandered at large in the field like animals," and there was "as yet no ordered system of religious worship nor of social duties."[20] It was then that a "great and wise" man "assembled and gathered" his uncivilized brothers and "introduced them to every useful and honorable occupation, though they cried out against it at first because of its novelty." Nevertheless, he gained their attention through "reason and eloquence" ("*propter rationem atque orationem*") and by these means he "transformed them from wild savages into a kind and gentle folk." Nor would it have been possible, Cicero adds, to have "turned men . . . from their habits" if wisdom had been "mute and voiceless"; only "a speech at the same time powerful and entrancing could have induced one who had great physical strength to submit to justice without violence." From that time on, "many cities have been founded, . . . the flames of a multitude of wars have been extinguished, and . . . the strongest alliances and most sacred friendships have been formed not only by the use of reason, but also more easily by the use of eloquence" (I, 1). Whereas in the foundationalist story an original purity (of vision, purpose, procedure) is corrupted when rhetoric's siren song proves too sweet, in Cicero's story (later to be echoed by countless others)[21] all the human virtues, and indeed humanity itself, are wrested by the arts of eloquence from a primitive and violent state of nature. Significantly (and this is a point to which we shall return), both stories are stories of power, rhetoric's power; it is just that in one story that power must be resisted lest civilization fall, while in the other that power brings order and a genuine political process where before there was only the rule of "physical strength."

The contrast between the two stories can hardly be exaggerated because what is at stake is not simply a matter of emphasis or priority (as it seems to be in Aristotle's effort to demonstrate an *alliance* between rhetoric and truth) but a difference in worldviews. The quarrel between rhetorical and foundational thought is itself foundational; its content is a disagreement about the basic constituents of human activity and about the nature of human nature itself. In Richard Lanham's helpful terms, it is a disagreement as to whether we are members of the species *homo seriosus* or *homo rhetoricus*. *Homo seriosus* or Serious Man

possesses a central self, an irreducible identity. These selves combine into a single, homogeneously real society which constitutes a referent reality for the men living in it.

This referent society is in turn contained in a physical nature itself referential, standing "out there" independent of man. Man has invented language to communicate with his fellow man. He communicates facts and concepts about both nature and society. He can also communicate a third category of response, emotions. When he is communicating facts or concepts, success is measured by something we call *clarity*. When he is communicating feelings, success is measured by something we call *sincerity, faithfulness to the self* who is doing the feeling.[22]

Homo rhetoricus or rhetorical man, on the other hand,

is an actor; his reality public, dramatic. His sense of identity, depends on the reassurance of daily histrionic reenactment. He is thus centered in time and concrete local event. The lowest common denominator of his life is a social situation.... He assumes a natural agility in changing orientations.... From birth, almost, he has dwelt not in a single value-structure but in several. He is thus committed to no single construction of the world; much rather, to prevailing in the game at hand.... He accepts the present paradigm and explores its resources. Rhetorical man is trained not to discover reality but to manipulate it. Reality is what is accepted as reality, what is useful. (p.4)

As rhetorical man manipulates reality, establishing through his words the imperatives and urgencies to which he and his fellows must respond, he manipulates or fabricates himself, simultaneously conceiving of and occupying the roles that become first possible and then mandatory given the social structure his rhetoric has put in place. By exploring the available means of persuasion in a particular situation, he tries them on, and as they begin to suit him, he becomes them.[23] "I hold," says Isocrates, "that people can become better and worthier if they conceive an ambition to speak well," for in the setting forth of his position the orator "will select from all the actions of men ... those examples which are the most illustrious and the most edifying; and habituating himself to contemplate and appraise such examples, he will feel their influence not only in the preparation of a given discourse but in all the actions of his life" (pp. 275, 277). What serious man fears – the invasion of the fortress of essence by the contingent, the protean, and the unpredictable – is what rhetorical man celebrates and incarnates. In the philosopher's vision of the world rhetoric (and representation in general) is merely the (disposable) form by which a prior and substantial content is conveyed; but in the world of *homo rhetoricus* rhetoric is *both* form and content, the manner of presentation and what is presented; the "improvising power of the rhetor" is at once all-creating and the guarantee of the impermanence of its creations: "to make a thing beautiful or unbeautiful, just or unjust, good or bad is both a human power and a sign of the insubstantiality of these attributes."[24] Having been made they can be made again.

Which of these views of human nature is the correct one? The question can only be answered from within one or the other, and the evidence of one party will be regarded by the other either as illusory or as grist for its own mill. When presented with the ever-changing panorama of history, serious man will see variation on a few basic themes; and when confronted with the persistence of essentialist questions and answers, rhetorical man will reply as Lanham does by asserting that serious man is himself a supremely fictional achievement; seriousness is just another style, not the state of having escaped style:

In a fallen cosmetic world, [plain Jane] is asking *not* to be considered, wants to be overlooked – or perhaps to claim attention by contrast. She is as rhetorical as her made up sister, proclaims as loudly an attitude. Thus the whole range of ornament from zero to 100 is equally rhetorical, equally deep or equally superficial. (p. 30)

That is to say, for rhetorical man the distinctions (between form and content, periphery and core, ephemeral and abiding) invoked by serious man are nothing more than the scaffolding of the theater of seriousness, are themselves instances of what they oppose. And on the other side, if serious man were to hear *that* argument, he would regard it as one more example of rhetorical manipulation and sleight of hand, an outrageous assertion that flies in the face of common sense, the equivalent in debate of "so's your old man." And so it would go, with no prospect of ever reaching accord, an endless round of accusation and counteraccusation in which truth, honesty, and linguistic responsibility are claimed by everyone: "from serious premises, all rhetorical language is suspect; from a rhetorical point of view, transparent language seems dishonest; false to the world."[25]

And so it *has* gone; the history of Western thought could be written as the history of this quarrel. And, indeed, such histories have been written and with predictably different emphases. In one version written many times, the mists of religion, magic, and verbal incantation (all equivalently suspect forms of fantasy) are dispelled by the Enlightenment rediscovery of reason and science; enthusiasm and metaphor alike are curbed by the refinement of method, and the effects of difference (point of view) are bracketed and held in check by a procedural rigor. In another version (told by a line stretching from Vico to Foucault) a carnivalesque world of exuberance and possibility is drastically impoverished by the ascendency of a soulless reason, a brutally narrow perspective that claims to be objective and proceeds in a repressive manner to enforce its claim. It is not my intention here to endorse either history or to offer a third or to argue as some have for a nonhistory of discontinuous *episteme* innocent of either a progressive or lapsarian curve; rather, I only wish to point out that the debate continues to this very day and that its terms are exactly those one finds in the dialogues of Plato and the orations of the sophists.

III

As I write, the fortunes of rhetorical man are on the upswing, as in discipline after discipline there is evidence of what has been called the interpretive turn, the realization (at least for those it seizes) that the givens of any field of activity – including the facts it commands, the procedures it trusts in, and the values it expresses and extends – are socially and politically constructed, are fashioned by man rather than delivered by God or Nature. The most recent (and unlikely) field to experience this revolution, or at least to hear of its possibility, is economics. The key text is Donald McCloskey's *The Rhetoric of Economics* (Wisconsin, 1985), a title that is itself polemical since, as McCloskey points out, mainstream economists don't like to think of themselves as employing a rhetoric; rather, they regard themselves as scientists whose methodology insulates them from the appeal of special interests or points of view. They think, in other words, that the procedures of their discipline will produce "knowledge free from doubt, free from metaphysics, morals and personal conviction" (p. 16). To this, McCloskey responds by declaring (in good sophistic terms) that no such knowledge is available, and that while economic method promises to deliver it, "what it is able to deliver [and] renames as scientific methodology [are] the scientist's and especially the economic scientist's metaphysics, moral, and personal convictions" (p. 16). Impersonal method, then, is both an illusion and a danger (as a kind of rhetoric it masks its rhetorical nature), and as an antidote to it McCloskey offers rhetoric, which he says, deals not with abstract truth, but with the truth that emerges in the context of distinctly human conversations (pp. 28–9). Within those conversations there are always

particular arguments good or bad. After making them there is no point in asking a last, summarizing question: "Well, is it True?" It's whatever it is – persuasive, interesting, useful, and so forth. . . . There is no reason to search for a general quality called Truth, which answers only the unanswerable question, "What is it in the mind of God?" (p. 47)

The answerable questions are always asked within the assumptions of particular situations, and both question and answer "will always depend on one's audience and the human purposes involved" (p. 150). The real truth, concludes McCloskey, is that "assertions are made for purposes of persuading some audience" and that, given the unavailability of a God's-eye view, "this is not a shameful fact," but the bottom line fact in a rhetorical world.

At the first conference called to consider McCloskey's arguments, the familiar anti-rhetorical objections were heard again in the land, and the land might have been fifth-century Athens as well as Wellesley, Massachusetts, in 1986. One participant spoke of "the primrose path to extreme relativism" which proceeds from "Kuhn's conception of the incommensurability of paradigms" to the "contention that there are no objective and unambiguous procedures for applying . . . rules since the meanings of particular actions and terms are entirely . . . context-dependent." Other voices proclaimed that nothing in McCloskey's position was new (an observation certainly true), that everyone already knew it, and that at any rate it didn't touch the core of the economists' practice. Still others invoked a set of related (and familiar) distinctions between empirical and interpretive activities, between demonstration and persuasion, between verifiable procedures and anarchic irrationalism. Of course, each of these objections had already been formulated (or reformulated) in those disciplines that had heard rhetoric's siren song long before it reached the belated ears of economists. The name that everyone always refers to (in praise or blame) is Thomas Kuhn. His *The Structure of Scientific Revolutions* is arguably the most frequently cited work in the humanities and social sciences in the past twenty-five years, and it is rhetorical through and through. Kuhn begins by rehearsing and challenging the orthodox model of scientific inquiry in which independent facts are first collected by objective methods and then built up into a picture of nature, a picture that he himself either confirms or rejects in the context of controlled experiments. In this model, science is a "cumulative process" (p. 3) in which each new discovery adds "one more item to the population of the scientist's world" (p. 7). The shape of that world – of the scientist's professional activities – is determined by the shapes (of fact and structure) already existing in the larger world of nature, shapes that constrain and guide the scientist's work.

Kuhn challenges this story by introducing the notion of a paradigm, a set of tacit assumptions and beliefs within which research goes on, assumptions which rather than deriving from the observation of facts are determinative of the facts that could possibly be observed. It follows, then, that when observations made within different paradigms conflict, there is no principled (i.e., nonrhetorical) way to adjudicate the dispute. One cannot put the competing accounts to the test of fact, because the specification of fact is precisely what is at issue between them; a fact cited by one party would be seen as a mistake by the other. What this means is that science does not proceed by offering its descriptions to the independent judgment of nature; rather, it proceeds when the proponents of one paradigm are able to present their case in a way that the adherents of other paradigms find compelling. In short, the "motor" by which science moves is not verification or falsification, but persuasion. Indeed, says

Kuhn, in the end the force of scientific argument "is *only* that of persuasion" (p. 94). In the case of disagreement, "each party must try, by persuasion, to convert the other" (p. 198), and when one party succeeds there is no higher court to which the outcome might be referred: "there is no standard higher than the assent of the relevant community" (p. 94). "What better criterion," asks Kuhn, "could there be?" (p. 170).

The answer given by those who were horrified by Kuhn's rhetoricization of scientific procedure was predictable: a better criterion would be one that was not captive to a particular paradigm but provided a neutral space in which competing paradigms could be disinterestedly assessed. By denying such a criterion, Kuhn leaves us in a world of epistemological and moral anarchy. The words are Israel Scheffler's:

Independent and public controls are no more, communication has failed, the common universe of things is a delusion, reality itself is made ... rather than discovered. ... In place of a community of rational men following objective procedures in the pursuit of truth, we have a set of isolated monads, within each of which belief forms without systematic constraints.[26]

Kuhn and those he has persuaded have, of course, responded to these accusations, but, needless to say, the debate continues in terms readers of this essay could easily imagine; and the debate has been particularly acrimonious because the area of contest – science and its procedures – is so heavily invested in as the one place where the apostles of rhetorical interpretivism would presumably fear to tread.

At one point in his argument Kuhn remarks that in the tradition he is critiquing scientific research is "reputed to proceed" from "raw data" or "brute experience"; but, he points out, if that were truly the mode of proceeding, it would require a "neutral observation language" (p. 125), a language that registers facts without any mediation by paradigm-specific assumptions. The problem is that "philosophical investigation has not yet provided even a hint of what a language able to do that would be like" (p. 127). Even a specially devised language "embodies a host of expectations about nature," expectations that limit in advance what can be described. Just as one cannot (in Kuhn's view) have recourse to neutral facts in order to settle a dispute, so one cannot have recourse to a neutral language in which to report those facts or even to report on the configuration of the dispute. The difference that divides men "is prior to the application of the languages in which it is nevertheless reflected" (p. 201). Whatever reports a particular language (natural or artificial) offers us will be the report on the world as it is seen from within some particular situation; there is no other aperspectival way to see and no language other than a situation-dependent language – an interested, rhetorical language – in which to report.

This same point was being made with all the force of philosophical authority by J. L. Austin in a book published, significantly, in the same year (1962) that saw the publication of *The Structure of Scientific Revolutions*. Austin begins *How to Do Things with Words* by observing that traditionally the center of the philosophy of language has been just the kind of utterance Kuhn declares unavailable, the context-independent statement that offers objective reports on an equally independent world in sentences of the form "He is running" and "Lord Raglan won the battle of Alma" (pp. 47, 142). Such utterances, which Austin calls "constative," are answerable to a requirement of truth and verisimilitude ("the truth of the constative . . . 'he is running' depends on his being running"); the words must match the world, and if they do not they can be criticized as false and inaccurate. There are, however, innumerable utterances that are not assessable in this way. If, for example, I say to you, "I promise to pay you five dollars" or "Leave the room," it would be odd were you to respond by saying "true" or "false"; rather, you would say to the first "good" or "that's not enough" or "I won't hold my breath" and to the second "yes, sir" or "but I'm expecting a phone call" or "who do you think you are?" These and many other imaginable responses would not be judgments on the truth or accuracy of my utterance but on its appropriateness given our respective positions in some social structure of understanding (domestic, military, economic, etc.). It is only if the circumstances are of a certain kind – that is, if five dollars is a reasonable rather than an insulting amount, if the room I order you to leave is mine not yours – that the utterances will "take" and achieve the meaning of being a promise or a command. Thus the very identity, and therefore the meaning, of this type of utterance – Austin names it "performative" – depends on the context in which it is produced and received. There is no regular – in the sense of reliable and predictable – relationship between the form of the linguistic marks (the words and their order) and their significance. Nothing guarantees that "I promise to pay you five dollars" will be either intended or heard as a promise; in different circumstances it could be received as a threat or a joke (as when I utter it from debtors' prison), and in many circumstances it will be intended as one act and understood as another (as when your opinion of my trustworthiness is much lower than my own). When the criterion of verisimilitude has been replaced by the criterion of appropriateness, meaning becomes radically contextual, potentially as variable as the situated (and shifting) understandings of countless speakers and hearers.

It is, of course, precisely this property of performatives – their force is contingent and cannot be formally constrained – that is responsible for their being consigned by philosophers of language to the category of the "derived" or "parasitic," where, safely tucked away, they are prevented from contaminating the core category of the constative. But it is this act of segregation and quarantining that Austin undoes in the second half of his book when he extends the analysis of performatives to constatives and finds that they too mean differently in the light of differing contextual circumstances. Consider the exemplary constative, "Lord Raglan won the battle of Alma." It is true, accurate, a faithful report? It depends, says Austin, on the context in which it is uttered and received (pp. 142–3). In a high school textbook it might be accepted as true because of the in-place assumptions as to what, exactly, a battle is, what constitutes winning, what the function of a general is, etc., while in a work of "serious" historical research all of these assumptions may have been replaced by others, with the result that the very notions "battle" and "won" would have a different shape. The properties that supposedly distinguish constatives from performatives – fidelity to preexisting facts, accountability to a criterion of truth – turn out to be as dependent on particular conditions of production and reception as performatives. "True" and "false," Austin concludes, are not names for the possible relationships between freestanding (constative) utterances and an equally freestanding state of affairs; rather, they are situation-specific judgments on the relationship between contextually produced utterances and states of affairs that are themselves no less contextually produced. At the end of the book constatives are "discovered" to be a subset of performatives, and with this discovery the formal core of language disappears entirely and is replaced by a world of utterances vulnerable to the sea change of every circumstance, the world, in short, of rhetorical (situated) man.

This is a conclusion Austin himself resists when he attempts to isolate (and thereby contain) the rhetorical by invoking another distinction between serious and nonserious utterance. Serious utterances are utterances for which the speaker takes responsibility; he means what he says, and therefore you can infer his meaning by considering his words in context. A nonserious utterance is an utterance produced in circumstances that "abrogate" (p. 21) the speaker's responsibility, and therefore one cannot with any confidence – that is, without the hazard of ungrounded conjecture – determine what he means:

a performative utterance will, for example, be . . . hollow or void if said by an actor on the stage, or if introduced in a poem, or spoken in a soliloquy. . . . Language in such circumstances is in special ways . . . used not seriously, but in ways *parasitic* upon its normal use. . . . All this we are *excluding* from consideration. Our performative utterances . . . are to be understood as issued in ordinary circumstances. (p. 22)

The distinction, then, is between utterances that are, as Austin puts it later, "tethered to their origin" (p. 61), anchored by a palpable intention, and utterances whose origin is hidden by the screen of a theatrical or literary stage setting. This distinction and the passage in which it appears were taken up in 1967 by Jacques Derrida in a famous (and admiring) critique of Austin. Derrida finds Austin working against his own best insights and forgetting what he has just acknowledged, that "infelicity [communication going astray, in an unintended direction] is an ill to which *all* [speech] acts are heir."[27] Despite this acknowledgment, Austin continues to think of infelicity – of those cases in which the tethering origin of utterances is obscure and must be constructed by interpretive conjecture – as special, whereas, in Derrida's view, infelicity is itself the originary state in that any determination of meaning must always proceed within an interpretive construction of a speaker's intention. The origin that supposedly tethers the interpretation of an utterance will always be the product of that interpretation; the special circumstances in which meaning must be inferred through a screen rather than directly are the circumstances of every linguistic transaction. In short, there are no ordinary circumstances, merely those myriad and varied circumstances in which actors embedded in stage settings hazard interpretations of utterances produced by actors embedded in other stage situations. All the world, as Shakespeare says, is a stage, and on that stage "the quality of risk admitted by Austin" is not something one can avoid by sticking close to ordinary language in ordinary circumstances, but is rather "the internal and positive condition" of any act of communication."[28]

In the same publication in which the English translation of Derrida's essay appeared, John Searle, a student of Austin's, replied in terms that make clear the affiliation of this particular debate to the ancient debate whose configurations we have been tracing. Searle's strategy is basically to repeat Austin's points and declare that Derrida has missed them: "Austin's idea is simply this: if we want to know what it is to make a promise we had better not *start* our investigations with promises made by actors on stage . . . because in some fairly obvious way such utterances are not standard cases of promises" (p. 204). But in Derrida's argument, the category of the "obvious" is precisely what is being challenged or "deconstructed." Although it is true that we consider promises uttered in everyday contexts more direct – less etiolated – than promises uttered in everyday contexts more direct – less etiolated – than promises made on a stage, this (Derrida would say) is only because the stage settings within which everyday life proceeds are so powerfully – that is, rhetorically – in place that they are in effect invisible, and therefore the meanings they make possible are experienced as if they were direct and unmediated by any screens. The "obvious" cannot be opposed to the "staged," as Searle assumes, because it is simply the achievement of a staging that has been particularly successful. One does not escape the rhetorical by fleeing to the protected area of basic communication and common sense because common sense in whatever form it happens to take is always a rhetorical – partial, partisan, interested – construction. This does not mean, Derrida hastens to add, that all rhetorical constructions are equal, just that they are equally rhetorical, equally the effects and extensions of some limited and challengeable point of view. The "citationality" – the condition of being in quotes, of being *in*direct – of an utterance in a play is not the same as the citationality of a philosophical reference or a deposition before a court; it is just that no one of these performatives is more serious – more direct, less mediated, less rhetorical – than any other. Whatever opposition there is takes place within a "general" citationality which "constitutes a violation of the allegedly rigorous purity of every event of discourse or every *speech act*" (p. 192).

Searle points out (p. 205) that in order to achieve a "general theory of speech acts," one must perform acts of exclusion or idealization like Austin's; but it is the possibility of a general theory – of an account that is itself more than an extension of some *particular* context or perspective – that Derrida denies. His is the familiar world of Rhetorical Man, teeming with roles, situations, strategies, interventions, but containing no master role, no situation of situations, no strategy for outflanking all strategies, no intervention in the arena of dispute that does not expand the arena of dispute, no neutral point of rationality from the vantage point of which the "merely rhetorical" can be identified and held in check. That is why deconstructive or post-structuralist thought is supremely rhetorical: it systematically asserts and demonstrates the mediated, constructed, partial, socially constituted nature of all realities, whether they be phenomenal, linguistic, or psychological. To deconstruct a text, says Derrida, is to "work through the structured genealogy of its concepts in the most scrupulous and immanent fashion, but at the same time to determine from a certain external perspective that it cannot name or describe what this history may have concealed or excluded, constituting itself as history through this repression in which it has a stake."[29] The "external perspective" is the perspective from which the analyst knows in advance (by virtue of his commitment to the rhetorical or anti-foundational worldview) that the coherences presented by a text (and an institution or an economy can in this sense be a text) rests on a contradiction it cannot acknowledge, rests on the suppression of the challengeable rhetoricity of its own standpoint, a standpoint that offers itself as if it came from nowhere in particular and simply delivered things as they really (i.e., nonperspectivally) are. A deconstructive reading will surface those contradictions and expose those suppressions and thus "trouble" a unity that is achieved only by covering over all the excluded emphases and interests that might threaten it. These exclusions are part of the text in that the success of its totalizing effort depends on them. Once they are made manifest, the hitherto manifest meaning of the text is undermined – indeed, is shown to have always and already been undermined – as "the rhetorical operations that produce the supposed ground of argument, the key concept or premise," are deprived of the claim to be *un*rhetorical, serious, disinterested.[30]

Nor is this act performed in the service of something beyond rhetoric. Derridean deconstruction does not uncover the operations of rhetoric in order to reach the Truth; rather, it continually uncovers the truth of rhetorical operations, the truth that all operations, including the operation of deconstruction itself, are rhetorical. If, as Paul de Man asserts, "a deconstruction always has for its target to reveal the existence of hidden articulations and fragmentations within assumedly monadic totalities," care must be taken that a new monadic totality is not left as the legacy of the deconstructive gesture. Since the course of a deconstruction is to uncover a "fragmented stage that can be called natural with regard to the system that is being undone," there is always the danger that the "natural" pattern will "substitute *its* relational system for the one it helped to dissolve."[31] The only way to escape this danger is to perform the deconstructive act again and again, submitting each new emerging constellation to the same suspicious scrutiny that brought it to light, and resisting the temptation to put in place of the truths it rhetoricizes the truth that everything is rhetorical. One cannot rest even in the insight that there is no place to rest. "Rhetoric," says de Man, "suspends logic and opens up vertiginous possibilities of referential aberration" (p. 10). But the rhetorical vision is foreclosed on and made into a new absolute if those "vertiginous possibilities" are celebrated as the basis of a new wisdom. The rhetorical beat must by definition go on, endlessly repeating the sequence by which "the lure of solid ground" is succeeded by "the ensuing demystification."[32] When de Man approvingly quotes Nietzsche's identification of truth with "a moving army of metaphors, metonymies and anthropomorphisms," a rhetorical construction whose origin has been (and must be) forgotten, he does not exempt Nietzsche's text from its own corrosive effects. If Nietzsche declares (well in advance of Kuhn and Austin, but well after Gorgias and Protagoras) that "there is no such thing as an unrhetorical, 'natural' language," for "tropes are not something that can be added or subtracted from language at will," the insight must be extended to that very declaration: "A text like *On Truth and Lie*, although it presents itself legitimately as a demystification of literary rhetoric, remains entirely literary, and deceptive itself" (p. 113). The "rhetorical mode," the mode of deconstruction, is a mode of "endless reflection," since it is "unable ever to escape from the rhetorical deceit it announces" (p. 115).

IV

That, however, is just what is wrong with deconstructive practice from the viewpoint of the intellectual left, many of whose members subscribe to Nietzsche's account of truth and reality as rhetorical but find that much of post-structuralist discourse uses that account as a way of escaping into new versions of idealism and formalism. Frank Lentricchia, for example, sees in some of de Man's texts an intention to place "discourse in a realm where it can have no responsibility to historical life" and fears that we are being invited into "the realm of the thoroughly predictable linguistic transcendental," the "rarified region of the undecidable," where every text "speaks synchronically and endlessly the same tale . . . of its own duplicitous self-consciousness."[33] Terry Eagleton's judgment is even harsher. Noting that in the wake of Nietzschean thought, rhetoric, "mocked and berated for centuries by an abrasive rationalism," takes its "terrible belated revenge" by finding itself in every rationalist project, Eagleton complains that many rhetoricians seem content to stop there, satisfied with the "Fool's function of unmasking all power as self-rationalization, all knowledge as a mere fumbling with metaphor."[34] Operating as a "vigorous demystifier of all ideology," rhetoric functions only as a form of thought and ends up by providing "the final ideological rationale for political inertia." In retreat "from market place to study, politics to philology, social practice to semiotics," deconstructive rhetoric turns the emancipatory promise of Nietzschean thought into "a gross failure of ideological nerve," allowing the liberal academic the elitist pleasure of repeatedly exposing "vulgar commercial and political hectorings" (pp. 108–9). In both his study of Benjamin and his influential *Literary Theory: An Introduction*, Eagleton urges a return to the Ciceronian–Isocratic tradition in which the rhetorical arts are inseparable from the practice of a politics, "techniques of persuasion indissociable from the substantive issues and audiences involved," techniques whose employment is "closely determined by the pragmatic situation at hand."[35] In short, he calls for a rhetoric that will do real work and cites as an example the slogan "black is beautiful," which he says is "paradigmatically rhetorical since it employs a figure of equivalence to produce particular discursive and extra-discursive effects without direct regard for truth."[36] That is, someone who says "black is beautiful" is not so much interested in the accuracy of the assertion (it is not constatively intended) as he is in the responses it may provoke – surprise, outrage, urgency, solidarity – responses that may in turn set in motion "practices that are deemed, in the light of a particular set of falsifiable hypotheses, to be desirable."[37]

For Eagleton, the desirable practices are Marxist–socialist and the rhetoric that will help establish them has three tasks:

First, to participate in the production of works and events which . . . so fictionalize the "real" as to intend those effects conducive to the victory of socialism. Second, as "critic" to expose the rhetorical structures by which non-socialist works produce politically undesirable effects. . . . Third, to interpret such words where possible "against the grain," so as to appropriate from them whatever may be valuable for socialism.[38]

It is, of course, the second of these tasks that presents conceptual and cognitive problems. If all cultural work is, as Eagleton says in the sentence just before this passage, rhetorical, then how does one's own rhetoric escape the inauthenticity it discovers in the rhetoric of others? Eagleton's answer is contained in his assumption of the superiority of the socialist program; any rhetorical work in the service of that program will be justified in advance, while conversely any rhetorical work done in opposition to socialist urgencies will flow from "false consciousness" and will deserve to be exposed. This confidence in his objectives makes Eagleton impatient with those for whom the rhetoricity of all discourse is something to be savored for itself, something to be lovingly and obsessively demonstrated again and again. It is not, he says, "a matter of starting from certain theoretical or methodological problems; it is a matter of starting from what we want to *do*, and then seeing which methods and theories will best help us to achieve these ends."[39] Theories, in short, are themselves rhetorics whose usefulness is a function of contingent circumstances. It is ends – specific goals in local contexts – that rule the invocation of theories, not theories that determine goals and the means by which they can be reached.

There are those on the left, however, for whom the direction is the other way around, from the theoretical realization of rhetoric's pervasiveness to a vision and a program for implementing it. In their view the discovery (or rediscovery) that all discourse and therefore all knowledge is rhetorical leads or should lead to the adoption of a *method* by which the dangers of rhetoric can be at least mitigated and perhaps extirpated. This method has two stages: the first is a stage of debunking, and it issues from the general suspicion in which all orthodoxies and arrangements of power are held once it is realized that their basis is not reason or nature but the success of some rhetorical/political agenda. Armed with this realization, one proceeds to expose the contingent and therefore challengeable basis of whatever presents itself as natural and inevitable. So far this is precisely the procedure of deconstruction; but whereas deconstructive practice (at least of the Yale variety) seems to produce nothing but the occasion for its endless repetition, some cultural revolutionaries discern in it a more positive residue, the loosening or weakening of the structures of domination and oppression that now hold us captive. The reasoning is that by repeatedly uncovering the historical and ideological basis of established structures (both political and cognitive), one becomes sensitized to the effects of ideology and begins to clear a space in which those effects can be combated; and as that sensitivity grows more acute, the area of combat will become larger until it encompasses the underlying structure of assumptions that confers a spurious legitimacy on the powers that currently be. The claim, in short, is that the radically rhetorical insight of Nietzschean/Derridean thought can do radical political work; becoming aware that everything is rhetorical is the first step in countering the power of rhetoric and liberating us from its force. Only if deeply entrenched ways of thinking and acting are made the objects of suspicion will we be able "even to *imagine* that life could be different and better."

This last sentence is taken from an essay by Robert Gordon entitled "New Developments in Legal Theory."[40] Gordon is writing as a member of the Critical Legal Studies Movement, a group of legal academics who have discovered the rhetorical nature of legal reasoning and are busily exposing as interested the supposedly disinterested operations of legal procedures. Gordon's pages are replete with the vocabulary of enclosure or prison; we are "locked into" a system of belief we did not make; we are "demobilized" (that is, rendered less mobile); we must "break out" (p. 291), we must "unfreeze the world as it appears to common sense" (p. 289). What will help us to break out, to unfreeze, is the discovery "that the belief-structures that rule our lives are not found in nature but are historically contingent," for that discovery, says Gordon, "is extraordinarily liberating" (p. 289). What it will liberate are the mental energies that were before prevented by the "paralysis-inducing" effects of received systems of thought from even imagining that "life could be different and better." In the words of Roberto Unger (another prominent member of the movement), if you start with an awareness of the insight "that no one scheme of human association has conclusive authority" and come to an understanding of the "flawed" nature of the schemes now in place, you can then "imagine the actualizations [i.e., present-day arrangements of things] transformed" and in time "transform them in fact."[41] The result will be a "cultural-revolutionary practice" that will bring about the "progressive emancipation from a background plan of social division and hierarchy" (p. 587). To the question, what is the *content* of that emancipation, given a world that is rhetorical through and through, those who work Gordon's and Unger's side of the street usually reply that emancipation will take the form of a strengthening and enlarging of a capacity of mind that stands to the side of, and is therefore able to resist, the appeal of the agenda that would enslave us. That capacity of mind has received many names, but the one most often proposed is "critical self-consciousness." Critical self-consciousness is the ability (stifled in some, developed in others) to discern in any "scheme of association," including those one finds attractive and compelling, the partisan aims it hides from view; and the claim is that as it performs this negative task, critical self-consciousness participates in the positive task of formulating schemes of associations (structures of thought and government) that are in the service not of a particular party but of all mankind.

It need hardly be said that this claim veers back in the direction of the rationalism and universalism that the critical/deconstructive project sets out to demystify. That project begins by rejecting the rationalities of present life as rationalizations and revealing the structure of reality to be rhetorical, that is, partial; but then it turns around and attempts to use the insight of partiality to build something that is less partial, less hostage to the urgencies of a particular vision and more responsive to the needs of men and women in general. Insofar as this "turn" is taken to its logical conclusion, it ends up reinventing at the conclusion of a rhetorically informed critique the entire array of anti-rhetorical gestures and exclusions. One sees this clearly in the work of Jürgen Habermas, a thinker whose widespread influence is testimony to the durability of the tradition that began (at least) with Plato. Habermas's goal is to bring about something he calls the "ideal speech situation," a situation in which all assertions proceed not from the perspective of individual desires and strategies, but from the perspective of a general rationality upon which all parties are agreed. In such a situation nothing would count except the claims to universal validity of all assertions. "No force except that of the better argument is exercised; and, . . . as a result, all motives except that of the cooperative search for truth are excluded."[42] Of course, in the world we now inhabit there is no such purity of motive; nevertheless, says Habermas, even in the most distorted of communicative situations there remains something of the basic impulse behind all utterance, "the intention of communicating a true [*wahr*] proposition . . . so that the hearer can share the knowledge of the speaker."[43] If we could only eliminate from our discourse performances those intentions that reflect baser goals – the intentions to deceive, to manipulate, to persuade – the ideal speech situation could be approximated.

What stands in our way is the fact that many of our speech acts issue from the perspective of local and historically contingent contexts, and these by definition cannot contribute to the building up of a general rationality. Therefore, it is incumbent upon us to choose and proffer utterances that satisfy (or at least claim and desire to satisfy) *universal* conditions of validity. This is the project Habermas names "Universal Pragmatics" and the name tells its own story. Habermas recognizes, as all modern and postmodern contextualists do, that language is a social and not a purely formal phenomenon, but he thinks that the social/pragmatic aspect of language use is itself "accessible to formal analysis" (p. 6) and that therefore it is possible to construct a universal "communicative competence" (p. 29) parallel to Chomsky's linguistic competence. Sentences produced according to the rules and norms of this communicative competence would be tied not to "particular epistemic presuppositions and changing contexts" (p. 29), but to the unchanging context (the context of contexts) in which one finds the presuppositions underlying the general possibility of successful speech. "A *general* theory of speech acts would... describe... that fundamental system of rules that adult subjects master to the extent that they can fulfill *the conditions of happy employment of sentences in utterances* no matter to which particular language the sentences may belong and in which accidental contexts the utterances may be embedded" (p. 26). If we can operate on the level of that fundamental system, the distorting potential of "accidental contexts" will be neutralized because we will always have one eye on what is essential, the establishing by rational cooperation of an interpersonal (nonaccidental) truth. Once speakers are oriented to this goal and away from others, oriented toward *general* understanding, they will be incapable of deception and manipulation: "Truthfulness guarantees the transparency of a subjectivity representing itself in language" (p. 57). A company of transparent subjectivities will join together in the fashioning of a transparent truth and of a world in which the will to power has been eliminated.

In his book *Textual Power* (New Haven, 1985), Robert Scholes examines the rationalist epistemology in which a "complete self confronts a solid world, perceiving it directly and accurately,... capturing it perfectly in a transparent language" and declares it to be so thoroughly discredited that it now "is lying in ruins around us" (pp. 132–3). Perhaps so, in some circles, but the fact of Habermas's work and of the audience he commands suggests that even now those ruins are collecting themselves and rising again into the familiar anti-rhetorical structure. It would seem that any announcement of the death of either position will always be premature, slightly behind the institutional news that in some corner of the world supposedly abandoned questions are receiving what at least appear to be new answers. Only recently the *public* fortunes of rationalist-foundationalist thought have taken a favorable turn with the publication of books like Allan Bloom's *The Closing of the American Mind* [New York, 1987] and E. D. Hirsch's *Cultural Literacy* [New York, 1988], both of which (Bloom's more directly) challenge the "new Orthodoxy" of "extreme cultural relativism" and reassert, albeit in different ways, the existence of normative standards. In many quarters these books have been welcomed as a return to the common sense that is necessary if civilization is to avoid the dark night of anarchy. One can expect administrators and legislators to propose reforms (and perhaps even purges) based on Bloom's arguments (the rhetorical force of anti-rhetoricalism is always being revived), and one can expect too a host of voices raised in opposition to what will surely be called the "new positivism." Those voices will include some that have been mentioned here and some others that certainly merit recording but can only be noted in a list that is itself incomplete. The full story of rhetoric's twentieth-century resurgence would boast among its cast of characters: Kenneth Burke, whose "dramatism" anticipates so much of what is considered avant-garde today; Wayne

Booth, whose *The Rhetoric of Fiction* [Chicago, 1961] was so important in legitimizing the rhetorical analysis of the novel; Mikhail Bakhtin, whose contrast of monologic to dialogic and heteroglossic discourse sums up so many strands in the rhetorical tradition; Roland Barthes, who in the concept of "jouissance" makes a (non) constitutive principle of the tendency of rhetoric to resist closure and extend play; the ethnomethodologists (Harold Garfinkel and company) who discover in every supposedly rule-bound context the operation of a principle (exactly the wrong word) of "ad-hocing"; Chaim Perelman and L. Olbrechts-Tyeca whose *The New Rhetoric: A Treatise on Argumentation* [Notre Dame, 1969] provides a sophisticated modern source book for would-be rhetoricians weary of always citing Aristotle; Barbara Herrnstein Smith who, in the course of espousing an unashamed relativism, directly confronts and argues down the objections of those who fear for their souls (and more) in a world without objective standards; Fredric Jameson and Hayden White who teach us (among other things) that "history...is unaccessible to us except in textual form, and that our approach to it and to the Real itself necessarily passes through its prior textualization";[44] reader-oriented critics like Norman Holland, David Bleich, Wolfgang Iser, and H. R. Jauss who, by shifting the emphasis from the text to its reception, open up the act of interpretation to the infinite variability of contextual circumstance; innumerable feminists who relentlessly unmark male hegemonic structures and expose as rhetorical the rational posturnings of the legal and political systems; equally innumerable theorists of composition who, under the slogan "process, not product," insist on the rhetorical nature of communication and argue for far-reaching changes in the way writing is taught. The list is already formidable, but it could go on and on, providing support for Scholes's contention that the rival epistemology has been vanquished and for Clifford Geertz's announcement (and he too is a contributor to the shift he reports) that "Something is happening to the way we think about the way we think."[45]

But it would seem, from the evidence marshaled in this essay, that something is always happening to the way we think, and that it is always the same something, a tug-of-war between two views of human life and its possibilities, no one of which can ever gain complete and lasting ascendancy because in the very moment of its triumphant articulation each turns back in the direction of the other. Thus Wayne Booth feels obliged in both *The Rhetoric of Fiction* and *A Rhetoric of Irony* [Chicago, 1974] to confine the force of rhetoric by sharply distinguishing its legitimate uses from two extreme-limit cases (the "unreliable narrator" and "unstable irony"); some reader-response critics deconstruct the autonomy and self-sufficiency of the text, but in the process end up privileging the autonomous and self-sufficient subject; some feminists challenge the essentialist claims of "male reason" in the name of a female rationality or nonrationality apparently no less essential; Jameson opens up the narrativity of history in order to proclaim one narrative the true and unifying one. Here one might speak of the return of the repressed (and thereby invoke Freud whose writings and influence would be still another chapter in the story I have not even begun to tell) were it not that the repressed – whether it be the fact of difference or the desire for its elimination – is always so close to the surface that it hardly need be unearthed. What we seem to have is a tale full of sound and fury, and signifying itself, signifying a durability rooted in inconclusiveness, in the impossibility of there being a last word.

In an essay, however, someone must have the last word and I give it to Richard Rorty. Rorty is himself a champion of the antiessentialism that under-lies rhetorical thinking; his neo-pragmatism makes common cause with Kuhn and others who would turn us away from the search for transcendental absolutes and commend to us (although it would seem superfluous to do so) the imperatives and goals already informing our practices. It is, however, not the polemicist Rorty whom I call upon to sum up, but the Rorty who is the brisk chronicler of our epistemological condition:

There . . . are two ways of thinking about various things . . . The first . . . thinks of truth as a vertical relationship between representations and what is represented. The second . . . thinks of truth horizontally – as the culminating reinterpretation of our pre-decessors' reinterpretation of their predecessors' reinterpretation. . . . It is the difference between regarding truth, goodness, and beauty as eternal objects which we try to locate and reveal, and regarding them as artifacts whose fundamental design we often have to alter.[46]

It is the difference between serious and rhetorical man. It is the difference that remains.

Notes

1 *Gorgias*, ed. and trans. W. C. Helmbold (Indianapolis, 1952), p. 18.
2 Plato, *Phaedrus*, ed. and trans. W. C. Helmbold and W. G. Rabinowitz (Indiana-polis, 1956), p. 46.
3 *The Works of Aristotle*, vol. 11, ed. and trans. W. Rhys Roberts (Oxford, 1946).
4 See A. C. Howell, "*Res et Verba*: Words and Things," in *Seventeenth Century Prose: Modern Essays and Criticism*, ed. S. Fish (Oxford, 1971).
5 Thomas Kuhn, *The Structure of Scientific Revolutions* (Chicago, 1962), p. 125.
6 See Andrew Lange, *The Artificial Language Movement* (Oxford, New York, and London, 1985).
7 Jürgen Habermas, *Legitimation Crisis* (Boston, 1975), p. 108.

8   This is the language of H. L. A. Hart's *The Concept of Law* (Oxford, 1961).

9   John Milton, "Areopagitica," in *Milton's Prose*, ed. J. Max Patrick et al. (New York, 1968), p. 297.

10   Rudolf Carnap, "The Elimination of Metaphysics," in *Logical Positivism*, ed. A. J. Ayer (Glencoe, Ill., 1959), p. 63.

11   See on this point George Kennedy, *The Art of Persuasion in Greece* (Princeton, NJ, 1963), p. 23.

12   See John Milton, "Reason of Church Government," in *The Complete Prose Works of John Milton*, ed. D. M. Wolfe et al., vol. 1 (New Haven, Conn., 1953), pp. 817–18.

13   *Rhetoric* (London, 1971), p. 14.

14   *Die Fragmente der Vorsokratiker*, ed. H. Diels and W. Kranz (Berlin, 1960), 371: 80, B4.

15   William K. Guthrie, *The Sophists* (Cambridge, 1971), p. 193.

16   Ibid., p. 186.

17   Ibid., p. 187.

18   Ibid., p. 51.

19   Isocrates, "Antidosis," in *Isocrates*, vol. 2, ed. and trans. George Norlin (Cambridge: Harvard University Press, 1962), pp. 275, 277.

20   Cicero, "De Inventione," in *Cicero*, vol. 2, ed. and trans. H. M. Hubbell (Cambridge: Harvard University Press, 1968), I, 2.

21   See, for example, John Lawson, *Lectures Concerning Oratory*, ed. E. N. Claussen and K. R. Wallace (Carbondale and Edwardsville: Southern Illinois University Press, 1972), p. 27.

22   *The Motives of Eloquence* (New Haven, Conn., 1976), p. 1.

23   See Thomas Sloane, *Donne, Milton, and the End of Humanist Rhetoric* (Berkeley, Los Angeles, and London, 1985), p. 87: "Rhetoric succeeded in humanism's great desideratum, the artistic creation of adept personhood." See also Stephen Greenblatt, *Renaissance Self-Fashioning* (Chicago, 1980).

24   Nancy Streuver, *The Language of History in the Renaissance* (Princeton, NJ, 1970), pp. 15, 12.

25   Lanham, *Motives*, p. 28.

26   *Science and Subjectivity* (Indianapolis, 1967), p. 19.

27   Jacques Derrida, "Signature Event Context," *Glyph* 1 (1977): 190.

28   Ibid.

29   Jacques Derrida, *Positions* (Chicago: University of Chicago Press, 1981), p. 6.

30   Jonathan Culler, *On Deconstruction* (Ithaca, NY, 1982), p. 86.

31   *Allegories of Reading* (New Haven, Conn., 1979), p. 249.

32   William Ray, *Literary Meaning* (Oxford, 1984), p. 195.

33   *After the New Criticism* (Chicago, 1980), pp. 310, 317.

34   *Walter Benjamin or Towards a Revolutionary Criticism* (London, 1981), p. 108.

35   Ibid., p. 104.

36   Ibid., p. 112.

37   Ibid., p. 113.

38   Ibid.
39   *Literary Theory* (Minneapolis, 1983), p. 211.
40   *The Politics of Law* (New York, 1983), p. 287.
41   "The Critical Legal Studies Movement," *Harvard Law Review* 96 (1983): 580.
42   *Legitimation Crisis* (Boston, 1975), pp. 107–8.
43   *Communication and the Evolution of Society* (Boston, 1979), p. 2.
44   *The Political Unconscious* (Ithaca, 1981), p. 35.
45   "Blurred Genres: The Refiguration of Social Thought," *The American Scholar* 49 (Spring 1980).
46   *Consequences of Pragmatism* (Minneapolis, 1982), p. 92.

6

There's No Such Thing as Free Speech, and It's a Good Thing, Too

Stanley Fish's provocative essay, "There's No Such Thing as Free Speech, and It's a Good Thing, Too," offers a challenge to left liberals who believe in First-Amendment absolutism, the notion not only that the First Amendment has paramount importance in the adjudication of free-speech issues, but that it is based on principles of neutrality that ought not to be abrogated under the pressure of political arguments of any kind. Fish argues instead that free speech, although appearing as a principle indifferent to political pressures, is inevitably invoked for political reasons, and that it has never been treated as an absolute and inviolable principle.

He takes issue with the notion that the First Amendment values speech for speech's sake, and that it is fundamentally indifferent to the content of what is said. In a logical vein, he argues that speech only becomes valuable by virtue of what it communicates and what it performs, and that it is a rare occasion in which simple, contentless yammering is held to be valuable in an absolute sense. In a clear formulation of his view, Fish writes, "speech, in short, is never a value in and of itself but is always produced within the precincts of some assumed conception of the good to which it must yield in the event of conflict." In other words, the value of speech must be weighed against other values, and difficult, pragmatic decisions must be made with respect to the relative merit of each of the values being asserted.

He not only argues, though, that free speech is not a neutral principle, but that the adjudication of the First Amendment constantly comes up against the question: What will and will not qualify as speech? The line that demarcates the field of speech is usually drawn in relation to conduct, whereby certain expressions are said to communicate, and others to act in some way. The former is protected by the First Amendment, whereas the latter remains unprotected. In the case of hate speech, the expression in question tends to be regarded as speech by those who would have it be protected by law, and tends to be regarded as conduct by those who would claim that it falls outside the reach of the First Amendment. Fish holds that there is no non-arbitrary way to make the distinction between speech and conduct, and that the distinction is invariably made in the service of one political strategy or another. The "absolute" value of speech thus relies on a fully arbitrary demarcation of what speech is. Moreover, any expression of speech can both communicate and perform, and there is no certain way to separate the expressive and performative dimensions of utterances.

Perhaps his most controversial claim, however, is the idea conveyed by the title of his essay, namely, that speech has never actually been free. By this claim, he means that any speech community is constituted by virtue of norms that govern what will and will not qualify as communicable speech, and that these norms necessarily render incommunicable or non-sensical certain forms of expression. These latter expressions form an "originary exclusion" by which the internal intelligibility of any delimited realm of speech is established. To be a member of a speech community means to have accepted as a first presupposition that certain kinds of expressions will not be possible: "speech only becomes intelligible against the background of what isn't being said." If censorship conditions the very possibility of speech, then no speech is absolutely free.

Finally, Fish's argument has implications for thinking about the relationship of legal and ethical principle to politics and policy. In general, he opposes the notion that we might seek recourse to abstract and neutral principles such as free speech in order to adjudicate the proper limits of speech-related policy issues. The invocation of abstract principle masks the operation of political strategy, and all principle, it appears, is reducible to "politics." What "politics" consists in is only gesturally indicated in this essay, but it seems to relate to positions that are "urgently" and "deeply" held, and are held not by virtue of principles, but by virtue of passionate investments. When we say that we adhere to free speech because we passionately adhere to the principle of safeguarding free speech, we speak in a way that is somewhat misleading. For Fish, our principles follow from our passionate convictions, and not vice versa. Politics is thus both masked and advanced through the language of principles, but "principles" can only be disingenuously invoked as neutral to politics. Whether passionate conviction suffices as a definition of the political sphere is an important critical question.

Practically, then, this means that Fish recommends that we make hard decisions regarding free speech through an inspection of the situation in which the conflict emerges. He remarks, for instance, that in the present day, the dangers of not considering the harms of hate speech are greater than those that attend the limitations on free-speech doctrine that such regulations may entail. But how does Fish delimit a "present situation," and how would agreement on what the "situation" is take place if there are no principles of selection at work in deciding what belongs to our situation and in what its salient contours consist? This seems to be a question left open by this probing essay.

Judith Butler

> Nowadays the First Amendment is the First Refuge of Scoundrels.
> S. Johnson and S. Fish

Lately, many on the liberal and progressive left have been disconcerted to find that words, phrases, and concepts thought to be their property and generative of their politics have been appropriated by the forces of neoconservatism. This is particularly true of the concept of free speech, for in recent years First Amendment rhetoric has been used to justify policies and actions the left finds problematical if not abhorrent: pornography, sexist language, campus hate speech. How has this happened? The answer I shall give in this essay is that abstract concepts like free speech do not have any "natural" content but are filled with whatever content and direction one can manage to put into them. "Free speech" is just the name we give to verbal behavior that serves the substantive agendas we wish to advance; and we give our preferred verbal behaviors *that* name when we can, when we have the power to do so, because in the rhetoric of American life, the label "free speech" is the one you want your favorites to wear. Free speech, in short, is not an independent value but a political prize, and if that prize has been captured by a politics opposed to yours, it can no longer be invoked in ways that further your purposes, for it is now an obstacle to those purposes. This is something that the liberal left has yet to understand, and what follows is an attempt to pry its members loose from a vocabulary that may now be a disservice to them.

Not far from the end of his *Areopagitica*, and after having celebrated the virtues of toleration and unregulated publication in passages that find their way into every discussion of free speech and the First Amendment, John Milton catches himself up short and says, of course I didn't mean Catholics, them we exterminate:

I mean not tolerated popery, and open superstition, which as it extirpates all religious and civil supremacies, so itself should be extirpate . . . that also which is impious or evil absolutely against faith or manners no law can possibly permit that intends not to unlaw itself.

Notice that Milton is not simply stipulating a single exception to a rule generally in place; the kinds of utterance that might be regulated and even prohibited on pain of trial and punishment constitute an open set; popery is named only as a particularly perspicuous instance of the advocacy that cannot be tolerated. No doubt there are other forms of speech and action that might be categorized as "open superstitions" or as subversive of piety, faith, and manners, and presumably these too would be candidates for "extirpation." Nor would Milton think himself culpable for having failed to provide a list of unprotected utterances. The list will fill itself out as utterances are put to the test implied by his formulation: would this form of speech or advocacy, if permitted to flourish, tend to undermine the very purposes for which our society is constituted? One cannot answer this question with respect to a particular utterance in advance of its emergence on the world's stage; rather, one must wait and ask the question in the full context of its production and (possible) dissemination. It might appear that the result would be ad hoc and unprincipled, but for Milton the principle inheres in the core values in whose name individuals of like mind came together in the first place. Those values, which include the search for truth and the promotion of virtue, are capacious enough to accommodate a diversity of views. But at some point – again impossible of advance specification – capaciousness will threaten to become shapelessness, and at that point fidelity to the original values will demand acts of extirpation.

I want to say that all affirmations of freedom of expression are like Milton's, dependent for their force on an exception that literally carves out the space in which expression can then emerge. I do not mean that expression (saying something) is a realm whose integrity is sometimes compromised by certain restrictions but that restriction, in the form of an underlying articulation of the world that necessarily (if silently) negates alternatively possible articulations, is constitutive of expression. Without restriction, without an inbuilt sense of what it would be meaningless to say or wrong to say, there would be no assertion and no reason for asserting it. The exception to unregulated expression is not a negative restriction but a positive hollowing out of value – we are for *this*, which means we are against *that* – in relation to which meaningful assertion can then occur. It is in reference to that value – constituted as all values are by an act of exclusion – that some forms of speech will be heard as (quite literally) intolerable. Speech, in short, is never a value in and of itself but is always produced within the precincts of some assumed conception of the good to which it must yield in the event of conflict. When the pinch comes (and sooner or later it will always come) and the institution (be it church, state, or university) is confronted by behavior subversive of its core rationale, it will respond by declaring "of course we mean not tolerated ——, that we extirpate," not because an exception to a general freedom has suddenly and contradictorily been announced, but because the freedom has never been general and has always been understood against the background of an originary exclusion that gives it meaning.

This is a large thesis, but before tackling it directly I want to buttress my case with another example, taken not from the seventeenth century but from the charter and case law of Canada. Canadian thinking about freedom of expression departs from the line usually taken in the United States in ways that bring that country very close to the *Areopagitica* as I have expounded it. The differences are fully on display in a recent landmark case, *R. v. Keegstra.* James Keegstra was a high school teacher in Alberta who, it was established by evidence, "systematically denigrated Jews and Judaism in his classes." He described Jews as treacherous, subversive, sadistic, money loving, power hungry, and child killers. He declared them "responsible for depressions, anarchy, chaos, wars and revolution" and required his students "to regurgitate these notions in essays and examinations." Keegstra was indicated under Section 319(2) of the Criminal Code and convicted. The Court of Appeal reversed, and the Crown appealed to the Supreme Court, which reinstated the lower court's verdict.

Section 319(2) reads in part, "Every one who, by communicating statements other than in private conversation, willfully promotes hatred against any identifiable group is guilty of . . . an indictable offense and is liable to imprisonment for a term not exceeding two years." In the United States, this provision of the code would almost certainly be struck down because, under the First Amendment, restrictions on speech are apparently prohibited without qualification. To be sure, the Canadian charter has its own version of the First Amendment, in Section 2(b): "Everyone has the following fundamental freedoms . . . (b) freedom of thought, belief, opinion, and expression, including freedom of the press and other media of communication." But Section 2(b), like every other section of the charter, is qualified by Section 1: "The Canadian Charter of Rights and Freedoms guarantees the rights and freedoms set out in it subject only to such reasonable limits prescribed by law as can be demonstrably justified in a free and democratic society." Or in other words, every right and freedom herein granted can be trumped if its exercise is found to be in conflict with the principles that underwrite the society.

This is what happens in *Keegstra* as the majority finds that Section 319(2) of the Criminal Code does in fact violate the right of freedom of expression guaranteed by the charter but is nevertheless a *permissible* restriction because it accords with the principles proclaimed in Section 1. There is, of course, a dissent that reaches the conclusion that would have been reached by most, if not all, US courts; but even in dissent the minority is faithful to Canadian ways of reasoning. "The question," it declares, "is always one of balance," and thus even when a particular infringement of the charter's Section 2(b) has been declared unconstitutional, as it would have been by the minority, the question remains open with respect to the next case. In the United States the question is presumed closed and can only be pried open by special tools. In our legal culture as it is now constituted, if one yells "free speech" in a crowded courtroom and makes it stick, the case is over.

Of course, it is not that simple. Despite the apparent absoluteness of the First Amendment, there are any number of ways of getting around it, ways that are known to every student of the law. In general, the preferred strategy is to manipulate the distinction, essential to First Amendment jurisprudence, between speech and action. The distinction is essential because no one would think to frame a First Amendment that began "Congress shall make no law abridging freedom of action," for that would amount to saying "Congress shall make no law," which would amount to saying "There shall be no law," only actions uninhibited and unregulated. If the First Amendment is to make any sense, have any bite, speech must be declared not to be a species of action, or to be a special form of action lacking the aspects of action that cause it to be the object of regulation. The latter strategy is the favored one and usually involves the separation of speech from consequences. This is what Archibald Cox does when he assigns to the First Amendment the job of protecting "expressions separable from conduct harmful to other individuals and the community." The difficulty of managing this segregation is well known: speech always seems to be crossing the line into action, where it becomes, at least potentially, consequential. In the face of this categorical instability, First Amendment theorists and jurists fashion a distinction within the speech/action distinction: some forms of speech are not really speech because their purpose is to incite violence or because they are, as the court declares in *Chaplinsky v. New Hampshire* (1942), "fighting words," words "likely to provoke the average person to retaliation, and thereby cause a breach of the peace."

The trouble with this definition is that it distinguishes not between fighting words and words that remain safely and merely expressive but between words that are provocative to one group (the group that falls under the rubric "average person") and words that might be provocative to other groups, groups of persons not now considered average. And if you ask what words are likely to be provocative to those nonaverage groups, what are likely to be *their* fighting words, the answer is anything and everything, for as Justice Holmes said long ago (in *Gitlow v. New York*), every idea is an incitement to somebody, and since ideas come packaged in sentences, in words, every sentence is potentially, in some situation that might occur tomorrow, a fighting word and therefore a candidate for regulation.

This insight cuts two ways. One could conclude from it that the fighting words exception is a bad idea because there is no way to prevent clever and unscrupulous advocates from shoveling so many forms of speech into the excepted category that the zone of constitutionally protected speech shrinks to nothing and is finally without inhabitants. Or, alternatively, one could conclude that there was never anything in the zone in the first place and that the difficulty of limiting the fighting words exception is merely a particular instance of the general difficulty of separating speech from action. And if one opts for this second conclusion, as I do, then a further conclusion is inescapable: insofar as the point of the First Amendment is to identify speech separable from conduct and from the consequences that come in conduct's wake, there is no such speech and therefore nothing for the First Amendment to protect. Or, to make the point from the other direction, when a court invalidates legislation because it infringes on protected speech, it is not because the speech in question is without consequences but because the consequences have been discounted in relation to a good that is judged to outweigh them. Despite what they say, courts are never in the business of protecting speech per se, "mere" speech (a nonexistent animal); rather, they are in the business of classifying speech (as protected or regulatable) in relation to a value – the health of the republic, the vigor of the economy, the maintenance of the status quo, the undoing of the status quo – that is the true, if unacknowledged, object of their protection.

But if this is the case, a First Amendment purist might reply, why not drop the charade along with the malleable distinctions that make it possible, and declare up front that total freedom of speech is our primary value and trumps anything else, no matter what? The answer is that freedom of expression would only be a primary value if it didn't matter what was said, didn't matter in the sense that no one gave a damn but just liked to hear talk. There are contexts like that, a Hyde Park corner or a call-in talk show where people get to sound off for the sheer fun of it. These, however, are special contexts, artificially bounded spaces designed to assure that talking is not taken seriously. In ordinary contexts, talk is produced with the goal of trying to move the world in one direction rather than another. In these contexts – the contexts of everyday life – you go to the trouble of asserting that X is Y only because you suspect that some people are wrongly asserting that X is Z or that X doesn't exist. You assert, in short, because you give a damn, not about assertion – as if it were a value in and of itself – but about what your assertion is about. It may seem paradoxical, but free expression could only be a primary value if what you are valuing is the right to make noise; but if you are engaged in some purposive activity in the course of which speech happens to be produced, sooner or later you will come to a point when you decide that some forms of speech do not further but endanger that purpose.

Take the case of universities and colleges. Could it be the purpose of such places to encourage free expression? If the answer were "yes," it would be hard to say why there would be any need for classes, or examinations, or departments, or disciplines, or libraries, since freedom of expression requires nothing but a soapbox or an open telephone line. The very fact of the university's machinery – of the events, rituals, and procedures that fill its calendar – argues for some other, more substantive purpose. In relation to that purpose (which will be realized differently in different kinds of institutions), the flourishing of free expression will in almost all circumstances be an obvious good; but in some circumstances, freedom of expression may pose a threat to that purpose, and at that point it may be necessary to discipline or regulate speech, lest, to paraphrase Milton, the institution sacrifice itself to one of its *accidental* features.

Interestingly enough, the same conclusion is reached (inadvertently) by Congressman Henry Hyde, who is addressing these very issues in a recently offered amendment to Title VI of the Civil Rights Act. The first section of the amendment states its purpose, to protect "the free speech rights of college students" by prohibiting private as well as public educational institutions from "subjecting any student to disciplinary sanctions solely on the basis of conduct that is speech." The second section enumerates the remedies available to students whose speech rights may have been abridged; and the third, which is to my mind the nub of the matter, declares as an exception to the amendment's jurisdiction any "educational institution that is controlled by a religious organization," on the reasoning that the application of the amendment to such institutions "would not be consistent with the religious tenets of such organizations." In effect, what Congressman Hyde is saying is that at the heart of these colleges and universities is a set of beliefs, and it would be wrong to require them to tolerate behavior, including speech behavior, inimical to those beliefs. But insofar as this logic is persuasive, it applies across the board, for all educational institutions rest on some set of beliefs – no institution is "just there" independent of any purpose – and it is hard to see why the rights of an institution to protect and preserve its basic "tenets" should be restricted only to those that are religiously controlled. Read strongly, the third section of the amendment undoes sections one and two – the exception becomes, as it always was, the rule – and points us to a balancing test very much like that employed in Canadian law: given that any college or university is informed by a core rationale, an administrator faced with complaints about offensive speech should ask whether damage to the core would be greater if the speech were tolerated or regulated.

The objection to this line of reasoning is well known and has recently been reformulated by Benno Schmidt, former president of Yale University. According to Schmidt, speech codes on campuses constitute "well intentioned but misguided efforts to give values of community and harmony a higher place than freedom" (*Wall Street Journal*, May 6, 1991). "When the goals of harmony collide with freedom of expression," he continues, "freedom must be the paramount obligation of an academic community." The flaw in this logic is on display in the phrase "academic community," for the phrase recognizes what Schmidt would deny, that expression only occurs in communities – if not in an academic community, then in a shopping mall community or a dinner party community or an airplane ride community or an office community. In these communities and in any others that could be imagined (with the possible exception of a community of major league baseball fans), limitations on speech in relation to a defining and deeply assumed purpose are inseparable from community membership.

Indeed, "limitations" is the wrong word because it suggests that expression, as an activity and a value, has a pure form that is always in danger of being compromised by the urgings of special interest communities; but independently of a community context informed by interest (that is, purpose), expression would be at once inconceivable and unintelligible. Rather than being a value that is threatened by limitations and constraints, expression, in any form worth worrying about, is a *product* of limitations and constraints, of the already-in-place presuppositions that give assertions their very particular point. Indeed, the very act of thinking of something to say (whether or not it is subsequently regulated) is already constrained – rendered impure, and because impure, communicable – by the background context within which the thought takes its shape. (The analysis holds too for "freedom," which in Schmidt's vision is an entirely empty concept referring to an urge without direction. But like expression, freedom is a coherent notion only in relation to a goal or good that limits and, by limiting, shapes its exercise.)

Arguments like Schmidt's only get their purchase by first imagining speech as occurring in no context whatsoever, and then stripping particular speech acts of the properties conferred on them by contexts. The trick is nicely illustrated when Schmidt urges protection for speech "no matter how obnoxious in content." "Obnoxious" at once acknowledges the reality of speech-related harms and trivializes them by suggesting that they are *surface* injuries that any large-minded ("liberated and humane") person should be able to bear. The possibility that speech-related injuries may be grievous and *deeply* wounding is carefully kept out of sight, and because it is kept out of sight, the fiction of a world of weightless verbal exchange can be maintained, at least within the confines of Schmidt's carefully denatured discourse.

To this Schmidt would no doubt reply, as he does in his essay, that harmful speech should be answered not by regulation but by more speech; but that would make sense only if the effects of speech could be canceled out by additional speech, only if the pain and humiliation caused by racial or religious epithets could be ameliorated by saying something like "So's your old man." What Schmidt fails to realize at every level of his argument is that expression is more than a matter of proferring and receiving propositions, that words do work in the world of a kind that cannot be confined to a purely cognitive realm of "mere" ideas.

It could be said, however, that I myself mistake the nature of the work done by freely tolerated speech because I am too focused on short-run outcomes and fail to understand that the good effects of speech will be realized, not in the present, but in a future whose emergence regulation could only inhibit. This line of reasoning would also weaken one of my key points, that speech in and of itself cannot be a value and is only worth worrying about if it is in the service of something with which it cannot be identical. My mistake, one could argue, is to equate the something in whose service speech is with some locally espoused value (e.g., the end of racism, the empowerment of disadvantaged minorities), whereas in fact we should think of that something as a now-inchoate shape that will be given firm lines only by time's pencil. That is why the shape now receives such indeterminate characterizations (e.g., true self-fulfillment, a more perfect polity, a more capable citizenry, a less partial truth); we cannot now know it, and therefore we must not prematurely fix it in ways that will bind successive generations to error.

This forward-looking view of what the First Amendment protects has a great appeal, in part because it continues in a secular form the Puritan celebration of millenarian hopes, but it imposes a requirement so severe that one would except more justification for it than is usually provided. The requirement is that we endure whatever pain racist and hate speech inflicts for the sake of a future whose emergence we can only take on faith. In a specifically religious vision like Milton's, this makes perfect sense (it is indeed the whole of Christianity), but in the context of a politics that puts its trust in the world and not in the Holy Spirit, it raises more questions than it answers and could be seen as the second of two strategies designed to delegitimize the complaints of victimized groups. The first strategy, as I have noted, is to define speech in such a way as to render it inconsequential (on the model of "sticks and stones will break by bones, but . . ."); the second strategy is to acknowledge the (often grievous) consequences of speech but declare that we must suffer them in the name of something that cannot be named. The two strategies are denials from slightly different directions of the *present* effects of racist speech; one confines those effects to a closed and safe realm of pure mental activity; the other imagines the effects of speech spilling over into the world but only in an ever-receding future for whose sake we must forever defer taking action.

I find both strategies unpersuasive, but my own skepticism concerning them is less important than the fact that in general they seem to have worked; in the parlance of the marketplace (a parlance First Amendment commentators love), many in the society seemed to have bought them. Why? The answer, I think, is that people cling to First Amendment pieties because they do not wish to face what they correctly take to be the alternative. That alternative is *politics*, the realization (at which I have already hinted) that decisions about what is and is not protected in the realm of expression will rest not on principle or firm doctrine but on the ability of some persons to interpret – recharacterize or rewrite – principle and doctrine in ways that lead to the protection of speech they want heard and the regulation of speech they want heard and the regulation of speech they want silenced. (That is how George Bush can argue *for* flag-burning statutes and *against* campus hate-speech codes.) When the First Amendment is successfully invoked, the result is not a victory for free speech in the face of a challenge from politics but a *political victory* won by the party that has managed to wrap its agenda in the mantle of free speech.

It is from just such a conclusion – a conclusion that would put politics *inside* the First Amendment – that commentators recoil, saying things like "This could render the First Amendment a dead letter," or "This would leave us with no normative guidance in determining when and what speech to protect," or "This effaces the distinction between speech and action," or "This is incompatible with any viable notion of freedom of expression." To these statements (culled more or less at random from recent law review pieces) I would reply that the First Amendment has always been a dead letter if one understood its "liveness" to depend on the identification and protection of a realm of "mere" expression distinct from the realm of regulatable conduct; the distinction between speech and action has always been effaced in principle, although in practice it can take whatever form the prevailing political conditions mandate; we have never had any normative guidance for marking off protected from unprotected speech; rather, the guidance we have has been fashioned (and refashioned) in the very political struggles over which it then (for a time) presides. In short, the name of the game has always been politics, even when (indeed, especially when) it is played by stigmatizing politics as the area to be avoided.

In saying this, I would not be heard as arguing either for or against regulation and speech codes as a matter of general principle. Instead my argument turns away from general principle to the pragmatic (anti)principle of considering each situation as it emerges. The question of whether or not to regulate will always be a local one, and we cannot rely on abstractions that are either empty of content or filled with the content of some partisan agenda to generate a "principled" answer. Instead we must consider in every case what is at stake and what are the risks and gains of alternative courses of action. In the course of this consideration many things will be of help, but among them will not be phrases like "freedom of speech" or "the right of individual expression," because, as they are used now, these phrases tend to obscure rather than clarify our dilemmas. Once they are deprived of their talismanic force, once it is no longer strategically effective simply to invoke them in the act of walking away from a problem, the conversation could continue in directions that are now blocked by a First Amendment absolutism that has only been honored in the breach anyway. To the student reporter who complains that in the wake of the promulgation of a speech code at the University of Wisconsin there is now something in the back of his mind as he writes, one could reply, "There was always something in the back of your mind, and perhaps it might be better to have this code in the back of your mind than whatever was in there before." And when someone warns about the slippery slope and predicts mournfully that if you restrict one form of speech, you never know what will be restricted next, one could reply, "Some form of speech is always being restricted, else there could be no meaningful assertion; we have always and already slid down the slippery slope; someone is always going to be restricted next, and it is your job to make sure that the someone is not you." And when someone observes, as someone surely will, that antiharassment codes chill speech, one could reply that since speech only becomes intelligible against the background of what isn't being said, the background of what has already been silenced, the only question is the political one of which speech is going to be chilled, and, all things considered, it seems a good thing to chill speech like "nigger," "cunt," "kike," and "faggot." And if someone then says, "But what happened to free-speech principles?" one could say what I have now said a dozen times, free-speech principles don't exist except as a component in a bad argument in which such principles are invoked to mask motives that would not withstand close scrutiny.

An example of a wolf wrapped in First Amendment clothing is an advertisement that ran recently in the Duke University student newspaper, the *Chronicle*. Signed by Bradley R. Smith, well known as a purveyor of anti-Semitic neo-Nazi propaganda, the ad is packaged as a scholarly treatise: four densely packed columns complete with "learned" references, undocumented statistics, and an array of so-called authorities. The message of the ad is that the Holocaust never occurred and that the German state never "had a policy to exterminate the Jewish people (or anyone else) by putting them to death in gas chambers." In a spectacular instance of the increasingly popular "blame the victim" strategy, the Holocaust "story" or "myth" is said to have been fabricated in order "to drum up world sympathy for Jewish causes." The "evidence" supporting these assertions is a slick blend of supposedly probative facts – "not a single autopsied body has been shown to be gassed" – and sly insinuations of a kind familiar to readers of *Mein Kampf* and *The Protocols of the Elders of Zion*. The slickest thing of all, however, is the presentation of the argument as an exercise in free speech – the ad is subtitled "The Case for Open Debate" – that could be objected to only by "thought police" and censors. This strategy bore immediate fruit in the decision of the newspaper staff to accept the ad despite a long-standing (and historically honored) policy of refusing materials that contain ethnic and racial slurs or are otherwise offensive. The reasoning of the staff (explained by the editor in a special column) was that under the First Amendment advertisers have the "right" to be published. "American newspapers are built on the principles of free speech and free press, so how can a newspaper deny these rights to anyone?" The answer to this question is that an advertiser is not denied his rights simply because a single media organ declines his copy so long as other avenues of publication are available and there has been no state suppression of his views. This is not to say that there could not be a case for printing the ad, only that the case cannot rest on a supposed First Amendment obligation. One might argue, for example, that printing the ad would foster healthy debate, or that lies are more likely to be shown up for what they are if they are brought to the light of day, but these are precisely the arguments the editor *disclaims* in her eagerness to take a "principled" free-speech stand.

What I find most distressing about this incident is not that the ad was printed but that it was printed by persons who believed it to be a lie and a distortion. If the editor and her staff were in agreement with Smith's views or harbored serious doubts about the reality of the Holocaust, I would still have a quarrel with them, but it would be a different quarrel; it would be a quarrel about evidence, credibility, documentation. But since on these matters the editors and I are in agreement, my quarrel is with the reasoning that led them to act in opposition to what they believed to be true. That reasoning, as I understand it, goes as follows: although we ourselves are certain that the Holocaust was a fact, facts are notoriously interpretable and disputable; therefore nothing is ever really settled, and we have no right to reject something just because we regard it as pernicious and false. But the fact – if I can use that word – that settled truths can always be upset, at least theoretically, does not mean that we cannot affirm and rely on truths that according to our present lights seem indisputable; rather, it means exactly the opposite: in the absence of absolute certainty of the kind that can only be provided by revelation (something I do not rule out but have not yet experienced), we must act on the basis of the certainty we have so far achieved. Truth may, as Milton said, always be in the course of emerging, and we must always be on guard against being so beguiled by its present shape that we ignore contrary evidence; but, by the same token, when it happens that the present shape of truth is compelling beyond a reasonable doubt, it is our moral obligation to act on it and not defer action in the name of an inter-pretative future that may never arrive. By running the First Amendment up the nearest flagpole and rushing to salute it, the student editors defaulted on that obligation and gave over their responsibility to a so-called principle that was not even to the point.

Let me be clear. I am not saying that First Amendment principles are inherently bad (they are *inherently* nothing), only that they are not always the appropriate reference point for situations involving the production of speech, and that even when they are the appropriate reference point, they do not constitute a politics-free perspective because the shape in which they are invoked will always be political, will always, that is, be the result of having drawn the relevant line (between speech and action, or between high-value speech and low-value speech, or between words essential to the expression of ideas and fighting words) in a way that is favorable to some interests and indifferent or hostile to others. This having been said, the moral is not that First Amendment talk should be abandoned, for even if the standard First Amendment formulas do not and could not perform the function expected of them (the elimination of political considerations in decisions about speech), they still serve a function that is not at all negligible: they slow down outcomes in an area in which the fear of overhasty outcomes is justified by a long record of abuses of power. It is often said that history shows (itself a formula) that even a minimal restriction on the right of expression too easily leads to ever-larger restrictions; and to the extent that this is an empirical fact (and it is a question one could debate), there is some comfort and protection to be found in a procedure that requires you to jump through hoops – do a lot of argumentative work – before a speech regulation will be allowed to stand.

I would not be misunderstood as offering the notion of "jumping through hoops" as a new version of the First Amendment claim to neutrality. A hoop must have a shape – in this case the shape of whatever binary distinction is representing First Amendment "interests" – and the shape of the hoop one is asked to jump through will in part determine what kinds of jumps can be regularly made. Even if they are only mechanisms for slowing down outcomes, First Amendment formulas by virtue of their substantive content (and it is impossible that they be without content) will slow down some outcomes more easily than others, and that means that the form they happen to have at the present moment will favor some interests more than others. Therefore, even with a reduced sense of the effectivity of First Amendment rhetoric (it can not assure any particular result), the counsel with which I began remains relevant: so long as so-called free-speech principles have been fashioned by your enemy (so long as it is *his* hoops you have to jump through), contest their relevance to the issue at hand; but if you manage to refashion them in line with your purposes, urge them with a vengeance.

It is a counsel that follows from the thesis that there is no such thing as free speech, which is not, after all, a thesis as startling or corrosive as may first have seemed. It merely says that there is no class of utterances separable from the world of conduct and that therefore the identification of some utterances as members of that nonexistent class will always be evidence that a political line has been drawn rather than a line that denies politics entry into the forum of public discourse. It is the job of the First Amendment to mark out an area in which competing views can be considered without state interference; but if the very marking out of that area is itself an interference (as it always will be), First Amendment jurisprudence is inevitably self-defeating and subversive of its own aspirations. That's the bad news. The good news is that precisely *because* speech is never "free" in the two senses required – free of consequences and free from state pressure – speech always matters, is always doing work; because every-thing we say impinges on the world in ways indistinguishable from the effects of physical action, we must take responsibility for our verbal performances – *all* of them – and not assume that they are being taken care of by a clause in the Constitution. Of course, with responsibility comes risks, but they have always been our risks, and no doctrine of free speech has ever insulated us from them. They are the risks, respectively, of permitting speech that does obvious harm and of shutting off speech in ways that might deny us the benefit of Joyce's *Ulysses* or Lawrence's *Lady Chatterley's Lover* or Titian's paintings. Nothing, I repeat, can insulate us from those risks. (If there is no normative guidance in determining when and what speech to protect, there is no normative guidance in determining what is art – like free speech a category that includes everything and nothing – and what is obscenity.) Moreover, nothing can provide us with a principle for deciding which risk in the long run is the best to take. I am persuaded that at the present moment, right now, the risk of not attending to hate speech is greater than the risk that by regulating it we will deprive ourselves of valuable voices and insights or slide down the slippery slope toward tyranny. This is a judgment for which I can offer reasons but no guarantees. All I am saying is that the judgments of those who would come down on the other side carry no guarantees either. They urge us to put our faith in apolitical abstractions, but the abstractions they invoke – the market-place of ideas, speech alone, speech itself – only come in political guises, and therefore in trusting to them we fall (unwittingly) under the sway of the very forces we wish to keep at bay. It is not that there are no choices to make or means of making them; it is just that the choices as well as the means are inextricable from the din and confusion of partisan struggle. There is no safe place.

Postscript

When a shorter version of this essay was first published, it drew a number of indignant letters from readers who took me to be making a *recommendation*: let's abandon principles, or let's dispense with an open mind. But, in fact, I am not making a recommendation but declaring what I take to be an unavoidable truth. That truth is not that freedom of speech should be abridged but that freedom of speech is a conceptual impossibility because the condition of speech's being free in the first place is unrealizable. That condition corresponds to the hope, represented by the often-invoked "marketplace of ideas," that we can fashion a forum in which ideas can be considered independently of political and ideological constraint. My point, not engaged by the letters, is that constraint of an ideological kind is *generative* of speech and that therefore the very intelligibility of speech (as assertion rather than noise) is radically depend-ent on what free-speech ideologues would push away. Absent some already-in-place and (for the time being) unquestioned ideological vision, the act of speaking would make no sense, because it would not be resonating against any background understanding of the possible courses of physical or verbal actions and their possible consequences. Nor is that background accessible to the speaker it constrains; it is not an object of his or her critical self-conscious-ness; rather, it constitutes the field in which consciousness occurs, and therefore the productions of consciousness, and specifically speech, will always be poli-tical (that is, angled) in ways the speaker cannot know.

In response to this, someone might say (although the letters here discussed do not rise to this level) that even if speech is inescapably political in my somewhat rarified sense, it is still possible and desirable to provide a cleared space in which irremediably political utterances can compete for the public's approval without any one of them being favored or stigmatized in advance. But what the history of First Amendment jurisprudence shows is that the decisions as to what should or should not enjoy that space's protection and the determination of how exactly (under what rules) that space will first be demarcated and then administered are continually matters of dispute; moreover, the positions taken in the dispute are, each of them, intelligible and compelling only from the vantage point of a deeply assumed ideology, which, like the ideology of speech in general, dare not, and indeed cannot, speak its name. The structure that is supposed to permit ideological/political agendas to fight it out fairly – on a level playing field that has not been rigged – is itself always ideologically and politically constructed. This is exactly the conclusion reached reluctantly by Robert Post in a piece infinitely more nuanced than the letter he now writes. At the end of a long and rigorous analysis, Post finds before him "the startling proposition that the boundaries of public discourse cannot be fixed in a neutral fashion" ("The Constitutional Concept of Public Discourse: Outrageous Opinion, Democratic Deliberation, and *Hustler v. Falwell*," *Harvard Law Review* 103, no. 3 [January 1990]: 683). "The ultimate fact of ideological regulation," he adds, "cannot be blinked." Indeed not, since the ultimate fact is also the *root* fact in the sense that one cannot get behind it or around it, and that is why the next strategy – the strategy of saying, "Well, we can't get beyond or around ideology, but at least we can make a good faith try" – won't work either. In what cleared and ideology-free space will the "try" be made? one must ask, and if the answer is (and it must be by Post's own conclusion) that there is no such cleared space, the notion of "trying" can have no real content. (On a more leisurely occasion I would expand this point into an argument for the emptiness of any gesture that invokes a regulative ideal.)

No such thing as free (nonideologically constrained) speech; no such thing as a public forum purged of ideological pressures or exclusions. That's my thesis, and waiting at the end (really at the beginning) of it is, as my respondents have said, politics. Not, however, politics as the dirty word it becomes in most First Amendment discussions, but politics as the attempt to implement some partisan vision. I place the word "vision" after "partisan" so as to forestall the usual reading of partisan as "unprincipled," the reading Post attributes to me when he finds me "writing on the assumption that there is some implicit and mutually exclusive dichotomy between politics and principle." In fact, my argument is exactly the reverse: since it is only from within a commitment to some particular (not abstract) agenda that one feels the deep urgency we identify as "principled," politics is the *source* of principle, not its opposite. When two agendas square off, the contest is never between politics and principle but between two forms of politics, or, if you prefer, two forms of principle. The assumption of an antagonism between them is not mine, but Post's, and it is an assumption he doubles when he warns of the danger of "unprincipled self-assertion." This is to imagine selves as possibly motivated by "mere" preference, but (and this is the same point I have already made) preference is never "mere" in the sense of being without a moral or philosophical rationale; preference is the precipitate of some defensible (and, of course, challengeable) agenda, and selves who assert it, rather than being unprincipled, are at that moment extensions of principle. Again, it is Post, not me, who entertains a picture of human beings "as merely a collection of Hobbesian appetites." I see human beings in the grip of deep (if debatable) commitments, commitments so constitutive of their thoughts and actions that they cannot help being sincere. Franklin Haiman and Cushing Strout (two other correspondents) could not be more off the mark when they brand me cynical and opportunistic. They assume I am counseling readers to set aside principle in favor of motives that are merely political, whereas in fact I am challenging that distinction and counseling readers (the counsel is superfluous) to act on what they believe to be true and important, and not to be stymied by a doctrine that is at once incoherent and (because incoherent) a vehicle for covert politics.

In general, the letter writers ignore my challenge to the binaries on which their arguments depend, and take to chiding me for failing to respect distinctions whose lack of cogency has been a large part of my point. Thus, Professor Haiman solemnly informs me that an open mind is not the same as an empty one; but, in my analysis – which Professor Haiman is of course not obliged to accept but is surely obliged to note – they *are* the same. An open mind is presumably a mind not unduly committed to its present contents, but a mind so structured, or, rather, *un*structured, would lack a framework or in-place background in relation to which the world (both of action and speech) would be intelligible. A mind so open that it was anchored by no assumptions, no convictions of the kind that order and stabilize perception, would be a mind without gestalt and therefore without the capacity of keeping anything *in*. A consciousness not shored up at one end by a belief (not always the same one) whose negation it could not think would be a sieve. In short, it would be empty.

Professor Strout ventures into the same (incoherent) territory when he takes me to task for "confusing toleration with endorsing" and "justifying" with "putting up with." The idea is that a policy of allowing hate speech does not constitute approval of hate speech but shifts the responsibility for approving or disapproving to the free choice of free individuals. But this is to assume that the machinery of deliberation in individuals is purely formal and is unaffected by what is or is not in the cultural air. Such an assumption is absolutely necessary to the liberal epistemology shared by my respondents, but it is one that I reject because, as I have argued elsewhere, the context of deliberation is cultural (rather than formal or genetic), and because it is cultural, the outcome of deliberation cannot help being influenced by whatever notions are current in the culture. (Minds are not free, as the liberal epistemology implies, for the same reason that they cannot be open.) The fact that David Duke was rudely and provocatively questioned by reporters on "Sixty Minutes" or "Meet the Press" was less important than the fact that he was on "Sixty Minutes" and "Meet the Press" in the first place, for these appearances legitimized him and put his views into national circulation in a way that made them an unavoidable component of the nation's thinking. Tolerating may be different from endorsing from the point of view of the tolerator, who can then disclaim responsibility for the effects of what he has not endorsed, but, if the effects are real and consequential, as I argue they are, the difference may be cold comfort.

It is, of course, *effects* that the liberal epistemology, as represented by a strong free-speech position, cannot take into account, or can take into account only at the outer limits of public safety ("clear and imminent danger," "incitement to violence"). It is, therefore, perfectly apt for Professor Haiman to cite Holmes's dissent in *Abrams*, for that famous opinion at once concisely states the modern First Amendment position and illustrates what I consider to be its difficulties, if not its contradictions. Holmes begins by acknowledging the truth basic to my argument: it makes perfect sense to desire the silencing of beliefs inimical to yours, because if you did not so desire, it would be an indication that you did not believe in your beliefs. But then Holmes takes note of the fact that one's beliefs are subject to change, and comes to the skeptical conclusion that since the course of change is unpredictable, it would be unwise to institutionalize beliefs we may not hold at a later date; instead, we should leave the winnowing process to the marketplace of ideas unregulated by transient political pressures.

This sounds fine (even patriotic), but it runs afoul of problems at both ends. The "entry" problem is the one I have already identified in my reply to Professor Post: the marketplace of ideas – the protected forum of public discourse – will be structured by the same political considerations it was designed to hold at bay; and therefore, the workings of the marketplace will not be free in the sense required, that is, be uninflected by governmental action (the government is given the task of managing the marketplace and therefore the opportunity to determine its contours). Things are even worse at the other end, the exit or no-exit end. If our commitment to freedom of speech is so strong that it obliges us, as Holmes declares, to tolerate "opinions . . . we . . . believe to be fraught with death" (a characterization that recognizes the awful consequentiality of speech and implicitly undercuts any speech/action distinction), then we are being asked to court our own destruction for the sake of an abstraction that may doom us rather than save us. There are really only three alternatives: either Holmes does not mean it, as is suggested by his instant qualification ("unless . . . an immediate check is required to save the country"), or he means it but doesn't think that opinions fraught with death could ever triumph in a free market (in which case he commits himself to a progressivism he neither analyzes nor declares), or he means it and thinks deadly opinions could, in fact, triumph, but is saying something like *"qué será, será,"* (as it would appear he is in a later dissent, *Gitlow v. New York*). Each of these readings of what Holmes is telling us in *Abrams* and *Gitlow* is problematic, and it is the problems in the position born out of these two dissents that have been explored in my essay. The replies to that essay, as far as I can see, do not address those problems but continue simply to rehearse the pieties my analysis troubles. Keep those cards and letters coming.

7

The Law Wishes to Have a Formal Existence

Paradox governs this 1991 essay in which Stanley Fish explores inconsistencies in the law. Weaving through layers of juristic incongruity in discussions of two fraught issues in contract law – the parol evidence rule and consideration – Fish shows that the deleterious influence of morality and the dangerously compromising possibility of interpretation that legal formalists fear erode the law are in fact what gives the law a formal existence in the first place. Fish argues that what governs court decisions is not the unambiguous application of law, but rather the most favorable or convincing narrative; like the courts, Fish also appeals to narrative as the most salutary story, as his way of accounting for how the law can function pragmatically within its thorny field of paradox and self-contradiction. Unable to resist resolving the apparent impasses exposed by a critical (even deconstructive) reading of case law, statute, and legal commentary, Fish offers his own narrative resolution to the paradoxes of law, legal philosophy, and the practice of critical legal studies.

This essay enters a debate about the status of the law, engaged in by legal formalists, natural law theorists, and critical legal theorists. What makes the law law, as Fish demonstrates, is paradoxically a function of how we approach the law. The law, which legal formalists wish to be self-evident with a plain, clear meaning that needs no interpretation, only enjoys its existence as law because of the activities of interpretation it invites. Exploring the contradictions in the parol evidence rule (wherein evidence of contracting parties' intentions or corollary agreements cannot be used to interpret the terms of an unambiguous written instrument), Fish shows that the rule paradoxically invites the interpretation of otherwise "unambiguous" contracts through the necessary admission of parol evidence. Demonstrating through case analysis that courts generally reach the result they wish by accepting the most plausible narrative offered by litigants, Fish suggests that the seeming "constraint" imposed by the parol evidence rule is not only something the courts can always work around, but that working around the constraint is actually what produces the law's formal existence.

Fish's paradoxical conclusion – "efficacious formalisms – marks and sounds that declare meanings to which all relevant parties attest – are always the product of the forces – desire, will, intentions, circumstances, interpretation – they are meant to hold in check" – paradoxically provides a model for a perspicacious critical legal study, an approach Fish characterizes throughout the essay as typically one that sees law's contradictions as a bar to its functioning. Situating his own argument as beyond any specific camp, the largest paradox of the essay is that Fish, through his merciless deconstructive readings, is perhaps the most critical of legal theorists, but also the most conciliatory and perhaps the most judicial, appealing to the sophisticated logic of the law's use of narrative as a way to adjudicate the dispute between formalists and critical legal scholars.

Judith Roof

Achieving Plain and Clear Meanings

The law wishes to have a formal existence. That means, first of all, that the law does not wish to be absorbed by, or declared subordinate to, some other – nonlegal – structure of concern; the law wishes, in a word, to be distinct, not something else. And second, the law wishes in its distinctness to be perspicuous; that is, it desires that the components of its autonomous existence be self-declaring and not be in need of piecing out by some supplementary discourse; for were it necessary for the law to have recourse to a supplementary discourse at crucial points, that discourse would be in the business of specifying what the law is, and, consequently, its autonomy would have been compromised indirectly. It matters little whether one simply announces that the principles and mechanisms of the law exist ready-made in the articulations of another system or allows those principles and mechanisms to be determined by something they do not contain; in either case, the law as something independent and self-identifying will have disappeared.

In its long history, the law has perceived many threats to its autonomy, but two seem perennial: morality and interpretation. The dangers these two pose are, at least at first glance, different. Morality is something to which the law wishes to be related, but not too closely; a legal system whose conclusions clashed with our moral intuitions at every point so that the categories *legally valid* and *morally right* never (or almost never) coincided would immediately be suspect; but a legal system whose judgments perfectly meshed with our moral intuitions would be thereby rendered superfluous. The point is made concisely by the Supreme Court of Utah in a case where it was argued that the gratuitous payment by one party of the other party's mortgage legally obligated the beneficiary to repay. The court rejected the argument, saying "that if a mere moral, as distinguished from a legal, obligation were recognized as valid consideration for a contract, that would practically erode to the vanishing point the necessity for finding a consideration."[1] That is to say, if one can infer directly from one's moral obligation in a situation to one's legal obligation, there is no work for the legal system to do; the system of morality has already done it. Although it might seem (as it does to many natural law theorists) that such a collapsing of categories recommends itself if only on the basis of efficiency (why have two systems when you can make do with one?), the defender of a distinctly legal realm will quickly answer that since moral intuitions are notoriously various and contested, the identification of law with morality would leave every individual his or her own judge; in place of a single abiding standard to which disputing parties might have recourse, we would have many standards with no way of adjudicating between them. In short, many moralities would make many laws, and the law would lack its most saliently desirable properties, generality and stability.

It is here that the danger posed by morality to law, or, more precisely, to the rule (in two senses) of law intersects with the danger posed by interpretation. The link is to be found in the desire to identify a perspective larger and more stable than the perspective of local and individual concerns. Morality frustrates that desire because, in a world of more than one church, recourse to morality will always be recourse to someone's or some group's challengeable moral vision. Interpretation frustrates that desire because, in the pejorative sense it usually bears in these discussions, interpretation is the name for what happens when the meanings embedded in an object or text are set aside in favor of the meanings demanded by some angled, partisan object. Interpretation, in this view, is the effort of a morality, of a particular, interested agenda, to extend itself into the world by inscribing its message on every available space. It follows then that, in order to check the imperial ambitions of particular moralities, some point of resistance to interpretation must be found, and that is why the doctrine of formalism has proved so attractive. Formalism is the thesis that it is possible to put down marks so self-sufficiently perspicuous that they repel interpretation; it is the thesis that one can write sentences of such precision and simplicity that their meanings leap off the page in a way no one – no matter what his or her situation or point of view – can ignore; it is the thesis that one can devise procedures that are self-executing in the sense that their unfolding is independent of the differences between the agents who might set them in motion. In the presence (in the strong Derridean sense) of such a mark or sentence or procedure, the interpretive will is stopped short and is obliged to press its claims within the constraints provided by that which it cannot override. It must take the marks into account; it must respect the self-declaring reasons; it must follow the route laid down by the implacable procedures, and if it then wins it will have done so fairly, with justice, with reason.

Obviously then, formalism's appeal is a function of the number of problems it solves, or at least appears to solve: it provides the law with a palpable manifestation of its basic claim to be perdurable and general; that is, not shifting and changing, but standing as a point of reference in relation to which change can be assessed and controlled; it enables the law to hold contending substantive agendas at bay by establishing threshold requirements of procedure that force those agendas to assume a shape the system will recognize. The idea is that once a question has been posed as a *legal* question – has been put into the proper *form* – the answer to it will be generated by relations of entailment between that form and other forms in the system. As Hans Kelsen put it in a book aptly named *The Pure Theory of Law*,

The law is an order, and therefore all legal problems must be set and solved as order problems. In this way legal theory becomes an exact structural analysis of positive law, free of all ethical-political value judgments.[2]

Kelsen's last clause says it all: the realms of the ethical, the political, and of value in general are the threats to the law's integrity. They are what must be kept out if the law is to be something more than a misnomer for the local (and illegitimate) triumph of some particular point of view.

There are at least two strong responses to this conception of law. The first, which we might call the "humanistic" response, objects that a legal system so conceived is impoverished, and that once you have severed procedures from value, it will prove enormously difficult, if not impossible, to relink them in particular cases. Since the answers generated by a purely formal system will be empty of content (that, after all, is the formalist claim), the reintroduction of content will always be arbitrary. The second response, which we might call "radical" or "critical," would simply declare that a purely formal system is not a possibility, and that any system pretending to that status is already informed by that which it purports to exclude. Value, of both an ethical and political kind, is already inside the gate, and the adherents of the system are either ignorant of its sources or are engaged in a political effort to obscure them in the course of laying claim to a spurious purity. In what follows, I shall be elaborating a version of the second response, and arguing that however much the law wishes to have a formal existence, it cannot succeed in doing so, because – at any level from the most highly abstract to the most particular and detailed – any specification of what the law is will already be infected by interpretation and will therefore be challengeable. Nevertheless, my conclusion will not be that the law fails to have a formal existence but that, in a sense I shall explain, it always succeeds, although the nature of that success – it is a political/rhetorical achievement – renders it bitter to the formalist taste.

We may see what is at stake in disputes about formalism by turning to a recent (July, 1988) opinion delivered by Judge Alex Kozinski of the United States Court of Appeals for the Ninth Circuit.[3] The case involved the desire of a construction partnership called Trident Center to refinance a loan at rates more favorable than those originally secured. Unfortunately (or so it seemed), language in the original agreement expressly blocked such an action, to wit that the "'[m]aker shall not have the right to prepay the principal amount hereof in whole or in part' for the first 12 years."[4]

Trident's attorneys, however, pointed to another place in the writing where it is stipulated that "[i]n the event of a prepayment resulting from a default . . . prior to January 10, 1996 the prepayment fee will be ten percent"[5] and argued that this clause gives Trident the option of prepaying the loan provided that it is willing to incur the penalty as stated. Kozinski is singularly unimpressed by this reasoning, and, as he himself says, dismisses it "out of hand,"[6] citing as his justification the clear and unambiguous language of the contract. Referring to Trident's contention that it is entitled to precipitate a default by tendering the balance plus the ten percent fee, Kozinski declares that "the contract language, cited above, leaves no room for this construction,"[7] a judgment belied by the fact that Trident's lawyers managed to make room for just that construction in their arguments. It is a feature of cases like this that turn on the issue of what is and is not "expressly" said that the proclamation of an undisputed meaning always occurs in the midst of a dispute about it. Given Kozinski's rhetorical stance, the mere citation (his word, and a very dangerous one for his position) of the contract language should be sufficient to end all argument, but what he himself immediately proceeds to do is argue, offering a succession of analyses designed to buttress his contention that "it is difficult to imagine language that more clearly or unambiguously expresses the idea that Trident may not uni-laterally [more is given away by this word than Kozinski acknowledges] prepay the loan during its first 12 years."[8] If this were in fact so, it would be difficult to imagine why Kozinski should feel compelled to elaborate his opinion again and again. I shall not take up his points except to say that, in general, they are not

particularly persuasive and usually function to open up just the kind of interpretive room he declares unavailable. Thus, for example, he reasons that
Trident's interpretation "would result in a contradiction between two clauses
of the contract" whereas the "normal rule of construction... is that courts
must interpret contracts, if possible, so as to avoid internal conflict."[9] But it is
no trick at all (or at least not a hard one) to treat the two clauses so that they
refer to different anticipated situations and are not contradictory (indeed that is
what Trident's lawyers do): in the ordinary course of things, as defined by the
rate and schedule of payments set down in the contract, Trident will not have
the option of prepaying; but in the extraordinary event of a default, the
prepayment penalty clause will then kick in. To be sure, Kozinski is ready
with objections to this line of argument, but those objections themselves trace
out a line of argument and operate (no less than the interpretations he rejects)
to fill out the language whose self-sufficiency he repeatedly invokes.

In short (and this is a point I shall make often), Kozinski's assertion of ready-
made, formal constraints is belied by his efforts to stabilize what he supposedly
relies on, the plain meaning of absolutely clear language. The act of construction for which he says there is no room is one he is continually performing.
Moreover, he performs it in a way no different from the performance he
castigates. Trident, he complains, is attempting "to obtain judicial sterilization
of its intended default,"[10] and the reading its lawyers propose is an extension of
that attempt rather than a faithful rendering of what the document says. The
implication is that *his* reading is the extension of nothing, proceeds from no
purpose except the purpose to be scrupulously literal. But his very next words
reveal another, less disinterested purpose: "But defaults are messy things and
they are supposed to be.... Fear of these repercussions is strong medicine that
keeps debtors from shirking their obligations...."[11] And he is, of course, now
administering that strong medicine through his reading, a reading that is
produced not by the agreement, but by his antecedent determination to
enforce contracts whenever he can. The contrast then is not (as he attempts
to draw it) between a respect for what "the contract clearly does... provide"[12]
and the bending of the words to an antecedently held purpose, but between
two bendings, one of which by virtue of its institutional positioning – Kozinski
is after all the judge – wins the day.

Except that it doesn't. In the second half of the opinion there is a surprise
turn, one that alerts us to the larger issue Kozinski sees in the case and explains
the vehemence (often close to anger) of his language. The turn is that Kozinski
rules for Trident, setting aside the district court's declaration that the clear and
unambiguous nature of the document leaves Trident with no cause of action
and setting aside, too, the same court's sanction of Trident for the filing of a
frivolous lawsuit. In so doing Kozinski is responding to Trident's second

argument, which is that "even if the language of the contract appears to be unambiguous, the deal the parties actually struck is in fact quite different" and that "extrinsic evidence" shows "that the parties had agreed Trident could prepay at any time within the first 12 years by tendering the full amount plus a 10 percent prepayment fee."[13] Kozinski makes it clear that he would like to reject this argument and rely on the traditional contract principle of the parol evidence rule, the rule (not of evidence but of law) by which "extrinsic evidence is inadmissible to interpret, vary or add to the terms of an unambiguous integrated written instrument."[14] He concedes, however, that this rule has not been followed in California since *Pacific Gas & Electric Co. v. G. W. Thomas Drayage & Rigging Co.*,[15] a case in which the state supreme court famously declared that there is no such thing as a clear and unambiguous document because it is not "feasible to determine the meaning the parties gave to the words from the instrument alone."[16] In other words (mine, not the court's), an instrument that seems clear and unambiguous on its face seems so because "extrinsic evidence" – information about the conditions of its production including the situation and state of mind of the contracting parties, etc. – is already in place and assumed as a background; that which the parol evidence rule is designed to exclude is already, and necessarily, invoked the moment writing becomes intelligible. In a bravura gesture, Kozinski first expresses his horror at this doctrine ("it . . . chips away at the foundation of our legal system")[17] and then flaunts it by complying with it.

While we have our doubts about the wisdom of *Pacific Gas*, we have no difficulty understanding its meaning, even without extrinsic evidence to guide us . . . we must reverse and remand to the district court in order to give plaintiff an opportunity to present extrinsic evidence as to the intentions of the parties.[18]

That is, "you say that words cannot have clear and constant meanings and that, therefore, extrinsic evidence cannot be barred; I think you are wrong and I hereby refute you by adhering strictly to the rule your words have laid down."

But of course he hasn't. The entire history of the parol evidence rule – the purposes it supposedly serves, the fears to which it is a response, the hopes of which it is a repository – constitutes the extrinsic evidence within whose assumption the text of the case makes the sense Kozinski labels "literal." When he prefaces his final gesture (the judicial equivalent of "up yours") by saying "As we read the rule," he acknowledges that it is *reading* and not simply receiving that he is doing.[19] And to acknowledge as much is to acknowledge that *Pacific Gas* could be read differently. Nevertheless, the challenge Kozinski issues to the Traynor court is pertinent; for what he is saying is that the question of whether or not it is possible to produce " 'a perfect verbal expression' "[20] – an expression that will serve as a "meaningful constraint on public and private conduct"[21] – will not be settled by the pronouncement of a court. Either it is or it isn't; either a court or a legislature or a constitutional convention can order words in such a way as to constrain what interpreters can then do with them or it cannot. The proof will be in the pudding, in what happens to texts or parts of texts that are the repository of that (formalist) hope. The parol evidence rule will not have the desired effect if no one could possibly follow it.

That this is, in fact, the case is indicated by the very attempt to formulate the rule. Consider, for example, the formulation found in section 2–202 of the Uniform Commercial Code.

Terms with respect to which the confirmatory memoranda of the parties agree or which are otherwise set forth in a writing intended by the parties as a final expression of their agreement with respect to such terms as are included therein may not be contradicted by evidence of any prior agreement or of a contemporaneous oral agreement but may be explained or supplemented.

(a) by course of dealing or usage of trade (Section 1–205) or by course of performance (Section 2–208); and

(b) by evidence of consistent additional terms unless the court finds the writing to have been intended also as a complete and exclusive statement of the terms of the agreement.[22]

One could pause at almost any place to bring the troubles lying in wait for would-be users of this section to the surface, beginning perhaps with the juxtaposition of "writing" and "intended," which reproduces the conflict supposedly being adjudicated. (Is the writing to pronounce on its own meaning and completeness or are we to look beyond it to the intentions of the parties?) Let me focus, however, on the distinction between explaining or supplementing and contradicting or varying. The question is how can you tell whether a disputed piece of evidence is one or the other? And the answer is that you could only tell if the document in relation to which the evidence was to be labeled one or the other declared its own meaning; for only then could you look at "it" and then at the evidence and proclaim the evidence either explanatory or contradictory. But if the meaning and completeness of the document were self-evident (a wonderfully accurate phrase), explanatory evidence would be superfluous and the issue would never arise. And on the other hand, if the document's significance and state of integration are not self-evident – if "it" is not complete but must be pieced out in order to become what "it" is – then the relation to "it" of a piece of so-called extrinsic evidence can only be determined after the evidence has been admitted and is no longer extrinsic. Either there is no problem or it can only be solved by recourse to that which is in dispute.

Exactly the same fate awaits the distinction between "consistent additional terms" and additional terms that are inconsistent. "Consistent in relation to what?" is the question; the answer is "consistent in relation to the writing." But if the writing were clear enough to establish its own terms, additional terms would not be needed to explain it (subsection *[b]*, you will remember, is an explanation of "explained or supplemented"), and if additional terms are needed there is not yet anything for them to be consistent or inconsistent with. The underlying point here has to do with the distinction – assumed but never examined in these contexts – between inside and outside, between what the document contains and what is external to it. What becomes clear is that the determination of what is "inside" will always be a function of whatever "outside" has already been assumed. (I use quotation marks to indicate that the distinction is interpretive, not absolute.) As one commentary puts it, "questions concerning the admissibility of parol evidence cannot be resolved without considering the nature and scope of the evidence which is being offered," and "thus the court must go beyond the writing to determine whether the writing should be held to be a final expression of the parties' . . . agreement."[23]

Nowhere is this more obvious than in the matter of *trade usage*, the first body of knowledge authorized as properly explanatory by the code. Trade usage refers to conventions of meaning routinely employed by members of a trade or industry, and is contrasted to *ordinary usage*, that is, to the meanings words ordinarily have by virtue of their place in the structure of English. The willingness of courts to regard trade usage as legitimately explanatory of contract language seems only a minor concession to the desire of the law to find a public – i.e., objective – linguistic basis, but in fact it is fatal, for it opens up a door that cannot be (and never has been) closed. In a typical trade usage case, one party is given the opportunity to "prove" that the words of an agreement don't mean what they seem to mean because they emerged from a special context, a context defined by the parties' expectations. Thus, for example, in one case it was held that, by virtue of trade usage, the shipment term "June–Aug." in an agreement was to be read as excluding delivery in August;[24] and in another case the introduction of trade usage led the court to hold that an order for thirty-six-inch steel was satisfied by the delivery of steel measuring thirty-seven inches.[25] But if "June–Aug." can, in certain persuasively established circumstances, be understood to exclude August, and "thirty-six" can be understood as meaning thirty-seven, then anything, once a sufficiently elaborated argument is in place, can mean anything: "thirty-six" could mean seventy-five, or, in relation to a code so firmly established that it governed the expectations of the parties, "thirty-six" could mean detonate the atomic bomb.

If this line of reasoning seems to slide down the slippery slope too precipitously, consider the oft cited case of *Columbia Nitrogen Corporation v. Royster*

Company.[26] The two firms had negotiated a contract by which Columbia would purchase from Royster 31,000 tons of phosphate each year for three years, with an option to extend the term. The agreement was marked by "detailed provisions regarding the base price, escalation, minimum tonnage and delivery schedules,"[27] but when phosphate prices fell, Columbia ordered and accepted only one-tenth of what was specified. Understandably, Royster sued for breach of contract, and was awarded a judgment of $750,000 in district court. Columbia appealed, contending that, in the fertilizer industry.

> because of uncertain crop and weather conditions, farming practices, and government agricultural programs, express price and quantity terms in contracts ... are mere projections to be adjusted according to market forces.[28]

One would think that this argument would fail because it would amount to saying that the contract was not worth the paper it was printed on. If emerging circumstances could always be invoked as controlling, even in the face of carefully negotiated terms, why bother to negotiate? Royster does not make this point directly, but attempts to go the (apparently) narrower route of section 202. After all, even trade usage is inadmissible according to that section if it contradicts, rather than explains, the terms of the agreement, and as one authority observes, "it is hard to imagine a ... 'trade usage' that contradicts a stated contractual term more directly than did the usage in *Columbia Nitrogen Corporation.*"[29] The court, however, doesn't see it that way. Although the opinion claims to reaffirm "the well established rule that evidence of usage of trade ... should be excluded whenever it cannot be reasonably construed as consistent with the terms of the contract,"[30] the reaffirmation undoes itself; for by making the threshold of admissibility the production of a "reasonable construal" rather than an obvious inconsistency (as in 31,000 is inconsistent with 3,100), the court more or less admits that what is required to satisfy the section is not a demonstration of formal congruity but an exercise of rhetorical skill. As long as one party can tell a story sufficiently overarching so as to allow the terms of the contract and the evidence of trade usage to fit comfortably within its frame, that evidence will be found consistent rather than contradictory. What is and is not a "reasonable construal" will be a function of the persuasiveness of the construer and not of any formal fact that is perspicuous before some act of persuasion has been performed.

The extent to which this court is willing to give scope to the exercise of rhetorical ingenuity is indicated by its final dismissal of the contention by Royster that there is nothing in the contract about adjusting its terms to reflect a declining market. "Just so," says the court, there is nothing in the contract about this and that is why its introduction is not a contradiction or inconsistency. Since "the contract is silent about adjusting prices and quantities ... it neither permits or prohibits adjustment, and this neutrality provides a fitting occasion for recourse to usage of trade ... to supplement the contract and explain its terms."[31] Needless to say, as an interpretive strategy this could work to authorize almost anything, and it is itself authorized by the first of the official comments on section 202 (and why a section designed supposedly to establish the priority of completely integrated writings is itself in need of commentary is a question almost too obvious to ask): "This section definitely rejects (a) any assumption that because a writing has been worked out which is final on some matters, it is to be taken as including all the matters agreed upon."[32] Or in other words, just because a writing says something doesn't mean that it says everything relevant to the matter; it may be silent on some things, and in relation to those things parol evidence is admissible. But of course the number of things on which a document (however interpreted) is silent is infinite, and consequently there is no end to the information that can be introduced if it can be linked narratively to a document that now becomes a mere component (albeit a significant one) in a larger contractual context.

One way of doing this is exemplified by the majority opinion in *Masterson v. Sine*,[33] a case in which the attempt of a bankruptcy trustee to exercise an option to purchase a particular piece of property (on the grounds that the right of option belongs to the estate) was challenged by parol evidence tending to show that it was the intention of the drafting parties to keep the property in the family (Mr Masterson and Mrs Sine were brother and sister) and "that the option was therefore personal to the grantors and could not be exercised by the trustee."[34] The trial court excluded the evidence, ruling that the written contract was a complete and final embodiment of the terms of the agreement and said nothing about the assignability of the option. The court, in the person of Chief Justice Traynor (the same Traynor who in Kozinski's eyes commits the villainy of *Pacific Gas*), responds by declaring that, yes, "the deed is silent on the question of assignability,"[35] but that this very silence was a reason for admitting the evidence, not as a gloss on the agreement as written, but as proof of a collateral agreement – an agreement made on a related, but adjoining matter – that was entered into orally. The beauty of this recharacterization of the situation is that it manages at once to save the integrity of the integrated agreement and to create another agreement whose honoring has the effect of setting aside what the integrated agreement seems to say. This is all managed by telling another story about the negotiations. The parties conducted not one, but two negotiations; in one, the question of the conveying of the land and the option of the conveyers to repurchase was settled; in another (orally conducted), the question of reserving the option to members of the family was settled. The demands of formalism are at once met and evaded, a result that led two dissenting justices to complain that the parol evidence rule had been eviscerated, that the decision rendered all instruments of conveyance, no matter how full and complete, suspect, and that the reliance one might previously have placed upon written agreements had been materially undermined.

This conclusion might seem to be the one I, myself, was moving toward in the course of presenting these examples, for surely the moral of *Columbia Nitrogen, Warren's Kiddie Shoppe, Dekker Steel, Pacific Gas*, and *Masterson v. Sine* (and countless others that could be adduced) is that the parol evidence rule is wholly ineffective as a stay against interpretive assaults on the express language of contracts and statutes. But the moral I wish to draw goes in quite another direction, one that reaffirms (although not in a way formalists will find comforting) the power both of the parol evidence rule and of the language whose "rights" it would protect, to "provide a meaningful constraint on public and private conduct."[36] It is certainly the case that *Masterson v. Sine*, like *Columbia Nitrogen* and the others, indicates that no matter how carefully a contract is drafted it cannot resist incorporation into a persuasively told story in the course of whose unfolding its significance may be altered from what it had seemed to be. But the same cases also indicate that the story so told cannot be any old story; it must be one that fashions its coherence out of materials that it is required to take into account. The important fact about *Masterson* is not that in it the court succeeds in getting around the parol evidence rule, but that it is the parol evidence rule – and not the first chapter of Genesis or the first law of thermodynamics – that it feels obliged to get around. That is, given the constraints of the institutional setting – constraints that help shape the issue being adjudicated – the court could not proceed on its way without raising and dealing with the parol evidence rule (and this would be true even if the rule had not been invoked by the eager trustee); consequently, the *path* to the result it finally reaches is constrained, in part, by the very doctrine that result will fail to honor.

One sees this clearly in the route the court takes to the discovery that there are not one, but two agreements. It is not enough, the court acknowledges, to observe that if an agreement is silent on a matter, information pertaining to it is admissible, for the official comment to section 2–202 adds that "if the additional terms are such that, if agreed upon, they would certainly have been included in the document in the view of the court, then evidence of their alleged making must be kept from the trier of fact."[37] In other words, the court must determine whether or not the additional terms that would make up a collateral agreement are such that persons contemplating the original agreement would certainly have considered including them; for if they were such and were not included, their exclusion was intentional and the original writing must be regarded as complete. In *Masterson*, the court reasons that the inexperience of the parties in land transactions made it unlikely that they would have been aware "of the disadvantages of failing to put the whole agreement in the deed" and rules that therefore "the case is not one in which the parties 'would certainly' have included the collateral agreement"[38] had they meant to enter into it. Again the point is not so much the persuasiveness of such reasoning (in another landmark case a New York court found the same reasoning unpersuasive),[39] but the fact that it must be produced, and this requirement would have held even if the reasoning had been rejected. It was open to the court (as a note to the case indicates) to find that in a particular instance what the parties would naturally have done was, in fact, not done and that "the unnatural actually happened";[40] but had the court so found, the official comment would have been honored even as it was declared to be inapposite, for that finding (or some other in the same line of country) would have been rendered obligatory by the existence of the comment. It is always possible to "get around" the comment as it is always possible to get around the parol evidence rule – neither presents an absolute bar to reaching a particular result; there is always work that can be done – but the fact that it is the comment you are getting around renders it constraining even if it is not, in the strict sense, a constraint.

In short, the parol evidence rule is of more service to the law's wish to have a formal existence than one might think from these examples. The service it provides, however, is not (as is sometimes claimed) the service of safeguarding a formalism already in place, but the weaker (although more exacting) service of laying down the route by which a formalism can be fashioned. I am aware, of course, that this notion of the formal will seem strange to those for whom a formalism is what is "given" as opposed to something that is made. But, in fact, efficacious formalisms – marks and sounds that declare meanings to which all relevant parties attest – are always the product of the forces – desire, will, intentions, circumstances, interpretation – they are meant to hold in check. No one has seen this more clearly than Arthur Corbin who, noting that "sometimes it is said that 'the courts will not disregard the plain language of a contract or interpolate something not contained in it,'"[41] offers for that dictum this substitute.

If, after a careful consideration of the words of a contract, in the light of all the relevant circumstances, and of all the tentative rules of interpretation based upon the experience of courts and linguists, a plain and definite meaning is achieved by the court, a meaning actually given by one party as the other party had reason to know, it will not disregard this plain and definite meaning and substitute another that is less convincing.[42]

There are many words and phrases one might want to pause over in this remarkable sentence (*relevant, tentative, experience, actually*), but for our purposes the most significant word is *achieved* and, after that, *convincing*. *Achieved* is a surprise because, in most of the literature, a plain meaning is something that constrains or even precludes interpretation, while in Corbin's statement it is something that interpretation helps fashion; once it is fashioned, the parol evidence rule can then be invoked with genuine force: you must not disregard this meaning – that is, the meaning that has been established in the course of the interpretive process – for one that has not been so established. *Convincing* names the required (indeed the only) mode of establishing, the mode of persuasion, and what one is persuaded *to* is an account (story) of the circumstances ("relevant" not before, but as a result of, the account) in relation to which the words of the agreement could only mean one thing. Of course, if an alternative account were to become more rather than less convincing – perhaps in the course of appeal – then the meanings that followed from *its* establishment would be protected by the rule from the claims of meanings to which the court had not been persuaded. As Corbin puts it in another passage, "when a court says that it will enforce a contract in accordance with the 'plain and clear' meaning of its words... the losing party has merely urged the drawing of inferences... that the court is unwilling to draw."[43] That is, the losing party has told an unpersuasive story, and consequently the meanings it urges – i.e., the inferences it would draw – strike the court as strained and obscure rather than plain.

There are, then, two stages to the work done by the parol evidence rule: in the first its presence on the "interpretative scene" works to constrain the path interpreters must take on their way to telling a persuasive story (an account of all the "relevant" circumstances); then, once the story has been persuasively told, the rule is invoked to protect the meanings that flow from that story. The phrase that remains to be filled in is *persuasive story*. What is one and how is it, in Corbin's word, *achieved?* The persuasiveness of a story is not the product merely of the arguments it explicitly presents, but of the relationship between those arguments, and other, more tacit, arguments – tantamount to already-in-place beliefs – that are not so much being urged as they are being traded on. It is this second, recessed, tier of arguments – of beliefs so much a part of the background that they are partly determinative of what will be heard as an argument – that does much of the work of fashioning a persuasive story and, therefore, does much of the work of filling in the category of "plain and clear" meaning. What kinds of arguments or (deep) assumptions are these? It is difficult to generalize (and dangerous, since generalization would hold out the false promise of a *formal* account of persuasion), but one could say first of all that they will include, among other things, beliefs one might want to call "moral" – dispositions as to the way things are or should be as encoded in maxims and slogans like "order must be preserved" or "freedom of expression" or "the American way" or "the Judeo–Christian tradition" or "we must draw the line somewhere." It follows, then, that whenever there is a dispute about the plain meaning of a contract, at some level the dispute is between two (or more) visions of what life is or should be like.

Consider, for example, still another famous case in legal interpretation, *In Re Soper's Estate*.[44] The facts are the stuff of soap opera. After ten years of marriage, Ira Soper faked his suicide and resurfaced in another state under the name of John Young. There he married a widow who died three years later, where-upon he married another widow with whom he lived for five years when he again committed suicide, but this time for real. The litigation turns on an agreement Soper–Young made with a business partner according to which, upon the death of either, the proceeds of the insurance on the life of the deceased would be delivered to his wife. The question of course is who is the wife, Mrs Young or the long-since deserted Mrs Soper, who, to the surprise of everyone, appeared to claim her rightful inheritance.

The majority rules for the second wife, Gertrude, while a strong dissent is registered on behalf of the abandoned Adeline. There is a tendency in both opinions to present the case as if it were a textbook illustration of a classic conflict in contract law between the view (usually associated with Williston) that determinations of the degree of integration and of the meaning of an agreement are to be made by looking to the agreement itself and the view (later to be associated with Corbin) that such issues can only be decided by ascertaining the intentions of the drafting parties, that is, by going outside the agreement to something not in it but in the light of which it is to be read. But, in fact, what the case illustrates is the impossibility of this very distinction. It is the minority that raises the banner of literalism, arguing that since a man can have only one lawful wife and since Adeline was, at the time of the agreement, "the only wife of Soper then living,"[45] the word *wife* must refer to her. The majority replies that by the same standard of literalism, the agreement contains no mention of a Mr Soper, referring only to a Mr Young whose only possible wife was a lady named Gertrude; and indeed, observes Justice Olson, the document can only be read as referring to Adeline by bringing in the same kind of oral evidence her lawyers (and the dissent) now wish to exclude. An inquirer merely looking at the document might well conclude "that two different men are involved," for after all,

in what manner may either establish relationship to the decedent as his "wife" except by means of oral testimony.... Adeline, to establish her relationship, was necessarily required to and did furnish proof, principally oral, that her husband, Ira Collins Soper, was in fact the same individual as John W. Young, [and] Gertrude by similar means sought to establish her claim.[46]

The moral is clear even though the court does not quite draw it: rather than a dispute between a reading confining itself to the document and one that goes outside it to the circumstances from which it emerged, this is a dispute between two opposing accounts of the circumstances. Depending on which of these accounts is the more persuasive – that is, on which of the two stories about the world, responsibility, and wives is firmly in place – the document will acquire one of the two literal meanings being proposed for it. The majority finds itself persuaded by Gertrude's story and thus can quite sincerely declare that the "agreement points to no one else than Gertrude as Young's 'wife,'"[47] and Justice Olsen with an *e* (I resist the temptation to inquire into the *différance* of this difference) can declare with equal sincerity that "I am unable to construe this word to mean anyone else than the only wife of Soper then living."[48] Indeed he *is* unable, since as someone who subscribes to the moral vision that underlies Adeline's claims – a vision in which responsibilities once entered into cannot be weakened by obligations subsequently incurred – *wife* can only refer to the first in what is, for him, a nonseries; just as, for Justice Olson with an *o* – in whose morality obligations in force at the time of agreement take precedence over obligations recognized by a legal formalism – *wife* can only refer to the person "all friends and acquaintances . . . recognized . . . as his wife."[49]

The majority says that the "question is not just what words mean literally but how they are intended to operate practically on the subject matter,"[50] but its own arguments show that words *never* mean literally except in the context of the intention they are presumed to be effecting, and that rather than being determined by the meanings the words already (by right) have, the intentional context – established when one or the other party succeeds in being convincing – determines the meaning of the words. In short, the issue is not nor could ever be the supposed choice between literal and contextual reading, but the relative persuasiveness of alternative contexts as they are set out in ideologically charged narratives. That is why it is no surprise to find Justice Olsen's confident declaration of linguistic clarity ("I am unable to construe") preceded by a rehearsal of the moralizing story that produces that clarity:

Much is said in the opinion as to the wrong done to the innocent woman whom he purported to marry. Nothing is said about the wrong done to the lawful wife. To have her husband abandon her and then purport to marry another, and live in cohabitation with such other, was about as great a wrong as any man could inflict upon his wife.[51]

The majority thinks that something else (setting aside as of no account the relationship between the deceased and Gertrude) is the greater wrong and therefore thinks, like the minority, that the meaning of the agreement is obvious and inescapable. Again, my point is not to discredit the reasoning of either party nor to dismiss the claim of each to have pointed to a formal linguistic fact; rather, I wish only to observe once again that such formal facts are always "achieved" and that they are achieved by the very means – the partisan urging of some ideological vision – to which they are then rhetorically (and not unreasonably) opposed.

Contract's Two Stories

That is to say – and in so saying I rehearse the essence of my argument – the law is continually creating and recreating itself out of the very materials and forces it is obliged, by the very desire to *be* law, to push away. The result is a spectacle that could be described (as the members of the critical legal studies movement tend to do) as farce, but I would describe it differently, as a signal example of the way in which human beings are able to construct the roadway on which they are traveling, even to the extent of "demonstrating" in the course of building it that it was there all the while. The failure of both legal positivists and natural law theorists to find the set of neutral procedures or basic moral principles underlying the law should not be taken to mean that the law is a failure, but rather that it is an amazing kind of success. The history of legal doctrine and its applications is a history neither of rationalistic purity nor of incoherence and bad faith, but an almost Ovidian history of transformation under the pressure of enormously complicated social, political, and economic urgencies, a history in which victory – in the shape of *keeping going* – is always being wrested from what looks like certain defeat, and wrested by means of stratagems that are all the more remarkable because, rather than being hidden, they are almost always fully on display. Not only does the law forge its identity out of the stuff it disdains, it does so in public.

If this is true of the law's relation to interpretation, it is equally true of its relation to morality, as one can readily see by inquiring into the doctrine of consideration. Consideration is a term of art and refers to the "bargain" element in a transaction, what X did or promised to do in return for what Y did or promised to do. It is an article of faith in modern contract law that only agreements displaying consideration – a mutuality of bargained-for exchange – are legally enforceable. The intention of this requirement is to separate the realm of legal obligation from the larger and putatively more subjective realm of moral obligation, and the separation is accomplished (or so it is claimed) by providing *formal* (as opposed to value-laden) criteria of the intention to be legally bound. There are all kinds of reasons why one might make promises or perform actions conferring benefits on another and all kinds of after-the-fact analyses of what the promise signified or what the action contemplated. But if there is something tangible offered in return for something tangible requested, the transaction is a legal one and the machinery of legal obligation kicks in.

The existence of consideration helps to provide *objective evidence* that the parties intended to make a binding agreement. It helps courts distinguish those agreements that were intended by the parties to be legally enforceable from . . . promises of gifts which neither party expected to be enforceable in court.[52]

By demarcating an area of legal obligation that is distinct from and independent of the larger matrix of obligations that make up our social existence, consideration plays a role similar to the role played (if it could be played) by the parol evidence rule. Just as Judge Kozinski says (or wants to say) to *Trident*, "you may not like the agreement you made, you may wish you could have it to do all over again, or that you had employed another negotiating team, but, nevertheless, this is the agreement you signed and this is what it says, and that's all there is to it," so might he or another judge say, "you may repent of your bargain because you know that someone will pay more for the automobile, but you promised to hand it over if he gave you $500; he has given you $500 and you must hand it over." Like absolutely express language (if there could be such a thing), consideration is a device for severing the moment of legal transaction from its surrounding circumstances and reducing it to a form that will stand out over the circumstances in which it is later examined by a court.

Consideration is, thus, a part of the law's general effort to disengage itself from history and assume (in two senses) a shape that time cannot alter. Consideration can be said to be such a shape because it has no content or, rather (it amounts to the same thing), can have any content whatsoever provided that there is an exchange and it is voluntary. That is why courts frequently declare that they will not inquire into the adequacy of the consideration,[53] will not, that is, inquire into whether or not the two parties were equally informed or received equivalent benefits from the exchange or were equally powerful actors in the market. To do so would be to reintroduce the very issues – of equity, of the distribution of resources, of fairness, of relative capacity, of *morality* – that consideration is designed to bracket. (All of those issues will return by routes students of contract law know very well, but the fact that such indirection is required is crucial.) With these issues bracketed, the act of contracting (or so it is claimed) becomes purely rational as the parties play out their formal roles in response to a mechanical requirement, the requirement of consideration. This, in turn, requires the court to be similarly mechanical (formal) lest it substitute for the bargain two free agents rationally made a bargain it would have preferred them to make.

Where a party contracts for the performance of an act...his estimate of the value should be left undisturbed.... There is...absolutely no rule by which the courts can be guided, if once they depart from the value fixed by the promisor. If they attempt to fix some standard, it must necessarily be an arbitrary one, and...then the result is that the court substitutes its own judgment for that of the promisor, and, in doing this, makes a new contract.[54]

That is, presumably the parties had reasons for bargaining as they did and the court should not set aside those reasons for reasons that seem to it to be more compelling. The court's responsibility is to "judge" the contract only in a weak sense, to determine whether or not it displays the requisite shape of consideration; were it to exercise judgment in a stronger sense by inquiring into the conditions of the contract, the court would pass from being an instrument of *the* law into an instrument of *a* morality. The result, should this occur, would be exactly the same result that attends the failure to constrain interpretation, the making of a new contract in place of the contract it is the job of the law to enforce. The conclusion is one toward which I have been pointing since the beginning of this essay: interpretation and morality are not simply twin threats to the autonomy and integrity of the law; they are the *same* threat. Interpretation is the name for the activity by which a particular moral vision makes its hegemonic way into places from which it has been formally barred.

If interpretation and morality pose the same threats to the law's self-identity, what is true of one is likely to be true of the other, and, as we have seen, what is true of interpretation is that it is already inside the precincts that would exclude it. The parol evidence rule does not – cannot – work because the integrated agreement it is designed to protect can only come into being – achieve integration – by the very (interpretive) means it stigmatizes. Similarly, the distinction between legal and moral obligation will not work because any specification of a legal obligation is itself already linked with a morality. The large point here is one that I cannot pause to argue (although it has been argued elsewhere by me and by others): that the requirement of procedures that are neutral between contending moral agendas cannot be met because, in order even to take form, procedures must promote some rationales for action and turn a blind eye to others. This is spectacularly true of the procedures built around the doctrine of consideration, a doctrine that finally makes sense not as an alternative to morality, but as the very embodiment of the morality of the market, a morality of arm's length dealing between agents without histories, gender, or class affiliation. Whatever one thinks of this conception of transaction and agency, it is hardly one that has bracketed moral questions; rather it has decided them in a particular way, and, moreover, in a way that is neither necessary nor inevitable. As E. Allan Farnsworth points out, the principle of "direct bilateral exchanges" is not the "only possible basis for an economic system." Other societies have "distributed their resources by sharing, based on notions of generosity, rather than by bargaining, based on notions of self-interest."[55] Historically, the morality of self-interest and with it the require-ment of consideration triumphed after a determined effort by Lord Mansfield to make contractual and moral obligations one and the same. The fact that he failed does not mean that morality had been eliminated as an issue in contract law, but that one morality – the morality of discrete, one-shot transactions – became so firmly established that it won the right to call itself "mere proce-dure" and was able to set up a watchdog – called "consideration" – whose job it was to keep the other moralities at bay.

In a way, this outcome is inevitable given what we have already noted about the law. In order to be law, it must define itself *against* particular moral traditions. It follows then that the first thing a moral tradition must do after having captured the law (or some portion of its territory) is present itself as being beyond or below (it doesn't really matter) morality. This, in turn, dictates the strategy by which any alternative morality will have to make its way: it will have materially to alter the law while maintaining all the while that it is preserving what it alters. Just as the winning interpretation of a contract must persuade the court that it is not an interpretation at all but a plain and clear meaning, so the winning morality must persuade the court (or direct the court in the ways of persuading itself) that it is not a morality at all but a perspicuous instance of fidelity to the law's form.

Contract law performs this feat of legerdemain by implanting within con-sideration theory a number of subversive concepts, chief among which is the concept of "contract implied in law." Nominally, a contract implied in law is a category in the taxonomy of contracts, but in fact it exceeds the taxonomy and threatens to render it incoherent. The category can be best grasped by con-trasting it with its two neighbors, the express contract and the contract implied in fact. An express contract is a written or oral agreement whose terms explicitly state the basis for consideration: I will do or promise to do this if you will do or refrain from doing or promise to do or promise to refrain from doing that. Now, it may be that the parties have entered into no formal agreement but comport themselves in relation to one another in ways that could only be explained by the existence of the requisite contractual intentions. If you bring a broken item to a repair shop and leave it, your action and the action of the shop's agent are intelligible only within the assumption that, in return for his professional skill, you have obligated yourself to the payment of a reasonable fee. In short, you and the shop have entered into a contract even though it has not been expressly stated; it is a contract implied in fact, implied, that is, by the behavior of the contracting parties.

Express contracts and contracts implied in fact are thus different ways of signifying an intention to be party to a bargained-for exchange. Contracts implied in law, on the other hand, are not attempts to ascertain and enforce the parties' intentions with respect to a contemplated transaction, but are imposed by a court on persons irrespective of the intentions they had or the actions they performed. Indeed, a contract implied in law is a judgment by a court that a party *ought* to have had a certain intention or performed in a certain way and for the purposes of justice and equity that intention or performance will now be imputed to him along with the obligations that follow. The notion of a contract implied in law springs all the bolts that consideration is designed to secure and provides the means for a court to do what, under contract law, a court is not supposed to do, make a new contract in accordance with its conception of morality. Contract implied in law is a wild-card category inserted into the heart of contract doctrine, and, moreover, courts that employ it often admit as much.

[A] contract implied in law is not a contract at all, but an obligation imposed by law for the purpose of bringing about justice and equity without reference to the intent or agreement of the parties and, in some cases, in spite of an agreement between the parties.
. . . It is a non-contractual obligation that is to be treated procedurally as if it were a contract. . . .[56]

In other words, the notion of implied in law contract does not belong in contract law, for as Stanley Henderson puts it, "the substantive right to recover benefits conferred upon another does not respect legal categories, particularly that of contract."[57]

What, then, is it doing there? The question implies that contract law would be better off were it not there or were its presence accounted for in ways that could better support a claim to consistency. Consistency, however, is not a feature of contract law but is its (always precarious) achievement, and it is an achievement whose possibility depends on *not* resolving the conflicts contract doctrine displays. It is *because* it is a world made up of materials that pull in diverse directions that contract law can succeed in its endless project of making itself into a formal whole. Rather than being an embarrassment, the presence in contract doctrine of contradictory versions of the enterprise is an opportunity. It is in the spaces opened by the juxtaposition of apparently irreconcilable impulses – to be purely formal and intuitively moral – that the law is able to exercise its resourcefulness.

These spaces continue to be opened up even in documents supposedly designed to close them. Here, for example, is section 86 of *Restatement Second*, a section that promises to adjudicate the tension between legal and moral notions of obligation, but ends up reproducing it.

86. Promise for Benefit Received
    (1) A promise made in recognition of a benefit previously received by the promisor from the promisee is binding to the extent necessary to prevent injustice.
    (2) A promise is not binding under Subsection (1)
        (a) if the promise conferred the benefit as a gift or for other reasons the promisor has not been unjustly enriched; or
        (b) to the extent that its value is disproportionate to the benefit.[58]

Although the form of the section is straightforward and declarative, its content, as Grant Gilmore has observed, is hesitant and even schizophrenic.[59] By recognizing promises for benefits received, subsection (1) seems to send us firmly in the direction of an expansive notion of legal obligations (in "classic doctrine" such promises are not enforceable because the benefit was unsought and is not part of a bilateral exchange); but wait, "what Subsection (1) giveth, Subsection (2) largely taketh away";[60] such a promise will not be binding if the benefit came to the promisor in the form of a gift, that is, in a form not involved in a mutual transaction, that is, in a form without consideration. As Henderson observes, the requirement of subsection (2) "means that events are to be screened by consideration tests in order to determine which promises are to be included within the category of promises binding without consideration"; and he concludes that the restriction as stated "erodes the policy of growth manifested" in subsection (1).[61] But this is to regard the section as if it were (or aspired to be) a logical statement when, in fact, it is a set of directions for accomplishing a particularly difficult (but essential) task, the task of maintaining the formal basis of contract law while at the same time making room for the substantive concerns formalism desires to exclude. By first opening the door to moral obligation (that is, to promises for benefits received) and then allowing it to enter only if it can be provided with an origin in a bargained-for exchange, section 86 delivers a message, and delivers it not despite but because of its schizophrenia: "Relax the requirement of consideration, but do so in the guise of honoring it." The message is repeated and given a rationale almost charming in its transparency in official comment (a):

Enforcement of promises to pay for benefit received has sometimes been said to rest on "past consideration" or on the "moral obligation" of the promisor, and there are statutes in such terms in a few states. Those terms are not used here: "past consideration" is inconsistent with the meaning of consideration stated in [section] 71, and there seems to be no consensus as to what constitutes a "moral obligation."[62]

Or in other words, "look, if we want to revise contract doctrine so as to bring it more into line with our moral intuitions, we would be well advised to do so in terms that contract doctrine, as presently formulated, will find acceptable. Neither past consideration nor moral obligation are such terms. The first fails because it is too obviously ex post facto with respect to the moment of exchange that constitutes a contract; it too nakedly asks us simply to declare that what had not been bargained for in the past – an unasked-for benefit – was in fact the basis of a bargain. The second fails because it provides us with no standard – there seems to be no consensus as to what constitutes a 'moral obligation' – and too nakedly acknowledges that the basis of law is variable. It is true that in some precincts these terms have been used, but the liabilities they present. are greater than the advantage of employing them. If we want our moral intuitions to be incorporated into the law we will have to make sure that they look like what the law wants them to look like."

That is to say, they must be worked into a form that matches the picture of consideration, the picture of a freely chosen giving up of something in return for something just as freely proffered. The fact (as I take it to be) that the notion of choosing one's obligations independently of historical pressures is a fiction, that the "inside" of the isolated and "free" transaction is always determined by an "outside" it does not acknowledge, may be philosophically compelling; but the morality of consideration – of exchanges uninfluenced by anything except the opportunities offered by the moment of transaction – is too firmly embedded in contract doctrine to be embarrassed by any analysis of it. So firmly is it embedded that anticonsideration impulses can be harbored and even nurtured in contract doctrine where, rather than undermining the orthodox view, they provide it with the flexibility it needs. Henderson notes that "the judicial process, in spite of a consistent adherence to the test of bargain, exhibits a recurring tendency to appeal to a code of moral duties in order to justify enforcement of a particular promise."[63] Henderson calls this a "fundamental inconsistency" that has been "built into contract analysis,"[64] but like most "buildings" this structure is neither accidental nor unproductive. In order to be what it claims to be – something, rather than everything or nothing – contract law must uphold a view of transaction in which its features are purely formal; but in order to be what it wants to be – sensitive to our always changing intuitions about how people ought to behave – contract law must continually smuggle in everything it claims to exclude. I must emphasize again that the so-called formal view of legal obligation was never really formal at all, but was the extension of a social vision from which it was detached at the moment of that vision's triumph. The tension between consideration doctrine with its privileging of the autonomous and selfish agent and the doctrine of moral obligation with its acknowledgment of responsibilities always and already in place is a tension between two contestable conceptions of life; it is just that one of them has won the right to occupy the pole marked *formal* (i.e., unattached to any particular agenda) in a powerful (because constitutive of an institutional space) opposition. Given that victory, the fact that the claim of consideration doctrine to be merely formal cannot finally be upheld is of no practical consequence; it is upheld by the rhetorical structure it has generated, and in order to alter that structure you must appear to be upholding it too. As I have already said, you can only get around consideration doctrine by elaborately honoring it.

And how do you do that? In many ways, including several we have already observed. You develop a taxonomy of contractual kinds, one of which violates the principles of the taxonomy; you produce a document (the *Restatement*) that, in the guise of clarifying the state of the law, presents its contradictions in a form that further institutionalizes them; you announce as a "principle of law" that the improver of another's land has no right to relief, and then in the next sentence you declare this principle "merely... technical" (i.e., legal) and dismiss it in favor of "an equitable remedy";[65] you develop and expand notions like promissory estoppel, duress, incapacity, unconscionability, and unjust enrichment and then expand them to the point where there is no action that cannot be justified in their terms; you invoke the distinction between public and private, even as you allow public pressures to determine the distinction's boundaries. In short, you tell two stories at the same time, one in which the freedom of contracting parties is proclaimed and protected and another in which that freedom is denied as a possibility and undermined by almost everything courts do. But in order to make them come out right, you tell the two stories as if they were one, as if, rather than eroding the supposedly formal basis of contract law, the second story merely refines it at the edges and leaves its primary assertions (which are also assertions of the law's stability) intact.

Illustrations of this process are everywhere in the law; indeed, as I have been arguing, the process *is* the law. For a conveniently concise and naked instance of the process at work, we can turn to a classic case of promise for benefit received, *Webb v. McGowin*.[66] Webb was an employee of a lumber company and one of his duties was to clear the upper floor of a mill by dropping pine blocks weighing 75 pounds to the ground below. "While so engaged" he saw McGowin directly below him, in the line of drop as it were, and rather than allowing the block to fall, he diverted its course by falling with it, "thus preventing injuries to McGowin," but causing himself to suffer "serious bodily injuries" as a result of which "he was badly crippled for life and rendered unable to do physical or mental labor." A grateful McGowin, "in consideration... [for] having prevented him from sustaining death or serious bodily harm" promised to pay Webb $15 every two weeks for the rest of his life.[67]

That sum was paid until McGowin's death, whereupon the payments were discontinued and Webb sued to recover the unpaid installments.

This recital of the facts is taken, the court acknowledges, from the appellant's brief, and therefore it is obvious from the beginning where the court's (moral) sympathies lie. It is also obvious what obstacles stand in the way of transforming those sympathies into a legal remedy. Webb's action seems, on its face, to be a spontaneous and gratuitous expression of fellow feeling and, as such, ineligible for a remedy that requires evidence of a transaction of a pecuniary nature. Late in the opinion, however, the court declares that

[t]he case at bar is clearly distinguishable from that class of cases where the consideration is a mere moral obligation or conscientious duty unconnected with receipt by promisor of benefits of a material or pecuniary nature.[68]

But as the facts are initially encountered, the category of "mere moral obligation or conscientious duty" seem to be the one they clearly instantiate. The clarity to which the court refers is not a clarity it finds, but a clarity it *achieves*, and, accordingly, the story the opinion really tells is of that achievement.

The work is already being done as the facts are rehearsed. Presumably the action that initiates the entire affair took place in a split second, but in the court's presentation of it (or rather, the presentation adopted wholesale from the appellant's brief), that action occurs in slow motion: from the first report that the appellant was "in the act of dropping the block" (a locution that already extends the duration of something that must have occurred in the blink of an eye) to his decision (if that is the word) to drop with it, four long sentences intervene. What these sentences do is transform an instantaneous and instinctive response to an unanticipated situation of crisis into a deliberative and considered act. The first sentence does this by beginning the sequence all over again and further dilating it: "As he started to turn the block loose" – "in the act" now has stages, starting and whatever is the next stage after starting. (Of course starting could itself be further subdivided; there is no end to the process of drawing out process.) This stop action technique then leads to the revelation of what is stopping the action: "he saw J. Greeley McGowin, testator of the defendants, on the ground below and directly under where the block would have fallen." The recital has now become a drama of the "Perils of Pauline" variety. Will the block fall? What will Webb do? The "would have fallen" tells us that it didn't, in fact, fall and provokes in us the desire to know how Webb prevented it from falling; but before that desire is fulfilled two additional sentences inform us, first of what "would have" happened if the block would have fallen ("Had he turned it loose it would have struck McGowin with such force as to have caused him serious bodily harm or death"), and, second, how (by what deliberative route) Webb arrived at the course of action he finally (by now this is a full-fledged melodrama) took: "The only safe and reasonable way to prevent this was for appellant to hold to the block and divert its direction in falling from the place where McGowin was standing and the only safe way to divert it so as to prevent its coming into contact with McGowin was for appellant to fall with it to the ground below." A teacher of freshman composition might be moved to criticize this sentence and the entire passage for repetition ("to the ground below" or some variant appears five times in almost as few sentences) and prolixity ("so as to prevent its coming into contact"), but such criticism would miss the effect and the intention behind it, to stretch a punctual moment into a sequence long enough to allow the playing out of freely chosen alternatives and consequences, so that when, in the next sentence, we are told (with a brevity whose force is in direct proportion to the prolixity of what comes before it) "Appellant did this," our sense of what he did is complicated enough, has a sufficient number of stages and spaces, so that we can regard it as the action of a rational and free agent.

So far, so good, but the court is only halfway home; conferring rationality and choice on Webb is quite an achievement, but in order to be truly efficacious it has to be matched by another: Webb's rationality and choice must be shown to exist in a reciprocal relation with the rationality and choice of McGowin. After all, on the facts, his promise to compensate occurs *after* the benefit has been received and the element of bargain for a consideration is conspicuously absent. The court deals with this difficulty in two simultaneously performed moves: it quantifies the benefit and it transforms the quantified benefit into one the promisor (McGowin) had requested. The benefit is quantified not by a legal or even an economic argument but by a blatantly moral one (remember that the point of these moves is to disengage the case from the realm of "mere moral obligation"). After all, the court reasons, the preservation of life is something for which physicians charge, and patients willingly pay a price; therefore, "[l]ife and preservation of the body have material, pecuniary values, measurable in dollars and cents."[69] That is to say, since if Webb were a physician and McGowin his patient what passed between them would be regarded as a transaction in relation to services rendered, let us so regard it. At the same time that an analogy is thus extended into a legal fact, the present case is related to an earlier one in which "a promise... to pay for the past keeping of a bull which had escaped from defendant's premises and had been cared for by plaintiff was valid," on the reasoning that in the circumstances the promise was "equivalent to a previous request."[70] The court conveniently ignores the fact about the case that would distinguish it from the one before it (since the bull is a fungible good, both its value to the owner and the value of the service rendered by the person who cares for it can be monetarized) and seizes the opportunity to exclaim that the service Webb rendered McGowin was "far more material than caring for his bull."[71] In this sentence, the two contradictory strains of the court's argument mesh perfectly: the moral argument that nothing could be more material than the saving of life becomes (through an equivocation on the notion of material) a reason for finding that the present instance of saving a life becomes (through an equivocation on the notion of material) a reason for finding that the present instance of saving life is both more and less than moral, that is, legal and quantifiable. The moral urgency of the court's desire produces the sleight of hand by which the case is disengaged from moral consideration. It is then that the court can triumphantly declare that "[t]he case at bar is clearly distinguishable from that class of cases where the consideration is a mere moral obligation."[72]

It remains only for the court to consolidate its gains in a final breathtaking move. Since it has now been shown that "the promisor received a material benefit constituting a valid consideration for his promise," we can regard the promise as "an affirmance or ratification of the services rendered carrying with it the presumption that a previous request for the service was made," and the court proceeds immediately to so regard it:

McGowin's express promise to pay appellant for the services rendered was an affirmance or ratification of what appellant had done raising the presumption that the services had been rendered at McGowin's request.[73]

And when was this request made? Why in that infinitely extended moment when all the alternative courses of action and all the attendant consequences passed through Webb's mind, and now we are told implicitly, passed through McGowin's mind also. The commercial transaction of voluntary and free agents that seemed so obviously lacking in this case is now supplied and given a location in the minds of two parties who never spoke a word to one another.

The conclusion is as inevitable as it is fantastic: "the services rendered by the appellant were not gratuitous." That is, they were bargained for. And how do we know that? Because of "[t]he agreement of McGowin to pay and the acceptance of payment by appellant." In other words, the meaning and shape of what McGowin did on August 3, 1925, becomes clear in the light of what the two parties did later. In "real-life" terms, the reasoning is familiar and uncontroversial; often we only know what we did when subsequent actions provide us with a retrospective understanding of our actions. But the world of contract is not "real life"; it is (or is supposed to be) formal, and in *that* world, events are discrete and discernible in terms of punctual intentions and foreseen (not retroactively constructed) consequences. The court is dangerously close, here, to falling into the language of "past consideration," but the danger is avoided because, in the context of the opinion's story (of which this is the conclusion), what Webb and McGowin did after the event (make a promise and accept a payment) becomes proof of what they actually (not as a matter imposed after the fact) did *in* the event, enter into a transaction. The fact that they never spoke or in any real sense ever met and the fact that the transaction they are said to have entered into is bizarre ("if you will risk being crippled for life I will pay you thirty dollars a month") might give one pause, but pausing is not what the opinion encourages (except in those earlier moments when the space in which this "bargain" will be inserted is being opened up) and the court quickly moves to a brisk exit: "Reversed and remanded."

In a brief but revealing concurring opinion, Judge William H. Samford further pulls back a curtain that had never really been closed. He admits that the opinion he now joins is "not free from doubt" and acknowledges that according to "the strict letter of the rule" Webb's recovery would be barred, but then he simply declares the "principle" the court has been following, a principle whose articulation he attributes to Chief Justice Marshall when he said "I do not think that law ought to be separated from justice."[74] The effect is complex but swift; what Justice Marshall says amounts to a denial of the law's independence, but the fact that he, the most respected jurist in US history, said it makes his pronouncement a *legal* one and therefore one that can be invoked as a legal justification for departing from the rule of law. Once again, and on several levels of constructions supporting constructions (Justice Samford legitimizes the creative work of his brethren by linking it in a narrative to the equally creative work of a now authoritative predecessor), the legal establishment reaffirms its commitment to a formal process it is in the act of setting aside. Once again, the two stories have been told and then made into the single story that assures the continuity of the tradition.

The Amazing Trick

An unsympathetic reader of the previous paragraph, or indeed of this entire essay, might say that what I have shown is that what works in the law is what you can get away with, precisely the observation made by some members of the critical legal studies movement in essays that point, as I have, to the contradictions that fissure legal doctrine. The difference between those essays and this one lies in the conclusions that follow (or are said to follow) from the analysis. The conclusion often (but not always) reached by critical legal studies proponents is that the inability of legal doctrine to generate logically consistent outcomes from rules and distinctions that have a clear formal basis means that the entire process is at once empty and insidious. The process is empty because its results are entirely ad hoc – lacking firm definitions or borders, the concepts of doctrine can be manipulated at will and in any direction one pleases – and the process is insidious because these wholly ad hoc determinations are presented to us as if they had been produced by an abstract and godly machine. Here is a representative statement from a well-known essay by Clare Dalton that anticipates many of my own arguments.

> ...we need...to understand...how doctrinal inconsistency necessarily undermines the force of any conventional legal argument, and how opposing arguments can be made with equal force. We need also to understand how legal argumentation disguises its own inherent indeterminacy and continues to appear a viable way of talking and persuading.[75]

By "doctrinal inconsistency" Dalton means (1) the inability of doctrine to keep itself pure – as she points out, the poles of supposedly firm oppositions are defined in terms of one another and thus cannot do the work they pretend to do – and (2) the presence in doctrine of contradictory justificatory arguments that are deployed by lawyers and jurists in an ad hoc and opportunistic manner. That is why "opposing arguments can be made with equal force": given the play in the logic of justification, the facts of a case can, with equal plausibility, be made to generate any number of outcomes, no one of which is deduced from a firm base of principle. Nevertheless, Dalton's complaint continues, the law's apologists present these outcomes as if they issued from a procedure that was as determinate as it was impersonal.

To this I would reply, first, that doctrinal inconsistency undoes conventional argument only when the arguments are removed from the local occasion of their emergence and then put to the test of fitting with one another independently of any particular circumstances. But since it is only in particular circumstances that arguments weigh or fail to weigh, the inconsistency Dalton is able to document is not fatal and is embarrassing only if the context is not law and its workings, but philosophy and its requirements. Law, however, is not philosophical (except when it borrows philosophy's arguments for its own purposes) but pragmatic, and from the pragmatic standpoint, the inconsistency of doctrine is what enables law to work. Dalton inadvertently says as much when, in the same sentence, she denies force to conventional argument because of its inconsistency, and then complains that conventional argument, again because of its inconsistency, has too much force. This is not so much a contradiction as it is a distinction (not quite spelled out) between two kinds of force, one good and one bad. The good force is the force of determinate procedure, and that is what the law lacks; the bad force is the force of rhetorical virtuosity, and that the law has in shameful abundance. But the rhetorical nature of law is a shameful fact only if one requires that it operate algorithmically, and that is the requirement (of which there are hard and soft versions) of the position Dalton rejects. By stigmatizing the law's rhetorical content, she makes herself indistinguishable from her opponents for, like them, she measures the law by a standard of rational determinacy; it is just that where they give the law high marks, she finds it everywhere failing.

My point is that while Dalton's description of the law is exactly right, it is a description of strengths rather than weaknesses. When Dalton observes that the law's normative statements are so vaguely formulated ("fairness," "what justice requires," "good faith") that the moment of "normative choice" is deferred "until an individual judge is required to make an individual decision,"[76] all she means is that while the law's normative formulations specify the vocabularly and conceptual "neighborhood" of decision making, they set no limits to what a judge can do with that vocabularly on the way to reaching a plausible (in the sense of recognizably legal) result. In the absence of a mechanical decision procedure there is ample room for judicial maneuvering (although, as I have shown, that maneuvering is itself far from free), and if the "individual decision" is strong enough – if the story it tells seems sufficiently seamless – it will have constituted the norm it triumphantly invokes as its justification. That is the trouble, Dalton might respond: the law is at once thoroughly rhetorical and engaged in the effacing of its own rhetoricity. Exactly, I would reply, and isn't it marvelous (a word intended nonevaluatively) to behold. It may be true that "we have no reliable, and therefore no legitimate, basis for allocating responsibility between contracting parties,"[77] but while the legitimacy is not ready-made in the form of some determinate system of rules and distinctions, it is continually being achieved by the very means Dalton rehearses in such detail.

Consider, for example, her discussion of the interplay between the doctrines of consideration and reliance. She has been retelling the story of *Second Restatement* sections 71 and 90 (one defining contract obligation in terms of consideration, the other concerning "Contracts Without Consideration") and notes the avoidance both in the *Restatement* and in the cases that invoke it of "the knotty questions of how their coexistence should be imagined."[78] The mechanisms of avoidance, as she describes them, include the sequential application of the doctrines so that each of them seems to be preserved and a clash between them is forever deferred; the stipulating of different measures of recovery in a way that suggests a distinction that an analysis of the cases does not support; and the elaboration of different vocabularies that cause "reliance rhetoric to sound different from consideration rhetoric," although when the occasion demands, the two vocabularies can draw together and begin "to appear indistinguishable."[79] Impressive as this is, it is only a partial catalog of the mechanisms at the law's disposal, mechanisms that allow a distinction that cannot finally be maintained to be reinforced and, at other times, relaxed and, at still other times, conveniently forgotten. The story is an amazing one, and Dalton accurately characterizes it as "the story of how what appears impossible is made possible."[80]

It is, in short, the story of rhetoric, the art of constructing the (verbal) ground upon which you then confidently walk. Reviewing a case that displays the law's virtuosity at its height, Harry Scheiber exclaims

One is reminded . . . of a dazzling double-feint, backhand flying lay-up shot by a basket-ball immortal. Only in slow motion replay does one comprehend the whole move; and only then does one realize that defiance of gravity is an essential component of it![81]

Scheiber calls this the law's "amazing trick," the trick by which the law rebuilds itself in mid-air without ever touching down. It is a trick Dalton and others decry, but it is the trick by which law subsists and it is hard to imagine doing without it. The alternatives would seem to be either the determinate rationality that every critical legal analysis shows to be impossible, or the continual exposure of the sleights of hand by means of which the "amazing trick" is performed. But if the latter alternative were followed, and every legal procedure turned into a debunking analysis of its enabling conditions, decisions would never be reached and the law's primary business would never get done. Perhaps this is the result we want, but somehow I doubt it, and therefore I tend to think that the law's creative rhetoricity will survive every effort to deconstruct it.

It need hardly be said that I am not the first to declare that the operations of law are rhetorical. That is, in fact, Dalton's point, although she makes it as an indictment, and it is the point of others who (in the tradition of Cicero) see the law's rhetoricity more positively. Under the rubric of "rhetorical jurisprudence," Steven J. Burton has elaborated a description of the law that accords on many points with one presented here. His basic thesis is that the "local law of a society represents a possible organization of human relations, and a public commitment to bring it into empirical being"; each application of the law "brings that imagined world into being in some respect."[82] In this argument, the organization of human relations is not something the law follows or replicates, but something the law produces, and produces by means it invents. Rather than proceeding as science does (at least in pre-Kuhnian characterizations) to adjust its presentation in order "better to fit the world," law is a practical discipline, operating to change the world so as "better to fit the representation."[83] That change is brought about by a discourse that creates the authorities it invokes. "A rhetorical understanding concerns the criteria of evidence implicit in a local legal discourse, and thus the effects of the discourse on what the participants will take seriously as law or legal argument, with or without good reasons."[84] A rhetorical jurisprudence does not ask timeless questions; it inquiries into the local conditions of persuasion, into the reasons that *work*; and what it finds interesting about the law's normative claims is not whether or not they can be cashed (in strict terms they cannot), but the leverage one can achieve by invoking them.

Whether such concepts of law are sound or not, they continue in legal discourses to influence the thoughts and actions of many legal actors. Accordingly, they are an important object for rhetorical study within the effort to understand legal practices.[85]

Not surprisingly, I find this very agreeable. I become nervous only when Burton shifts from describing the law as rhetorical to a claim that this description, if heeded, could have beneficial consequences for legal practice: "A rhetorical criticism draws attention to features of law that are neglected by a legal discourse as a first step toward possibly improving that discourse as *legal*."[86] The course of this improvement is not spelled out, but it seems to follow from the reasoning that once we know the law to be rhetorical we will be better able to function within it, better able to "listen, deliberate and justify action."[87] But knowing that the law is rhetorical could improve it only if we were thereby insulated against that rhetoricity – in which case Burton would be harboring a desire for the scientific jurisprudence his essay rejects – or if that knowledge made the law *more* rhetorical than it already is – a goal that is incoherent since the condition of being rhetorical, of being tied to the exigencies and pressures of the moment, admits of no degree. Once "the law is understood from the practical point of view as a system of reasons for action,"[88] one does not either gain a distance from those reasons or become more compelled by them because one has achieved that understanding. They will still be *local* reasons, as they were before they were so named by Burton, and they will still occur in the context of local pressures rather than in the context of some overall recognition that they are local. The lesson of the law's rhetoricity – the lesson that reasons are reasons only within the configurations of practice and are not reasons that generate practice from a position above it – must be extended to itself. It can no more serve as a master thesis than the formalist theses it replaces. Formalists at least make their mistake legitimately, since it is *their* position that local practices follow or should follow from master principles; it cannot, without internal contradiction, be a rhetorician's position, even when the master principle is rhetoric itself.

Burton's flirtation with what I have elsewhere called "antifoundationalist theory hope" (the hope that by becoming aware of the rhetoricity of our foundations we gain a [nonrhetorical] perspective on them that we didn't have before) is a fully developed romance in the work of James Boyd White. White defines the law (correctly in my view) as "a set of resources for thought and argument."[89] This set, he argues, is open and includes the concepts thought to be basic to the enterprise. As a result, the law is at every level creative, constructing its principles even as it applies them.

For in speaking the language of the law the lawyer must always be ready to try to change it: to add or to drop a distinction, to admit a new voice, to claim a new source of authority, and so on. One's performance is in this sense always argumentative, not only about the result one seeks to obtain but also about the version of the legal discourse that one uses – that one creates – in one's speech and writing. That is, the lawyer is always saying not only "here is how this case should be decided," but also "here – in this language – is the way this case and similar cases should be talked about. The language I am speaking is the proper language of justice in our culture."...in this sense legal language is always argumentatively constitutive of the language it employs.[90]

To this point I am more or less with White, but he loses me when his description of the way the law works leads to a demand for a new form of legal practice: "This means that one question constantly before us as lawyers is what kind of culture we shall have."[91] But the question "before us" is always a legal one, couched in terms of legal categories and possible courses of action. The fact that a legal question can always be shown to have a source in presupposed cultural values does not mean that it is the business of a legal inquiry to discover or revise those values. Of course one could always engage in that business, but to do so would not be to practice law as the institution's members now recognize it. White himself makes the point when he observes again and again that the workings of the law are local; "it always starts in a particular place among particular people," and therefore "one cannot idealize" it by saying "here is how it should go in general."[92] But here is White, idealizing it and saying how it should go in general: it should provoke a continuing philosophical discussion of the society's values and goals. But were it to do that, it would not be law but moral philosophy; the irremediably local perspective of the law – its rootedness in particular disputes requiring particular, and timely, solutions – leaves no room for the extended reflections White recommends and indeed brands them as inappropriate. The judge who was always stopping to "put his (or her) fundamental attitudes and methods to the test of sincere engagement with arguments the other way"[93] would not be doing his or her job as a judge, but would be doing something else, something valuable no doubt but, in legal terms, something inept and even irresponsible (unless the exercise were preliminary, strategically, to the announcing of a conclusion, in which case the practice of testing one's attitudes against alternatives would not be engaged in for its own sake – as an effort to expand one's consciousness – but for the sake of a goal to which a limited consciousness was precommitted).

White's mistake is to conflate the perspective from which one might ask questions about the nature of law (is it formal or moral or rhetorical?) with the perspective from which one might ask questions in the hope that the answers will be of use in getting on with a legal job of work. It is from the first perspective (the perspective of metacritical inquiry) that one might decide that the law is a process in which "we, and our resources, are constantly remade by our own collective activities,"[94] but those who are immersed in that process do not characteristically act with the intention of furthering that remarking, but with the intention either of winning or deciding. With respect to that intention, an account of the law's rhetoricity will either be irrelevant (i.e., it does not touch on the isues the case raises) or dangerous (introducing it could weaken the position you are defending) or, in some circumstances, marginally helpful (as when you remind yourself and your fellows that the law is not an exact science and is less severe than science in its demand for proof). But even in this last instance, the thesis of the law's rhetoricity will not have generated a new way of practicing law; it will merely have added one more resource to a practice that will still be shaped, in large measure, by the goals the law will continue to have, the goals of winning an argument or crafting an opinion. These are result-oriented activities, and to engage in them seriously is to have already foreclosed on the openness to alterity that White would have us adopt.

White doesn't see this because he thinks that if openness to alterity characterizes the law (as opposed to the more closed characterizations offered by formalist theorists), then legal actors should themselves be open; since history shows that the law "provides a ground for challenge and change,"[95] it is with the motives of challenge and change that we should act. But while challenge and change are often the by-products of the resourcefulness legal actors display, they are not the motives for which legal action is usually taken. It may be, as White contends, that, as a rhetorical process, the law can never be closed to the interpretive pressures of alternative conversations and displays a "structural openness,"[96] but it does not follow that those who practice the law do so with the intention of being thus open. That is the intention of those who would practice a form of critical self-consciousness. As it turns out, this is precisely the future White envisions for the law: the legal agent will continually "doubt the adequacy of any language, and seek to be aware of the limits of her own forms of thought and understanding"; she will be committed to "many-voicedness" and be "profoundly against monotonal thought and speech, against the single voice, the single aspect of the self or culture dominating the rest."[97] White calls this vision "rhetorical," but it is a strange rhetoric that imagines conflict finally dissolved in the wash of a many-voiced pluralism. The truth is that White's hopes for the law are not rhetorical, but transcendental; he regards the scene of persuasion as only temporary, and, like Habermas, he looks forward to a time when all parties will lay down their forensic arms and join together in the effort to build a new and more rational community. This "commitment to openness,"[98] this determination to "be tentative and poetic,"[99] may be admirable, but it is hard to see what place it could have in a process that *demands* single-voiced judgments, even if that voice can be shown to be plurally constituted. White may begin by acknowledging and celebrating difference, but in the end he cannot tolerate it.

The same can be said of Peter Goodrich, a British-style critical legal scholar who, in books and essays of enormous erudition and sophistication, elaborates "a concept of a rhetoric of legal language" that emphasizes "the rhetorical, socio-linguistic and loosely pragmatic dimensions and contexts of any communicational practice."[100] Goodrich begins by observing that a "defining feature of all formalism" is the "rejection of history,"[101] that is, of the circumstantial background that informs the supposedly self-sufficient and self-declaring rule or doctrine. He then finds the source of the formalist dream in "the distinction between logic and rhetoric,"[102] a distinction that produces the traditional categories of the philosophy of language with a pure semantic kernel at their center and the meanings generated by social and political conditions on the stigmatized periphery. Of course, Goodrich insists, this pure center is a "mythology,"[103] "palpably more rhetorical than actual,"[104] a device for diverting attention away from "the actual 'social facts' or historical and particular 'forms of life' that determine the substantive meaning of legal rules."[105] Once we realize that meaning is "the product or outcome of communication between socially organized individuals and groups," we will see that there could not possibly be any "self-articulated unities of discourse" because every text, no matter how apparently autonomous "implies other meanings, other texts, other discourses, and will constantly exceed the boundaries of any given instance of discourse."[106]

Once again I find myself in agreement both with the analysis and its conclusion: rather than a formal mechanism applying determinate rules to self-declaring fact situations, the law is "preeminently the discourse of power,"[107] that is, a discourse whose categories, distinctions, and revered formulas are extensions of some political program that does not announce itself as such. Goodrich supports and extends this conclusion by analyzing cases in which, as he shows, it is "the persuasive function of particular rhetorical techniques"[108] rather than any independent logic that generates decisions, even though the decision will always be presented as one that reinforces "the distinction between the formal normative character of the legal process and the substantive content . . . of a dispute."[109] The law, in short, is continually engaged in effacing the ideological content of its mechanisms so that it can present itself as "a discourse which is context independent in its claims to universality and reason."[110] In this way it rhetorically establishes its independence from the very social and political values that are its content, exercising a "constant, centripetal, endeavor to maintain itself by differentiation and by exclusion of the discourses and languages which surround it."[111] By "avoiding or excluding the . . . implications of its own institutionalization," its status as a historical and contingent discourse, and "by treating legal problems of syntax or of a lexico-grammatical kind . . . the law manages and controls . . . the hierarchy of social and political relations . . . while apparently doing no more than prohibiting and facilitating certain generic and inherently uncontroversial, legally specific, activities and functions."[112]

Except for the somewhat inflated vocabulary, this is precisely my account of the law as a discourse continually telling two stories, one of which is denying that the other is being told at all. The difference is that for Goodrich this account amounts to a scandal, whereas for me it simply brings to analytical attention the strategy by which the law fashions out of alien materials the autonomy it is obliged to claim. Were the law to deploy its categories and concepts in the company of an analysis of their roots in extralegal discourses, it would not be exercising, but dismantling its authority; in short it would no longer be law. Goodrich quite correctly sees that one can become an adept in the law only by forgoing an inquiry into the sources of the norms you internalize: "the entire process of socialization into the legal institution is a question of learning deference and obedience, a question of explicit and implicit education into the requisite modes of interaction – the forms, procedures and languages – of the different levels, functions and topics of the legal system."[113] But he thinks that we can and should undo this education and bring into the foreground everything it labored to occlude. We must "challenge the hermetic security . . . of substantive jurisprudence";[114] we must make visible the "alternative meanings"[115] that legal meanings ignore:

In reading the law, it is constantly necessary to remember the compositional, stylistic and semantic mechanisms which allow legal discourse to deny its historical and social genesis. It is necessary to examine the silences, absences and empirical potential of the legal text, and to dwell upon the means by which it appropriates the meaning of other discourses and of social relations themselves, while specifically denying that it is doing so.[116]

Now, it may be that "in reading the law" – that is, in subjecting it to a sociological or deconstructive analysis – one must remember everything forgotten in the course of its self-constitution, but the practice of law requires that forgetting, requires legal discourse to "appropriate the meaning of other discourses... while specifically denying that it is doing so." And if you reply that a practice so insulated from a confrontation with the contingency of its foundations is unworthy of respect, I would reply, in turn, that every practice is so insulated and depends for its emergence as a practice – as an activity distinct from other activities – on a certain ignorance of its debts and complicities. As I have put the matter elsewhere,

"Forgetfulness," in the sense of not keeping everything in mind at once, is a condition of action, and the difference between activities... is a difference between differing species of forgetfulness.[117]

This is true even of the practice of remembering what other practices have forgotten, for in order to engage in that practice, Goodrich must himself forget (or at the very least bracket) the empirical conditions that give rise to law and constrain its operation, conditions including the need for procedures to adjudicate disputes, and the pressure for prompt remedies and decisions. I am not criticizing Goodrich, only pointing out that his project is no more free of forgettings than the project he excoriates. His mistake is to think that it could be so free, and he thinks *that* because he believes in the possibility of a general discourse that takes account of everything and excludes nothing. There is no such discourse, only the particular discourses that gain their traction by the very means Goodrich laments. And, indeed, it is more than a little ironic that Goodrich finally scorns the material setting of the law's exercise and seeks to set it, instead, in the leisurely precincts (no less material but differently so) of a philosophy seminar. The law, however, is not philosophy; it is law, although, like everything else it can become the object of philosophical analysis, in which case it becomes something different from what it is in its own terms. To be sure, the phrase "in its own terms" refers to the very construct Goodrich would expose, and exposing it as a construct is a perfectly respectable thing to do. That is not, however, what the law can do and still remain operative as law. It is certainly true, as Goodrich both asserts and demonstrates, that the law is not "best read in its own terms,"[118] but that does not mean that the law is best not *practiced* in its own terms, for it is only by deploying its own terms confidently and without metacritical reservation that it can be practiced at all. Goodrich ends his book with a call for the "interdisciplinary study of law... aimed... at breaking down the closure of legal discourse."[119] This is a worthy project and one that (with his help) is already succeeding; but it is an academic project determined in its shape by norms of academic inquiry (themselves forms of closure): once the seminar is over and the grip of philosophy's norms has been relaxed, legal discourse will once again be closed (although the shape of its closure will be endlessly revisable) and the law will resume the task of simultaneously declaring and fashioning the formal autonomy that constitutes its precarious, powerful being.

I cannot conclude without speaking briefly to three additional points. First of all, my account and defense of the law's rhetoricity – of the strategies by which it generates outcomes from concerns and perspectives it ostentatiously disavows – should not be taken as endorsing those outcomes. Although much of legal theory is an effort to draw a direct line between some description of the law's workings and the rightness (or wrongness) of particular decisions, it has been my (antitheoretical) point that "rightness" is automatically conferred on any decision the system produces, that is to say, any decision that follows from the persuasive marshalling of certain arguments. As soon as an argument has proven to be persuasive to the relevant parties – a court, a jury – we say of it that it is right, by which we mean that it is now the law (nothing succeeds like success), that it is *legally* right. Of course, we are still free to object to the decision on other grounds, to find it "wrong" in moral terms or in terms of the long-range health of the republic. In that event, however, our recourse would not be to an alternative form of the legal process but to alternative arguments that would be successful – that is persuasive – within the same general form. In my view, the legal process is always the same, an open, though bounded, forum where forensic battles are contingently and temporarily won; therefore, preferred outcomes are to be achieved not by changing the game but by playing it more effectively (and what is and is not "more effective" is itself something that cannot be known in advance). In short, even if the cases I discuss were to be decided differently, were to be reversed or overturned, the routes of decision would be as I have described them here.

This brings me to my second point. It might seem that, by saying that the legal process is always the same, I have made the law into an ahistorical abstraction and endowed it with the universality and stability my argument so often denies. However, this objection (which I raise myself because others will certainly raise it) turns on a logical quibble and on the assumption that one cannot at the same time be true to history and contingency and make flat categorical statements about the way things *always* are. But what I am saying is that things always are historical and contingent; that is, I am privileging history by refusing to recognize a check on it – a determinate set of facts, a monumentally self-declaring kind of language – and it is only a philosophical parlor trick that turns this insistence on historicity into something ahistorical. The alternative to my account would be one in which the law's operations were grounded in a reality (be it God or a brute materiality or universal moral principles) independent of historical process, and it seems curious to reason that, because I do not allow for that reality, I am being unhistorical. To be sure, the possibility that such an independent reality may reveal itself to me tomorrow remains an alive one, but it is not a possibility that can weigh on my present understanding of these matters, nor would it be the case that the act of ritually acknowledging it (as Dalton, Burton, White, and Goodrich urge) would be doing anything of consequence. Nevertheless, there is a sense in which the present essay is not historical: it doesn't do historical *work*; that is, it does not chart in any detail any of the differently contingent courses the law has taken in the areas it has marked out for its own. That work, however, is in no way precluded by my thesis and, indeed, the value of doing it is greatly enhanced once that thesis is assented to; once contingency (or ad-hocness or makeshiftness or rhetoricity) is recognized as constitutive of the law's life, its many and various instantiations can be explored without apology and without any larger (that is, grandly philosophical) rationale.

This brings me to my final point. Assuming, for the sake of argument, that I am right about the law and that it is in the business of producing the very authority it retroactively invokes, why should it be so? Why should law take *that* self-occluding and perhaps self-deceiving form? The short answer is that that's the law's job, to stand between us and the contingency out of which its own structures are fashioned. In a world without foundational essences – the world of human existence; there may be another, more essential one, but we know nothing of it – there are always institutions (the family, the university, local and national governments) that are assigned the task of providing the spaces (or are they theaters) in which we negotiate the differences that would, if they were given full sway, prevent us from living together in what we are pleased to call civilization. And what, after all, are the alternatives? Either the impossible alternative of grounding the law in perspicuous and immutable abstractions, or the unworkable alternative of intruding that impossibility into every phase of the law's operations, unworkable because the effect of such intrusions would be so to attenuate those operations that they would finally disappear. That leaves us with the law as it is, something we believe in because it answers to, even as it is the creation of, our desires.

Notes

1   *Manwill v. Oyler*, 11 Utah 2d 433, 361 P. 2d 177 (1961).
2   P. 192. Trans. Max Knight from the 2nd (rev. and enl.) German ed. (Berkeley: University of California Press, 1967).
3   *Trident Center v. Connecticut General Life Insurance Company*, 847 F. 2d 564 (9th Cir. 1988).

4   Ibid., 566.
5   Ibid.
6   Ibid.
7   Ibid., 567.
8   Ibid., 566.
9   Ibid.
10 Ibid., 568.
11 Ibid.
12 Ibid., 567 n.1.
13 Ibid., 568.
14 Ibid.
15 68 Cal. 2d 33, 442 P. 2d 641 (1968).
16 *Trident Center v. Connecticut General*, 568 (citing 69 Cal. 2d 38).
17 Ibid., 569.
18 Ibid., 569–70.
19 Ibid., 569.
20 Ibid. (citing 69 Cal. 2d 37).
21 Ibid., 569.
22 *Uniform Commercial Code*, 10th ed. (St Paul, Minn.: West Publishing, 1987), 71.
23 Gordon D. Schaber and Claude D. Roher, *Contracts in an Nutshell*, 2nd ed. (St Paul, Minn.: West Publishing, 1984), 243.
24 *Warren's Kiddie Shoppe, Inc. v. Casual Slacks, Inc.*, 120 Ga. App. 578, 171 S.E. 2d 643 (1969).
25 *Dekker Steel Co. v. Exchange National Bank of Chicago*, 330 F. 2d 82 (1964).
26 451 F.2d 3 (1971).
27 Ibid., 9.
28 Ibid., 7.
29 Steven Emanuel and Steven Knowles, *Contracts* (Larchmont, NY: Emanuel Law Outlines, 1987), 160.
30 *Columbia Nitrogen v. Royster Company*, 451 F.2d 3 (1971), 9.
31 Ibid., 9–10.
32 *Uniform Commercial Code*, 71.
33 65 Cal. Rptr. 545, 436 P. 2d 561 (Cal. Sup. Ct. 1968).
34 Ibid., 562.
35 Ibid., 565.
36 *Trident Center*, 569.
37 *Uniform Commercial Code*, 72.
38 *Masterson*, 731–2.
39 *Mitchill v. Lath*, 247 N.Y. 377, 160 N.E. 646 (1928).
40 *Masterson*, 731n.
41 Corbin, *Corbin on Contracts*, one-volume edition (St Paul, Minn.: West Publishing, 1952), 496.
42 Ibid., 497.

43 Ibid., 515.
44 196 Minn. 60, 264 N.W. 247 (1935).
45 Ibid., 433.
46 Ibid., 431.
47 Ibid.
48 Ibid., 433.
49 Ibid., 431.
50 Ibid., 433 (citing *City of Marshall v. Gregoire*, 193 Minn. 188, 198–9, 259 N.W. 377, 381–2).
51 Ibid., 433.
52 Emanuel and Knowles, *Contracts*, 72.
53 *Restatement of the Law Second, Contracts Second*, vol. 1 (St Paul, Min.: American Law Institute Publishers, 1981), sec. 79.
54 *Wolford v. Powers*, 85 Ind. 294 (1882), 303.
55 E. Allan Farnsworth, *Contracts* (Boston: Little, Brown, 1982), 6.
56 *Continental Forest Products, Inc. v. Chandler Supply Company*, 95 Idaho 739, 743, 518 P. 2d 1201 (1974), 1205.
57 Stanley Henderson, "Promises Grounded in the Past: The Idea of Unjust Enrichment and the Law of Contracts," *Virginia Law Review* 57 (1971): 1141.
58 *Restatement Second, Contracts Second*, 233.
59 Grant Gilmore, *The Death of Contract* (Columbus: Ohio State University Press, 1974), 74–5.
60 Ibid.
61 Henderson, "Promises Grounded in the Past," 1127.
62 *Restatement Second, Contracts Second*, 233–4.
63 Henderson, "Promises Grounded in the Past," 1122–3.
64 Ibid., 1122.
65 *Pull v. Barnes*, 142 Colo. 272, 350 P. 2d 829 (1960).
66 27 Ala. App. 82, 168 So. 196 (1935).
67 Ibid., 196–7.
68 Ibid., 198.
69 Ibid.
70 Ibid., 197.
71 Ibid.
72 Ibid., 198.
73 Ibid.
74 Ibid., 199.
75 Clare Dalton, "An Essay in the Deconstruction of Contract Doctrine," *Yale Law Review* 94 (1985): 1007.
76 Ibid., 1035.
77 Ibid., 1066.
78 Ibid., 1084.
79 Ibid., 1091.
80 Ibid., 1087.

81   Harry Scheiber, "Public Rights and the Rule of Law in American Legal History," *California Law Review* 72 (1984): 236–7.
82   Steven J. Burton, "Rhetorical Jurisprudence: Law as Practical Reason" (unpublished manuscript), 69.
83   Ibid., 63.
84   Ibid., 9.
85   Ibid., 2.
86   Ibid., 9.
87   Ibid., 69.
88   Ibid.
89   James Boyd White, *Heracles' Bow: Essays on the Rhetoric and Poetics of the Law* (Madison: University of Wisconsin Press, 1985), 33.
90   Ibid., 34.
91   Ibid., 42.
92   Ibid., 39.
93   Ibid., 47.
94   Ibid., 45.
95   Ibid.
96   Ibid.
97   Ibid., 124.
98   Ibid.
99   Ibid., 125.
100 Peter Goodrich, *Legal Discourse: Studies in Linguistics, Rhetoric, and Legal Analysis* (New York: St Martin's Press, 1987), 5–6.
101 Ibid., 27.
102 Ibid., 61.
103 Ibid., 77.
104 Ibid., 58.
105 Ibid., 57.
106 Ibid., 147.
107 Ibid., 88.
108 Ibid., 90.
109 Ibid.
110 Ibid., 175.
111 Ibid.
112 Ibid., 176.
113 Ibid., 173.
114 Ibid., 132.
115 Ibid., 183.
116 Ibid., 204.
117 Stanley Fish, *Doing What Comes Naturally* (Durham, NC: Duke University Press, 1989), 397.
118 Goodrich, *Legal Discourse*, 212.
119 Ibid.

8

The Young and the Restless

One of the ironies attending "The Young and the Restless," Stanley Fish's homily in professional complacency addressed to New Historicists, is that its message is, arguably, one reason that New Historicism no longer has much claim as a practice. Once the subversion/containment debate was launched, it defined the terms in which the conservatism of the New Historicism came to be recognized, and its promise of newness was dismantled. Fish does not refer to these terms in his essay, but his argument, in which the theory (supposedly) behind the New Historicism is declared unrelated to its practice, produces the same effect, especially when Fish assures New Historicists that all they do is perform "another move in the practice of history as it has always been done." For Fish, this is meant as consolation. His odd claim that history is always the same may not contradict his earlier endorsement of Hayden White on the textuality of history, since Fish would seem to be suggesting that no matter what textual form history takes, its object remains unchanged. One can perhaps see this as the point in the only ill-tempered moment in the piece, when Fish (supposedly) dismantles (actually misreads) a sentence by Jon Klancher, demanding of it transparency, specificity, and referentiality. These procedures reproduce Fish's argument, in which theory and practice are separated, and their relationship is declared inconsequential, nonexistent. That is: "theory" is, for Fish, a word that might be found in what he calls elsewhere "just a fancy phrase." As purveyor of the truth, Fish delivers the facts.

For Fish, one fact that follows from the inherent conservatism of all practice is that there can be no difference between or among practices. Seeing that "difference" divides New Historicists from their detractors, Fish makes difference into sameness; that is, by offering a theoretical abstraction rather than any terms for difference (e.g., race, gender, sexuality, class), Fish turns differences into the general question of difference. At this (inconsequential) level, Fish can grant anything – for instance that all practice is political, because for Fish to say that everything is political, or ideological, or textual is to say the same thing, merely to be using fancy words. Fish conjures up the truth of the political in a scene in which "a new reading of *The Scarlet Letter*" is debated "on the floor of Congress." Presenting his readers with this (supposedly) absurd spectacle of academic freedom in peril, Fish acts as if Congress were the only place in which anything worthy of the name "politics" occurs, and as if no one in Congress ever bothered about what academics do. Not only are both beliefs odd about where and what politics might be, they also seem rather strange in relationship to New Historicist practice, here misrecognized as nothing other than the familiar literary critical production of readings, elsewhere in the piece misrecognized as a new kind of history.

If Fish misrecognizes in these ways, it is, of course, to conserve what he represents as the only game in town, one that he needs to insist everyone plays. Yet, his everyone, following Fish's refusal to countenance difference in any form, must be a version of the same (just as Fish's version of psychology offered in the piece imagines consciousness as always undivided, the self as necessarily so singular as to be incapable even of self-reflection, which must necessarily be empty). Eviscerated, emptied, New Historicists and their opponents – characterized by Fish as "materialists," whether they are left or right in their politics – all play that game, or could if they knew it: the price is right. And – final irony, or proof that Fish is right? – for some time now, the media have embraced Fish as a voice against conservatism.

Jonathan Goldberg

This essay appeared at the conclusion of The New Historicism, *a volume in which a group of well-known scholars and critics present the case for and against the movement named by Stephen Greenblatt.*

As a privileged first reader of these essays I want to comment on the many and varied pleasures they provide. Whatever the New Historicism is or isn't, the energies mounted on its behalf or in opposition to its (supposed) agenda are impressive and galvanizing. In a brief afterword, as this is intended to be, I cannot do justice to the arguments and demonstrations of more than twenty pieces, but some things, while perhaps obvious, should at least be noted. The footnotes to some of the essays (see particularly Newton, Klancher, Pecora, Montrose, Marcus, and Fineman) are alone worth the price of admission; they illustrate even more than the essays themselves the richness and diversity of concerns that cluster around the questions raised by the banner of a New Historicism. One is grateful also for the glimpse into new (and at least for this literary scholar) uncharted territories – the politics of modern Indonesia (Pecora), the political emplotment of Latin American narrative (Franco), the fortunes of feminism in the First World War (Marcus), the history of art's efforts to be historical (Bann). These, however, are pleasures along the way, and even when they are provided, they are more often than not ancillary to whatever pleasure is to be derived from polemical debate, which is to say, from theory. For the most part (and this is a distinction to which I shall return) these essays are not doing New Historicism, but talking about doing New Historicism, about the claims made in its names and the problems those claims give rise to; and ungenerous though it may be, those problems will be the focus of my discussion.

The chief problem is both enacted and commented on in more than a few essays: it is the problem of reconciling the assertion of "wall to wall" textuality – the denial that the writing of history could find its foundation in a substratum of unmediated fact – with the desire to say something specific and normative. How is it (the words are Newton's) that one can "recognize the provisionality and multiplicity of local knowledge" and yet "maintain that it is possible to give truer accounts of a 'real' world"?[1] On what basis would such a claim be made if one has just been arguing that all claims are radically contingent and therefore vulnerable to a deconstructive analysis of the assumptions on which they rest, assumptions that must be suppressed if the illusion of objectivity and veracity is to be maintained? One can see this "dilemma" with Brook Thomas as a tension between the frankly political agenda of much New Historicist work and the poststructuralist polemic which often introduces and frames that same work. Thomas notes the tendency of many New Historicists to insist that any representation "is structurally dependent on misrepresentation" (184), on exclusions and forgettings that render it suspect, and wonders how their own representations can be proffered in the face of an insight so corrosive: "If all acts of representation are structurally dependent on misrepresentation, these new histories inevitably create their own canons and exclusions" (185).[2] Thomas's chief exhibit is Jane Tompkins who, he says, switches from asking the meta-critical question, "Is there a text in this classroom" to asking the political and normative question, "What text should we have in the classroom?" and thereby "abandons her up-to-date poststructuralist pose and returns to old--

fashioned assumptions about literature and historical analysis" (185). It would seem, he concludes, that "the very poststructuralist assumptions that help to attack past histories seem necessarily forgotten in efforts to create new ones" (186). We shall return to the idea of "forgetting" which appears more than once in this collection, and I shall suggest that as an action of the mind it is less culpable than Thomas seems to suggest; but for the time being, I shall let his formulation stand since it clearly sets out a problematic to which many in this volume are responding.

One response to this problematic is to refuse it by denying either of its poles. Thus Elizabeth Fox-Genovese, Vincent Pecora, Jane Marcus, and (less vehemently) Jon Klancher simply reject the poststructuralist textualization of history and insist on a material reality in relation to which texts are secondary. For these authors the "dance" of New Historicism substitutes the ingenuity and cobbled-up learning of the critic for the "history" he or she supposedly serves: "When New Historicism plays with history to enhance the text," objects Marcus, "its enhancement is like the coloring of old movies for present consumption.... To learn political lessons from the past we need to have it in black and white" (133). Her effort is to remove from the history of literary women in the First World War the coloring imposed by Sandra Gilbert; she wants, she says, to do "justice to women's history" (144). In a similar vein Pecora contrasts "the kinds of symbolic significance Geertzian anthropology creates" (264) in its so-called "thick descriptions" of Indonesian life to the "complex and polymorphous internecine struggles of the Indonesian people for self-determination" and finds that in his analyses Geertz reduces historical experience to "a well-known Western myth" (262), to "anthropological abstraction in spite of [his] claim to greater specificity" (266). "What, for many historians, would be... 'basic' categories such as material want and material struggle...lose their privileged position" in Geertzian New Historicism and become, like everything else, "merely culturally constructed sign systems" (244). New Historicist accounts, Pecora concludes, "are theoretically and anthropologically given and not historically determined" (269).

Fox-Genovese is even more blunt. History, she declares, is not simply "a body of texts and a strategy of reading or interpreting them"; rather, "history must also be recognized as what did happen in the past – of the social relations and, yes, 'events' of which our records offer only imperfect clues." It may be possible "to classify price series or...hog weights...as texts – possible, but ultimately useful only as an abstraction that flattens historically and theoretically significant distinctions" (216). "Distinctions" is a key word in this sentence and in many of the essays, and indeed it names a place of emphasis for both New Historicists and their materialist critics, finally reducing the difference between them in a shared devotion to difference. I shall return to this point, but for the moment I want simply to note the materialist position and to observe that its large vulnerability is one of the subjects of Hayden White's essay. While the materialist critics of New Historicism criticize the ideological program of its practitioners and declare that program to be ahistorical, the grounds for this condemnation "are themselves functions of the ideological positions of these critics" (296). The implicit claim of the materialists to be more immediately in touch with the particulars of history cannot be maintained, because all accounts of the past (and, I might add, of the present) come to us through "some kind of natural or technical language" (297) and that language must itself proceed from some ideological vision. "Every approach to the study of history presupposes some model for construing its object of study"; and it is from the perspective of that model, whatever it is, that one distinguishes "between what is 'historical' and what is not" (296). What this means is that "the conflict between the New Historicists and their critics" is not a conflict between textualists and true historians, but "between different theories of textuality" (297). Thus everyone's history is textual – "there is no such thing as a specifically historical approach to the study of history" (302) – and while one can always lodge objections to the histories offered by one's opponents, one cannot (at least legitimately) label them as nonhistorical. In the words of Lynn Hunt, herself a respected historian, "there is no such thing as history in the sense of a referential ground of knowledge."[3]

Of course, such remarks return us to the dilemma with which we began and invite the familiar question, "but if you think *that* about history, how can you, without contradictions, make historical assertions?" How, in other words, can you theorize your own position in a way that escapes the critique you want to make of those who have been historians before you? It would seem that one must either give up the textualist thesis as the materialists urge (which leaves them open to the charge of being positivist at a time when it is a capital offense to be such) or stand ready to be accused of the sin of contradiction. Some New Historicists outflank this accusation by making it first, and then confessing to it with an unseemly eagerness. In this way they transform what would be embarrassing if it were pointed out by another into a sign of honesty and methodological self-consciousness.

In this mode Louis Montrose may be thought a virtuoso. His now familiar formula, "the textuality of history, the historicity of texts," is a succinct expression of the (supposed) problem. By the textuality of history Montrose means "that we can have no access to a full and authentic past, a lived material existence, unmediated by the surviving textual traces of the society in question,... traces ... that ... are themselves subject to subsequent textual mediations when they are construed as the 'documents' upon which historians ground their own texts, called 'histories'" (20). By the historicity of texts,

Montrose means "the cultural specificity, the social embedment, of all modes of writing" (20). The problem is to get from the quotation marks put around "documents" and "histories" to the specificities, or more pointedly, to the strong assertion of the specificities that have now, it would seem, dissolved into a fluid and protean textuality. Once you have negotiated the shift, as Montrose puts it later, from "history to histories," that is, to multiple stories and constructions no one of which can claim privilege, how do you get back?

At one point Montrose seems to say "no problem," as he simply declares the passage easy. "We may simultaneously acknowledge the theoretical indeterminacy of the signifying process and the historical specificity of discursive practices" (23). More often, however, he allows the dilemma to play itself out as he tacks back and forth between the usual claims for the special powers of the New Historicist methodology and the admission that his own epistemology seems to leave no room for those special powers. The climax of this drama late in his essay finds Montrose bringing these two directions of his argument together in a moment of high pathos. In one sentence he asserts that by foregrounding "issues such as politics and gender" in his readings of Spenser and Shakespeare, he is participating both in the "re-invention of Elizabethan culture" and in the "re-formation" of the constraints now operating in our own; and in the next, he acknowledges that his work is "also a vehicle for my partly unconscious and partly calculating negotiation of disciplinary, institutional and societal demands" and that therefore "his pursuit of knowledge and virtue is necessarily impure" (30). The conclusion, which seems inescapable, is that you cannot "escape from ideology," but this insight is itself immediately converted into an escape when the act of having achieved it is said to have endowed the agent (in this case Montrose) with a special consciousness of the conditions within which he lives:

However, the very process of subjectively *living* the confrontations or contradictions within or among ideologies makes it possible to experience facets of our own subjection at shifting internal distances – to read as in a refracted light, one fragment of our own ideological inscription by means of another. A reflexive knowledge so partial and unstable may, nevertheless, provide subjects with a means of empowerment as agents. (30)

Partiality and instability – the very impediments to achieving any distance from our situation – become the way to that distance when one becomes reflexively aware of them. The questions one might ask of this reflexivity – what is its content, where does it come from? – are never asked. Montrose is content to solve his dilemma by producing (but not recognizing) another version of it in the claim that while he, like all the rest of us, is embedded and impure, he and some of his friends *know* it, and thus gain a perspective on their impurity which mitigates it.

Elsewhere I have named this move antifoundationalist-theory-hope and declared it illegitimate,[4] but here I am interested in it largely as one response to the dilemma New Historicists and materialists negotiate in different (and sometimes opposing) ways. What I want to say in the rest of this essay is that it is a false dilemma ("no problem" is the right answer) that is generated by the conflation and confusion of two different questions:

1. Can you at once assert the textuality of history and make specific and positive historical arguments?
2. Can you make specific and positive historical arguments that follow from – have the form they do as a consequence of – the assertion that history is textual?

The answer to the first question is "yes," and yes without contradiction (whether it is a contradiction one castigates or wallows in) because the two actions – asserting the textuality of history and making specific historical argument – have nothing to do with one another. They are actions in different practices, moves in different games. The first is an action in the practice of producing general (i.e. metacritical) accounts of history, the practice of answering such questions as "where does historical knowledge come from?" or "what is the nature of historical fact?" The second is an action in the practice of writing historical accounts (as opposed to writing an account of how historical accounts get written), the practice of answering questions such as "what happened" or "what is the significance of this event?" If you are asked a question like "what happened" and you answer "the determination of what happened will always be a function of the ideological vision of the observer; there are no unmediated historical perceptions," you will have answered a question from one practice in the terms of another and your interlocutor will be justifiably annoyed. But isn't it the case, one might object, that the two are intimately related, that you will answer the question "what happened" differently if you believe that events are constructed rather than found? The answer to that question is no. The belief that facts are constructed is a *general* one and is not held with reference to any facts in particular; particular facts are firm or in question insofar as the perspective (of some enterprise or discipline or area of inquiry) within which they emerge is firmly in place, settled; and should that perspective be dislodged (always a possibility) the result will not be an indeterminancy of fact, but a new shape of factual firmness underwritten by a newly, if temporarily, settled perspective. No matter how strongly I believe in the constructed nature of fact, the facts that are perspicuous for me within constructions not presently under challenge (and there must always be some for perception even to occur) will remain so. The conviction of the textuality of fact is logically independent of the firmness with which any particular fact is experienced.

I would not be read as flatly denying a relationship between general convictions and the way facts are experienced. If one is convinced of the truth of, say, Marxism or psychoanalysis, that conviction might well have the effect of producing one's sense of what the facts in a particular case are;[5] but a conviction that all facts rest finally on shifting or provisional grounds will not produce shifting and provisional facts because the grounds on which facts rest are themselves particular, having to do with traditions of inquiry, divisions of labor among the disciplines, acknowledged and unacknowledged assumptions (about what is valuable, pertinent, weighty). Of course, these grounds are open to challenge and disestablishment, but the challenge, in order to be effective, will have to be as particular as they are; the work of challenging the grounds will have to be as particular as they are; the work of challenging the grounds will not be done by the demonstration (however persuasive) that they are generally challengeable. The conclusion may seem paradoxical, but it is not: although a conviction strongly held can affect perception and the experience of fact, the one exception to this generality is the conviction that all convictions are tentative and revisable. The only context in which holding (or being held by) *that* conviction will alter one's sense of fact is the context in which the fact in question is the nature and status of conviction. In any other context the conviction of general revisability – the conviction that things have been otherwise and could be otherwise again – will be of no consequence whatsoever.

You may have noticed that by answering my first question – can you at once profess a textual view of history and make strong historical assertions? – in the affirmative, I have at the same time answered my second question – can you do history in a way that follows from your conviction of history's textuality? – in the negative. The fact that the textualist views of the New Historicists do not prevent them from making specific and polemic points means that those points will be made just as everyone else's are – with reference to evidence marshaled in support of hypotheses that will in the end be more or less convincing to a body of professional peers. In short, in my argument New Historicists buy their freedom to do history (as opposed to meta-accounts of it) at the expense of their claim to be doing it – or anything else – differently. But of course that is a price the New Historicists will not be willing to pay, for, like their materialist critics, they have a great deal invested in being different, and, again like their materialist critics, the difference they would claim is the difference of being truly sensitive to difference, that is, to the way in which orthodox historical narratives suppress the realities whose acknowledgement would unsettle and deauthorize them. Whatever their disagreements on other matters, both New Historicists and materialists are united in their conviction that current modes of historiography are (wittingly or unwittingly) extensions of oppressive social and political agendas, and this conviction brings with it an agenda: what has been marginalized must be brought to the center; what has been forgotten or left out must be brought to consciousness; what has been assumed must be exposed to the corrosive operation of critique. The materialists believe that the New Historicists default on this program by aestheticizing it; the New Historicists respond by claiming, as Montrose does, that by producing readings of Shakespeare that foreground the politics of gender and the contestation of cultural constraints they participate in the redrawing of the lines of authority and power. Both camps are committed to cultural reformation, and both believe that cultural reformation can be effected by opening up the seams and fissures that a homogenized history attempts to deny.

The idea, although it is never stated in quite this way, is not to allow prevailing schemes of thought and organization to filter out what might be embarrassing to the interests they sustain. The byword or watchword is "complexity," a value that is always being slighted by the stories currently being told. Jane Marcus makes the point with the notion of "forgetting." She quotes Milan Kundera to the effect that "the struggle of man against power is the struggle of memory against forgetting. . . . [M]an has always harbored the desire to . . . change the past, to wipe out tracks, both his own and others" (133). Of course, what tracks are wiped out by are other tracks; for it is the nature of assertion to be selective and the path it lays down will always have the result of obscuring other paths one might have taken. This is what Richard Terdiman means when he observes that "classification always entails symbolic violence" (228). "It is not only that the class you take determines what class you get into. It is that *in classes we learn to class*" (227), that is, learn to draw lines, establish boundaries, set up hierarchies. Classification in all of its forms, says Terdiman (following Bourdieu), "forcefully excludes what it does not embrace" (227).

This is no doubt true, and indeed it is so true that one wonders whether there is anything one can do about it. "Symbolic violence" seems to be just a fancy phrase for what consciousness inevitably does in the act of seeing distinctions, whether they be social, political, moral, or whatever. However, several writers in this volume think that there is something to be done, something that will counter the violence of "received evaluations of fundamental social operators" (Terdiman, 229). Montrose counsels a "refusal to observe strict boundaries between 'literary' and other texts" (26); we should instead "render problematic the connections between literary and other discourses, the dialectic between the text and the world" (24). Newton would have us behave in a manner appropriate to a self that is now thought to be not stable, but "multiple, contradictory and in process," and she praises those feminist theorists who "have embraced multiplicity and provisionality."[6] These and other contributors urge us to the same course of action: We should reject the exclusionary discourses that presently delimit our perceptions and abrogate our freedom of action in favor of the more flexible and multidirectional mode of being that seems called for by everything we have recently learned about the historicity of our situatedness; we should classify less, remember more, refuse less, and be forever open in a manner befitting a creature always in process.

The trouble with this advice is that it is impossible to follow. While openness to revision and transformation may characterize a human history in which firmly drawn boundaries can be shown to have been repeatedly blurred and abandoned, openness to revision and transformation are not methodological programs any individual can determinedly and self-consciously enact. One cannot wake up in the morning and decide, "today I am going to be open" – as opposed to deciding that today I am going to eat less or pay more attention to my children or get my finances in order. Someone who declares "today I am going to be more open" is in turn open to the question, "open with respect to what?" That is an answerable question and the answer can make sense, as in, "with respect to my habit of dismissing relevant student comments I am going to be open" or "where up to now I have refused to consider sex and race as criteria for admission to this program, I am henceforth going to be open." But of course *that* kind of openness is nothing more (or less) than a resolution to be differently closed, to rearrange the categories and distinctions within which some actions seem to be desirable and others less so; whereas the openness (apparently) desired by several of the contributors to this volume is something very much more, a *general* faculty, a distinct muscle of the spirit or mind whose exercise leads not to an alternative plan of directed action but to a plan (if that is the word) to be directionless, to refuse direction, to resist the drawing of lines, to perform multiplicity and provisionality.

This is not a new goal. It is, as Catherine Gallagher points out, a familiar component of the left radical agenda, at least since the sixties. She calls it "indeterminate negativity" (interestingly, Roberto Unger's name for it is "negative capability"[7]) and characterizes it correctly as the attempt "to live a radical culture" (41), an attempt in which Montrose thinks we partially succeed when we live – that is, consciously employ as part of our equipment – "the contradictions ... of our own subjection" (30). What I am saying is that radical culture – understood as the culture of oppositional action, not opposition in particular contexts, but just *opposition* as a principle – cannot be lived, and it cannot be lived for the same reason that the textualist view of history cannot yield an historical method: it demands from a wholly situated creature a mode of action or thought (or writing) that is free from the entanglements of situations and the lines of demarcation they declare; it demands that a consciousness that has shape only by virtue of the distinctions and boundary lines that are its content float free of those lines and boundaries and remain forever unsettled. The curious thing about this demand, especially curious as a component of something that calls itself the New Historicism, is that what it asks us to be is unhistorical, detached at some crucial level from the very structures of society and politics to which the New Historicism pledges allegiance. My point again is that the demand cannot be met; you cannot not forget; you cannot not exclude; you cannot refuse boundaries and distinctions; you cannot live the radical or indeterminate or provisional or textualist life.

What you can do is write sentences like this:

English Romantic writings were staged within an unstable ensemble of older institutions in crisis (state and church) and emerging institutional events that pressured any act of cultural production – the marketplace and its industrializing, the new media and their reading audiences, the alternative institutions of radical dissent, shifting modes of social hierarchy. (Klancher, 80)

It is tempting (and it is a temptation many of my generation would feel) to mount a full-scale close reading of this sentence, but I will content myself with pointing out the efforts of the prose to keep itself from settling anywhere: English Romantic writings are barely mentioned before they are said to be "staged," i.e. not there for our empirical observation, but visible only against a set of background circumstances that must be the new object of our attention; but before those circumstances are enumerated they are declared to be "unstable" and also an "ensemble" (not one particular thing); and then this instability itself is said to be "in crisis," but in a crisis that is only "emerging" (not yet palpable); and this entire staged, unstable, emerging and "ensembling" crisis is said to put pressure on "any act of cultural production." At this point it looks, alarmingly, as if there is actually going to be a reference to such an act, but anything so specific quickly disappears under a list of the "institutional events" through which "it" is mediated; and finally, lest we carry away too precise a sense of those events (even from such large formulas as "the new media" and "radical dissent") they are given one more kaleidoscopic turn by the phrase "shifting modes." The question is, how long can one go on in *this* shifting mode? Not for many sentences and certainly not for entire essays. Klancher himself touches down to tell a quite linear (and fascinating) story of the institution of Romantic criticism, and indeed no one of the authors in this volume is able to sustain the indeterminacy of discourse that seems called for by the New Historicist creed.

The problem, if there is one, is illustrated by Jean Franco's criticism of allegorical or homogenizing stories. Repeatedly in her essay Franco opposes allegorical readings to enactments of contradiction and difference (see 208, 210). The last few pages of the piece resound with the praise of that which "def[ies] categorization," of the "uneasy and unfinished," of that which "generic boundaries cannot really contain," of the "unclassifiable," of "pluralism," of clashing styles, of the "kaleidoscope [that] constantly shifts to form different and unreconcilable patterns." "We need," she says in conclusion, "density of specification in order to understand the questions to which literary texts are an imaginary response" (212). But while she opposes "density of specification" to allegorical reading, in her own reading of Latin American novels this same insistence on density and the deferral of assertion becomes an allegory of its own. If density of specification is put forward as an end in itself, it is an allegory as totalizing as any, an allegory of discontinuities and overlappings; and if it is urged as a way to flesh out some positive polemical point, it is an allegory of the more familiar kind. Not that I am faulting Franco for falling into the trap of being discursive and linear; she could not do otherwise and still have as an aim (in her terms an allegorical aim) the *understanding* – the bringing into discursive comprehension – of anything. In the end you can't "defy categorization," you can only categorize in a different way. (Itself no small accomplishment.)

Where then does this leave us? Precisely where we have always been, making cases for the significance and shape of historical events with the help of whatever evidence appears to us to be relevant or weighty. The reasons that a piece of evidence will seem weighty or relevant will have to do with the way in which we are situated as historians and observers, that is, with what we *see* as evidence from whatever angle or perspective we inhabit. Of course, not everyone will see the same thing, and in the (certain) event of disputes, the disputing parties will point to their evidence and attempt to educe more. They will not brandish fancy accounts of how evidence comes to be evidence or invoke theories that declare all evidence suspect and ideological, because, as I have already said, that would be another practice, the practice not of giving historical accounts, but the practice of theorizing their possibility. If you set out to determine what happened in 1649, you will look to the materials that recommend themselves to you as the likely repositories of historical knowledge and go from there. In short, you and those who dispute your findings (a word precisely intended) will be engaged in empirical work, and as Howard Horwitz has recently said, arguments about history "are not finally epistemological but empirical, involving disputes about the contents of knowledge, about evidence and its significance" ("I Can't Remember: Skepticism, Synthetic Histories, Critical Action," *South Atlantic Quarterly* 87: 4 [Fall 1988]: 798).

Another way to put this is to say what others have said before me: the New Historicism is not new. But whereas that observation is usually offered as a criticism – it should be new and it's not – I offer it as something that could not be otherwise. The only way the New or any other kind of historicism could be new is by asserting a new truth about something in opposition to, or correction of, or modification of, a truth previously asserted by someone else; but that newness – always a possible achievement – will not be *methodologically* new, will not be a new (nonallegorical, nonexcluding, nonforgetting, non-boundary-drawing) way of doing history, but merely another move in the practice of history as it has always been done.

If New Historicist methodology (as opposed to the answers it might give to thoroughly traditional questions) is finally not different from any other, the claim of the New Historicism to be politically engaged in a way that other historicisms are not cannot be maintained. The methodological difference claimed by New Historicism is the difference of not being constrained in its gestures by narrow disciplinary and professional boundaries. The reasoning is that since New Historicists are aware of those boundaries and aware, too, of their source in ultimately revisable societal (and even global) structures, they can angle their actions (or interventions as they prefer to call them) in such a way as to put pressure on those structures and so perform politically both in the little world of their institutional situation and the larger world of POLITICS. Now in essence this picture of the radiating or widening out effects of institutional action is an accurate one; for since all activities are interrelated and none enables itself, what is done in one (temporarily demarcated) sphere will ultimately have ramifications for what goes on in others. The question is can one perform institutionally with an eye on that radiating effect? Can one grasp the political constructedness and relatedness of all things in order to do one thing in a different and more capacious way? Given that disciplinary performance depends on the in-place force of innumerable and enabling connections and affiliations (both of complicity and opposition), can I *focus* on those connections in such a way as to make my performance self-consciously larger than its institutional situation would seem to allow?[8]

The answer to all these questions is "no," and for the same reason that it is not possible to practice openness of a general rather than a context specific kind. The hope that you can play a particular game in a way that directly affects the entire matrix in which it is embedded depends on there being a style of playing that exceeds the game's constitutive rules (I am not claiming that those rules are fixed or inflexible, just that even in their provisional and revisable form they define the range of activities – including activities of extension and revision – that will be recognized as appropriate, i.e. in the game); depends, that is, on there being a form of destabilization that is not specific to particular practices, but is simply DESTABILIZATION writ large. If there is no such form – no destabilizing act that does not leave more in place than it disturbs – the effects of your practice will be internal to that practice and will only impinge on larger structures in an indirect and etiolated way.

In short, there is no road, royal or otherwise, from the insight that all activities are political to a special or different way of engaging in any particular activity, no politics that derives from the truth that everything is politically embedded. Interrelatedness may be a fact about disciplines and enterprises as seen from a vantage point uninvolved in any one of them (the vantage point of another, philosophical, enterprise), but it cannot be the motor of one's performance. Practices may *be* interrelated but you cannot *do* interrelatedness – simultaneously stand within a practice and reflectively survey the supports you stand on. One often hears it said that once you have become aware of the political and constructed nature of all actions, this awareness can be put to methodological use in the practices (history, literary criticism, law) you find yourself performing; but (and this is the argument about openness, provisionality, and interrelatedness all over again) insofar as awareness is something that can be put into play in a situation it will be awareness relative to the demarcated concerns of that situation, and not some separate capacity that you carry with you from one situation to another.

I do not mean to deny that New Historicist practice may be involved in a politics, only that it could not be involved in the (impossible) politics that has as its goal the refusing of boundaries as in "I refuse to think of literature as a discrete activity" (sometimes you do, sometimes you don't) or "I refuse to think in terms of national or regional identities" (it depends on what you're thinking about), and the exclusion of exclusions, as in "I will remember everything" (which means you will be unable to think of anything) or "I close my ears to no voice" (which means that no voice will be heard by you). Nor am I saying that New Historicist practice has no global implications; only that the global implications of New Historicist practice cannot be operated by its practitioners. Of course, this is not true of all practices. The actions, say, of members of Congress or of officials of the national administration will have far-reaching and immediate consequences and those consequences can be held in mind as those actions are taken; moreover, it is not impossible that literary criticism could in time become a practice with similarly far-reaching effects.

One can imagine general political conditions such that the appearance on Monday of a new reading of *The Scarlet Letter* would be the occasion on Tuesday of discussion, debate, and proposed legislation on the floor of Congress; but before that can happen (if we really want it to happen) there will have to be a general restructuring of the lines of influence and power in our culture; and while such a restructuring is not unthinkable, it will not be brought about by declarations of revolutionary intent by New Historicists or materialists or anyone else. So long as literary studies are situated as they are now, the most one can hope for (at least with respect to aims that are realistic) is that your work will make a difference in the institutional setting that gives it a home.

And that, as Catherine Gallagher points out, is quite a lot. She observes that New Historicist and allied practices have already altered the institutional land-scape by influencing "the curricula in the literature department, introducing non-canonical texts into the classroom . . . making students more aware of the history and significance of . . . imperialism, slavery and gender differentiation" (44–5). She also notes that for many on the left these changes are insufficient, and there is evidence in the present volume that in the minds of some they are downright suspicious. Montrose, as we have seen, is uneasy at the thought that the successes of New Historicism may be merely professional, and that his own labors may be "a vehicle for . . . partly unconscious and partly calculating negotiation of disciplinary, institutional and societal demands and expecta-tions." He is nervous, that is, at the thought that his career may be going well. Vincent Pecora is distressed at the alacrity at which the New Historicism has turned into a "new kind of formalism" (272), and he complains that cultural semiotics for all its pretensions remains determinedly literary and that its effect has been to make our activities not "more political . . . but . . . less so." It is hard to know whether such anxieties are a sign of large ambitions that have been frustrated – do these critics want to be the acknowledged legislators of the world? – or a sign of the familiar academic longing for failure – we must be doing something wrong because people are listening to us and offering us high salaries. But whatever the source of the malaise, I urge that it be abandoned and that New Historicists sit back and enjoy the fruits of their professional success, wishing neither for more nor for less.[9] In the words of the old Alka-Seltzer commercial, "try it, you'll like it."

Notes

1   The quoted passages appear in a longer version: Judith Newton, "History as Usual," *Cultural Critique* 9 (Spring 1988), 98.
2   I would reply that histories create their own exclusions not because they are misrepresentations – a word that requires for its intelligibility the possibility of a representation that is not one – but because as narratives that tell one story rather than all stories they will always seem partial and inaccurate from the vantage point of other narratives, themselves no less, but differently, exclusionary.

3   From a talk delivered at a meeting of the English Institute, August 27, 1988.

4   See my "Consequences," *Critical Inquiry* 11 (March 1985): 440–1; p. 95 above.

5   But one could be strongly committed to Marxism or psychoanalysis at one level and still practice history (or literary criticism or pedagogy) in a way that was free of Marxist or psychoanalytic assumptions (although the practice would flow from some other assumptions). This might hold true even if in answer to a direct question about your practice you declared that it was Marxist or psychoanalytic. Your theory of what you do is logically independent of what you in fact do (although, as I acknowledge above, a relationship, at least in some cases, is always possible). Thus someone might reasonably disagree with your account of your practice and agree wholeheartedly with its assertions. To demand a perfect homology between practice and theory and between theory and politics is, as Catherine Gallagher says, to surrender "to the myth of a self-consistent subject impervious to divisions of disciplinary boundaries and outside the constraints of disciplinary standards" (46).

6   The quoted passage appears in a longer version of Newton's essay in *Cultural Critique* 8 (Spring 1988), note 33, p. 99.

7   See Roberto Unger, "The Critical Legal Studies Movement, *Harvard Law Review* 96 (1983), and see my "Unger and Milton," in *Doing What Comes Naturally: Change, Rhetoric, and the Practice of Theory in Legal and Literary Studies* (Durham, NC: Duke University Press, 1989).

8   In fact, were I to adopt such a focus I would no longer be doing literary criticism, I would be doing something else, sociology or anthropology or systems analysis, etc. It is once again a question of forgetting and remembering: one cannot keep in mind everything at once and still perform specific tasks (except perhaps the specific – and impossible – task of fully enumerating everything). The very possibility of performing a specific task depends on *not* attending to (i.e. forgetting) concerns that would, if they were given their due, involve one in the performing of a different specific task.

9   Cf. Gallagher: "There may be no political impulse whatsoever behind [the] desire to historicize literature. This is not to claim that the desire for historical knowledge is itself historically unplaced or 'objective'; it is, rather, to insist that the impulse, norms, and standards of a discipline called history, which has achieved a high level of autonomy in the late twentieth century, are a profound part of the subjectivity of some scholars and do not in all cases require political ignition" (46). I would only add that the antiprofessionalism displayed by Pecora and Montrose is yet another indication of the idealizing and ahistorical vision that generates their complaints and anxieties.

9
Why Literary Criticism Is Like Virtue

It was within the blooming, buzzing hive of the 1996 Modern Language Association Convention – at the book displays, in the Duke University Press booth – that I finally met Stanley Fish. The professor had by this time suffered two decades' worth of essays promising once and for all to catch Fish, bait Fish, harpoon Fish. And all they ever seemed to prove was that there was no attack from which Fish could not slither free. A year earlier, though, I had published a review of his latest book, *Professional Correctness: Literary Studies and Political Change*, which I thought had finally netted the man.

The problem with his other critics, I reasoned, *was that they took his arguments on his own terms*. All Fish's works are variations on a single, elegantly maddening theme: human beings (to cite the title of the book that contains the essay below) can only "do what comes naturally"; that is to say, do things according to rules we understand so implicitly we cannot reflect on them, but rules we ourselves "do" into naturalness simply by unreflectively living our everyday lives. It is a vicious circle, and to his critics who claim to have broken it, Fish is always able to handily point out the unreflective ways they obey, and thus reproduce, rules they had not before known they were following in writing the very essay under consideration.

In *Professional Correctness*, Fish rang the familiar changes: English professors could not save their profession from the dominant culture's abuse by infiltrating the dominant culture's media, for to do so they would have to do what came naturally within those media, thus abandoning the very practices which give them whatever cultural power they possess, which flows from their unique practice as literary professionals. QED: public intellectualism would likely cause them to lose their cultural autonomy, not preserve it. The only thing that could, in fact, preserve the profession of literary studies, was to preserve literary studies' distinctiveness from all other realms of human endeavor.

I found this argument airless and irrelevant – but how to criticize it without Fish catching me in his circle? I chose to outflank him. The profession's autonomy came not from its unique practices but – where else? – from decades of flush Cold War funding for the humanities, a stream now so threatened that English departments are hiring only one new professor for every four professors who retire. To preserve what autonomy that remained, I argued, required just the sort of cagey worldliness that Fish derides. I drove the harpoon home: "He might note that employees of the Interstate Commerce Commission may well have been able to boast impeccable professionalism, but little good it did them when their agency fell to the budget ax this year."

Meanwhile, at the MLA convention. Spotting Fish's turtleneck from across a crowded room, I approached him to wrest from him the concession speech that surely was my due. Alas, he said, he *loved* my review.

"But it was a negative review."

"No, I agreed with it totally."

"So you've changed your views."

"Not at all. You see, you made the same mistakes all my critics do ...."

Well. And here I had thought I had diverged radically from his critics. I wish I could reproduce here what happened in the ten minutes that followed as Fish, somehow, spun out the reasons why my views accorded perfectly with his own, *as set out in the book*. He left me gasping, as he had so many before, with nothing left to do but concede. That he could do so is the very reason his work deserves to be collected in such a book as this.

Fish writes, in *Professional Correctness*, of literary studies' distinctiveness from all other realms of human endeavor: "Literary critics do not traffic in wisdom, but in metrics, narrative structures, double, triple, and quadruple meanings, recondite allusions, unity in the midst of apparent fragmentation, fragmentation, despite surface unity, reversals, convergences, mirror images, hidden arguments, climaxes, denouements, stylistic registers, personae." If you believe Fish is indeed right that continuing to so traffic is what it will take to keep and preserve literary criticism for future generations, study the quietly brilliant tropology below – literary criticism at its most literary-criticismish – with exquisite care. If not: well, just sit back and enjoy the ride.

Rick Perlstein

One of the pleasures of giving these lectures, over and above the general pleasures of being in Oxford, has been a number of chance meetings with members of the audience who pause on the street or in a café or in a bookshop to say hello and ask a question, usually in the form of a mild (at least in tone) objection. One of you (Professor Avraham Oz) even took the time to send me a substantial letter, in which the main thesis of these lectures – that academic work is one thing and political work another – was strongly contested. Let me share with you some of the letter-writer's points and my replies.

His first point, which he acknowledged is in no way in conflict with what I have been saying, is that, as an Israeli, he inhabits a culture where the relationship between academic productions and political acts is much closer than in the United States; indeed, given the fact that in his country some of the leading literary intellectuals have also been among the nation's most prominent politicians, it is inevitable that those who perform and consume exegetical labours do so with a strong sense of the potential connection between them and the urgent questions of the day; and this holds true when the text being explicated is Shakespeare, and especially true if it is *The Merchant of Venice*.

As he and I agree, however, this coincidence of the literary and the political contexts is not generalizable since it flows from the particular fact of a society in which being Jewish, being a citizen, being a patriot, and being a cultural critic are all bound up with one another. Moreover, even in this situation, where the link between politics and interpretive acts of a literary kind is close and pressuring, interpretive acts will still not be political acts in the strong sense, because while they might well have political consequences (by virtue of a network of reciprocal attention) they will still have as their immediate aim – as the purpose that gets them going – the telling of the truth about some text or group of texts. In the United States, literary interpretive acts are both limited in their immediate aim and without consequences outside the precincts in which that aim is properly taken, and therefore those who perform interpretive acts need not feel at their backs the pressure exerted by their civic and religious identities.

My correspondent's second point is more directly challenging. No matter where we live, he points out, we carry with us histories as members of racial or ethnic groups, social classes, and political parties that surely have an influence on the areas of scholarship to which we gravitate and the questions we think to ask when we do our academic work. This is certainly true, and I can offer my own experience as a corroborating, if imperfectly understood (by me), example. A second-generation American Jew and the first in my family to attend college, it can hardly be an accident that I have made my life's work non-dramatic literature of the sixteenth and seventeenth centuries, with a special emphasis on the relationship between Christian theology and aesthetic structures. Nor am I alone. I remember looking around my department at Berkeley in the late 1960s and saying (to myself), "My God, all the Christian humanists are Jews."

How is this phenomenon to be read? What does it mean? Presumably it means that for many young Jews of my generation the process of assimilation included a decision, less than consciously made, to identify with that part of the field most invested in the assumptions, both cultural and theological, of the main stream tradition. But while such a consideration, however mediated, might well have been a reason (less than conscious) for my getting into a certain line of work, it was not a reason that guided me in *doing* that work once I became committed to it. That is, when I set out, for example, to account for the peculiarly astringent power of Herbert's poetry, I did not begin with an awareness of my position as a Jew explicating Christian verse; rather I began with an awareness of what had been done and said by those who had preceded me in attempting that task, and it was in reference to their prior efforts – with its record of successes, failures, and unresolved problems – that I mounted my own. What I am invoking here, despite my earlier jibes at the discipline of philosophy, is the familiar philosophical distinction between the context of justification – the context that determines what will count as evidence in the eyes and ears of one's peers – and the context of discovery – the personal history that brought one into this arena of evidence rather than into another.

This brings me to my correspondent's third point, which is, I think, the most telling: that insofar as the question is the relationship between academic practices and social or political change, it is finally "a matter of degree, rather than of essence." I couldn't agree more. In some countries – Israel would seem to be an example – academic and political practices, even in the case of literary studies, overlap to such an extent that one cannot engage in the former without having the latter strongly in mind (although, I would hasten to add, they remain distinctive, even when because of contingent circumstances, they become linked up). But in some other countries, and I have been saying that the United States is one, the overlap, while theoretically possible, is simply not a feature of the situation, and the two go their way with only chance meetings that will seem odd when they occur. This is not to deny that even in the United States alterations in the structure of academic life will sometimes have an effect on the society as a whole. As Catherine Gallagher has observed, new historicist and allied movements have already altered the institutional landscape by influencing "curricula in literature departments ... introducing non-canonical texts into the classroom... making students...more aware of the history and significance of...imperialism, slavery and gender differentiation" (in H. Aram Veeser, ed., *The New Historicism*, New York, 1989, 44–5). And it is no doubt true that in some cases (although by no means all or even the majority) students introduced to these new texts and topics will factor them into their thinking in ways that will markedly affect their performances as citizens, churchgoers, parents, doctors, lawyers, etc. (The so-called "Sixties" generation can stand as a convenient collective instance.) But, to repeat a point I have made often, such consequences of one's disciplinary activities cannot be counted on. They may or may not occur; and, more importantly, such consequences are not what one intends when engaging in a piece of literary analysis; not because such an intention is incapable of realization in any context, but because in the context now in force in the United States, it cannot be responsibly formed.

To this one might respond, "So much the worse for the United States." But I am not so sure. Being sequestered in the academy has its advantages as well as its liabilities; many who wished for increased public attention to their labors got it in the past few years of the right-wing backlash and found that, rather than bringing respect and influence, it brought danger and the elimination of progressive programs. Perhaps it is not so bad a thing after all that in the United States those who operate the levers of commerce and government do not give much heed to what goes on in our classrooms or in our learned journals.

Again one must note the exception that proves the rule. In the years of the Reagan and Bush administrations a number of government officials had links to a network of Straussians, students and followers of the late Leo Strauss, a political philosopher who strongly attacked what he saw as the corrosive relativism of modern thought and urged a return to the normative thinking of the ancients. Strauss's views or versions of them were alive and well in the persons of William Bennett, Lynne Cheney, Chester Finn, Dianne Ravitch, and Quayle's Chief of Staff, William Kristol, and it is at least arguable that these and others close to the administration were able to influence its policies especially in matters of education, the arts, and civil rights. It would seem, then, that this was an instance in which intellectuals had a direct impact on the political life of the nation. But if these men and women were influential it was not because of their teachings and writings but because they managed through non-academic connections to secure positions that gave their teachings and writings a force they would not have had if they had remained in the academy where they would have had to wait for some accidental meeting between their "great thoughts" and the powers that be. Absent such an accident or an appointment to public office only contingently related to those thoughts (government officials don't say, "He wrote a great book on the English novel; let's make him Secretary of Education"), there are no regular routes by which the accomplishments of academics in general and literary academics in particular can be transformed into the currency of politics.

This is not an inevitable condition: there is nothing in theory to prevent such routes from being established, but literary theorists will not be the people to establish them; the initiative has to come from the other direction, from those who are so situated as to have the power (although they do not yet have the reasons) to introduce into their councils news from the world of cultural studies, or feminist theory or reader-response criticism. As things stand now such a development is not easily imaginable (and even if it were realized, the news would have to be translated into political terms, at which point it would no longer be literary), for it would require alterations in the existing spheres of influence and routes of communication so great that the culture of which we are all members would be unrecognizable. Until that happens, or until some unlikely political event surprises us – such as, for instance, the election to the presidency of a literary critic; and in order for it to count he or she would have to be elected *as* a literary critic, and not as someone otherwise qualified who *also* laid claim to this curious little talent – literary critics will have to be content with the 'trickle-down' consequences that may or may not flow from the fact that generations of young adults pass through their classrooms. It goes without saying that such consequences – associated in earlier pedagogical fantasies with Mr Chips – will not be sufficient for those who want to participate in "the revolutionary transformation of social relations all at one go" (Tony Bennett, *Outside Literature*, London, 1990, 237). All one can offer such would-be shakers and movers is an unhappy choice: they must either content themselves with the successes achieved in the context of specifically literary goals and purposes, or they must look forward to a life of continual frustration as the desire to extend the effects of such successes into precincts incapable of recognizing them (never mind responding to them) goes forever unrealized.

The unhappiness of this choice has not been lost on those it confronts. Critics who begin with "revolutionary" aspirations regularly lament the fact that their efforts have been appropriated – and, to add insult to injury, rewarded – by the very institution they thought to transcend. Immediately after claiming to be reforming his own culture by reforming the received picture of the culture of Spenser and Shakespeare, Montrose ruefully acknowledges "that my professional practice as a teacher-scholar is also a vehicle for my partly unconscious and partly calculating negotiation of disciplinary, institutional, and societal demands and expectations" ("Professing the Renaissance," in Veeser, ed., *The New Historicism*, 30). "I have," he admits, "a complex and substantial stake in sustaining and reproducing the very institutions whose operations I wish to call into question." In the same vein, Don Wayne worries that in the work of new historicists power relations replace other themes in what amounts to little more than a "new formalism." The danger, he observes, is that the new terms, with their apparent political edge, will "operate in our criticism in the way that generic categories, narrative functions, and stylistic devices did formerly" ("Power, Politics, and the Shakespearen Text," in J. Howard and M. O'Connor, eds., *Shakespeare Reproduced: The Text in History and Ideology*, New York, 1987, 61). That is, they will operate as components of a practice that continues to be shaped by the imperative to explicate poems. The face of the practice may continually change as new topics are drawn into its orbit, but, once in, anything "new" is immediately rendered very familiar by the questions – with what does it cohere? of what is it a conversion? with what is it in tension? – the practice is obliged (by its own sense of itself) to ask. That is why supposedly "critical scholarship," scholarship driven by the determination to read "against the grain," is, as Michael Bristol sadly notes, "likely to result in legitimation rather than in practically effective critique" ("Lenten Butchery: Legitimation Crisis in *Coriolanus*," in Howard and O'Connor, eds., *Shakespeare Reproduced*, 220), likely, in other words to extend rather than challenge the discipline that finds room for it. "Just at the moment when its presence in the . . . university seems assured," John Beverley laments, "cultural studies has begun to lose the radicalizing force that accompanied its emergence as a field" (*Against Literature*, Minneapolis, 1993, 21).

The fear that this loss has already been suffered haunts a huge anthology entitled *Cultural Studies* (ed. Lawrence Grossberg, Cary Nelson, and Paula Treichler, New York, 1992), the record of a conference held at the University of Illinois in 1990. The papers at that conference were many and varied in their focus, but they shared a desire to link the practice of cultural studies in the classroom to the project of restructuring society. In almost every question period, however, someone would raise the obvious point that this very meeting, with all of its talk about interventions, radical questionings, and transgressions, was taking place at a large, publicly funded university and bore all the marks of the hierarchies, factional rivalries, and personal agendas that were so often the objects of scathing criticism. Where at a different kind of conference a speaker might have been challenged because he cited an outdated edition or failed to take account of newly discovered facts, a speaker at this conference was challenged because "a certain Eurocentrism" (368) had been detected in his argument. He replied in kind, finding the comments of his questioner "problematic" because "you seek to give them moral force by situating yourself as a representative of a number of marginalized or repressed constituencies" (368). The game here is not "my scholarship is better than yours," but "my marginalization is greater and more authentic than yours," but the difference is, as Chomsky might say, a notational variant, and at bottom the games are pretty much the same.

This sense of the game weights heavily on the participants who wish they were not playing it, but doing something else. "I don't mind listening to people I admire," one participant declares, "but it seems to me we need four days of discussion about how we can intervene in the institutions in which we work, rather than four days reproducing the same kind of hierarchy we already have" (294). It is hard to see why he thinks that an additional four days would be less shadowed by the institutions that would structure and sponsor them or less hierarchical in their unfolding than the days he has already endured, or more likely to produce strategies other than those he has learned to perform in the schools he now despises. "What we have to understand," says another participant, "is that we too are held by institutionalized practices and discourses ... I'm often frustrated with my own inability to rethink these standard practices" (528–9). Stuart Hall is more than frustrated; he is "completely dumbfounded" by American cultural studies, which seems to him the very emblem of the "moment of profound danger" that always attends "institutionalization" (285). If that is the danger, it surrounds this conference; it *is* this conference.

The basic point has been made with devastating authority by Evan Watkins. Academic literary work, he says,

occupies a marginal position and circulation within the dominant formation. And studying TV commercials or films or rock music or political speeches rather than a "traditional" literary canon does little in and of itself to effect any social change. That sort of "territory shift" doesn't mean we're now playing for big stakes ... It just means we're playing for the same marginal stakes with new material ... that the one-way street remains a dead end, unable to convey the work involved anywhere else. (*Work Time: English Departments and the Circulation of Cultural Value*, Stanford, Calif., 1989, 271.)

After such things have been said, it is hard to imagine saying anything else. But the dream of intervening in the world more effectively than the profession of literary criticism seems to allow dies hard. Within a few paragraphs Watkins is urging his readers/colleagues to "forge connections to popular cultures ... and to use the connections to educate a support structure for the next step, the next shift in territory in a prolonged war of position" (273), and in the penultimate sentence of his book he is calling on his fellow critics "to change the conditions of all our work" (276). It could be that in time all or almost all of the conditions of our work might be changed (as they have in fact changed since the days of Sidney, Jonson, and Milton), but the change will not come about because literary critics have *willed* it; for we could change the conditions of all our work only by standing outside them (but then it is hard to say why they would then be *our* conditions). So long as we labor within them the changes we might make will be in the nature of modifications rather than ruptures. If, for example, we "forge connections to popular culture" by writing about it in addition to or in place of writing about Shakespeare and Spenser we will merely have added another room to our academic house. This will make a difference in the way the profession looks, but it will not mean that the boundaries of the profession will have been pushed outward. Bringing new grist to your mill does not in itself alter the basic manner of its operation. It would seem from much of his book that Watkins knows this, but the knowledge weighs heavily on him and when the lure of political hope captures him, he forgets it.

Sometimes the forgetting is instantaneous. Montrose asserts strongly (and correctly) that the "possibility of political and institutional agency cannot be based upon the illusion of an escape from ideology" ("Professing the Renaissance," 30), of an escape, that is, from the presuppositions within which one thinks to act. However, the very next sentence begins with "However": "However, the very process of subjectively *living* the confrontations or contradictions within or among ideologies makes it possible to experience facets of our own subjection . . . to read, as in a refracted light, one fragment of our ideological inscription by means of another." Montrose underlines "living," but what he really means by it is "thinking about" or "being self-consciously aware of." The idea is that while ideological subjection is unavoidable, we can at least gain a perspective on it, either by moving back and forth "among" ideological formations in a way that gives us a purchase on one even as we are "inscribed" in another, or by surfacing the contradictions "within" an ideology and thus distancing ourselves from its full sway. We may not be able to escape ideology, but we can, in moments of strenuous self-consciousness, loosen its hold.

There are two theses here. The first is that every ideological formation gains its apparent plausibility only by suppressing elements within it that would, if they were brought to light, subvert its claims to coherence. The second thesis is that once we are aware of this truth about a particular ideology, its force will have been lessened, if only slightly. ("A reflexive knowledge so partial and unstable may, nevertheless, provide subjects with a means of empowerment as agents.") The first thesis seems to me obviously right: when the apparent unity of an ideological system is strongly interrogated one will always discover the embarrassing exceptions, concessions, and barely disguised duplicities that tell the "real story" of an agenda cobbled together out of the most disparate and contradictory elements. An easy, because familiar to me, example is the body of American contract law, which ceaselessly presents a master narrative in which autonomous agents freely enter into bargained-for exchanges that courts inspect only for procedural flaws while refusing on principle to import into their rulings any considerations of value. But even a cursory knowledge of the case-law reveals that this master narrative is kept afloat by invoking (under rubrics like unconscionability) just those considerations that have been most loudly banished by the rhetoric of the enterprise. In its every operation contract law is telling *two* stories while pretending that the second one has been ruled out of court.

Should we conclude then (as proponents of the Critical Legal Studies Movement tend to) that this news should be broadcast from the rooftops, and that if it were, a shamefaced profession would give up its shabby ways and face the basic contradictions of its inauthentic existence? I'm afraid not, if only because this is news that everyone already knows, and not only knows but utilizes in the course of getting through the mercantile and juridical day. It is by virtue of the contradictions it harbours that contract law is able to exhibit the flexibility required by the double obligation to adhere to an official morality of contractual autonomy while adjusting its rulings to the reality of a world in which such autonomy has always and already been compromised. An analysis of contract law that foregrounded its contradictions would be embarrassing to its project only if the goal of that project were to be philosphically consistent. But that is not the goal of any project except for the project of philosophy itself. Other projects have the less abstract goal (which philosophy also shares) of wanting to flourish. I would have thought that the last word on the relationship between the foregrounding of contradiction and the impulse to reform was said by Joe E. Brown in Billy Wilder's classic movie *Some Like It Hot*. Brown, you will remember, has been courting Jack Lemmon in drag and is about to propose to him on a boat. Thinking to end this farce once and for all by revealing a fatal contradiction in the structure of Brown's desire, Lemmon cries, "I can't marry you; I'm a man," to which Brown sublimely replies, "Nobody's perfect."

The moral here is that the awareness of contradiction doesn't make any necessary difference and certainly will not make the difference (claimed by Montrose) of allowing us at once to experience constraint (or as he calls it subjection) and to stand apart from it. This is the hope and the dream of critical self-consciousness, the thesis that ye shall know that what passes for the truth is socially and historically constructed and that knowledge shall set you free. The critically self-conscious agent, the argument goes, is just as embedded as anyone else, but he is *aware* of it and that makes all the difference, or at least the difference that keeps the hope of boundary-breaking behaviour alive. This will work, however, only if the knowledge that we are embedded is stored in a part of the mind that floats free of the embeddedness we experience at any one time; but that would mean that at least a part of our mind was not somewhere but everywhere and that would mean that we were not human beings but gods. In a frankly religious tradition the internalization of deity is not only possible, it is obligatory; but in the militantly secular tradition of the new historicism and cultural studies, what is internalized are the routines and deep assumptions of human practices which resemble deity only in that they are jealous of rivals and say to us "Thou shalt have no other gods before me."

Critical self-consciousness, conceived of as a mental action independent of the setting in which it occurs, is the last infirmity of the mind that would deny its own limits by positioning itself in two places at the same time, in the place of its local embodiment and in the disembodied place (really no place) of reflection. It is to this latter place that cultural studies promises to bring us by relaxing the grip of forms of thought and categorization specific to particular disciplines. It should be the "result of practicing Cultural Studies," declares Fred Inglis, "that they teach both the feasibility *and* the moral necessity of . . . displacement of the self into the fourth dimension" (*Cultural Studies*, Oxford, 1993, 210). By the "fourth dimension," Inglis means a dimension removed from the pressures of everyday institutional and political life: "I detach myself from myself and consider my life as if it were not mine, considering by what historical road it came to this pass." Refreshed by this sojourn in the ether of disembodied reflection, Inglis reports, "I step back into myself, and the torrential demands of my life."

In an older tradition this is the sequence enacted by penitents, pilgrims, and flagellants who ascend not to cultural studies but to the mount of Contemplation (see *The Faerie Queene*, 1. x) and a vision of deity (see Plato's *Phaedrus* and Augustine's *On Christian Doctrine*). Cultural studies, it would seem, has replaced poetry as the replacement for religion; it is the new altar before which those who would cast off their infirmities worship. Cultural studies, Inglis intones only half-jokingly, "will make you good" (229). Henry Giroux isn't joking at all when he declares that "cultural studies offers the possibility for extending the democratic principles of justice, liberty, and equality to the widest possible set of social relations and institutional practices that constitute everyday life' (*Cultural Studies Times*, Fall 1994, A15). Somewhat less dramatically, but no less ambitiously, S. P. Mohanty finds in cultural and political criticism the key to being fully human "not merely the capacity to act purposefully but also to *evaluate* actions and purposes in terms of larger ideas we might hold about, say, our political and moral world" ("Us and Them: On the Philosophical Bases of Political Criticism," *Yale Journal of Criticism*, 2/2, 1989, 22). It is this "capacity for self-aware historical agency" that informs cultural-political criticism and is presumably enlarged by it. A discipline that resists this "second order understanding" refuses to know the conditions of its own possibility and, in Bruce Robbins's words, "shirks the responsibility to think through the issue of its own vocation, its own authorities, its own grounding" (*Secular Vocations*, London, 1993, 110).

These claims for the effects of cultural studies follow from (and are the mirror image of) the description of cultural studies as a more inclusive, deeper form of inquiry than is permitted by the self-policing parameters of traditional disciplines. My response to that description is also my response to this expression of hoped-for effects: cultural studies is not larger or more penetrating than the modes of interrogation it seeks to displace; it is merely different and will bring different – not higher or truer – yields. And while it will bring you to a different place than, say, the study of Renaissance pastoral, it will not bring you to any fourth dimension, only to the dimension of its own *specialized* practice. The practice of cultural studies will not make you good, it will make you proficient in the routines that are its content. Cultural studies involves no "second-order" understanding, only the understanding of the phenomena its questions bring into view.

Moreover, what is true of cultural studies is true of reflection in general, that mode of mental activity of which cultural studies is supposedly the institutional form. It is not that reflection is impossible – most of us engage in it every day; it is just that rather than floating above the practices that are its object and providing a vantage-point from which those practices can be assessed and reformed, reflection is either (*a*) an activity *within* a practice and therefore finally not distanced from that practice's normative assumptions or (*b*) an activity grounded in its own normative assumptions and therefore one whose operations will reveal more about itself than about any practice viewed through its lens. If, for example, I "reflect" on the relationship between literary studies and the study of history, the course of my reflection – the direction it takes – will be a function of the fact that literary studies (and everything it presupposes) is its starting-point. Such a reflection will yield answers, but they will be answers to the questions literary studies (as it is now constituted) poses and not to its own questions, and if they *were* the answers to reflection's own questions – to questions posed in reflection's own language, a language in no way hostage to literary imperatives – the answers could not be connected up with literary studies (or anything else) in anything but an arbitrary way. While it is always possible to interrogate a literary work by applying to it the categories of some philosophical system, absent any pre-established link between that system and the work's origin in an intentional project, the resulting description will be without any particular significance or, rather, will be available to any significance an interpreter happens to prefer. Again, either reflection is the extension of a practice and can claim no distance from it or it is itself a practice and has no privileged relationship to, or even any necessary significance for, practices other than itself.

What this means, as I argue elsewhere (in *Doing what Comes Naturally*, Oxford, 1989, ch. 19), is that there is no such thing as critical self-consciousness, no separate "muscle of the mind" that can be flexed in any situation, no capacity either innate or socially nurtured for abstracting oneself from everyday routines in the very act of performing them, no buffer zone that allows us to assess critically what we are doing, no possibility of a discipline's thinking through "the issue of its own grounding," no strategy for loosening the constraints that bind us whenever we set ourselves a particular task. And what *that* means is that any rewards or pleasures we might look for will come from particular tasks and not from their transcendence.

What are those rewards and pleasures? This is again the question of justification, now given new urgency because, in light of the arguments I have been making, the usual justifications are unpersuasive. The old justification made literary critics the custodians of a human treasure, a repository of wisdom good for all problems and all times. The new justification, fashioned by deconstructionists, new historicists, cultural materialists, postmodernists, etc., gives literary critics, now called discourse analysts, a role in the forming of new subjectivities capable of forming a counter-disciplinary practice as part of the construction of an "oppositional public sphere" (Patrick Brantlinger, *Crusoe's Footprints*, New York, 1990, 24). The old justification won't work because the strong historicism to which many of us have been persuaded rules out a set of texts that float above all historical conditions dispensing wisdom to those fit to receive it. The new justification won't work because the same strong historicism leaves no room for the special and ahistorical brand of reflective consciousness that discourse analysis supposedly engenders.

If literary interpretation will neither preserve the old order nor create a new one, what can it do and why should anyone practice it? I can't tell you in so many words – a general answer to the question is precisely what my argument will not allow – but perhaps I can show you. My vehicle will be a single line from *Paradise Lost*. It occurs mid-way in book I, just as Milton's narrator is about to call the roll of fallen angels, who, he says, will in future times pass themselves off as gods to credulous mortals. They manage to so corrupt "the greatest part of Mankind" (367–8) that men and women "forsake God their creator' (379) and fall to worshipping brutes. The contempt the narrator feels for those who are thus deceived is bitingly expressed in the line that interests me:

And Devils to adore for Deities. (373)

That is, how stupid can you be? Of all the mistakes to make, the mistaking of a devil for a deity seems the most reprehensible and the most inexplicable. How could you fail to tell the difference between the creator and the most base of his creatures, hardly a creature at all in his rebellious infidelity? That is surely the sense of the line, at least in paraphrase which, if it is a heresy, is one we all necessarily and endlessly practice.

But, even as that sense unfolds, the medium of its expression begins to undo it; for while the sense of the line insists on the great difference between devils and deities and registers incredulity at anyone's inability to tell them apart, the sound-pattern of the line — what would have been called in Milton's age its "schematic figures" — is blurring the difference and making it hard to tell them apart. Not only are the two main nouns, Devils and Deities, linked by alliteration and assonance, but their acoustic similarity is quite literally mirrored in the words — "to adore for" — that separate them, but do not really separate them since the effect of mirroring is to bring them even closer together.

What then is the line finally saying: that there is a huge difference between devils and deities or that there is practically (a word precisely intended) no difference between devils and deities? The answer — inevitable given the underlying assumptions of literary interpretation as I described them earlier — is that the line is saying both: the difference is huge; the difference is very small, and there is no paradox because the largeness and smallness exist on different levels. The difference is small if we think to discern it with the physical eye or ear. Devils can make themselves up to look or sound like deities any time; appearance, after all, is the diabolical realm, is what they worship, is what they are. True discernment requires an *inner* eye capable of penetrating to essences, an eye that does not rest on surfaces, but quite literally sees through them, the eye in short, of faith, famously defined in Hebrews II as the "evidence of things not seen." The inner eye has only God as its object; and the difference between God and anything else looms large and immediately; if the gaze wanders, if the eye is distracted by some glittering simulacrum, the difference is blurred and becomes difficult to "tell." Those who mistake devils for deities do not experience an empirical failure; they experience the failure that is empiricism, the failure to distinguish between the things that are made and the maker, who is, of course, invisible.

The failure that is empiricism is graphically on display in book II when Mammon, admiring the "Gems and Gold" beneath the soil of hell, declares "what can Heav'n show more?" (273). He really means it; for Mammon there is nothing more than show, appearance, surface; that is all he can see — and hell to adore for heaven — because that is all he is. The master text for all of this is the *Areopagitica*:

Good and evill . . . in the field of the World grow up together almost inseparably; and the knowledge of good is so involv'd and interwoven with the knowledge of evil, and in so many cunning resemblances hardly to be discern'd, that those confused seeds which were imposed on *Psyche* as an incessant labour to cull out, and sort asunder, were not more intermixed. ([Milton's] *Complete Prose Works* [gen. ed. Don M. Wolfe, 8 vols., New Haven, 1953–82], ii. 514)

Both the difficulty and the necessity of discerning are Milton's great subject and he presents it by repeatedly displaying "cunning resemblances" and then asking his readers to sort them asunder. The result is "incessant labour," an interpretive labour, whose yield is not the calculation of the right answer but the experience of how difficult it is "in the field of this World" to determine what the right answer is, how difficult it is to tell the difference between devils and deities.

For me the reward and pleasure of literary interpretation lie in being able to perform analyses like this. Literary interpretation, like virtue, is its own reward. I do it because I like the way I feel when I'm doing it. I like being brought up short by an effect I have experienced but do not yet understand analytically. I like trying to describe in flatly prosaic words the achievement of words that are anything but flat and prosaic. I like savouring the physical "taste" of language at the same time that I work to lay bare its physics. I like uncovering the incredibly dense pyrotechnics of a master artificer, not least because in praising the artifice I can claim a share in it. And when those pleasures have been (temporarily) exhausted, I like linking one moment in a poem to others and then to moments in other works, works by the same author or by his predecessors or contemporaries or successors. It doesn't finally matter which, so long as I can *keep going*, reaping the cognitive and tactile harvest of an activity as self-reflexive as I become when I engage in it.

It is no small irony that in making this confession I have come round to the very position Terry Eagleton articulates when he declares "what the aesthetic imitates in its very glorious futility, in its pointless self-referentiality, in all its full-blooded formalism, is nothing less than human existence itself, which needs no rationale beyond its own self-delight, which is an end in itself and which will stoop to no external determination" ("The Ideology of the Aesthetic," in S. Regan, ed., *The Politics of Pleasure: Aesthetics and Cultural Theory*, Buckingham, Penn., 1992, 30). I couldn't have said it better, and I also agree with that part of Eagleton's analysis which finds aesthetic pleasure operating both as a support and guarantor of dominant modes of thought and as a challenge to those same modes. But at the moment I am neither supporting nor challenging, but just plain enjoying.

Indeed I will take my enjoyment wherever I can find it. Thus when I run out of sources and analogues, similarities and differences, I go to the history of the criticism which not only allows me to continue the game, but to secure my place in it by linking my own efforts to those of past giants. In the case of "And Devils to adore for Deities" I would head straight back to F. R. Leavis and his famously infamous attack on Milton's style, which, he says, "compels an attitude toward itself that is incompatible with sharp concrete realization" ("Milton's Verse," in C. A. Patrides, ed., *Milton's Epic Poetry*, Baltimore, 1967, 22). That is, rather than pointing the reader to something beyond itself, Milton's language, Leavis complains, calls attention to itself, to the relationships between its components. Milton "exhibits a feeling *for* words rather than a capacity for feeling *through* words." For Leavis, this refusal of the lived complexities of sensuous experience in favour of a verbal universe that traps us in its own intricacies is a fault of both style and character. The character is "disastrously single-minded" (28) and its narcissistic obsessiveness is reflected in a "tyrannical stylization" that in its "remoteness" (22) from English speech totally ignores the needs of the reader. Milton, Leavis concludes, "often produces passages that have to be read through several times before one can see how they go" (24).

To all of this I would say "precisely so," but where Leavis sees perversity and a "defect of imagination" (28), I see an intention brilliantly realized. The intention is to make the verse of the poem into a set of exercises in which the reader is forced to confront the difficulty of interpretive choices that must nevertheless be made. In relation to this intention the last thing Milton wants us to do is feel through his words to something else; rather he wants to *arrest* our attention, to slow down the reading experience to the extent that *its* problems become its content. It is just as Leavis says: the words of the poem *do* "value themselves . . . highly" (26), occupying our attention to the exclusion of any referent beyond them; but that is because the field of reference Milton is interested in is abstract, is a philological and philosophical field populated by the great moral and theological problems with which the age was obsessed. It is, to borrow a phrase from Francis Bacon, "a country in the mind," and if Milton wants us to remain in it and undergo its salutary trials, he must prevent us from escaping into the rich particulars of Leavis's "concretely realized" world. If "passages have to be read through several times before one can see how they go," it is because the *cognitive* acts such readings and rereadings involve are the acts Milton wants us to perform.

I see that in the course of presenting an example of literary criticism I have fallen under the sway of its imperatives and am now pursuing my analysis seriously rather than as a mere illustration. That's the way it is for me. I can't stay away from the stuff. It's what I do; and that, finally, is the only justification I can offer for its practice. It is usually said that justification, in order to be valid, must not borrow its terms from the activity being justified. Only a justification that did not presuppose the value of the activity under scrutiny would be legitimate; otherwise one would be trading on a value while pretending to establish it. This picture of justification will work, however, only if there is a normative structure in relation to which any and all practices can be assessed; but if, as I have been arguing, there is no such structure and each practice is answerable to the norms implicit in its own history and conventions, then justification can only proceed *within* that history and in relation to those conventions. It is not that an external justification could not be mounted, but that it would tell you more about the justificatory mechanism than about the enterprise supposedly being justified. Justification is always internal and can only get off the ground if the value it seeks to uncover or defend is presupposed and is (surreptitiously) guiding the process at the end of which it is triumphantly revealed. Justification never starts from scratch, and can only begin if everything it seeks to demonstrate is already taken for granted.

It is because justification is internal and never starts from scratch that no one chooses a profession by surveying available options and settling on the one whose claims to moral and philosophical coherence seem most persuasive. (The scenario is the same one that imagines Montrose *choosing* to believe in his readings of Spenser and Shakespeare.) Choice of that kind is never the route by which you "discover" your life's work; rather, one day, after many false starts, or in the wake of "starts" you do not recall attempting, you find yourself in the middle of doing something, enmeshed in its routines, extending in every action its assumptions. And when the request for justification comes, you respond *from the middle*, respond with the phrases and platitudes of disciplinary self-congratulation, respond with a rehearsal of canonical achievements and ancient claims to universal benefit, respond, as Weinrib says, by ploughing over the same ground in ever deeper furrows. Justification is not a chain of inferences, but a circle, and it proceeds, if that is the word, by telling a story in which every detail is an instantiation of an informing spirit that is known only in the details but always exceeds them.

Moreover, it is hard, if not impossible, to tell that story to those who do not already know it, or, rather, are not already living it. If you ask me, "Why is it a good thing to explicate *Paradise Lost?*," I can do nothing better or more persuasive than *do* it, spinning it out in directions at once familiar and surprising, ringing the changes, sounding the notes in the hope that the song is one you know or that it will be infectious enough to start you singing. Literary interpretation, Michael Carter has recently said, has no purpose external to the arena of its practice; it is the "constant unfolding" to ourselves "of who we are" as practitioners; its audience is made up of those who already thrill to its challenges and resonate to its performances (Michael Carter, "Scholarship as Rhetoric of Display," *College English*, 54/3, Mar. 1992, 310). Richard Rorty makes the same point when the rejects the idea that "humanities departments should have aims" – goals external to their own obsessions – and counsels us simply to think of departments as oases for "a bunch of wayfaring pilgrims who happened to take shelter in the same inn, or in the same section of the stacks" ("Tales of Two Disciplines," *Callaloo*, 17/2, 1994, 575). That's all there is to it; there's nothing more to be said, but it's enough for those who long ago ceased to be able to imagine themselves living any other life. Last year, an old friend whom I hadn't seen for a while called me to catch up. "What are you doing this summer?" he asked. "Writing on *Paradise Lost*," I answered. "But that's what you said thirty years ago," he responded. "Right," I replied, "yet once more"; and if I had thought of it I would have borrowed a line from my friend David Lodge, who borrowed it from George and Ira Gershwin: "Nice work if you can get it."

10

No Bias, No Merit: The Case Against Blind Submission

To this article on the protocols of submission, presented in two parts – the first written in 1979 and the second, a much shorter section, in 1988 – we can add a missing third. This was an op-ed piece on the Sokal affair (the case of the physicist publishing a hoax essay in the journal *Social Text*) that Fish wrote in the pages of the *New York Times* in 1996.[1] In that op-ed, Fish was once again commenting on the ethics of submission and professional codes. In each of these instances, his remarks on publishing are also larger reflections on academic professionalism, and hence, I'd argue, their importance for debate amongst us.

In the earlier article, Fish tells us, for example, that he is personally opposed to blind submission because the fact of his name attached to an article greatly increases its chances of being accepted. He doesn't have any reason to be apologetic: "I have paid my dues and...don't see why others shouldn't labor in the vineyards as I did." There is a blind submission here to the invisible hand of the professional market which is assumed in some transhistorical sense to always deal fairly. And the assumption doesn't get examined – Fish doesn't hear the voice of an adjunct, juggling three or even four jobs, protesting weakly that this ain't a level playing-field – because, I suspect, Fish is invested precisely in the transcendence that he purports to attack in the essay below. Fish closes "No Bias, No Merit" by describing his position as "for politics and against Politics (the new transcendence)"; in reality, such a position, I'm arguing, is one that is against politics and for a narrow professionalism (the uninterrogated, commonsensical rationality of our unfair system).

This investment in a depoliticized rationality is echoed in Fish's op-ed in the *New York Times* written nearly a decade later. Fish castigates Sokal for various things, including the violation of the time-honored trust between scholars conducting academic business. (Incidentally, in the prior piece, "No Bias, No Merit," Fish writes of two research scientists who took twelve articles and resubmitted them under fictitious names to the same journals that had earlier published them. In commenting on this experiment, Fish doesn't sense any breach of academic trust. In the later article, however, Fish, writing as the director of the press that publishes *Social Text*, waxes eloquent on the theme of "corrosive" distrust bred by deception.) More seriously, Fish does not address the basic political issue of exploitative hierarchies – in this instance, the divisions between the scientific priesthood and the common citizens – that, as the editors of *Social Text* insisted in various venues, are at the heart of the so-called "Science Wars."[2] Fish focuses on Sokal's fraud and its impact in the offices of learned journals instead of examining, say, the threat to privileged, professional scientists when public-interest critiques come from outside science. In doing so, Fish produces a constrained, conservative sense of what we should understand by both "profession" and "politics."

"No Bias, No Merit" shows the robust and broad-ranging wit of Stanley Fish arguing against the unexamined shibboleths of our professional institutions. The essay could also stake the further claim to revealing Fish's criticism as being centrist and also complacent. The essay enacts attractive space-clearing gestures, because, indeed, "strictly speaking, there is no such thing as blind submission." At the same time, Fish announces his difference only by levelling all other differences, and accusing all positions of eschewing the taint of professionalism. This is patently false. For quite some time now, whether Fish has noticed this or not, professors of English have been addressing precisely the question of what it means to be in this profession.[3] Now, of course, we have a more urgent sense of the threat to the profession. The vineyards might not be there to labor in anymore.

Amitava Kumar

Notes

1   Stanley Fish, "Professor Sokal's Bad Joke," *The New York Times* (May 21, 1996).

2   See, for instance, Bruce Robbins and Andrew Ross, "Scientific Priesthood," *The New York Times* (May 23, 1996), Editorials/Letters.

3   The publication of Fish's essay "No Bias, No Merit" in the *Proceedings of the Modern Language Association* had been preceded by several inquiries into the status of the literary profession, some of the well known among them being the following: Richard Ohmann, *English In America: A Radical View of the Profession* (New York, 1976), Gerald Graff, *Professing Literature: An Institutional History* (Chicago, 1987), and, Jonathan Arac, *Critical Genealogies: Historical Situations for Postmodern Literary Studies* (New York, 1987).

I 1979

When members of an institution debate, it may seem that they are arguing about fundamental principles, but it is more often the case that the truly fundamental principle is the one that makes possible the terms of the disagreement and is therefore not in dispute at all. I am thinking in particular of the arguments recently marshaled for and against blind submission to the journal of the Modern Language Association. Blind submission is the practice whereby an author's name is not revealed to the reviewer who evaluates his or her work. It is an attempt, as William Schaefer explained in the *MLA Newsletter,* "to ensure that in making their evaluations readers are not influenced by factors other than the intrinsic merits of the article."[1] In his report to the members Schaefer, then executive director of the association, declared that he himself was opposed to blind submission because the impersonality of the practice would erode the humanistic values that are supposedly at the heart of our enterprise. Predictably, Schaefer's statement provoked a lively exchange in which the lines of battle were firmly, and, as I will argue, narrowly, drawn. On the one hand, those who agreed with Schaefer feared that a policy of anonymous review would involve a surrender "to the spurious notions about objectivity and absolute value that . . . scientists and social scientists banter about"; on the other hand, those whose primary concern was with the fairness of the procedure believed that "[j]ustice should be blind."[2] Each side concedes the force of the opposing argument – the proponents of anonymous review admit that impersonality brings its dangers, and the defenders of the status quo acknowledge that it is important to prevent "extraneous considerations" from interfering with the identification of true merit.[3]

It is in phrases like "true merit" and "extraneous considerations" that one finds the assumptions to which all parties subscribe. The respondent who declares that "the point at issue is how to avoid the bias of a reviewer upon grounds other than those intrinsic to the article under review"[4] is making an

unexceptional statement. Everyone agrees that intrinsic merit should be protected; it is just a question of whether or not the price of protection – the
possible erosion of the humanistic community – is too high. In what follows I
would like not so much to enter the debate as to challenge its terms by arguing
that merit is not in fact identifiable apart from the "extraneous considerations"
that blind submission would supposedly eliminate. I want to argue, in short,
that there is no such thing as intrinsic merit, and, indeed, if I may paraphrase
James I, "no bias, no merit."

We might begin by noting that while in the course of this debate everyone
talks about intrinsic merit, no one bothers to define it, except negatively as
everything apart from the distractions of rank, affiliation, professional status,
past achievements, ideological identification, sex, "or anything that might be
known about the author."[5] Now this is a list so inclusive that one might
wonder what was left once the considerations it enumerates were eliminated.
The answer would seem to be that what is left is the disinterested judgment as
to whether or not an article does justice to the work or works it purports to
characterize. But that answer will be satisfactory only if the notion "does justice
to" can be related to a standard or set of standards that operates independently
of the institutional circumstances that have been labeled extraneous. My thesis
is, first of all, that there is no such standard (which is not the same thing as
saying there is no standard) and, second, that while we may, as a point of piety,
invoke it as an ideal, in fact we violate it all the time by practices that are at
once routine and obligatory. Consider, for example, the practice of referring, at
the beginning of an essay, or in the course of its unfolding, or in a succession of
footnotes (the conditions under which it would be proper to do it one way
rather than another could themselves be profitably studied) to the body of
previous scholarship. This is a convention of the profession, and a failure to
respect it will sometimes be grounds for rejecting an article. The reason is
obvious. The convention is a way of acknowledging that we are engaged in a
community activity in which the value of one's work is directly related to the
work that has been done by others; that is, in this profession you earn the right
to say something because it has not been said by anyone else, or because it is a
reversal of what is usually said, or because while it has been said, its implications
have not yet been spelled out. You do not offer something as the report of a
communion between the individual critical sensibility and a work or its author;
and if you did, if your articles were all written as if they were titled "What I
Think about *Middlemarch*" or "The *Waste Land* and Me" they would not be
given a hearing. (The fact that this is not true of some people does not disprove
but makes my point.) Instead, they would be dismissed as being a waste of a
colleague's time, or as beside the point, or as uninformed, or simply as
unprofessional. This last judgment would not be a casual one; to be unprofes-

sional is not simply to have violated some external rule or piece of decorum. It is to have ignored (and by ignoring flouted) the process by which the institution determines the conditions under which its rewards will be given or withheld. These conditions are nowhere written down, but they are understood by everyone who works in the field, and, indeed, any understanding one might have of the field is inseparable from (because it will have been produced by) an awareness, often tacit, of these conditions.

What are they? A full answer to the question would be out of place here, but a partial enumeration would include a canon of greater and lesser works and hence a stipulation as to what is or is not a major project, a set of authorized and unauthorized methodologies along with a recognized procedure by which members of one set can be moved into another, a list of the tasks that particularly need doing and of those that have already been well done, a specification of the arguments that are properly literary and of the kinds of evidence that will be heard as telling and/or conclusive (authorial statements, letters, manuscript revisions, etc.). Of course, these conditions can and do change — and the process by which they change is one of the things they themselves regulate — but they always have some shape or other, and one cannot, without risk, operate independently of them.

Everyone is aware of that risk, although it is usually not acknowledged with the explicitness that one finds in the opening sentence of Raymond Waddington's essay on books XI and XII of *Paradise Lost*. "Few of us today," Waddington writes, "could risk echoing C. S. Lewis's condemnation of the concluding books of *Paradise Lost* as an 'untransmuted lump of futurity.'"[6] The nature of the risk that Waddington is about *not* to take is made clear in the very next sentence, where we learn that a generation of critics has been busily demonstrating the subtlety and complexity of these books and establishing the fact that they are the product of a controlled poetic design. What this means is that the kind of thing that one can now say about them is constrained in advance, for, given the present state of the art, the critic who is concerned with maintaining his or her professional credentials is obliged to say something that makes them better. Indeed, the safest thing the critic can say (and Waddington proceeds in this essay to say it) is that, while there is now a general recognition of the excellence of these books, it is still the case that they are faulted for some deficiency that is in fact, if properly understood, a virtue. Of course, this rule (actually a rule of thumb) does not hold across the board. When Waddington observes that "few of us today could risk," he is acknowledging, ever so obliquely, that there are some of us who could. Who are they, and how did they achieve their special status? Well, obviously C. S. Lewis was once one (although it may not have been a risk for him, and if it wasn't, why wasn't it?), and if he had not already died in 1972, when Waddington was writing, presumably he could have been one again. That is, Lewis's status as an authority on Renaissance literature was such that he could offer readings without courting the risk facing others who might go against the professional grain, the risk of not being listened to, of remaining unpublished, of being unattended to, the risk of producing something that was by definition – a definition derived from prevailing institutional conditions – without merit.

With this observation we return to the notion of "intrinsic merit" as it relates to the issue of blind submission; for what the Waddington-Lewis example shows (among other things) is that merit, rather than being a quality that can be identified independently of professional or institutional conditions, is a product of those conditions; and, moreover, since those conditions are not stable but change continually, the shape of what will be recognized as meritorious is always in the process of changing too. So that while it is true that as critics we write with the goal of living up to a standard (of worth, illumination, etc.) it is a standard that had been made not in eternity by God or by Aristotle but in the profession by the men and women who have preceded us; and in the act of trying to live up to it, we are also, and necessarily, refashioning it. My use of "we" might suggest a communal effort in which everyone pulls an equal weight and exerts an equal influence. But, of course, this is not the case. Ours is a hierarchical profession in which some are more responsible for its products than others; and since one of those products is the standard of merit by which our labors will, for a time, be judged, there will always be those whose words are meritorious (that is, important, worth listening to, authoritative, illuminating) simply by virtue of the position they occupy in the institution. It is precisely this situation, of course, that the policy of blind submission is designed to remedy; the idea is to prevent a reviewer from being influenced in his or her judgment of merit by the professional status of the author; but on the analysis offered in this essay, merit is inseparable from the structure of the profession and therefore the fact that someone occupies a certain position in that structure cannot be irrelevant to the assessment of what he or she produces.

The point is made in passing by a respondent (anonymous, I am afraid) to the Executive Council's survey who asserts that "[i]f Northrop Frye should write an essay attacking archetypal criticism, the article would by definition be of much greater significance than an article by another scholar attacking the same approach."[7] The reason is that the approach is not something independent of what Northrop Frye has previously said about it; indeed, in large part archetypal criticism *is* what Northrop Frye has said about it, and therefore anything he now says about it is not so much to be measured against an independent truth as it is to be regarded, at least potentially, as a new pronouncement of what the truth will hereafter be said to be. Similarly, an article by Fredson Bowers on the principles of textual editing would automatically be of "general interest to the membership" because the sense the membership has of what the principles of textual editing could possibly be is inseparable from what Fredson Bowers has already written. However, it is not necessary to search for a hypothetical example. The fact that the judgment on *Paradise Lost* XI and XII was made by C. S. Lewis in a book that was immediately recognized as authoritative – a recognition that was itself produced in no small part by the prior authority of *The Allegory of Love* – was sufficient to ensure that it would be over fifteen years before a group of scholars could begin the rehabilitation of those books and another fifteen before Waddington could pronounce their effort successful by declaring that few of us today could risk echoing C. S. Lewis.

It could be argued that these are special cases, but they are special only in that Frye, Bowers, and Lewis are (or were) in the position of exerting a general authority over the entire discipline; but in the smaller precincts of subdisciplines and subsubdisciplines there are words that matter more than other words spoken by those who address a field that they themselves have in large part constituted. These are men and women who are identified with a subject (Frances Yates on arts of memory), with a period (M. H. Abrams on Romanticism), with a genre (Angus Fletcher on allegory), with a poet (Hugh Kenner on Pound), with a work (Stephen Booth on Shakespeare's *Sonnets*). When Geoffrey Hartman speaks on Wordsworth, is his just another voice, or is it the voice of someone who is in great measure responsible for the Wordsworth we now have, insofar as by that name we understand an array of concerns, formal properties, sources, influences, and so on? Of course, Geoffrey Hartman's Wordsworth is not everyone's, but everyone's Wordsworth is someone's; that is, everyone's Wordsworth is the product of some characterization of him that has been put forward (within constraints that are already in place) and has been found to be persuasive by a significant number of workers in the profession. The point is that whatever Wordsworth we have he will not be available independently of the institution's procedures; rather he will be the product of these procedures, and of the work of certain men and women, and therefore the identity of the men and women who propose to speak about him cannot be irrelevant to a judgment of the merit of what they have to say.

I make the point in order to anticipate an obvious objection to the preceding paragraphs: it may be the case that the merit of pieces of literary criticism is a function of conditions prevailing in the profession, but surely the merit of literary works themselves is another matter, for they precede the profession and are the occasion of its efforts and the justification of its machinery. This is a powerful objection because it is rooted in the most basic myth the profession tells itself, the myth that it is secondary in relation to literary works that are produced independently of its processes; but it is precisely my contention that literary works have the shape they do because of the questions that have been put to them, questions that emerge from the work of the profession and are understood by members of the profession to be the proper ones to ask. We often think of our task as the *description* of literary works, but description requires categories of description, and those categories, in the form of the questions we think to ask, will limit in advance the kinds of things that can be described, which in turn will limit the shapes that can even be seen. That is to say, the objects of our professional attention – texts, authors, genres, and so on – are as much the products of the institution as are the acceptable forms that attention can take. It follows then that the machinery of the institution does not grow up to accommodate needs that are independently perceived but that, rather, the institutional machinery comes first and the needs then follow, as do the ways of meeting them.

In short, the work to be done is not what the institution responds to but what it *creates*, and it was not long ago that this truth was brought home to me when I received the first of many mailings from the then fledgling Spenser Society of America. So fledging was that society in 1977 that I hadn't yet heard of it, and I was therefore somewhat surprised to open a letter from its treasurer thanking me for my support. What became clear as the letter proceeded was that my ignorance of the society in no way exempted me from its operations. "We are almost two hundred strong," read the second sentence of the letter, and the suggestion of a military organization into which I had been conscripted was unmistakable. Moreover, that organization was already fully articulated. I was informed of the identity of "my" officers, who had arranged "our lunch-eon," for which I was urged to make an immediate reservation because my fellow members had already spoken for thirty of the fifty available seats. By the end of the second paragraph I was not only firmly placed in the rank and file of a marching army but informed that I was already behind in my dues. It was not until the third and final paragraph, however, that the true significance of the society's operation was revealed in the announcement of an annual volume to be called *Spenser Studies*, the first number of which was already scheduled by an editorial board that had already signed an agreement, in my name, I suppose, with a prominent university press. We would be happy, wrote my treasurer, "if you would inform colleagues and students that we Spenserians now have another possibility for publication." Here is the real message of the letter and the real rationale of the Spenser Society of America: to multiply the institutional contexts in which writing on Spenser will at once be demanded and published. It so happens that the letter was written before the society's first meeting, but as this sentence shows, the society need never have met at all, since its most important goal – the creation of a Spenser industry with all its attendant machinery – had already been achieved.

In later communications that machinery was further elaborated, first of all by the calling of an International Conference on Cooperation in the Study of Edmund Spenser. The scheduled panels indicate the directions the cooperative studies will take: "Cooperation in the Study of Spenser's Medieval English Backgrounds," "Cooperation in the Study of Spenser's Continental Backgrounds." What is emerging here is not simply the shape of an organization but the shape of Edmund Spenser. Nor will that shape be allowed to grow like Topsy. The topic of the first panel is the *limits* of cooperative study; the same document at once calls into being an activity and begins to regulate it. It is not long before both cooperation and regulation take on a more substantial form in the promised production of a Spenser *Encyclopedia* (if a category or subject is not in the encyclopedia, it will not be in Spenser), plans for which, I was informed, were already "well advanced." It is a feature of this correspondence that the world it declares is provided with a past and a future that tend to obscure its purely documentary origin. Things are always "well advanced" or "previously discussed" in a way that suggests events are being reported rather than made. But it takes only a moment's reflection to see that in a paragraph like this one every event is brought into being by a piece of paper that is underwritten by a bureaucracy that is itself created and sustained by other pieces of paper:

Plans are now all advanced for the projected *Spenser Encyclopedia*, which was discussed at conferences last October and December. (See reports on these conferences in the latest issue of *Spenser Newsletter*, 10, no. 1.) An official announcement of the *Encyclopedia* will be made on 4th May 1979 at Kalamazoo, Michigan, where we hope to continue the cooperative spirit of the International Conference at Duquesne.

It may seem that I am overestimating the power of a series of letters, even if the first in the series was written on the 4th of July; and it is true that this letter and subsequent ones did not create the society's machinery and the possibilities attendant upon it in a vacuum or ex nihilo: there is, it turns out, an authority that legitimizes these documents and accounts for their immediate force. The identity of that authority was revealed in the reporting of a lack. The Spenser Society, it seems, was, at the time of its birth, without a constitution, and therefore the framing of a constitution was declared to be the first order of business at the first meeting. Before that meeting was held, however, a second letter arrived, written this time by "my" president, informing me that the constitution was in fact already available in the form of the constitution, ready-made as it were, of the Milton Society, which also, the letter went on to say, was to provide the model for a banquet, a reception, an after-dinner speaker, an honored scholar, and the publication of a membership booklet, the chief function of which was to be the listing of the publications, recent and forth-coming, of the members. The manner in which work on Spenser is to be recognized and honored will have its source not in a direct confrontation with the poet or his poem but in the apparatus of an organization devoted to another poet. Spenser studies will be imitative of Milton studies; the anxiety of influence, it would seem, can work backward. Moreover, it continues to work. The recent mail has brought me, and some of you, an announcement of a new publication, the *Sidney Newsletter*, to be organized, we are told, "along the lines of the well-established and highly successful *Spenser Newsletter*," which was organized along the lines of the well-established and highly successful *Milton Newsletter*.

Now I wouldn't want to be understood as criticizing the Spenser Society for its colonizing activities or for having been colonized, in its turn, by the Milton Society. My account of these matters is offered with affection and, indeed, with gratitude, for were it not for the opportunities made available by these organ-izations there would be nothing for us to do. As I have already said, the work to be done is not what the institution responds to but what it *creates*, and it is the business of these societies first to create the work and second to make sure that it will never get done. I say this from a position of authority, as a past president of the Milton Society, an office whose only duty is to preside over an annual meeting. At the meeting over which I presided the members of the society heard reports on the *Milton Encyclopedia*, the *Variorum Commentary, The Com-plete Prose*, the friends of Milton's cottage, the Milton Society Archive and Library, the Milton Society awards, and "upcoming panels and conferences at which members of the society might speak." These were labeled as "progress reports," and to some extent the label was accurate; but the rate of progress was reassuringly slow, and there were signs that mechanisms were already in motion to ensure that it would never get too far. *The Complete Prose* was threatening to become, in fact, complete; but there was an announcement that the seventh volume would soon be reissued in a revised and improved version, and if the seventh volume, could the first, second, third, fourth, fifth, and sixth be far behind? The volumes of the *Variorum* have hardly begun to appear, but already there is talk that the *Paradise Regained* is inadequate and will have to be redone. I myself was aghast to discover that antinomianism was not even an entry in the *Milton Encyclopedia* and began to think that similar omissions might necessitate the issuing of a new and improved edition. In so thinking I was not being cynical or opportunistic; I was responding with an honest act of judgment to a project that was called into being by the needs of the field. The fact that those needs corresponded to the need of the workers in the field to have something to do is worth noting; to note it, however, is not to call into question the sincerity of their efforts but to point out that those efforts are first and foremost professional and that therefore the motives one might have for engaging in them are professional too. To say this is to say what should go without saying: we do not write articles in order to report to no one in particular in no context in particular our unmediated experience of a literary work; articles are written by men and women who have something to contribute as "contribution" is defined by the conditions prevailing in the institution, an institution that provides both the questions and acceptable ways of answering them and provides too the canon of works to which the questions can be put. Indeed, the very writing of an article only makes sense within an institutional framework, and when an article gets published it is not because some independent agency has validated its merit but because in the machinery of a *political* agency – the Milton Society, the Spenser Society, the MLA – there is already a place for it.

With the word *political* we come to the heart of the matter, for that word names everything that so many in the profession would like to deny. It is the mark of a profession to claim that its activities are not tied to any one set of economic or social circumstances but constitute a response to needs and values that transcend particular times and places.[8] The profession of literary criticism carries this claim to an extreme that is finally self-destructive by declaring that its activities finally have very little value at all. The explanation for this curious maneuver lies in the relationship between what literary critics do and the commodity that occupies the center of the enterprise – literature. It is an article of faith in the profession that this commodity precedes the profession's efforts, which are seen as merely exegetical; and that means that from the very first the profession has a sense of itself as something secondary and superfluous. If the work itself is all-sufficient (a cardinal principle of twentieth-century aesthetics), the work of the critic is ultimately unnecessary, and criticism would seem to have compromised its claim to be a profession, even before that claim has been made.

One sees this clearly, for example, in John Crowe Ransom's "Criticism Inc.," a manifesto in which the literary community is urged to become more self-consciously professional. "Criticism," Ransom declares, "must become more scientific, or precise and systematic, and this means that it must be developed by the collective and sustained effort of learned persons – which means that its proper seat is in the universities."[9] This is the very language of professionalism, and it is accompanied by a disdain for amateurs[10] and by a rejection of the notion that criticism "is something which anyone can do."[11] But when it comes time to describe this new profession, its principles turn out to be unlike any other in that they are directed *away* from the public. To the question "What is criticism?" Ransom answers with what it is not, and what it is not is anything that might recommend it to the community at large; it does not report on the "moral content" of literature; it is not concerned with the lives of authors, or with literature's relationship to science, politics, the law, or geography; it must not make claims that its commodity is "moving" or "exciting" or "entertaining" or "great"; and above all it must not suggest that "art comes into being because the artist . . . has designs upon the public, whether high moral designs or box-office ones."[12] In this last phrase, high moral designs (which might include the design to enlighten one's readers, or to make them better, or to enlist them in some social or religious cause) are tarred, by association, with the brush of vulgarity; they are just another version of box-office designs because the intention of those who have them is to move others to this or that action in relation to this or that quotidian concern. Poetry, by contrast, is an effort deliberately abstracted from such concerns; the poet, Ransom writes, "perpetuates in his poem an order of existence which in actual life is constantly crumbling beneath his touch";[13] and the critic must attend only to that order and avoid attending to anything that would deny or compromise "the autonomy of the work itself as existing for its own sake."[14] In practice this means an exclusive focus on technique as it exists apart from any social or moral end,[15] a focus that promotes rapt contemplation as the only attitude that can properly belong to an activity defined in opposition to the business of everyday life, or to the everyday life of business.

The result is a professionalism that is divided against itself. It claims for itself the exclusive possession of a certain skill (the skill of attending properly to poems), but then it defines that skill in such a way as to remove its exercise from the activities of the marketplace where professions compete for the public's support. Indeed, it is a skill that can be exercised only if the conditions of the marketplace are resolutely ignored in favor of the *eternal* conditions that obtain, or should obtain, between poem and reader. So long as it is a first principle that poetry must be studied "for its own sake," the profession of literary criticism will exist in a shamefaced relationship with professional machinery, which will be regarded as a temporary and regrettable excrescence.

That is why the literary community teaches its members a contradictory lesson: literary criticism is a profession – it is not something that anyone can do – but it is not professional – it is not done in response to marketplace or political pressures. A policy of blind submission is an extension of that lesson and is also the extension of a general practice by which the profession hides from itself the true (political) nature of its own activities. As we have seen, the case for blind submission is that it protects the intrinsic from the extraneous; but what I have been trying to show, from a variety of perspectives, is that everything labeled extraneous – considerations of rank, professional status, previous achievement, ideology, and so on – is essential to the process by which intrinsic considerations are identified and put into place. I said at the beginning of this essay that there is no such thing as the intrinsic, and I would say it again if by "intrinsic" was meant a category of value that was in place for all time; but if we think of the intrinsic as something the profession determines, then there is always a category of the intrinsic, but it isn't always the same one. It therefore cannot be defined in opposition to the profession because it is a part of the profession's work to produce it, and then, in the course of discussion and debate, to produce it again.

The intrinsic, in short, is a political rather than an essential category, and as such it will always reflect the interests – wholly legitimate because without interest there would be no value – of those who have had a hand in fashioning it. In the process the interests of others will have been excluded or slighted, and those groups will, more often than not, protest their exclusion in the name of intrinsic merit; but what they will really be doing is attempting to replace someone else's notion of intrinsic merit with their own; that is, they will be playing politics. This is precisely what the proponents of blind submission are doing, whether they know it or not, and therefore the one claim they cannot legitimately maintain, although they make it all the time, is that they are doing away with politics. There are certainly arguments that can be made for blind submission, but they are frankly political arguments and if they were presented as such they might even receive a more sympathetic hearing. As things stand now, for example, I am against blind submission because the fact that my name is attached to an article greatly increases its chances of getting accepted. But that is just the condition we wish to change, someone might object, and to this I might reply that I have paid my dues and earned the benefit of the doubt I now enjoy and don't see why others shouldn't labor in the vineyards as I did. I would, that is, be responding in terms of my own self-interest, by which I don't mean *selfish* interests but interests that appear to me to be compelling given a sense of myself as a professional with a history and with a stake in the future of the profession.

A similar point is made by some of the participants in a discussion of peer review published in *The Behavorial and Brain Sciences: An International Journal of Current Research and Theory with Open Peer Commentary*.[16] The occasion was the report of research conducted by D. P. Peters and S. J. Ceci. Peters and Ceci had taken twelve articles published in twelve different journals, altered the titles, substituted for the names of the authors fictitious names identified as researchers at institutions no one had ever heard of (because they were made up), and resubmitted the articles to the journals that had originally accepted them. Three of the articles were recognized as resubmissions, and of the remaining nine eight were rejected. The response to these results ranged from horror ("It puts at risk the whole conceptual framework within which we are accustomed to make observations and construct theories"[17]) to "so what else is new." Almost all respondents, however, agreed with the researchers' call for the development of "fair" procedures, "fair . . . defined here as being judged on the merit of one's ideas, and not on the basis of academic rank, sex, place of work, publication record, and so on."[18] Nevertheless, there were a few who questioned that definition of fairness and challenged the assumption that it was wrong for reviewers to take institutional affiliation and history into considera-tion. "We consider a result from a scientist who has never before been wrong much more seriously than a similar report from a scientist who has never before been right. . . . It is neither unnatural nor wrong that the work of scientists who have achieved eminence through a long record of important and successful research is accepted with fewer reservations than the work of less eminent scientists."[19] "A reviewer may be justified in assuming at the outset that [well-known] people know what they are doing."[20] "Those of us who publish establish some kind of track record. If our papers stand the test of time . . . it can be expected that we have acquired expertise in scientific methodology."[21] (This last respondent is a woman and a Nobel laureate.) What this minority is saying is that a paper identified with a distinguished record is a better bet than a paper not so identified. I would go even further and say that a paper so identified will be *a different paper*. In a footnote to his *The Structure of Scientific Revolutions* Thomas Kuhn reports that when Lord Rayleigh submitted a paper to the British Association, his name was "inadvertently omitted" and the paper was rejected "as the work of some 'paradoxer.' "[22] But when his name was subsequently restored the paper was accepted immediately. On its face this might seem to be a realization of the worst fears of those who argue for blind submission, but I would read the result differently: shorn of its institutional lineage the paper presented itself as without direction, and whimsical; but once the reviewers were informed of its source they were able to see it as the continuation of work – of lines of direction, routes of inquiry – they already knew, and all at once the paper made a different kind of sense than it did when they were considering it "blindly."

Of course, they were not considering it blindly at all. Reviewers who receive a paper from which the identifying marks have been removed will immediately put in place an (imagined) set of circumstances of exactly the kind they are supposedly ignoring. Indeed, in the absence of such an imaginative and projective act, the paper could not be read *as* a paper situated in a particular discipline. Strictly speaking, there is no such thing as blind submission. The choice is not between a reading influenced by "extraneous" information and a reading uninflected by "extraneous" information but between readings differ-ently inflected. The pure case of a reading without bias is never available, not because we can never remove all our biases but because without them there would be nothing either to see or to say. A law school colleague told me the other day of a judge who was asked to disqualify himself from a case involving a black plaintiff and a white defendant on the grounds that since he himself was black he would be biased. The judge refused, pointing out that "after all, he had to be one color or the other." The moral is clear and it is my moral: bias is just another word for seeing from a particular perspective as opposed to seeing from no perspective at all, and since seeing from no perspective at all is not a possibility, bias is a condition of consciousness and therefore of action. Of course, perspectives differ, as do the actions that follow from them, and one can predict that a *PMLA* after blind submission will not be the same journal; but to the extent that it is different, that difference will be the result not of a process that has been depoliticized but of the passage from one political agenda to another.

II 1988

I wrote the preceding pages in 1979 and revised them slightly in 1982, and by one of those accidents that attend professional life the collection for which the piece was intended was never published. It is of course now out-of-date, but its out-of-dateness can be seen as extension of my point, that it is the conditions currently obtaining in the profession rather than any set of independent and abiding criteria that determine what is significant and meritorious. The point still holds, although many of the examples used to illustrate it will now strike readers as either obvious (and hence not worth elaborating) or simply wrong. The examples that are obvious will be so in part because of work subsequently done by me and by others. The reference to the status of books XI and XII of *Paradise Lost* has been expanded into a study of the critical history of that poem. The "professional anti-professionalism" of literary studies has been explored in a series of essays that show it to be a constituent of professional ideology. (To be a professional is to think of oneself as motivated by something larger than marketplace conditions – by, for instance, a regard for justice or for the sanctity of human life or for the best that has been thought and said – even as that larger something is itself given shape and being by the very market conditions it supposedly transcends.) These essays have been vigorously criticized by James Fanto, Drucilla Cornell, Bruce Robbins, Steven Mailloux, Samuel Weber, Martha Nussbaum, David Luban, Gerald Graff, Walter Davis, and others, and the resulting dialogue has done its part (along with the work of Michel Foucault, Pierre Bourdieu, Michel de Certeau, Terry Eagleton, Robert Scholes, Paul Bové, William Cain, John Fekete, Jonathan Arac, and Russell

Jacoby) in making the question of professionalism a more familiar and respectable one than it was in 1979.

Other things have changed since 1979. Antinomianism is no longer absent from the *Milton Encyclopedia*, having been added as an entry in a special supplement to the final volume. The Spenser Society is fully established and its activities are ritualized no less than are the activities of the Milton Society, which of course goes on as it always has. (Some things never change.) Romanticism is no longer firmly identified with M. H. Abrams or with anyone else. The canon of greater and lesser works is no longer firmly in place. Indeed, it never was except as an assumption continually belied by history; now the fact of the canon is no longer even assumed; new challenges emerge every day and have become as orthodox as the orthodoxy they indict.

But perhaps the greater change is the one that renders the key opposition of the essay – between the timeless realm of literature and the pressures and exigencies of politics – inaccurate as a description of the assumptions prevailing in the profession. To be sure, there are those who still believe that literature is defined by its independence of social and political contexts (a "concrete universal" in Wimsatt's terms), but today the most influential and up-to-date voices are those that proclaim exactly the reverse and argue that the thesis of literary autonomy is itself a political one, part and parcel of an effort by the conservative forces in society to protect traditional values from oppositional discourse. Rather than reflecting, as Ransom would have it, an "order of existence" purer than that which one finds in "actual life," literature in this New (Historicist) vision directly and vigorously "participates in historical processes and in the political management of reality."[23] Moreover, as Louis Montrose observes, if literature is reconceived as a social rather than a merely aesthetic practice, literary criticism, in order to be true to its object, must be rearticulated as a social practice too and no longer be regarded as a merely academic or professional exercise.[24]

It is with this turn in the argument that one begins to see something strange (or perhaps not so strange): in at least one of its aspects the New Historicism is the old high formalism writ political. I say "in one of its aspects" because the kind of work produced by the two visions is markedly different in many important ways, in the questions asked, in the materials interrogated, in the structures revealed, and in the claims made for the revelation – on one hand the claim to have reaffirmed a distinct and abiding aesthetic realm, on the other the claim to have laid bare the contradictions and fissures that an ideology can never quite manage to contain. Within these differences, however, one thing remains the same: the true and proper view of literature and literary studies defines itself against academic politics, which are seen by the aestheticians as being too much like the politics of "actual life" and by the new historicists as being not enough like the politics of "actual life." The complaint is different, but its target – the procedures and urgencies of professional activity – is familiar, and so is the opposition underlying the different complaints, the opposition between an activity in touch with higher values and an activity that has abandoned those values for something base and philistine. Whether the values are generality, detachment, disembodied vision, and moral unity on the one hand or discontinuity, rupture, disintegration, and engagement on the other, the fear is that they will be compromised by the demands that issue from the pressures of careerism, the pressure to publish, to say something new, to get a job, to get promoted, to get recognized, to get famous, and so on. In the context of the aesthetic vision these pressures are destructive of everything that is truly intellectual; in the context of the historicist vision, they are destructive of everything that is truly (as opposed to merely institutionally) political. Not only do the two visions share an enemy, they share a vocabulary, the vocabulary of transcendence, for in the discourses of both we are urged to free ourselves from parochial imperatives, to realize the true nature of our calling, to participate in that which is *really* and abidingly important. It is just that in one case the important thing is the life of the poetic mind, while in the other it is the struggle against repression and totalization; but that is finally only the difference between two differently pure acts, both of which are pure (or so is the claim) by *not* being the acts of an embedded professional. In 1979 (and in the years before) I was arguing for politics and against transcendence; now I am arguing for politics and against Politics (the new transcendence). As Donne might have said, small change when we are to (materialist) bodies gone.

It would seem then that there is some point to publishing this essay even nine years later (I have heeded, involuntarily, Horace's advice), since its argument is still being resisted, although from another direction. That argument, to rehearse it one last time, is that professional concerns and urgencies, rather than being impediments to responsible (meritorious) action, are determinative of the shape responsible action can take. One does not perform acts of criticism by breaking free of the profession's norms and constraints whether in the service of timeless masterpieces or in the name of political liberation, and whenever the claim to have broken free is made you can be sure that it is underwritten, authorized, and rendered intelligible by the very disciplinary boundaries it purports to have left behind.

Notes

1   William D. Schaefer, "Anonymous Review: A Report from the Executive Director," *MLA Newsletter* 10.2 (1978): 4.

2   "Correspondence," *MLA Newsletter* 10.3 (1978): 4.

3   Ibid., p. 5.

4   Ibid.

5   Schaefer, p. 5.

6   Raymond Waddington, "The Death of Adam: Vision and Voice in Books XI and XII of *Paradise Lost,*" *Modern Philology* 70 (1972): 9.

7   Schaefer, p. 5.

8   For the topic of professionalism, see B. J. Bledstein, *The Culture of Professionalism* (New York: Norton, 1977); Thomas L. Haskell, *The Emergence of Professional Social Science* (Urbana: University of Illinois Press, 1977); and M. S. Larson, *The Rise of Professionalism* (Berkeley: University of California Press, 1977).

9   John Crowe Ransom, *The World's Body* (Baton Rouge: Louisiana State University Press, 1938), p. 329.

10 Ibid., p. 327.

11 Ibid., p. 335.

12 Ibid., p. 343.

13 Ibid., p. 348.

14 Ibid., p. 343.

15 Ibid., p. 346.

16 D. P. Peters and S. J. Ceci, "Peer-review practices of psychological journals: The fate of published articles, submitted again," *The Behavioral and Brain Sciences: An International Journal of Current Research and Theory with Open Peer Commentary* 5 (1982): 187–255 (with commentary by R. K. Adair et al.).

17 Ibid., p. 245.

18 Ibid., p. 253.

19 Ibid., p. 196.

20 Ibid., p. 211.

21 Ibid., p. 244.

22 Thomas Kuhn, *The Structure of Scientific Revolutions* (Chicago: University of Chicago Press, 1962), p. 153.

23 Jean Howard, "The New Historicism in Renaissance Studies," *English Literary Renaissance* 16 (1986): 25.

24 Louis Montrose, "Renaissance Literary Studies and the Subject of History," *English Literary Renaissance* 16 (1986): 11–12.

11

Anti-Professionalism

In "Profession Despise Thyself," written amid the opening cannonades of the culture wars, Fish observed that journalistic mockery of academic criticism echoed the self-loathing of the critics themselves. Literature seemed unpleasantly unique among disciplinary objects: it was defined such that to analyze it professionally was necessarily to betray it.

"Anti-Professionalism" extends this paradox to the professions in general. Literature in its romantic idealization is only one example of those higher, external standards (truth, justice) by which all professionals, like literary critics, are forever judging and condemning themselves. Such standards deserve no special authority, Fish argues, for their disinterestedness is an illusion. All values, like professional values, emerge from local contexts and institutional constraints. Why then do professions torture themselves with such masochistic relish? Professionalism generates its own self-critique, Fish concludes, in its effort to resolve the various contradictions of professional existence. The effort is vain but inescapable. Self-critique is how professionalism works.

What appears to be a scathing critique of X is really only the normal functioning of X: such arguments can be read as either radical refusal of or eager acquiescence in the status quo. (This ambiguity is part of their appeal.) But they assume the status quo will endure. Of late the institutional existence of academic criticism has been too profoundly threatened to permit this assumption. In his haste to show that any given reproach is not a real indictment, Fish shows no interest in asking what *would* be a real indictment. By refusing to grant the validity of the question, he loses a chance to answer the profession's antagonists. But is the demand that the profession serve the public welfare merely an idealist phantasm? It comes from inside as well as outside the profession, and in a democracy it might seem as legitimately authoritative as anything else. In an exchange with Gerald Graff published with "Anti-Professionalism" in *New Literary History* (17:1, Autumn 1985), Fish conceded that "[n]o intepretive community exists in a hermetically sealed or monolithic state." A given profession must appeal for legitimation to "the more general interests of the larger society . . . when the activities of the community are interrogated by those who are not members of it" (126). But he dropped this exchange when the essay was published in *Doing What Comes Naturally* (1989) and left his earlier argument unchanged.

Still, the fact that this argument has had so little effect is strong testimony to its acuteness. Professionals cling to their self-loathing, however incoherent and inconsequential. The term "professionalism" continues to be used as if it were a self-evidently devastating accusation rather than a category that can be filled, as Fish suggests, with very diverse ideological contents. Yet Fish does not leave the routine of interpretation unchanged. "Anti-Professionalism" ups the anti, so to speak: it usefully calls the bluff of loose, inflated claims to critique – all the reversals, transgressions, and subversions that serve as less than convincing contemporary equivalents of "aesthetic value" – and thus clears the way for tighter, more publicly credible ones. We have to work harder in order to make something into critique – a critique that will satisfy those interested outsiders whose perspective Fish denies so pointedly that one suspects it is never far from his mind.

Bruce Robbins

I

Every so often one hears the story of the editor who is sent a relatively minor Shakespeare sonnet or an early poem by Keats and rejects it as mannered and artificial. The story is usually tagged by one of two morals. Either it indicates that we have been deceived by custom and critical orthodoxy into venerating something without value, or, alternatively, it indicates how easy it is for something of value to go unrecognized by those whose judgments are in bondage to this or that critical fashion. It would seem that these morals are contradictory and are drawn from opposing positions; but, in fact, the positions are finally the same in one important respect: they both affirm, although in different ways and with different emphases, the independence of value from the judgments delivered by the agencies of professional authority, whether that authority is seen as supported only by unexamined tradition or as representing nothing more than the partisan opinion of the most recent victor in the struggle for institutional power. Both the moralist who thinks that a poem of little intrinsic worth has been kept afloat by the vested interests of an entrenched elite and the moralist who thinks that a great work of art is in danger of being sacrificed to the ever-changing interests of academic opportunists make the very same assumption about the relationship between a socially organized activity and the objects of its attention – the assumption that questions of merit have nothing essentially to do with the acts of description and judgment that have their source in the largely political machinery of professional bureaucracies.

I want to call that the anti-professional assumption, and I define anti-professionalism as any attitude or argument that enforces a distinction between professional labors on the one hand and the identification and promotion of what is true or valuable on the other. In some formulations that distinction is very firm and amounts to an equation of professionalism with everything that is evil and corrupting. It is in this spirit that Burton Bledstein ends his study of *The Culture of Professionalism*,[1] calling his readers to an awareness of the "arrogance, shallowness, and potential abuses...by venal individuals who justify their special treatment and betray society's trust by invoking professional privilege, confidence, and secrecy."[2] In many of Bledstein's examples this betrayal takes the form of allowing professional considerations to overwhelm considerations of public and client welfare. Thus he cites late nineteenth-century "[g]ynecologists and psychiatrists" who "diagnosed female hysteria as a pathological problem with a scientific etiology related to an individual's physical history rather than anger the public by suggesting that it was a cultural problem related to dissatisfied females in the middle-class home."[3] Underlying this criticism is something like the following scenario: faced with a situation in which they could choose from a number of explanations, these doctors chose that explanation that would strengthen their already entrenched interest by solidifying rather than alienating the support of middle-class America. It is a perfectly reasonable scenario, especially given the anti-professionalist perspective, but it depends on assumptions about the nature of choice and the freedom of choosing agents that I will later challenge. For the meantime, however, we may note that in this particular example the professional's betrayal of his clients is simultaneously a betrayal of the truth. This is a particularly damning charge because, as M. S. Larson points out in *The Rise of Professionalism*,[4] professions characteristically justify their special status by claiming "cognitive exclusiveness,"[5] a unique access to some area of knowledge that is deemed crucial to the well-being of society; but that claim is more than compromised if knowledge is withheld from the public so that the profession's privileged position can remain secure. In the popular mind this particular form of professional abuse is typified by the behavior of lawyers who are entrusted with the determination and protection of truth, but who in practice deliberately obfuscate it by deploying procedural stratagems that constitute the real center of their craft and, finally, of their commitment. In the process, or so the story goes, the very values for which the enterprise supposedly exists – justice and the promotion of the general welfare – are sacrificed to the special interests that the legal profession at once represents and embodies.

The list of casualties left in the wake of professionalism grows – the client, society, truth, value; but perhaps the casualty most often lamented in anti-professionalist polemics is the self or soul of the professional himself. For it follows that if a profession has given itself over to hypocrisy, secrecy, expansion for expansion's sake, mindless specialization, and the like, its members have necessarily surrendered their values and ideals to these same false priorities. Indeed, in this view, it is not too much to say (and many have said it) that in the act of becoming a professional one is in danger of losing his very humanity. This is the burden, for example, of a recent book-length complaint by a number of lawyers and law professors against the narrowing effects of their own education and professional experience. "We become accultured," they write,

to an unnecessarily limiting way of seeing and experiencing law and lawyering, a way which can separate lawyers (as well as the other actors in the legal system) from their sense of humanity and their own values. When that separation occurs, the profession easily becomes experienced as only a job or role, and human problems as only legal issues. Care and responsibility yield to exigencies and stratagems; and legal education, instead of reflecting the aspiration and searching that embody law and lawyering, can all too easily become an exercise in attempted mastery and growing cynicism.[6]

In these sentences the authors produce a virtual compendium of anti-professionalist attitudes and arguments. Professionalism is indicted as a threat to humanity and to values; the openness of disinterested inquiry is replaced by the unworthy goal of "mastery" or manipulation, and, in the course of achieving mastery the professional is himself mastered (that is, taken over) by the constricted "roles and patterns" that are at once his weapons and his prison.[7] The professional, in short, becomes his own victim as the cynicism he practices transforms him into its image, leaving him with the base motives of an empty and self-serving careerism.

In addition to illustrating with force and concision what anti-professionalists are against, this paragraph allows us to infer what anti-professionalists are *for*: along with care, responsibility, humanity, and value, they are for openness, freedom, and sincerity – that is, for the real self as opposed to the self that has been lost or submerged in a "role." When the authors speak here of "actors in the legal system" their vocabulary is not neutrally employed; it is clear that acting or playing a "part" is an inferior form of behavior, not least because it binds the acting agent to the motivations of the "legal system"[8] and deprives him of the motivations he would have otherwise (and freely) chosen. In short, the actor enmeshed in a system is doing things for the wrong reasons, not for the reasons that would recommend themselves to him if he were not thus "constricted," but for reasons that attach to the limited and suspect goals of the professional enterprise. This complaint is often heard in anti-professional literature and is perhaps most familiar to us in the context of academic professionalism where it is regularly lamented that scholars are constrained in what they do by the desire to be promoted or by the fear that they won't be, and that therefore they write and publish only in order to augment their bibliographies and not out of true conviction or in response to an independently perceived need. As a result (the complaint continues), our journals are filled with publications that offer novelty rather than truth, since, as Richard Levin scathingly observes, university teachers "know that their interpretations are not likely to be published unless they say something . . . that has never been said before, which all too often means . . . that they must say something very strange."[9] Levin has in mind teachers of literature (and his indictment has been echoed recently by W. J. Bate, and was anticipated by Richard Ohmann, Mel Topf, and many others),[10] but the point is a general one: the pressure of professional life leads to the proliferation of work (research projects, publications, etc.) that has no justification in anything but the artificial demands of an empty and self-serving careerism.

Typically, careerism is seen not only as the corrupter of motives, but as the perverter of judgment. Not only does it tempt professionals to do things for the wrong — that is, "merely professional" — reasons, it tempts them to find authority in the accidental fact of professional status rather than in the true authority of carefully marshaled evidence and perspicuously powerful arguments. In the words of Frederick Crews, the authority inherent in some official or quasi-official professional position is "seized" rather than "earned"; it is false authority which proceeds not from "independent criteria of judgment," but from the anticipation of reward or punishment at the hands of "entrenched leaders."[11] Consequently, we have the spectacle of younger professionals who obsequiously adopt the opinions of their bureaucratic superiors, "imitating their mannerisms, praising their cleverness, using their favorite code words."[12] Observers like E. D. Hirsch fear that if such behavior were to become normative, the communal enterprise itself would be in danger of collapsing as the march of intellectual progress was interrupted (if not stopped altogether) by every "drift in the currents of intellectual fashion."[13]

In Hirsch's apocalyptic scenario "fashion" is an enemy named by an even larger word, "rhetoric," which he sees as the most serious threat to the "logical integrity of inquiry."[14] "Obviously," he declares, "the consolidated knowledge within a discipline has nothing directly to do with rhetoric."[15] Obviously, this is not only an observation; it is an exhortation. Rhetoric *should* have nothing to do with the consolidated knowledge of a discipline, and the fear that it may have all too much to do with it is what animates Hirsch's enterprise. Hirsch thus stands in a long line that begins with Aristotle when, in the opening paragraphs of the third book of *The Rhetoric*,[16] he confesses himself uneasy and even ashamed that he must now descend to a discussion of so meretricious a topic as style. "Nobody," he declares wistfully, "uses fine language when teaching geometry."[17] Aristotle's point is that geometrical proofs strike the reason with an immediate and self-sufficient force, and therefore there is no need to wrap them up in some attractive verbal package. In this opposition of the central or essential to the superficial or ephemeral, we have the essence of the long quarrel between rhetoric and philosophy, a quarrel that philosophy has by and large won since more often than not rhetoric is identified as the art of illegitimate appeal, as a repertoire of tricks or manipulative techniques by means of which some special interest, or point of view, or temporary fashion, passes itself off as the truth. The rhetorical, then, is that which stands between us and the truth, obscuring it, preventing us from allying ourselves with it, and tying us instead to some false or partial god. These are exactly the charges that are leveled against professionalism, and it seems clear that anti-professionalism is basically an up-to-date, twentieth-century form of the traditional hostility to rhetoric.

In identifying anti-professionalism with anti-rhetoricity, I am not doing anything simple or simply dismissive. The anti-rhetorical stance, which is also the anti-professional stance, is complex and comprehensive, and in the preceding paragraphs I have been trying to build up a sense of its complexity by demonstrating that underlying its polemics are an epistemology, a theory of values, and a conception of the self. In the context of that effort Hirsch is particularly helpful. His arguments are more reasoned than any we have yet examined, and he allows us to be more precise both about the components of anti-professionalism and about the positive program in relation to which professionalism is the negative example. In the space of just two pages rhetoric and professional irresponsibility are identified with "advocacy," "vanity," "ideology," and a "decline in commitment,"[18] and each word or phrase directs us to an important feature of the anti-professional stance. The linking of advocacy and vanity is especially illuminating because it specifies for us the nature of the "real self," in whose name anti-professionalism levels its indictment. By "advocacy" Hirsch means the urging of a particular or partisan point of view, of a special interest, and it follows, at least in his arguments, that one who advocates does so in the "spirit of vanity"[19] because he prefers an interest to which he is personally attached to the *dis*interested pursuit of truth. This is made clear when Hirsch contrasts both advocacy and vanity (components, as he sees them, or runaway professionalism) with "selfless devotion to the communal enterprise."[20] As it is used here, "selfless" should be read quite literally. What is required is a self that has no interests "of its own" or has set them aside in favor of something larger; for only that selfless self will be able to espy and embrace a piece of rationality or truth that is itself independent of any interest. In order to be such a self, however, one must resist or turn away from the lure of one's "self-interest" or of other partial and partisan appeals and commit oneself to the communal enterprise (also identified as an enterprise without or above interest); one must, that is, perform an act of the will in which a choice is made against ideology and for the truth. If this choice is not made, there will be a "decline in commitment to the critical testing of hypotheses against all the known relevant evidence";[21] skepticism will become "widespread" as "the process of knowledge ceases,"[22] and rhetoric – in the form of activities grounded in nothing but "[m]ere individual preference,"[23] and the selfish exploitation of the institutions of scholarship[24] – will triumph. In short, professionalism will triumph as the "logic of inquiry"[25] is supplanted by "anti-rationalism, faddism, and extreme relativism."[26]

These are strong words, and they show us what is at stake in anti-professionalist polemics – the protection and nourishing of a set of related and finally equivalent acontextual entities. First, there is a truth that exists independently of any temporal or local concern; and then there is knowledge about this truth, a knowledge that is itself dependent on no particular perspective but has as its object this same transperspectival truth; and finally, and most importantly, there is a self or knowing consciousness that is under the sway of no partial vision, and is therefore free (in a very strong sense) first to identify and then to embrace the truth to which a disinterested knowledge inescapably points. On the other side, this happy eventuality is continually threatened by the contingent, the accidental, the merely fashionable, the narrowly political, the superficial, the blindly interested, the inessential, the merely historical, the rhetorical, by everything that seems to so many to be the content of professionalism once it has been divorced from or has forgotten the higher purposes and values it is supposed to serve.

Now one can quarrel with this picture of things, as I shall before this essay concludes, but within its own terms it is powerful and perfectly coherent. That is, if one is operating from within what we might call an ideology of essences – a commitment to the centrality and ultimate availability of transcendent truths and values – one will necessarily view with suspicion and fear activities and structures that are informed by partisan purposes (the spirits of advocacy and vanity) and directed toward local and limited (i.e., historical) goals. Anti-professionalism, in short, follows inevitably from essentialism, so much so that an essentialist who wishes in some sense to give professionalism its due cannot avoid falling into the anti-professionalist stance. A case in point is Stephen Toulmin, who has devoted a large volume (and two successors are promised) to a project that at first glance looks like the opposite of anti-professionalism. Toulmin's thesis in *Human Understanding*[27] is that it is "a mistake to identify rationality and logicality – to suppose, that is, that the rational ambitions of any historically developing intellectual activity can be understood entirely in terms of the propositional or conceptual systems in which its intellectual content may be expressed at one or another time."[28] A rational activity, he continues, is not to be explained by reference to " 'fixed and universal' principles of understanding" or to some " 'invariant forms of reason' ";[29] rather, "it is an *intellectual enterprise* whose 'rationality' lies in the procedures governing its historical development and evolution."[30] His conclusion is worth quoting in full:

[N]o system of concepts and/or propositions can be 'intrinsically' rational, or claim a sovereign and necessary authority over our intellectual allegiance. From now on, we must attempt instead to understand the historical processes by which new families of concepts and beliefs are generated, applied, and modified in the evolution of our intellectual enterprises. . . .[31]

It would seem that anyone who wrote these sentences must be insulated against making the mistake (which he himself names) of devaluing history and historical process; but even as he elaborates this argument, Toulmin is invoking and developing a set of related distinctions that will finally subvert it. The first distinction is between "reasons" and "causes." By "reasons" he means an analysis of intellectual activity that is made "in terms of reasons, . . . arguments, and justifications – that is in terms of 'rational' categories"; while by "causes" he means an analysis that is made "in terms of forces, causes, compulsions, and explanations – that is, in terms of 'causal' categories."[32] Causal categories turn out to include such things as the centers of professional influence (what Toulmin calls "current reference-group[s]"), learned societies, the "invisible colleges," journals that "define the forum of competition within which the effective disciplinary contest . . . is conducted,"[33] the "roles, offices, and positions"[34] held by prominent workers in the field, and the institutional authority of essays and books produced by such workers – in short, all of the factors and considerations that make up what one understands by the notion of "professionalism."

As one comes upon it, the distinction between reasons and causes seems innocent and even promising because, after all, it is Toulmin's argument that "causal categories," and therefore the activities of intellectuals as *professionals*, have been too long ignored and dismissed to the detriment of our understanding of intellectual change. But simply by making the distinction – by assuming that rational categories are one thing and causal categories another – Toulmin has assured that sooner or later the latter will be dismissed in the context of a reassertion, in some form, of the opposition of the essential to the contingent. That is to say, unless one argues (as I shall finally argue) that the rational is itself an historical category – fashioned and refashioned by the very causal forces to which Toulmin draws our attention – the rational will inevitably be seen as a category that is transhistorical and therefore as a category that is finally independent of the "causal" forces that either nourish or threaten it.

This is exactly what happens when the distinction between reasons and causes is folded into yet another distinction between the "disciplinary" and the "professional," where the "disciplinary" refers to the "rational [and] justificatory"[35] aspect of an enterprise, and the "professional" to the "organizations, institutions, and procedures"[36] by means of which the rational *happened* to have come to light. The overt assertion is that these aspects are "complementary"[37] and "interact,"[38] but the real assertion emerges in the questions that more and more rule Toulmin's inquiry and reveal its bias:

How far do the structure, performance, and distribution of power within the professional institutions . . . enable them to meet the proper needs of the discipline for which they are acting?
. . .

How . . . do we recognize one set of factors or considerations as relevant to the intellectual content of a science, another to its human activities and institutional organizations?[39]

In these questions one clearly hears the silent "mere" before "human activities and institutional organizations," and one can easily infer the list of "improper needs" that stand in a relation of opposition and thwarting to the needs that are proper. Improper needs are the needs created by professional institutions, needs fueled by the spirits of advocacy and vanity, needs that threaten to blur the crucial distinction "between the intrinsic authority of ideas" (Toulmin apparently forgets that the notion of the intrinsic is one he has just challenged) and the "magisterial authority of books, men and institutions."[40] With this third distinction joining that between reasons and causes and between the disciplinary and the professional, the independence and (ideal) self-sufficiency of the rational is firmly established, notwithstanding Toulmin's claims to be establishing the contrary, and his pages begin to ring with the familiar anti-professionalist indictments. The observation that "even the best argument in the world could win the institutional authority merited by its intrinsic intellectual authority only if the professional circumstances were favourable,"[41] soon turns into a complaint against the "tyranny" of professional power, as a result of which "[p]apers are refused publication, academic posts are denied, professional honours are withheld . . . not for lack of worthwhile disciplinary arguments, but through professional disagreement with the editor, the research director, or the influential professor."[42] Presumably, the "best argument" should be recognizable independently of the criteria for judgment employed by any particular professional group, criteria that must be *seen through* if the best is not to be bested by the "merely" influential or institutionally authoritative; and presumably too, "professional disagreements" have only to do with base matters of patronage, preferment, and political infighting, and could only accidentally hook up with the rational considerations that are truly central to a discipline. In statements like these the deliberate and calm surface of Toulmin's prose (in its way a model of discursive decorum) gives way to the shrillness characteristic of Bate, Levin, Crews, and Bledstein and the full voice of anti-professionalism has emerged.[43]

That voice is underwritten by exactly the essentialist epistemology of which anti-professionalism is a manifestation, and the very center of that epistemology is revealed in what Paul de Man would call a moment of blindness and insight. The insight is that throughout Western history, words like "'force,' 'weight', and 'power'"[44] have been used to characterize and evaluate both rational arguments and arguments that proceed from institutional and professional authority; that is, the same vocabulary has been used to assess arguments "which are intellectually 'weighty' on their own account" and arguments which "'carry weight with' the actual participants in a scientific debate."[45] One would think that this observation might lead to the conclusion – supported by the evidence of long practice – that the two kinds of argument are not finally to be distinguished, that what seems "weighty" on its own account and without any further (rhetorical) justification seems so because the justification has already been made and made so persuasively that what follows from it seems to follow as a matter of course. One would think, in other words, that Toulmin would be led by his own project to see that an intrinsically rational argument is nothing more (or less) than a rhetorical or interested argument that has become so deeply established that its truth seems (for anyone operating in the relevant community) to be self-evident. Toulmin, however, sees something else; he sees confusion, a blurring of differences and of a distinction that he cannot let go of because at a basic level it is within its confines that he does his thinking. Those confines are securely and historically identified when he sighs, "No doubt a 'weighty' argument deserves to 'carry weight with' all informed reasoners, but it may not succeed in doing so."[46] Or, in other words, no one uses fine language when teaching geometry.

II

The foregoing remarks should be read less as a criticism of Toulmin than as a demonstration of the way in which his deepest convictions take over his argument and turn it in a direction different from the one he announces. One might even say that I am praising Toulmin for finally being consistent with his first principles; his blindness to the constitutive power of history, to its ability even to shape and reshape the category of the rational, follows "naturally" from his insight (a mistaken one in my opinion) that "[r]ationality . . . . has its own 'courts' in which all clear-headed men . . . are qualified to act" even when they represent different "'jurisdictions' of rationality."[47] In short, as a member of the intellectual "right" – defined here by its commitment to essence and foundations – Toulmin comes by his antihistoricism and his anti-professionalism honestly.

Not so the anti-professionalists of the intellectual left. By "intellectual left" I mean all those who have contributed to the assault on foundationalism and who have argued, from a variety of directions and with differing purposes, that the present arrangement of things – including, in addition to the lines of power and influence, the categories of knowledge with their attendant specification or factuality or truth – is not natural or given, but is conventional and has been instituted by the operation of historical and political (in the sense of interested) forces, even though it now wears the face of "common sense." Members of the intellectual left would include, among others, followers and readers of Marx, Vico, Foucault, Derrida, Barthes, Althusser, Gramsci, Jameson, Weber, Durkheim, Schutz, Kuhn, Hanson, Goffman, Rorty, Putnam, and Wittgenstein, and their common rallying cry would be "back (or forward) to history."

It would follow or seem to follow that the left would be an infertile ground for anti-professionalism, since anti-professionalism is grounded so firmly in a way of thinking that identifies the historical with the merely contingent. But the reverse is true. Anti-professionalist indictments are found as readily on the left as on the right, and, if anything, the left-wing version tends to be the more shrill. Moreover, what is consistency (of a challengeable kind) on the right is obvious – and hence almost mysterious – self-contradiction on the left. When an intellectual on the left makes a turn to anti-professionalism, the move is quite literally breathtaking and involves a forgetting of one's own declared principles that provokes admiration (in the old-fashioned sense of "wonder").

As a spectacular example, consider Robert W. Gordon's essay "New Developments in Legal Theory."[48] Gordon is writing as a member of the Critical Legal Studies Movement, a group of left-leaning lawyers and law professors who have discovered that legal reasoning is not "a set of neutral techniques available to everyone"[49] but is everywhere informed by policy, and that judicial decisionmaking, despite claims to objectivity and neutrality, rests on "[s]ocial and political judgments about the substance, parties, and context of a case...even when they are not the explicit or conscious basis of decision."[50] They have discovered, in short, that rather than being grounded in natural and logical necessity, the legal process always reflects the interests and concerns of some political or economic agenda, and they move from this discovery to a "critical exercise, whose point is to unfreeze the world as it appears to common sense as a bunch of more or less objectively determined social relations and to make it appear as (we believe) it really is: people acting, imagining, rationalizing, justifying."[51]

Now this is a traditional enough project – it is the whole of the sociology of knowledge; it is what the Russian Formalists meant by defamiliarization, and what the ethnomethodologists intend by the term "overbuilding"; and it is the program, if anything is, of deconstruction – but in Gordon's pages and in the pages of his cohorts, it takes a turn that finally violates the insight on which it is based. That turn turns itself, in part, on an equivocation in the use of the word "constructed." Used in one sense, it is part of the assertion that "[t]he way human beings experience the world is by collectively building and maintaining systems of shared meanings that make it possible for us to interpret one another's words and actions."[52] That is to say, "systems of shared meaning" do not have their source in distinctions and possibilities (for action) that precede and constrain human activity; rather human activity is itself always engaged in constructing the systems in relation to which its own actions and their meanings become at once possible and intelligible; and "'[l]aw' is just one among many such systems of meaning that people construct."[53] In sentences like this the notion of "construction" functions primarily as a counterassertion to the notion of the natural or inevitable, to the *unconstructed*; it does not suggest anything so specific or discreetly agential as implementing a "construction *plan*." That however, is precisely what is suggested in a sequence that turns the philosophical force of "construction" into a political accusation:

In the West, legal belief-structures, together with economic and political ones, have been constructed to accomplish this sorting out. The systems, of course, have been built by elites who have thought they had some stake in rationalizing their dominant power positions, so they have tended to define rights in such a way as to reinforce existing hierarchies of wealth and privilege.[54]

All of a sudden "constructed" means "fabricated" or "made up," and the scenario is one in which the act of construction is performed by persons who build "belief-structures" in order to impose them on those they would dominate. The trouble with this scenario is that it makes sense only within the assumptions – of neutrality and pure rationality – that Gordon is at pains to deny. For as soon as beliefs have been identified, as they are here, with the materials of fabrication, they have been implicitly (and negatively) contrasted to something that is *not* fabricated, something that is natural and objective. But it is the natural and the objective – or at least their presumption – that Gordon proposes to dislodge in favor of these historical realities created by "people acting, imagining, rationalizing, justifying"; that is to say, by people who are implementing their beliefs. By making beliefs into the material of conspiracy and deception, he covertly reintroduces as a standard the very vantage point – independent at once of both belief and history – he is supposedly rejecting; and that reintroduction becomes overt and explicit when we are urged "to struggle against being demobilized by our own conventional beliefs ... to try to use the ordinary rational tools of intellectual inquiry to expose belief-structures that claim that things as they are must necessarily be the way they are."[55] In other words, let us free ourselves from the confining perspective of particular beliefs (even when they are our own) and with the help of an *acontextual* and transcultural algorithm ("the ordinary rational tools of intellectual inquiry")[56] come to see things as they really are. This counsel would make perfect (if problematical) sense were it given by a Hirsch or a Toulmin, but given by Gordon it amounts to saying, "Now that we understand that history and convention rather than nature deliver to us our world and all its facts and all our ways of conceiving and constructing it, let us remove the weight of history from our backs and start again."

The full force of this contradiction becomes clear in the next paragraph when Gordon declares that the "discovery" that the "belief-structures that rule our lives are not found in nature but are historically contingent" is "liberating"; but the discovery can only be liberating (in a strong sense) if by some act of magic the insight that one is historically conditioned is itself not historically achieved and enables one (presumably for the first time) to operate outside of history. Gordon's capitulation to the essentialist ideology he opposes is complete when he fully specifies what he means by liberating: "This discovery is ... liberating ... because uncovering those [belief-] structures makes us see how arbitrary our categories for dividing up experience are."[57] By "arbitrary" Gordon can only mean not grounded in nature, for by his own account they are not arbitrary, in the sense of being whimsical or without motivation; rather, they are part and parcel of very motivated (that is, interested) ways of building and living within social structures, ways that have themselves been instituted against a background of other ways, no less interested and no less historical. What Gordon wants (although by his own principle he should want no such thing) are categories uninvolved in interest; and it is in the context of that absolutist and essentialist desire that the ways and categories we have can be termed arbitrary.

Exactly the same line of reasoning is displayed by Gordon's colleague Duncan Kennedy when he moves from the observation that legal reasoning is everywhere informed by policy to the conclusion that those who teach legal reasoning teach "nonsense," "*only* argumentative techniques," "policy and nothing more."[58] But arguments based on policy can be devalued and declared nonsensical only if one assumes the existence and availability of arguments (not really arguments at all) based on a sense beyond policy, a sense which, because it is apolitical or extrapolitical, can serve as a reference point from which the merely political can be identified and judged. Kennedy is right to say that teachers who persuade students that "legal reasoning is distinct, *as a method . . .* from ethical and political discourse in general"[59] have persuaded them to something false; but that is not the same as saying that they teach nonsense; they teach a very interested sense and teach it as if there were no other. The way to counter this is to teach or urge some other interested sense, some other ethical or political vision, by means of alternative arguments which, if success-ful, will be the new content of legal reasoning. This is in fact what Kennedy is doing in his essay, but it isn't what he thinks he's doing — he thinks he's clearing away the "mystification" (the word is his)[60] of mere argument and therefore replacing nonsense with sense; but he can only think that in relation to a sense that is compelling apart from argument, a sense informed not by policy, but by something more real; and once he begins to think that way he has already bought into the ahistorical vision of his opponents, a vision in which essential truths are always in danger of being obscured by the special (i.e., rhetorical) pleading of partisan interest.

He buys into that vision again when he declares that "the classroom distinc-tion between the unproblematic, legal case and the policy-oriented case is a *mere artifact.*"[61] "Artifact" functions in Kennedy's discourse as "construction" does in Gordon's: it is a "hinge" word, poised between the insight that reality as we know and inhabit it is institutional and therefore "man-made" and the desire (which contradicts the insight) for a reality that has been made by nature. That desire is the content of "mere," a word that marks the passage (already negotiated) from an observation — that the distinction between the unproblem-atic and the policy-oriented case is conventional — to a judgment — that because it is conventional, it is unreal. By delivering that judgment, Kennedy not only invokes a standard of reality – as extraconventional and ahistorical – that more properly belongs to his opponents, but he also mistakes the nature of his own project. He thinks that what he must do is expose as "merely" interested or artifactual the distinctions presently encoded in legal reasoning; and he thinks too that once this is done distinctions of a more substantial kind will emerge and exert their self-sufficient (disinterested) force. But what will really happen is that one set of interested distinctions will be replaced by another. That is to say, the distinction between unproblematic and policy-oriented cases is not the product of some ideological conspiracy practiced upon an unwitting and deceived laity; rather, it reflects a set of historically instituted circumstances in which some issues are regarded as settled and others are regarded as "up for grabs"; and if Kennedy succeeds in unsettling what now seems settled so that the lines between the unproblematic and the policy-oriented are redrawn, he will not have exchanged a mere artifact for the real thing, but he will have dislodged one artifact – understood nonpejoratively as a man-made structure of understanding – in favor of another.

Kennedy's inability to see this is of a piece with Gordon's inability to see that the alternative to "conventional beliefs" is not "liberation," but other conventional beliefs, urged not in a recently cleared space by a recently cleared vision, but in the institutional space that defines both the present shape of things and the possible courses of action by which that shape might be altered. Both men proceed, in an almost unintelligible sequence, from the insight that the received picture of things is not given but historically contingent to the conclusion that history should be repudiated in favor of a truth that transcends it.

It is only a short step (really no step at all) from this sequence to the reinvocation of the acontextualities that underwrite anti-professionalism: a self that is able to see through the mystification of "rhetoric" and achieve an independent clarity of vision; a truth that is perspicuous independently of argument, and which argument tends only to obscure; and a society where pure merit is recognized and the invidious rankings imposed by institutional hierarchies are no more. If Kennedy's specific targets are institutional practices like grading and tenure, his real target is the institution itself in all of its manifestations, from law school to clerkships to apprenticeships to full partnerships to judgeships and beyond; and his essay, like Gordon's, takes its place in the general project of the Critical Legal Studies movement, a militantly anti-professional project whose goal is "to abolish . . . hierarchies, to take control over the whole of our lives, and to shape them toward the satisfaction of our real human needs."[62] The key word in this last sentence – taken from Peter Gabel and Jay Feinman's essay "Contract Law as Ideology" – is "real," for it identifies both the complaint and the program of anti-professionalism wherever it appears, and one of my contentions is that it appears everywhere. The complaint is that a set of related and finally equivalent realities – real truth, real values, real knowledge, real authority, real motives, real need, real merit, the real self – is in continual danger of being overwhelmed or obscured or usurped by artifacts (fictions, fabrications, constructions) that have been created (imposed, manufactured) by forces and agencies that are merely professional or merely institutional or merely conventional or merely rhetorical or merely historical; and the program is simply to sweep away these artifacts – and with them professions, institutions, conventions, rhetorics, and history – so that uncorrupted and incorruptible essences can once again be espied and embraced. What is surprising, as I have already noted, is to find this the declared program of intellectuals who think of themselves as being on the left, and who therefore begin their considerations with a strong sense of the constitutive power of history and convention, and this leads me to the declaration of a rule that is already implicit in my analysis: at the moment that a left-wing intellectual turns anti-professional, he has become a right-wing intellectual in disguise.

Consider, as a case in point, Richard Ohmann, whose *English in America*[63] is a story of conversion. As Ohmann tells it, he was once a more or less typical liberal humanist who believed in "the redemptive power of literature," which, because it transcends politics, helps us to build "a world apart from the utilitarian one where words and forms advance pragmatic interests."[64] Not surprisingly, he saw professions and professional structures (departments, committees, organized research, institutional hierarchies, etc.) as obviously utilitarian and pragmatic and therefore as "destructive of community."[65] More precisely, they are destructive of the value of literary experience, an experience that puts us in touch with "an infinitely complicated and irreducible reality"[66] by immersing us in language that is "ordered in special ways": "[I]t is divorced from present circumstances and from utilitarian concerns. It neither conveys information nor furthers an argument nor embodies a command nor passes a judgment."[67] But, of course, in active professional life judgments are passed all the time, argument and counter-argument form the primary mode of transaction, and information (about contexts, lives, and even institutional happenings) is the chief currency. Obviously, then, the profession exists in a negative and corrupting relationship to the value it supposedly serves and as mere "machinery" constitutes a "barrier to free development."[68] That development will be encouraged only if we "relinquish the mind-forged manacles of our . . . categories"[69] and repudiate the merely professional practices of "more research, more . . . articles . . . more seeking out of neglected works, more coverage . . .

more minute specialization" – all of which are equated with "time serving and ambition."[70]

It hardly need be said that this is the classical anti-professionalist indictment, and it has the additional (expository) virtue of being absolutely explicit about its assumptions and imperatives: an atemporal value capable of lifting those who embrace it to an answerable level of transcendence is threatened by the all too temporal pressures of bureaucracies, committees, hierarchies, promotion, etc. The case is particularly pure because it is a literary one; for while in other disciplines anti-professionalism requires a conscious effort to detach the service or commodity from the social and cultural contexts in which it seems inextricably embedded, in literary studies, at least as they have been practiced for much of this century, the commodity is *defined* by its independence of those same contexts, and anti-professionalism is the very content of the profession itself. It is Ohmann's claim, however, to have seen through all of this and to have realized that in taking this line he was falling in with "assumptions . . . so familiar among literate people of the last 175 years that I was unaware of them as challengeable premises and thought of them as plain facts."[71] Ohmann, in short, has discovered history and with it the fact that "institutions don't exist in vacuums or in the pure atmosphere of their ideals," but "are part of the social order."[72] Armed with this insight, he proceeds to a reexamination of the profession of English, an examination in which, presumably, both the questions to be asked and the answers one hopes to find will be very different.

Everything, however, turns out to be the same. The goal is still the "free development" of human potential and the barrier to that goal is still professional and institutional procedures which are declared to be in a relation of subversion and corruption to genuine values.[73] To be sure, the freedom to be sought is not, as it was earlier, the freedom to enter into a contemplative relationship with the great works of literature, but the freedom to build a just and equitable society; that society, however, is imagined just as it was before the conversion, a "world apart from the utilitarian one where words and forms advance pragmatic interests,"[74] and the great works of literature are once again the vehicle by which captive selves will be liberated from the false visions of partial perspectives and turned toward abiding truths. Rather than serving to lift us above the ordinary and everyday, literature (especially poetry) now enables us to see through the ordinary and the everyday ("small change when we are to bodies gone")[75] and thereby puts us in a position to change what we have seen through. "[E]very good poem, play, or novel," Ohmann declares, "is revolutionary, in that it strikes through well-grooved habits of seeing and understanding";[76] and again, "[t]he poem disrupts the routine perceptions of everyday, and makes us see the world with new vision."[77]

It is tempting to linger over the obviously Neoplatonic sources of this supposedly revolutionary doctrine and to point out how traditional and how romantic a conception of literature this is; but for our purposes it is enough to observe that the entire program rests on the hope (and the possibility) of a self that can rise above its historical situation to a state where the false imperatives of merely institutional forms will be exchanged for the true imperatives that can now be espied by a newly cleaned vision, that is, by a newly free self. Much of Ohmann's analysis is devoted to demonstrating how and why the self is not yet free, imprisoned as it is in the perspectives imposed by professional structures; and the main indictment of those structures is that they impose choices on persons who would choose otherwise if they were truly liberated. Here a chief exhibit is a listing placed by the English department of Missouri Southern College in a publication entitled *Vacancies in College and University Departments of English for Fall 1971*.[78] Missouri Southern is described in the listing as a "new and growing four year institution," and the announced vacancy is for a specialist in Renaissance literature.[79] Ohmann interrogates the announcement by asking whose needs will be served by the presence of a Renaissance specialist in a small college in Joplin, Missouri. He observes that the prospective candidates for the position probably did not enter the profession with the expectation or hope of being anything "as specific as a Renaissance scholar"; instead, they probably "chose graduate work because they like[d] literature";[80] but that choice did not survive the coercing pressures of graduate education and, by the end of five or six years, lovers of literature have been made into technicians capable of filling one of the slots mandated by the professional bureaucracy. An even greater coercion has been practiced on the people of Missouri and the students of Missouri Southern who certainly did not themselves "feel a need to have this field covered at Joplin."[81] But if the choice either to be or to hire a Renaissance scholar does not originate with the state or with the students or even with the scholar himself, what is its source? Ohmann's answer is that its source is the internal requirements of the profession itself, conceived of as a grid of institutional or bureaucratic spaces that create needs and the actions that fill them independently of what anyone or any group "really" wants. In short, professional activity is not authorized by anything more substantive than the procedural exigencies built into the profession: "The profession exists so that there may be a means of accreditation and advancement for people in the profession, not out of any inner necessity and certainly not out of cultural need or the need of individual teachers."[82]

This answer seems to me to be the right one, but it does not seem to me, as it does to Ohmann, to be the matter of scandal; it is merely a recognition of the fact that needs and values do not exist independently of socially organized activities but emerge simultaneously with the institutional and conventional structures within which they are intelligible. When Ohmann says of the decisions to be or to hire a Renaissance specialist that "each choice is embedded in a network of decisions that were *not* choices,"[83] he is right; these decisions are only thinkable in relation to the already-in-place forms of socially organized activity that mark them as options; but when he turns this observation into an indictment and complains that such choices – enabled by structural possibilities that were not themselves consciously chosen – are not real choices, he falls into the trap of reserving "real" for choices that depend on no previously instituted circumstances whatsoever – choices that would be, in some strong sense, original. The problem is that it is hard even to imagine what those choices would be like; by what noninstitutional standards would they be made? What kinds of persons, at once abstracted from the concerns and alternatives built into conventional forms of behavior and yet *still acting*, would make them? The answers to these questions are distressingly familiar: What Ohmann desires are wholly free choices, made according to standards more objective than any attached to a particular perspective or partisan vision and by persons who are themselves above faction and entirely disinterested. The fact that this desire flatly contradicts his call for behavior that is "*more* political"[84] indicates the extent to which his "conversion" from mainstream liberalism to radical socialism is undone by his continuing anti-professionalism and constitutes dramatic proof of my general rule that a left-wing anti-professional is always a right-wing intellectual in disguise.

To put it another way, Ohmann's new historicism turns out to be barely skin-deep and amounts finally to a distrust of the historical more thorough-going than any he had evidenced before. In effect, he makes the same breath-taking move we have already seen in Gordon and Kennedy. Once, he tells us, I was blind to history's force, believing innocently in the availability and power of essences; now I see that the deposits of history everywhere surround us and even inform our ways of thinking; therefore let us resolve to think our way past or through history so that we may once again be free. Even when he is trying to be militantly historicist, Ohmann's essential essentialism shows through. "There is just no sense," he says, "in pondering the function of literature without relating it to the actual society that uses it, to the centers of power within that society, and to the institutions that mediate between literature and the people."[85] This all seems fine until one notices that the "it" in the sentence remains constant and is simply put to different uses by different interests. Literature, in short, stays the same; only its historical fortunes change; more-over, although its function may vary with varying political conditions, it does have a *true* function, the function of being iconoclastic and revolutionary. It never seems to occur to Ohmann that not only the uses of literature, but the items and qualities subsumed under the category, can change; it never occurs to him that literature is not an essential, but a conventional category, the content and scope of which is continually a matter of debate and adjudication between historically conditioned agents.

No such failure of insight can be attributed to Terry Eagleton who begins his recent *Literary Theory: An Introduction*[86] by historicizing what Ohmann leaves essential. Literature, Eagleton argues, is not a "definite signified,"[87] that is, a "distinct bounded object of knowledge"[88] with unique and stable properties; rather, he asserts (following Barthes), literature is what gets taught;[89] and what gets taught is at once incredibly diverse and continually changing. The line between the literary and nonliterary is continually being renegotiated; the content of key terms like "poetic diction" is continually in dispute; and the items in what is called "the canon" don't survive from one anthology to the next. In fact, "you cannot engage in an historical analysis of literature without recognizing that literature itself is a recent historical invention."[90] And if that is true of literature, it is even more true of literary theory, an activity that has no stable object to be theoretical about and is therefore indistinguishable "from philosophy, linguistics, psychology, cultural and sociological thought."[91] It follows, then, that literary theorists, critics, and teachers are custodians not of an essence, but "of a discourse," and their task is "to preserve this discourse, extend and elaborate it as necessary, defend it from other forms of discourse, initiate newcomers into it and determine whether or not they have successfully mastered it."[92]

From the point of view I will finally urge, this is exemplary, for it draws a straight (and to my mind correct) line from a thoroughgoing historicism to the insight that the features of the literary landscape are the products of institutional and professional forces. But then, inexplicably, Eagleton comes to a conclusion that puts him in the same camp with Ohmann, Gordon, Kennedy, and all the rest. "Literature," he declares, "is an illusion," and, moreover, "literary theory is an illusion too."[93] "Illusion" is a word like "construction" as Gordon uses it or "artifact" as Kennedy uses it; it marks the passage (apparently unnoticed by the author) from observation to judgment, from the description of something as conventional and historical to the declaration that therefore it is unreal. But one cannot say that because literature and literary theory are conventional – that is, effects of discourse – they are illusory without invoking as a standard of illusion a reality that is independent of convention, an essential reality; and once one has done that (however knowingly or unknowingly), the familiar anti-professionalist complaint against structures and practices that stand between us and what is true and valuable and sincere cannot be far behind.

In Eagleton's case, it arrives immediately. After having pointed out (quite correctly) that "[b]ecoming certified...as proficient in literary studies is a matter of being able to talk and write in certain ways," he comments indignantly, "[i]t is this which is being taught, examined and certificated, not what you personally think or believe."[94] This is just like Ohmann's complaint that in composition courses a student's sense of purpose "emerges from the matrix of the theme assignment" rather than from anything "he brings from life."[95] Behind both statements is the assumption that true purposes and genuine beliefs exist apart from social and institutional forms which provide artificial or manufactured motives that are subversive of the real self. It is hardly surprising that in a few pages Eagleton's fulminations are indistinguishable from those of Bate, Toulmin, Hirsch, et al., as reasoned analysis gives way to formulaic and shrill diatribes against "the largely wasted energy which postgraduate students are required to pour into obscure, often spurious research topics in order to produce dissertations which are frequently no more than sterile academic exercises, and which few others will ever read."[96] After something like this, the conclusion that "professionalism . . . is . . . bereft of any social validation of its activities"[97] is at once expected and incomprehensible; expected because it has long since become the content of every description/accusation; incomprehensible because "social validation" is precisely the kind of validation that professional activities have. Indeed, Eagleton's real complaint (although he would hardly acknowledge it) is that the validation of professional activities is "merely" social.

How do we account for this? How do we explain an argument that begins so promisingly, but then degenerates into the automatic and confused thinking displayed in these last quotations? The answer is to be found in a moment when it is possible to register one of two responses to the crucial insight impelling the work of left-wing intellectuals – the insight that our sense of what is obligatory, routine, ordinary, reasonable, authoritative, matter-of-fact, and even possible is grounded neither in nature nor in inevitability but in background conditions and assumptions that have been put into place by interested agents. One response, and the one almost always given, is outrage and horror, more or less equivalent to the discovery of the worm in the apple; and the reaction to that response is, as we have seen, first, indictment and then a call for action designed to free us from the impositions and deceptions to which we have become captive. The other response is less dramatic and takes the form of a project, of new research, in which the goal is to provide a full and analytical map of what have been called the "conditions of possibility," the conditions that underlie what at any point in the history of a society or an institution are taken to be the components of common sense.

Now, of course, these two responses are not mutually exclusive. One can engage in research of this kind and find oneself opposed to what it uncovers, but that is quite different from assuming at the outset that what is to be opposed is institutionalization or professionalization per se rather than this or that form of it, for that assumption (indistinguishable from essentialism) will work to preclude the sustained and serious investigation of institutional arrangements, since the investigator will be in a rush to deplore the fact that such arrangements exist. Just such a rush marks and mars the writings of those engaged in the GRIP project. One can hardly quarrel with the announced agenda of that project:

We would study the entire process of training and professional life that form a professional literary critic. We would examine how the professional comes to recognize only certain objects as worthy of study, for instance, how he or she regards only specifically defined work as important to perform; how he or she learns the rules for social behavior in the profession.[98]

The statement is by James Fanto, but the title of his piece – "Contesting Authority: The Marginal" – indicates in advance why its promise will never be fulfilled. He wishes to examine the lines of authority and influence not in order to understand them or even to propose that they be altered, but to express outrage that these or any other lines should be in place. Consequently, when he comes to describe the hierarchical form of the profession, he can only view it as a grand deception practiced on the public and on victimized initiates: "The profession . . . establishes a hierarchy and sets some individuals . . . at its summit together with the symbols associated with their names. . . . [T]hose new to the profession receive these symbols – they are formed by them; they submit to their authority."[99] What is missing here is any notice of the *content* of what Fanto calls "symbols," the research accomplishments, methodological techniques, powerful interpretations, pedagogical innovations, etc., that bring some men and women to the "summit" and form the basis of the authority that in Fanto's account is magically and arbitrarily conferred (seized rather than earned). He is so convinced beforehand that the deference accorded to institutional superiors is without foundation that he never bothers to catalog the tasks, longstanding puzzles, crucial problems, the negotiation and completion of which leads to professional recognition and promotion. To be sure, these tasks, problems, and puzzles can be challenged as not worth doing, and there are some who "rise" independently of any such accomplishments; but, nevertheless, there is a great deal more to the acquiring of professional power than "the frequent celebration of the master in reviews"[100] and other such gestures of servility that seem to make up Fanto's entire understanding of the matter.

Fanto writes his essay as a tribute to the "marginal" figure, the man or woman who struggles against the profession's hegemony in the name, supposedly, of values that exist independently of the profession and of any institution whatsoever. At one point, however, he acknowledges that the stance of opposition is not really "outside" but "remains within the perspective of the profession and perhaps even falls into a position already inscribed in the profession."[101] Indeed, he adds, "an appeal to one's own professional purity . . . can often serve as a strategy for displacing individuals and groups above one on the professional hierarchy."[102] But this moment of insight is brief and soon gives way to the familiar anti-professional blindness, as Fanto, in the very next paragraph, urges "resistance" to "institutions and social networks" and a continual scrutiny of "one's own position to guard against the reappearance of . . . professional power in one's own discourse and actions."[103] We could pause here to ask on the basis of what non-institutional standards and from what asocial position this resistance will be mounted, but by now, I trust, the questions are superfluous and the answer obvious.

What Fanto and his fellows in the GRIP project seem never to realize (despite the fact that they are all readers of Foucault) is that power not only constrains and excludes, but also enables, and that without some institutionally articulated spaces in which actions become possible and judgments become inevitable (because they are obligatory), there would be nothing to do and no values to support. David Shumway, for example, is only able to see tyranny and the mechanism of exclusion in the "disciplinary regime" of the modern academy, and he lists among the chief mechanisms the examination and the hiring process:

Beginning with the tests that one takes as an undergraduate, continuing through qualifying examinations, to the dissertation itself and the examination on it, disciplines exclude and categorize their adherents by means of examination. The hiring process with its *vitae*, dossiers, and interviews – all disciplinary instruments – is today perhaps the most powerful means of disciplinary exclusion.[104]

It is hard to see what this can mean except that some people get hired and others don't, and it is even harder to imagine an alternative arrangement, one that would result (presumably) in some form of universal academic employment with each of us conferring on ourselves the appropriate degrees and titles. (Although perhaps there would be none, since titles are evidence of invidious distinctions.) Of course, it could certainly be the case that the procedures and criteria by which the academy makes its judgments are in need of revision or even of a total overhauling, but one cannot completely jettison those procedures and criteria or refrain from those judgments without eliminating the achievements that are at once thinkable and recognizable only because they are in place. What Shumway doesn't see is that the very values he would protect – true judgment, true merit, true authority – are functions of the forms and structures he sees as dangers; and he doesn't see that because, like all anti-professionals, he is finally committed to an essentialism that renders *all* forms and structures automatically suspect, even when they are the very heart of one's project. It is this that explains why Shumway can at once observe that a paradigm is displaced when those at the institutional center of "intellectual authority" believe it to be "inadequate" and yet complain that it has not been "proven to be inadequate."[105] Again, what could this possibly mean except that Shumway is holding out for a standard of proof that is altogether independent of the standards in force in an institution? What could it mean except that at the very moment of embarking on a study of the constitutive power of disciplines and professions, he displays an inability to see that power as anything but the vehicle of conspiracy, even though he himself has declared that the "issue of conspiracy is almost always a red herring."[106]

It may be a red herring, but it is one that leads the entire GRIP project astray in a way that is concisely illustrated by three successive sentences in James Sosnoski's "The *Magister Implicatus* as an Institutionalized Authority Figure."[107] Sosnoski begins by announcing that "[t]he 'official' set of beliefs linking individuals to institutions are the subject of my investigation."[108] He then declares that "[t]hese beliefs are quite powerful." And he adds immediately, "They make us behave in ways that we would choose not to."[109] What this third sentence does is assure that the investigation of his "subject" will be impoverished even before it begins; for having decided in advance that the effect of institutions on individuals is disabling – depriving them of choices and of meaningful forms of behavior – Sosnoski is himself disabled from considering the many ways in which institutions *enrich* individual possibilities by making available alternative courses of action, including action designed to supply perceived deficiencies and remedy existing ills. The result is a performance in which observations that could be the basis of a rich and textured analysis are too soon transformed into indictments. Sosnoski points out, for example, that critical discourse is informed by questions, and that both the questions and their acceptable answers make "sense only within the context of the conceptual framework that identified the problem"[110] in the first place. Moreover, he adds, institutional questions – such as those found in textbooks and on examinations – are in fact instructions "to perform a particular task in a particular manner,"[111] and thus "are the principal instruments of literary training."[112] It looks for a moment as if this insight will generate an inquiry into the history of these questions, a history that might then lead to an exploration of the relationship between the shape of literary studies and the larger intellectual shape of the culture; but while Sosnoski makes some gestures in that direction, he quickly returns to his limited (and limiting) focus and falls to deploring the deadening effects of discipleship ("Critical schooling produces critical schools")[113] and complaining that the net result of literary training is to substitute mere professional authority for the authority that should be reserved for true "competence."[114] By invoking this distinction, Sosnoski reveals himself as one more card-carrying anti-professional, interested in studying institutions only so that he can expose their tendency to replace "real" values and "genuine" motives with values and motives that have their source only in a desire to manipulate and control; and he reveals too (and inevitably) that his goal is not the reform of institutions and professions, but a world in which their "warranting frameworks" and practices of initiation and directing questions are no longer operative.

A sense of what that world would be like emerges in the final pages of the essay when Sosnoski presents his positive recommendations. We should, he counsels, "introduce a protocol to AGREE TO AGREE to replace our present polemical protocol to AGREE TO DISAGREE."[115] This statement is remarkable in several respects, but chiefly for its suggestion that agreeing and disagreeing are *styles* of intellectual behavior rather than evidence of deeply held beliefs that may or may not be in conflict. But if one sees that disagreement reflects differences in commitment rather than a mere fashion in intellectual inquiry, the recommendation to leave off disagreeing will sound rather strange; it will sound like a recommendation to put off one's beliefs, and that recommendation will make sense only if beliefs are thought to be acquired and discarded much as one acquires and discards pieces of clothing. Like Gordon, Sosnoski has a picture of the way we come to hold our beliefs and of the ease of changing them (simply by changing a rule of operating procedure) that allows him to see them as obstacles to genuine action by persons who agree to "share ideas." But simply to identify that picture is to raise some familiar questions: what would persons who had divested themselves of belief be like, and where would the ideas they share come from if they didn't come from interested (and therefore polemical) perspectives, and if they came from those perspectives how could they be meaningfully shared unless there were a way to discriminate between them, and if there were such a way, what could it be except some calculus that transcended polemic because it transcended politics? Either these questions are unanswerable because there could be no such persons or such ideas and because there is no such calculus, or they can be answered only by invoking and affirming the acontextual fictions – unsituated selves, presuppositionless ideas, disinterested action, independent criteria – that Sosnoski, himself so polemical and political, should be loath to embrace. Once again we see that for an intellectual of the left, anti-professionalism is at once debilitating because it precludes action on any level except the Utopian, and contradictory because it leads inevitably to an essentialism that has its proper home on the right.

III

It is time to take stock of our argument and see where it has taken us. What I have tried to demonstrate is that anti-professionalism, as a set of attitudes and arguments, is indefensible no matter what forms it takes: it is indefensible on the right because it begins with incorrect assumptions (about the possibility of free selves choosing extrainstitutional values by means of independent criteria), and it is indefensible on the left because it contradicts the correct (historicist and conventional) assumptions with which left-wing intellectuals, as I have defined them, begin. Having said as much and said it at such length, I still have left unanswered the questions most readers would probably want to raise: First of all, if anti-professionalism is as vulnerable (not to say silly) as I have made it out to be, why is there so much of it? And, second, if one gives up anti-professionalism as a way of responding to institutional life, what then remains? What is the alternative?

To take the second question first, it might seem that the only alternative to anti-professionalism is quietism or acquiescence in the status quo because by discrediting it I have taken away the basis on which this or that professional practice might be criticized. But, in fact, the only thing that follows from my argument is that a practice cannot (or should not) be criticized *because* it is professional, because it is underwritten by institutionally defined goals and engaged in for institution-specific reasons; since here are no goals and reasons that are not institutional, that do not follow from the already-in-place assumptions, stipulated definitions, and categories of understanding of a socially organized activity, it makes no sense to fault someone for acting in the only way one can possibly act. This does not, however, rule out opposition, for someone can always be faulted for acting in institutional ways that have consequences you deplore; and you can always argue that certain institutional ways (and their consequences) should be altered or even abolished, although such arguments will themselves be made on behalf of other institutional ways (and *their* consequences). In short, the alternative to anti-professionalist behavior (which on my account is impossible) is behavior of the kind we are already engaged in. One could call it business as usual so long as "business as usual" is understood to include looking around (with institution-informed eyes) to see conditions (institutionally established) that are unjust or merely inefficient (with justice and efficiency institutionally defined) and proposing remedies and changes that will improve the situation. Of course, what is a change and what is a remedy and what is an improvement will be matters of dispute between agents embedded in different organizational settings with different priorities and interests, but none of the parties to the dispute will be acting purely, that is, with no ax to grind; and no one will be grinding an ax that is not an extension of some rationally defensible sense of the enterprise.

Doing away with anti-professionalism, then, will have as little effect as anti-professionalism itself; if action independent of institutions is impossible, it hardly seems to matter whether it is advocated or derided; it will still be impossible. And yet anti-professionalism thrives, and I return to my first question. Why is there so much of it? The answer is to be found in the history of professionalism and in the way it has defined itself as a project. As M. S. Larson recounts it, professionalism is a "typical product of the 'great transformation,' "[116] the passage from a decentralized and rural society where status is a function of birth and of geography to the modern urbanized state in which status is acquired by climbing the ladder provided by corporate and professional organizations. In this new world, power, influence, and authority are achieved not by the "accidents" of class but by the demonstration of merit on the part of individuals who rise to prominence by virtue of their native ability. This, at any rate, is the story the rising or bourgeois class tells itself and also tells those others who do not rise and who for the most part are excluded from even approaching the ladder by the new mechanisms of selection and discrimination (religion, ethnic background, examinations, degrees, etc.). Professionalism, then, at least as it presents itself, promotes and enhances individual effort; it gives people the opportunity to "make it on their own," and it allows those who do make it to believe they deserve everything they receive; and it allows them to believe too that those who fail simply didn't work hard enough or didn't have "what it takes" in the first place.

Larson calls this story the "ideology of professionalism," and she identifies it with democratic liberalism: "The notion that 'the individual is essentially the proprietor of his own person and capacities, for which he owes nothing to society,' is a cornerstone of the bourgeois theory of democratic liberalism."[117] It is an ideology both because it serves certain well-defined interests (despite its claims to neutrality and to equal access) and because it is at variance with the facts as Larson understands them. She points out that rather than owing nothing to society, the professional owes everything to society, including the self whose independence is his strongest claim and justification. That is, it is only with reference to the articulation and hierarchies of a professional bureaucracy that a sense of the self and its worth – its merit – emerges and becomes measurable. The ladder of advancement is not only a structural fact, it is a fact that tells the person who occupies a place on it who he is and what he has accomplished; by providing goals, aspirations, and alternative courses of action, the ladder also provides the "means of self-assertion."[118] "[C]areer," she concludes in a powerful aphorism, "is a pattern of organization of the self,"[119] which is another way of saying that the self of the professional is constituted and legitimized by the very structures – social and institutional – from which it is supposedly aloof.

Given this analysis (which seems to me entirely persuasive), it is obvious that professional life is a continual attempt to mediate and ameliorate this tension. A professional must find a way to operate in the context of purposes, motivations, and possibilities that precede and even define him and yet maintain the conviction that he is "essentially the proprietor of his own person and capacities." *The way he finds is anti-professionalism.* As we have seen again and again, anti-professionalism is by and large a protest against those aspects of professionalism that constitute a threat to individual freedom, true merit, genuine authority. It is therefore the strongest representation within the professional community of the ideals which give that community its (ideological) form. Far from being a stance taken at the margins or the periphery (as someone like Fanto would have it), anti-professionalism is the very center of the professional ethos, constituting by the very vigor of its opposition the true form of that which it opposes. Professionalism cannot do without anti-professionalism: it is the chief support and maintenance of the professional ideology; its presence is a continual assertion and sign of the purity of the profession's intentions. In short, the ideology of anti-professionalism – of essential and independent values chosen freely by an independent self – is nothing more or less than the ideology of professionalism taking itself seriously. (The more seriously it is taken, the more virulent will be the anti-professionalism; thus the peculiar form of literary anti-professionalism, which is more often than not the overt form of literary practice.)

This, then, is the answer to the question, why, if anti-professionalism is incoherent, is there so much of it? Anti-professionalism is professionalism itself in its purest form. Does this mean that at the heart of professional life is a blatant contradiction that should be recognized and extirpated? Not at all, for if it is, in some sense, a contradiction, it is also emblematic of a necessary condition of human life. Let me explain. Throughout this essay I have been urging what might be called a strong interpretivist or conventionalist view, a view in which facts, values, reasons, criteria, etc., rather than being independent of interpretive history, are the products of that history. But, at the same time, I have resisted any suggestion that those who stipulate to those facts or hold those values or advance those reasons are operating under a delusion that would be removed if they came to realize that their ways of thinking and evaluating were conventional rather than natural. Such a realization could only have that effect if it enabled the individual who was constituted by historical and cultural forces to "see through" those forces and thus stand to the side of his own convictions and beliefs. But that is the one thing a historically conditioned consciousness cannot do – scrutinize its own beliefs, conduct a rational examination of its own convictions; for in order to begin such a scrutiny, it would first have to escape the grounds of its own possibility and it could only do that if it were not historically conditioned and were instead an acontextual or unsituated entity of the kind that is rendered unavailable by the first principle of the interpretivist or conventionalist view.

What this means, finally, is that even if one is convinced (as I am) that the world he sees and the values he espouses are constructions, or, as some say, "effects of discourse," that conviction will in no way render that world any less perspicuous or those values any less compelling. It is thus a condition of human life always to be operating as an extension of beliefs and assumptions that are historically contingent, and yet to be holding those beliefs and assumptions with an absoluteness that is the necessary consequence of the absoluteness with which they hold – inform, shape, constitute – us. Professionalism is, as I have said, a very emblem of that condition. The professional who is "spoken" in his every thought and action by the institution and yet "speaks" in the name of essences that transcend the institution and provide a vantage point for its critique is not acting out a contradiction, but simply acting in the only way human beings can. From the beginning, my argument has been that anti-professionalism is indefensible because it imagines a form of life – free, independent, acontextual – that cannot be lived; that argument now takes its final and curious turn by concluding that professionalism itself cannot be lived apart from such an imagining. In my efforts to rehabilitate professionalism, I have come full circle and have ended up by rehabilitating anti-professionalism too.

Notes

1   B. Bledstein, *The Culture of Professionalism* (1976).
2   Ibid., p. 334.
3   Ibid., p. 330.
4   M. S. Larson, *The Rise of Professionalism* (1977).
5   Ibid., p. 15.
6   Introduction to *Becoming a Lawyer: A Humanistic Perspective on Legal Education and Professionalism* 2 (E. Dvorkin, J. Himmelstein, and H. Lesnick eds. 1981).
7   Ibid.
8   Ibid.
9   R. Levin, *New Readings vs. Old Plays* 196 (1979).
10 Bate, "The Crisis in English Studies," *Harvard Magazine*, September–October 1982, p. 85; R. Ohmann, *English in America* (1976); Topf, "Specialization in Literary Criticism," *College English* 39 (1977); Crews, "Deconstructing a Discipline," *University Publishing*, Summer 1980. For a critique, see S. Fish, "Profession Despise Thyself: Fear and Self-Loathing in Literary Studies," *Critical Inquiry* 10 (1983).

11   Crews, "Deconstructing a Discipline," p. 2.
12   Ibid.
13   E. D. Hirsch, *Aims of Interpretation* (1976), p. 155.
14   Ibid.
15   Ibid., p. 153.
16   *The Works of Aristotle, Rhetorica* (W. D. Ross ed. 1924).
17   Ibid., p. 1404.
18   Hirsch, *Aims of Interpretation*, pp. 152–3.
19   Ibid., p. 152.
20   Ibid.
21   Ibid., p. 153.
22   Ibid.
23   Ibid., p. 90.
24   Ibid., p. 13.
25   Ibid., p. 154.
26   Ibid., p. 13.
27   S. Toulmin, *Human Understanding* (1972).
28   Ibid., p. 84.
29   Ibid., p. 97.
30   Ibid., p. 85.
31   Ibid.
32   Ibid., p. 76.
33   Ibid.
34   Ibid., p. 267.
35   Ibid., p. 311.
36   Ibid., p. 142.
37   Ibid., p. 311.
38   Ibid., p. 268.
39   Ibid., p. 281, 309.
40   Ibid., p. 117.
41   Ibid., p. 272–3.
42   Ibid., p. 280.
43   Of course, anti-professionalism's voice need not be shrill. All it requires is that there be a sharp distinction between the knowledge provided by professional communities or disciplines, and a better knowledge that would proceed from some acontextual and abiding source. This kind of anti-professionalism informs many of the essays in *The Authority of Experts* (T. Haskell ed. 1984). Haskell, for example, writes in his preface, "[w]hat shapes my belief is as much psychological and sociological as logical" (preface to ibid., p. xi). Like Toulmin, he thinks that he is giving the psychological and the sociological their due, but again, like Toulmin, simply by assuming the distinction between the logical and the sociological, he grants the former a priority that implicitly reduces the status of the latter either to that of a helpmate or an enemy. Other essays in this volume make the same move with varying degrees of self-consciousness. For a particularly egregious example,

see ibid., pp. 239–40, where Stephen Stitch and Richard Nisbett oppose the rational to the social, the personal, and the historical.

44 Toulmin, *Human Understanding*, p. 312.
45 Ibid.
46 Ibid., pp. 312–13.
47 Ibid., p. 95.
48 Gordon, "New Developments in Legal Theory," in *The Politics of Law* 3 (D. Kairys ed. 1982).
49 Ibid., p. 284.
50 Kairys, "Introduction," in *The Politics of Law* 3.
51 Gordon, "New Developments in Legal Theory," p. 289.
52 Ibid., p. 287.
53 Ibid., p. 288.
54 Ibid.
55 Ibid., p. 289.
56 Ibid.
57 Ibid.
58 Kennedy, "Legal Education as Training for Hierarchy," in *The Politics of Law* 3, p. 47.
59 Ibid.
60 Ibid., p. 45.
61 Ibid., p. 47 (emphasis added).
62 Gabel and Feinman, "Contract Law as Ideology," in *The Politics of Law* 3, p. 173.
63 Ohmann, *English in America*.
64 Ibid., p. 334.
65 Ibid., p. 12.
66 Ibid., p. 16.
67 Ibid., p. 6.
68 Ibid., p. 20.
69 Ibid.
70 Ibid., p. 17.
71 Ibid., p. 20 (emphasis omitted).
72 Ibid., p. 22 (emphasis omitted).
73 Ibid., p. 30.
74 Ibid., p. 334.
75 J. Donne, "The Ecstasy," line 76.
76 Ohmann, *English in America*, p. 48.
77 Ibid., p. 58.
78 Association of Departments of English, *Vacancies in College and University Departments of English for Fall 1971* (1971).
79 Ibid.
80 Ohmann, *English in America*, p. 210.
81 Ibid.
82 Ibid., p. 40.

83   Ibid., p. 211.
84   Ibid., p. 332.
85   Ibid., p. 303.
86   T. Eagleton, *Literary Theory: An Introduction* (1983).
87   Ibid., p. 201.
88   Ibid., p. 205.
89   Ibid., p. 197.
90   Ibid., p. 204.
91   Ibid.
92   Ibid., p. 201.
93   Ibid., p. 204.
94   Ibid., p. 201.
95   Ohmann, *English in America*, p. 147.
96   Eagleton, *Literary Theory*, p. 213.
97   Ibid., p. 214.
98   In what follows I am quoting from the GRIP Report, volume one, second draft
      (presented on May 6–8, 1983). The GRIP Report is not a publication, but a set of
      working papers circulated among those associated with the Group for Research
      in the Institutionalization and Professionalization of Literary Studies ("GRIP"),
      sponsored by the Society for Critical Exchange, Inc., and headquartered at the
      English Department, University of Miami, Oxford, Ohio. The quotation is from
      Fanto, "Contesting Authority: The Marginal," in the GRIP Report, p. 6.
      Pagination refers to the manuscript pages of individual essays.
99   Fanto, "Contesting Authority," p. 17.
100   Ibid.
101   Ibid., p. 24.
102   Ibid.
103   Ibid., p. 25.
104   D. Shumway, "Interdisciplinarity and Authority in American Studies," in the
      GRIP Report, p. 16.
105   Ibid., pp. 13–14.
106   Ibid., pp. 16–17.
107   J. Sosnoski, "The *Magister Implicatus* As An Institutionalized Authority Figure,"
      in the GRIP Report, p. 98.
108   Ibid., p. 5.
109   Ibid.
110   Ibid., p. 10.
111   Ibid., p. 12.
112   Ibid., p. 14.
113   Ibid.
114   Ibid., p. 18.
115   Ibid., pp. 53–4.
116   Larson, *The Rise of Professionalism*, p. 76.
117   Ibid., pp. 221–2 (footnote omitted).

118   Ibid., p. 199.
119   Ibid., p. 229.

Index